THE FAMILY BOND

Marriage, Love, and Sex in America

CONSULTING EDITOR MARVIN BRESSLER PRINCETON UNIVERSITY

THE FAMILY BOND

LEONARD BENSON *North Texas State University*

Random House
NEW YORK

Marriage, Love, and Sex in America

ISBN: 0-394-31658-4

Library of Congress Catalog Card Number: 78-143552

Manufactured in the United States of America by The Book Press, Brattleboro, Vt.

First Edition

9 8 7 6 5 4 3 2 1

Design by James M. Wall

Cover design by Hermann Strohbach
Cover photo by Elliott Landy
Photo for Part One © Look Magazine
Photos for Parts Two, Three, and Four by George W. Gardner
Photo for Part Five by Charles Gatewood

To Good Marriages and Wise Parents

The family changes slowly. As a result, textbooks about it do not lag behind the reality they attempt to explain as much as textbooks in most other areas. Still the dangers of being dated and obsolete are always present. The family does change, and uncertainties about its future seem to be as numerous as those for other aspects of life. Sex is not the taboo subject it once was, monogamy now has zealous critics, and some contemporary women feel that the family is a scourge for them, designed and perpetuated for the benefit of men. Traditional ideals are by no means dead, but the actual behavior of people is quite variable. New standards can be and are being introduced.

At the most general level, our commitment to the principles of family life remains very strong. But a closer look reveals that family bonds have been weakened at certain critical points. Perhaps they were rarely as strong as presumed in the past, but community pressures allowed very little exploration of alternatives until recently. To keep up to date, one must study the changing relationship between popular themes and behavior as it actually occurs. In this book an attempt is made to do just that.

This approach has one very useful advantage. It helps break down the barrier that often separates academic study of the family from the more practical considerations of marriage and family living. Some texts attempt to generalize about the family and its changing social nature, stressing broad, institutional patterns; others stress the more or less typical day-to-day problems that people have in setting up families, living in them, and escaping from them when they do not work. But new problems become typical in a society only as the general nature of the family and its place in the social order change. They reflect strains in the interplay between our ideals on the one hand and the realities we face on the other.

To explore this interplay is to be relevant in the most fundamental sense of the term. This text is designed to make such an exploration, following the individual through his life cycle from childhood and adolescence to maturity and old age. In the process, each of us acquires basic attitudes and commitments toward the family, enters the dating and courtship stages of life, has experiences with love, experiments with sex, and (in the case of most people) embarks upon the marriage and parenthood phases of life. The text is intended to provide useful information along with a broad awareness of alternative possibilities and theories for all major aspects of marriage and family participation.

I am deeply indebted to hundreds of people who have contributed to our impressive current collection of information about family patterns and problems. The bibliography at the end of the book identifies many of these people, but certainly not all. I would like to express my special gratitude for useful comments to Elizabeth Almquist and James Kitchens, to my consulting editor, Marvin Bressler, and to editors Theodore Caris, Arthur Strimling, and David Bartlett for their continuing help and encouragement. I am indebted to Marilyn Brunner for her very valuable assistance, to Judy Schapiro of Random House for her excellent work in editing the final draft of the manuscript, and to Lynne Farber of Random House for performing the indispensable task of getting the manuscript ready for production and seeing it through. All of these people have given moral support and suggested improvements in the text; they certainly cannot be held responsible for any of its shortcomings. That responsibility is mine.

Denton, Texas   L.B.

PART ONE
Introduction

PART TWO
Anticipation of Marriage

PART THREE
Married Life: Adjustment and Change

PART FOUR
Breakup

PART ONE

Introduction

CHAPTER 1

Family Fundamentals

Because family life faces unusual problems in the modern metropolis, and the inner city is particularly hostile, people are scrambling to the suburbs in ever greater numbers, as the 1970 census shows. Many families, however, will not find tranquillity in the suburbs; marriage problems and parent-child relations will simply take a few new turns. The suburban family has become the typical American family, and, except for its affluence, it has much in common with the earlier small town model.

Traditional family customs and the problems associated with them have remained remarkably stable. They do change, of course, but slowly—except at critical times in history. It is possible that we are now living in such a critical period, but we cannot be too sure about that. The fall of the traditional family has been predicted repeatedly in the past, and it has repeatedly survived. Apparently it meets human needs as well as any alternative yet devised, but obviously it does not satisfy them so well that the search for something better is dropped altogether. The search never seems to end.

Interest in the *communal family* is the most striking current alternative (although it is by no means new). Many group-living arrangements have been tried, and a number of them now flourish, in the United States. Members (sometimes fifteen or more) live in intimate social and physical relationships, share food and other basic necessities, and have very strong feelings for one another. Monogamous pairing-off among adults is the most common pattern, although other sex arrangements are sometimes made. Usually there is a strong emphasis on the sharing of work and responsibilities. But individuals come and go, and the group itself may not last very long. New ones are constantly being formed, attracting people from more conventional homes or from disbanded communal groups (Downing 1970). A recent study of college students, based on a sample of approximately 8,000 persons, revealed that about one student in twenty strongly approves of communal family arrangements, and another twelve percent show an interest in joining one. About half of the students (48 percent) consider them "all right for some people," but not for themselves (Groves, Rossi, and Grafstein 1970).

The communal family arrangement is spreading much more slowly than suburbia, however, mainly because people are extremely conservative in family matters. Most of us are reared in conventional homes, and only rarely are we prepared to experiment with novel arrangements. The communal family therefore seems strange and unworkable—perhaps even immoral. We usually expect others to act like ourselves or in ways that make sense by our standards. Only after we get to know other people can we appreciate their odd customs—and maybe not even then. One of the most famous anthropologists of all time spent years with the natives of New Guinea, describing their customs in great detail, but could never really bring himself to like them or approve of their behavior (Malinowski 1967). Nowhere is our suspicion of cultural differences more intense than in the area of the family, but nowhere is it so important that we allow ourselves to seek the very best.

Despite inertia, conventional family life does find itself under attack on a broad front at the present time. The purposes of this book are to bring the nature of the family into sharp focus; to examine its strengths, its weaknesses, its hidden characteristics; and to point out where modern social developments seem to be taking us. The standard American family and the problems of its individual members will be our primary concerns, but it helps to know something about the entire range of family types, here and abroad.

FAMILY APPEALS

The family is a very sentimental institution. It is all too often romanticized in the mass media, but it should not be viewed wholly in that light. To the serious student it is a social structure possessing certain essential properties; it exists and thrives because it works, and it works despite the fact that it is the setting for man's most intense bitterness and hatred. (Murders are family affairs more often than not, and your own bedroom is one of the most dangerous places.)

A key problem faced by all nations is how to organize the most basic forms of social life, bringing order to relations between the sexes and among people of different ages. In the musical *Funny Girl* a song tells about "people who need people"—they are supposed to be the luckiest ones of all. But the fact is that everybody needs people, because we can survive only through cooperative efforts in orderly groups.

Although each person must cooperate with others, he must also keep some degree of independence. A separate, personal identity is essential for the individual's sense of integrity. The need to both cooperate and stay separate poses a problem that each person has to work out in his own fashion, but there are several common ways of doing it. If there is any help to be had in bridging the gap between social conformity on the one hand and personal independence on the other, it is most likely to come from the family.

Thus, the family is probably the most basic of all human groups, and loyalty to it is deeper and more intense than any other social loyalty. Its fundamental appeal is *familism*, a complex set of values that directly or indirectly create a sense of family commitment. Each one of us is familistic to some extent, varying in terms of our personal experiences at home and the kind of society we live in. All nations have ways of making family obligations reasonably clear and of encouraging people to fulfill them.

Of course some countries demand more wholehearted commitment than others. The Japanese, for example, have difficulty thinking of themselves as separate individuals. The conception of "self" in Japan is overlaid with a powerful sense of family membership (Caudill and Weinstein 1966), but this is true in many other parts of the world as well. In the United States (and in Japan, too) the family has become less necessary for sheer survival, but it is still an enormously useful halfway house between personal isolation and the indifference of the crowd. One of its strongest appeals is that it provides a relatively manageable slice of life within a much bigger and more chaotic society. This may seem more true in the modern city than in a peasant village, but even peasant families give people their most immediate assurance of continuing security (Foster 1962). There is one key difference in the city, however. If the family gives no pleasure, it is not too difficult to look around for something better. In many parts of the world there is simply no place else to go.

The idea that the *intrinsic* pleasures of family life are increasingly needed to keep the family together has been argued very effectively by Ernest Burgess and Harvey Locke (1960). They point out that social and economic pressures could be counted on to hold the family together in most agricultural societies, but the large industrial city changes all that and may even encourage people to leave home. A computerized economy places a premium on freeing talent and creative ability from family control, and thus it tends to weaken traditional family ties (Goode 1968). Where the family loses its importance for physical survival, it becomes relatively easy to leave, but under these circumstances it also becomes easy to create new ones.

Thus, any particular family may be unstable, but most people live in families most of the time. Americans who seek divorce, for example, usually marry again very soon, and their new marriages are more stable as a rule than their previous ones, though they are still relatively unstable (Monahan

1968). Even so, John Belcher (1967) found that the number of people living alone in "one-person households" in the United States is increasing much more rapidly than the total population, and this increase cannot be totally accounted for by the changing age structure of the population (more older people, for example).

Although all societies have ways to embarrass people who fail to meet their family responsibilities, they cannot rely on threats and embarrassments alone. The key is always a feeling of *personal obligation*, or even compulsion. Broadly speaking, there are two sources for this: *direct* and *symbolic*. Together they comprise the foundations of familism. The family has a direct appeal because in the course of our daily experiences with it, most of our basic emotional and survival needs are met (ego support, food, sleep, shelter). Symbolically, it is supported by the many favorable references made almost everywhere we go. If you watch television for an hour or so almost any time of the day you will probably see the family presented in a positive, sentimental, or dramatic way, even during the commercials. The idea that families are "warm," while people without families are lonely, is restated in a thousand different ways. The family is sometimes the butt of mock criticism, as in the cartoons that make fun of hapless fathers and nagging wives, but the effect of this is usually just the opposite of its apparent intent. We can make fun of the family only because it is so absolutely and unmistakably secure.

The appeal of the family is documented by a 1968 survey conducted by the American Council on Education. The council asked thousands of freshmen in public universities what objectives in life they considered essential or very important. Having a family ranked second. The top ten, with the percentage of students citing each, were:

To develop a philosophy of life	84 percent
To raise a family	70 percent
To have friends with different backgrounds	68 percent
To help others in difficulty	63 percent
To be an authority in my field	59 percent
To have an active social life	59 percent
To keep up with political affairs	57 percent
To succeed in my own business	45 percent
To be very well-off financially	44 percent
To obtain recognition from peers	42 percent

These results are all the more significant when you consider that the college years are not the ones of greatest interest in the family. Our need for family reassurance changes enormously at different times in life. Small children, for example, are almost totally involved in family affairs, although not necessarily by choice. People in old age endlessly mull over their earlier family experiences. By contrast, adolescents (especially teen-age boys) usually have other things on their minds. Girls are attracted to both marriage and parenthood when they are very young, but boys stand rather aloof to such things until late adolescence, when they become almost obsessed with thoughts of sex, or perhaps by the sheer prettiness of girls. They are rarely excited about becoming fathers, however, and are by no means anxious to take on family obligations.

Perhaps this simply means that the general excitement of dating leads rather slowly to marriage, but it does in fact lead there sooner or later. Thus, men and women are drawn into family commitments in different ways. How they handle their conflicting views will be crucial in determining how well they succeed in marriage.

FAMILY PROCESSES

Family activities include four very broad processes: anticipation, formation, accommodation, and dissolution. These vary from one culture to the next, occurring at different ages for different people, and some individuals may not experience all of them. *Anticipations* of marriage occur during the preparatory phase of life—in childhood and adolescence when the person forms his first conceptions of family matters and as he enters the dating, romantic, and premarital sex stage of life. The *formation* phase takes over in late adolescence or early maturity, when mate selection becomes a serious concern, and extends into the engagement period. The process of *accommodation* continues throughout marriage, but we shall view it in terms of three stages: the early marriage period, the middle years of marriage, and then old age. *Dissolution* occurs as family members leave home or die, or when accommodation breaks down, leading to problems of separation, divorce, desertion, widowhood, and several other situations for which we have no convenient names.

Underlying these processes are the basic forms of cooperation and solidarity essential to both social and family stability. In the broadest possible sense, there are two kinds of cooperative behavior. One is the *specialized* variety, where individuals work together, each contributing a rather unique skill or competence. This is most obvious in economic affairs. We are all part of an extremely complicated division of labor, making it possible to accomplish things no single individual (or group of unspecialized individuals) could ever achieve. One man may not be able to make an automobile, for example, but it can still be done because tens of thousands of very different skills are organized to do it. The other kind of cooperation is *nonspecialized,* where people work together with roughly equal skills and competencies. When friends gather to talk and "socialize" they have to cooperate, even though there may be no clear-cut division of labor. They must at least take turns speaking, for example, and allow each member of the group to have his say. Of course some people may talk more than others, but friendship groups are marked by lack of specialization and involve no formal assignment of tasks.

In the family, both specialized and nonspecialized cooperation occur. But, compared to most other groups, the family is highly unspecialized. Even if mother does most of the cooking, for example, she may not be a very good cook, and it is possible that on those occasions when father fixes the meal it is a little better than usual. The family is a *primary group*; in it people live together in intimacy and spontaneity, jointly solving their basic living problems. They manage the basic survival needs of food, shelter, clothing, and close human relations in a constantly adaptive way—without recourse to written rules and regulations. The exact responsibility of each member of the household is usually left unstated. (In fact, one of the continuing sore spots in family life is the problem of fixing blame when things go wrong, though ideally the question of blame never comes up.)

This doesn't mean that family members are free to do anything they please, however. People are notoriously unfree at home. Family behavior is controlled in countless ways by mores and customs, which can be traced back several thousand years in many cases. (We still respond to a number of rules for household behavior found in the Old Testament; see Chapter 15.) But we rarely think of family discipline as a specialized skill, since it is more often *stereotyped* than *skilled* behavior. It is the acting out of deeply entrenched notions about how people ought to behave.

What specialization there is in the family usually centers on two distinguishing traits: age and sex. Older members have certain responsibilities and privileges, especially in decision-making and use of family property, while younger members are expected to defer to the elders in a number of ways (though not without reservations and complaints). Males and females each have certain obligations and rights, and neither rights nor responsibilities are allotted to the overwhelming advantage of one sex—or of one age group—in most societies. But they are allotted unequally. An effective women's liberation movement may help equalize opportunities, probably to the advantage of both sexes.

THREE BASIC ROLES—THREE BASIC RELATIONSHIPS

Families are composed of men, women, and children, and each is expected to act in certain prescribed ways. Ideally, each will behave in accordance with the social expectations for people of his age and sex. When the man works at his job away from home, he is expected to perform a skill, and that is all; he is paid for his specialized work. At home, however, he is expected to act like a "man" in the most general sense of the term. And in this way family roles epitomize *manliness*, *womanliness*, and *childishness*. Basically, it is hoped that the husband will be a "good man," just as his wife is expected to be a "good woman." There may be fathers who earn the full respect of their families because of one outstanding ability, but most of them are judged by a range of behavior. These reveal the man's total measure, and it is only in the family that it can be seen.

Just as there are three key roles in the family, there are also three key *role relationships:* husband-wife, parent-child, and sibling-sibling. The family can be thought of as a small social system, divided into three subsystems. Not only will the general style of the family vary from place to place, nation to nation, class to class, religious group to religious group, race to race, and so on, but each of the three basic types of relationships will also vary—because stereotypes for family members will reflect differences in social conditions.

HUSBAND-WIFE RELATIONS

Marriage relations can take many forms, but in all societies there is *marriage work* to be done. Certain basic obligations are assumed when couples marry. It is appropriate to call them "marriage work" because in most cases they do require an effort. Some can be handled more spontaneously than others, but none are completely effortless. Unfortunately, there are usually neither clear-cut standards of excellence nor infallible models for failure for the role of "spouse."

Six kinds of marriage responsibilities are found in most societies (but it would be stretching the point to say that they are universal; the study of precisely what is expected of spouses in the world's many cultures is as yet poorly developed).

1. Truthfulness and Dependability. Spouses are expected to tell each other the truth and to be dependable. This is obvious enough, and in a sense it is not really "work." Ideally, people learn honesty long before they marry, so they do not have to think much about it after the wedding. For anyone who has to struggle to tell the truth, trouble already runs deep. There may be a few places where spouses are actually expected to be deceitful (Mead 1935), but even so, they complain about it.

2. Sharing the Work. Another common expectation is that married partners will share the work, although it is not uncommon for couples to get the feeling that one or the other is not pulling his load. Wives virtually always have one kind of work to do, husbands another, and many contemporaries feel that the traditional division of labor weighs heavily in favor of men.

3. Mutual Ego Support and Sympathy. Married couples are usually expected to listen sympathetically to each other's troubles and to make an effort to boost one another's ego. This seems to be especially true in

modern society where couples work together relatively less and offer companionship relatively more. In this connection James Hawkins (1968) attempted to distinguish between the companionship activities of couples (when they express affection or endearment and have recreational activities together) and hostility (angry outbursts aimed at deflating the partner's self-image). He found that companionship correlated with marital satisfaction in his sample at a modest level, but lack of hostility correlated even higher. It seems possible that mutual ego support is less a positive activity than avoidance of a negative one—that of humiliating the spouse. It is wise to give one's spouse a good word—an ego lift—every once in a while. But it may take about two of these to make up for every put-down, and the latter is usually so much easier to do.

4. Talking and Listening. Couples are supposed to talk to each other about the things that are of interest to either and to listen to what the other has to say. Again there are exceptions; and truly intimate, confidential relations between men and women seem most likely where the sexes are roughly equal in status and training—in interests, in the ability to express their views, and in opportunities to wield interpersonal influence. Good communication is difficult to achieve; it is "marriage work" in the most profound sense, and it involves more than just being sympathetic or giving ego support. It is the obligation to make some effort to hear what your spouse is interested in and to take these interests seriously.

5. Sex Satisfaction and Physical Warmth. Couples are expected to try to give each other sex fulfillment, and we know now that this does not come without effort—at least not for many people (Masters and Johnson 1970). It is often a task. Sex relations tend to decline in frequency and intensity in the course of marriage, becoming routine and even monotonous. The ideal of lifelong monogamy is the basic marriage pattern throughout the world (although polygyny is preferred by men of high status in many preindustrial countries), and the restriction of sex relations to monogamous pairs is not the best way to promote maximum sexual excitement. But it does seem to be a workable arrangement for organizing sex behavior, giving the greatest good to the greatest number. Couples in the middle stages of life often find that close physical relations (typified by simply sleeping in the same bed) are more basic for their continuing sense of personal security than wildly ecstatic sex relations.

6. Volunteering. Spouses are expected to at least occasionally show a willingness to do something for their partners above and beyond routine duty. One might object, saying that this is a bonus in marriage, not a basic expectation. But most people entering marriage do in fact expect something of this sort from the person they marry.

The point of this brief review of the basic work for married couples is to isolate the marriage relationship in family life and to suggest that there are similarities throughout the world. There are also differences. In later chapters it will be suggested that mutual ego support is the core marriage work in modern society. But it has certainly not always been so, and even today we find that many couples do poorly in this crucial task.

No particular attention has been given to the fact that obligations for husbands and wives are not exactly the same. That, too, will be discussed later. Suffice it to say that the husband's work differs from his wife's not only in kind, but in degree. There is still reason to believe that greater pressures are exerted on women to work at their marriages than men, but the pattern is rapidly changing.

PARENT-CHILD RELATIONS

Parents have their work cut out for them in rearing children in all societies. There are now many labor-saving devices—for mothers in particular—but it would be foolish to say that rearing children is any easier today than it has been in the past. It may be easier physically, but the psychological strains seem to be as great as ever. As physical problems are reduced, the psychological ones seem to grow.

But children have work to do, too. Above all, they still have to adjust to their parents, at least while they are young. As with parents, their physical chores have diminished (to the dismay of people who feel children need to work hard in order to learn the true meaning of life), but the psychological rigors of growing up are getting much more attention then ever before.

Parent Work

Just as there is marriage work for husbands and wives, "parent work" awaits mothers and fathers. And here, too, certain basic similarities are found across national boundaries.

1. Maintenance. The fundamental task of parents in virtually all societies is to take care of the survival needs of their children—food, shelter, clothing, sleep, bowel and bladder training, body care. And mother does most of the work. As yet there has never been an alternative to this basic pattern, not one that can be used to care for masses of children in a large, complex society—nor even in a simple one. Parents are relieved of much of the work in some places, as in the Israeli kibbutzim (more on this arrangement later), but most children in Israel are in fact taken care of by their parents in traditional ways. If we could ever devise a practical substitute for parent work in caring for infants and small

children, we would have a real family revolution on our hands. In the meantime, the growth and improvement of day-care centers for the children of working mothers will offer many new opportunities for women.

2. Guidance. In all cultures parents are expected to guide their children with regard to more than basic living habits; they influence their children's moral training and thought processes on all kinds of subjects. Parents exert an influence less by what they tell their children to do than by the example they set. If they want children to tell the truth, the best thing they can do is to be truthful themselves. This principle applies everywhere. Obviously the form and content of parental guidance changes as nations develop formal public school systems, but the essential function remains.

3. Discipline. Parents in all cultures must occasionally punish their children or withhold privileges or in one way or another see to it that certain minimal standards of behavior are met. This is indeed a task, a responsibility, although children often view it as a parental privilege (and one that is easily abused). As a task, it involves thought and self-discipline on the part of parents themselves. It is usually handled in traditional ways, however, and so it tends to become unthinking—like a ritual. The modern parent is much more likely than parents in the past to be insecure as a disciplinarian because we are now so conscious of the fact that traditional authority often does not work. Parents must still discipline their children, of course; we have simply opened up the question of how and when.

4. Assistance. Parents are expected to assist their children above and beyond the basic survival functions. In many ways this is a modern parental duty, since historically the emphasis has been on the obligations of children to their parents, not on obligations of parents to children. The contemporary parent helps his children with schoolwork, for example, and as children begin to leave home in the late teens, the parent makes financial contributions and helps out in other ways—especially in seeing them through college and helping them set up households of their own.

5. Love and Respect. The idea that parents should "love" their children is a truly modern idea. They are expected to want them in the first place (or else use contraceptives to keep pregnancy from occurring), to love them when they are small, and to gradually transform this early love to respect for the maturing person. Stress on "respect" is even newer than stress on love; the recent popularity of Haim Ginott's (1965) advice to parents is symptomatic of this trend. Ginott stresses the fact that contemporary parents must act toward their children the way they would act toward people in general, always showing respect for their essential

human integrity. Implicit is the realization that parents too often treat children as objects to be manipulated and disciplined, rather than as individuals who develop independent egos at a very early age and who are capable of much more self-direction and mutual trust than the traditional parent is likely to appreciate.

6. Release. Finally, a new parental task is to let the children go. Offspring not only can leave home now, they should and must. Even while the parent is caring for, guiding, disciplining, loving, respecting, and helping his children, there must be an implicit awareness that in the late teens the child will move out. He will then be on his own to a remarkable degree by premodern standards.

Differences between mothering and fathering have not been stressed in this discussion, but they will be clarified in later chapters. As in the case of marriage work, the trend seems to be toward greater similarity between men and women as parents. As mothers leave home to work, earning an increasing percentage of the family income, fathers are drawn into both household chores and child care to a much greater extent.

Duties of Children

Children have family duties in all societies. For centuries they were expected to be obedient and to do much of the menial work. Now they go to school, and their primary task is to please their teachers. Obligations to parents become ambiguous in the process. Children clearly have no preconceptions about their responsibilities in infancy, so their duties are established in the course of living within the family. They are almost exclusively products of "on the job training." The most important "work" for children, as it applies to relations with parents, shows up as their parents grow older, and this will be discussed in later chapters on family life for middle-aged and aging couples. But it should be obvious enough that concepts of "filial duty" and "filial respect" are ancient and that their content changes as society changes.

SIBLING RELATIONS

Sibling relations are the least studied aspect of family life and the part that is probably the most underrated—especially in terms of its impact on the character development of children. So much stress has been placed on the importance of parents, and more recently on the importance of teachers and peers, that the fundamental importance of brothers and sisters is easily overlooked.

Attention will be turned to this subject in later chapters, but information drawn from careful research is not available. We should like to know more about the changing relations between brothers and sisters as they mature and grow old. We know much about competition, jealousy, and rivalry in childhood, but what about the later developments? Even sibling relations in the teen-age years have been grossly neglected. Many brothers and sisters keep surprisingly close contact throughout life. But even more important is the fact that they have a great deal of influence upon each other's character development in childhood. An older brother or sister *can* be as influential as a parent, and efforts to impress or outdo a sibling can become a lifelong mission.

RELATIONS WITH KINSMEN

This discussion has been concerned mainly with relationships within the immediate family, but of course family relations also extend to "blood" relatives and in-laws. These *extended* family ties are found in all cultures, though rules governing them differ, and their importance varies. The most important ones are extensions of those already mentioned—between parents and children after the children set up households of their own and between brothers and sisters, again after they leave home. Most people never lose their special feeling for parents and siblings.

But cousins, aunts, uncles, nieces, and nephews can have extensive obligations to one another, too, especially in preindustrial societies. These relationships are usually not as important as primary ones in the modern city, however, as we shall see. Only relations between grandparents and their grandchildren cling to their longstanding significance, linking family members across three generations.

SUMMARY AND PROSPECTUS

The family is subject to extraordinary pressures in the modern industrial city, enough for some writers to call ours an anti-family society. People look for new domestic arrangements with almost the same eagerness that they look for new life styles in other areas. We not only find more alternatives available now than ever before, but almost all of them are subject to intense criticism from one side or another. The mass media spread new ideas quickly, and they spread disenchantment with them just as fast.

But traditional family forms persist with remarkable tenacity. The marriage rate is holding up at an extremely high level and, though the divorce rate stays up too, there is abundant evidence that most couples still try to make their marriages work. The family retains an appeal that is both direct and symbolic. In fact, it still seems to work reasonably well for masses of people.

The purpose of this brief chapter has been to identify the most fundamental characteristics of the human family and its basic subdivisions: husband-wife relations, parent-child relations, sibling relations, and relations with kinsmen. The remainder of the text will explore these roles in detail, with special emphasis on American family life. Chapter 16 delves into the fundamental nature of the family in greater depth, considering the enormous variety throughout the world. And Chapter 15 explores the historical and evolutionary background of American family practices.

Chapters in between trace the individual's family involvement through each stage of the *family cycle*. Anticipations of marriage are discussed in Chapters 3, 4, 5, and 6. This is the preparatory period of childhood and adolescence, including childhood indoctrination, dating, love, and premarital sex. The formation of marriage is taken up in Chapters 7 and 8 on mate selection, engagement, and the legal requirements for marriage. Accommodation is discussed in Chapters 9, 10, 11, and 12, covering adjustment in the early stages of marriage and then the later developments of middle and old age. The dissolution process is discussed in Chapters 13 and 14.

But before tackling these four processes it seems appropriate to take a closer look at the very real difficulties faced by contemporary family life, especially in the city, which exposes and aggravates almost every domestic weakness. This general problem is examined in Chapter 2 where the basic theme of the text is stated.

SELECTED READINGS

BARASH, MEYER, AND ALICE SCOURBY (eds.). *Marriage and the Family: A Contemporary Analysis of Contemporary Problems.* (New York: Random House, 1970).

GLASSER, PAUL H., AND LOIS N. GLASSER (eds.). *Families in Crisis* (New York: Harper & Row, 1970).

LEMASTERS, E. E. *Parents in Modern America* (Homewood, Ill.: Dorsey Press. 1970).

NIMKOFF, M. F. (ed.). *Comparative Family Systems* (Boston: Houghton Mifflin, 1965).

QUEEN, STUART A., ROBERT W. HABENSTEIN, AND JOHN B. ADAMS (eds.). *The Family in Various Cultures* (New York: Lippincott, 1961).

RODMAN, HYMAN (ed.). *Marriage, Family, and Society* (New York: Random House, 1965).

STEPHENS, WILLIAM N. *The Family in Cross-Cultural Perspective* (New York: Holt, Rinehart and Winston, 1963).

CHAPTER 2

Families Under Stress

The family has a special attraction for behavioral scientists, who are drawn to it by the many problems it poses—not only its psychological stresses and social strains, but also its remarkable capacity to satisfy human needs. Even this capacity stands as a problem, since it has not yet been fully explained. Research into the family and discourse about it are now flourishing popular interests—part of the swelling concern about the "quality" of America life. The general tone of this interest plays an important role in establishing the substance of our national mood, a mood of uncertainty and uneasiness about the future.

THE PROFESSIONAL APPROACH

Family research in the three related fields of psychology, sociology, and anthropology has grown to gigantic proportions in the twentieth century. Numerically, contributions to family sociology have always ranked in the top four of the twenty-four fields recognized by the American Sociological Association, and this is true in most other industrial nations as well (Mogey 1969). Books and extended monographs on the subject run into the tens of thousands. Scholarly papers and research reports are published in such a steady stream that it is far beyond the capacity of any one person to keep up with them all.

Therefore, professionals now specialize, knowing much more about some aspects of the subject than others. The National Council on Family Rela-

17

tions has emerged as the most important professional society in the area of family research and education, covering a great number of special interest areas. It publishes the leading periodical in the field, the *Journal of Marriage and the Family*. Founded in 1938, the National Council has grown in thirty-three years from an original membership of 200 to over 5,000, and its annual meetings attract people from all over the world.

Professional literature on the family radiates in all directions. Some of it is strictly fact-finding in nature. Almost all of it is concerned with understanding how the family functions, and it frequently leads to recommendations for improvement. A reasonably stable family system is considered absolutely necessary for continuing social order by almost all authorities. For example, one feature of familism in all societies is the concern for "legitimacy" (Malinowski 1964). Certain conditions must be met when pregnancy occurs in order to provide some assurance that the child will be adequately taken care of. Although the conditions are not always met, and in some places a large percentage of "illegitimate" babies are born, the standard of legitimacy exists in every culture, and the majority of births do in fact meet its requirements.

Professional literature on the family is critical of conventional wisdom in many ways, and it often debunks empty myths, sentimental nonsense, and wrong-headed ideas about "domesticity." Still, it is generally supportive of the family. It is guided by what has become almost a professional code: an effort to find useful solutions to both the old family problems that have existed for centuries and the new ones brought on by modern cities. The professional support for family life is more discriminating and less dogmatic than folklore, but it remains overwhelmingly positive in its purpose. Almost every issue of *The Journal of Marriage and the Family* is sprinkled with material that could be classified as part of a "family life movement," designed to spread ideas, information, and programs to improve family life.

There is also a long record of attempts to explain why the family is of such fundamental importance to mankind. To the professional, "the family" is an abstraction which is arrived at by making a mental leap from particular cases to the more general idea. Thus, the family becomes "the typical family," which changes as cities grow, as the population increases, as women gain more status, as children are given more freedom, and so on. Conversely, non-family affairs also change as the typical family unit becomes smaller, as fathers lose their patriarchal authority, or as mothers and fathers live together longer because life lasts longer.

One well-known sociologist, Kingsley Davis (1949), argues that there are four main functions of the family: *reproduction, maintenance, placement,* and *socialization* of the young. (Not everyone agrees with him, but his approach is rather typical.) The meaning of "reproduction" is obvious enough; families are childbearing units and they take care of their young.

"Maintenance" consists of the daily tasks of sheltering, feeding, clothing, and bathing members of the family. Infants and children are particularly dependent on the family for these services. Of course the family also provides emotional support. Ideally it contributes a sense of security to its members and adds a feeling of pleasure or significance to daily affairs. "Placement" refers to the role of the family in conferring a social position upon its children. Assuming that adults play a wide variety of social roles and that it is necessary for each new generation to fill roughly the same positions, it is convenient for children to follow in their parents' footsteps. Their general status is usually established by the father's economic position in the community; the son will therefore wind up in a job or career rather similar to his father's. Thus, the family, through its placement function, preserves the existing social order. Obviously this is a status quo system, and the family can be criticized because of it. But more will be said about that later. "Socialization" refers to the process by which children learn to play social roles and to live according to community standards. The child is not only taught basic rules of social behavior at home, he also acquires his own personal style. He will probably have a combination of the features of his parents—both the best ones and the worst.

Actually, there are few, if any, services that must *necessarily* be performed by the family. In all societies some children are born out of wedlock and some of them are cared for almost totally outside of conventional families. Decisions as to which religious views the child should learn or what school he should go to can be made by nonkinsmen. Food, clothing, shelter, and even emotional support can also be provided by people other than parents. Furthermore, there have been attempts to rear *all* children in the community away from the traditional home, as in some of the Israeli kibbutzim. Here small children are separated from their parents except during stated visiting hours. The children live together in small groups and are reared largely by nurses and teachers (Spiro 1956).

It is not surprising that many writers have toyed with the idea of replacements for the family—not emergency substitutes, but permanent, progressive replacements. Some claim that the day may come when man will devise a superior social form, with the ability to do everything the family has done in the past, perhaps more, but without the troublesome side effects. The idea that the family represents a "primitive" form of social organization, to be superseded by something else when people become truly civilized, has been expressed many times. And yet it is only as the survival functions of the family are reduced that its usefulness is seriously questioned. The power of the family to persist is therefore increasingly based on its ability to do the one thing that it is now best able to do—provide emotional support and ego security to people in mass society.

DISSENTING VIEWS

One very influential view of the modern family appeared in an article entitled "The Changing Family," written by William F. Ogburn (1938). In it Ogburn argues that the family has a number of important functions (he has a longer list than Kingsley Davis—economic, educational, protective, religious, recreational, status conferring, and affectional), but he feels that in every case except one the family is losing ground in modern society. Only in the area of affection has it moved ahead. Technological change, he argues, is the main reason for this "loss of functions." It forces a conflict between the needs of society and traditional family values, and the family simply does not respond to new developments as fast as it should.

Ogburn forecasts increasing competition between the family and other groups for people's loyalty. Although he has personal misgivings about this trend, he sees no way for the family to reverse it. The bonds holding married couples together and those holding children to their parents must become weaker and fewer unless love and affection can somehow be strengthened. The result is *individualization,* by which the individual is able to handle fewer of his personal problems within the family; he is increasingly on his own.

If Ogburn's position has any validity (most contemporary observers would seem to grant that it does, although with some reservations), the main chance for the family rests in the fact that it does retain one primary function—and this may actually take on more rather than less significance in the future. Although families have provided companionship throughout history, only in modern times are husbands and wives *supposed* to fall in love before they marry, and only recently have parents been advised to love their children rather than to act as authorities over them. But this is not a truly critical approach to the family, and Ogburn never intended it to be. He was hopeful that the family would become more stable as people learn how to make it come alive in the industrial city. Nevertheless, his point of view has been regarded by some writers as the culmination of a long history of criticism of the family, going all the way back to the fourteenth and fifteenth centuries.

More than any other person, Carle C. Zimmerman (1947) has attempted to sort out the kinds of criticism that the family has run up against. He argues that during the nineteenth and early twentieth centuries, while family sociology was developing, certain characteristic ideas dominated our thinking; their combined impact had the effect of undermining the family. Almost all intellectuals became *agents provocateurs* of "atomism," underminers of tradition, rather than defenders of the family and the beliefs that make it strong.

The key idea underlying their point of view, he argues, was the theory of continuous *social evolution* moving in a progressive direction. At the heart of this approach is the belief that all social institutions are contractual—man-made—and hence they can be changed or even eliminated by man himself. Social science took as its main duty the task of explaining evolution, and social critics were trained to attack anything and everything that they considered out of place, obstructive, or simply conservative.

One institution picked out for particular abuse, Zimmerman argues, was the family. Social evolution involved the shearing away of family bonds, as seen in trends toward easier divorce, liberation of the family from patriarchal control, easing of the burdens of child rearing, development of more sensuous and uninhibited sex play, stress on individual happiness through romantic courtship, and many other developments. The entire process, he claims, received a firm boost from the rise of nationalism and also from the Protestant contention that the family bond, though holy perhaps, was not a sacrament.

Thus, modern thinking about the family is largely a product of the Reformation according to Zimmerman. It attributes to the family all the elements of *secularism* and *contractualism* so prevalent since the Reformation. Virtually all of the great, early works in family sociology stressed the idea that the traditional family stands in the way of progress. Just as religion has been viewed as the opium of the people, the old-fashioned family was believed to have a deadening, "know-nothing" effect on social change. These works pointed out that important social improvements almost always occur in the nonfamily areas—in industry, science, and education, for example— while the family, with indifferent haste, slowly adapts to progressive changes. Familistic societies were shown to have sacred, slow-changing ideas about social order, while nonfamilistic societies were shown to be more innovative and dynamic (Becker 1957).

THREE KINDS OF CRITICISM

Currently, criticism of the family falls into three broad categories: one claims that the family is a conservative institution in its very nature and tends to hold back new social developments; a second claims that the traditional family stifles freedom, hence it conflicts with the leading theme of modern history—personal liberty; a third approach can be called the *cognitive incapacity theory*. It holds that the contemporary knowledge explosion calls for extraordinary new ways of transmitting our cultural heritage from one generation to the next. The family as it is now constituted may not be able to do the job.

The Conservative Argument

The essential reason for the alleged conservatism of the family is its role in child rearing; parents almost always try to teach their children the traditions of the past. The schools now take children at an early age, but parents are still in a position to mold their children's moral outlook, and they usually stress traditional ideas. This is not always true, however; Peter Morris (1967) has shown that families in different societies can promote both creative achievement and conventional attitudes.

As an employee or professional man, a father may be thoroughly up-to-date and eager to experiment in his field, but as a father he will probably speak for the familiar wisdom and against new ideas in morality, politics, and religion. Most children learn of novel ethical and philosophical ideas away from home if they learn about them at all, and they often do not hear such ideas until they reach college (though television and the mass media now make an earlier impact, and their power to liberate seems to be growing).

The family is perhaps most completely conservative in its economic outlook. It strives to hold on to its accumulated wealth and urges its members to protect any economic advantage they may have. If the family is wealthy, it not only wants to keep its money in the family but will also favor a variety of laws to protect it. (The full legal implications of this pattern are discussed in Chapter 8.)

The family is also conservative politically, since children usually take on the political views of their parents. If we can assume that these views were most appropriate for the time when parents developed their political consciousness—that is, for a previous political generation—then the effect of parents on children is an influence of the past on the present. But if parents are progressive in politics, then their children will probably be, too. In fact, teen-agers often become more liberal than their parents (Lipset 1968), but only because they are pushed by forces outside the family, rarely by those at home.

Some observers say that even in the schools education on family life tends to be moralistic, class bound, ethnocentric, and a fortress for the status quo (Kerckhoff 1957). Reuben Hill (1960), on the other hand, argues that marriage and family instruction is in fact "subversive," because it challenges the traditional assumption that the family is a "natural" institution (for which no special preparation is necessary). Perhaps much of the family material taught in public schools is tradition-bound and moralistic, but Hill does have a point. Family life education almost inevitably raises questions in an area of explosive sensitivity; it can be very threatening to tradition (which is why so many people are opposed to sex education).

This conservative argument is obviously double-edged. One of the strongest historical defenses for the family is that it brings the "wisdom of the ages" to bear on the training of children. This is an important part of its survival function. Parents can be painfully conservative—especially when they adhere stubbornly to old approaches to changing problems—but certainly not all of their experience and advice is outdated.

The Freedom Argument

Another criticism of the family is that it restricts our freedom. This complaint is voiced wherever concern for personal liberty is highly developed. It has been used rather facetiously among men—when they say that they have to give up more freedom in marriage than women (a questionable point of view). Now, with a reverse twist, feminists use the same argument. Both sexes give up at least some autonomy when they marry, but people who are steeped in the values of their society are always taught to forgo personal pleasures for the good of the family. One should not spend money without some thought for the family budget, for example, and sex is supposed to be avoided by single girls in many societies because it violates family taboos. The taboo against adultery for married people, however, is almost always stronger. Margot Hentoff (1969) says that nothing short of abolition of the family system and its control of the reproduction process will allow women to be free. Even romantic love is rarely freed from family restrictions.

But this, too, is a double-edged argument, since freedom is something that many people find hard to handle. An important function of the family has always been to protect people from themselves, that is, from the potential disasters of unlimited personal freedom. (The family's role in this regard is rarely mentioned when discussing the essential functions of the family, but perhaps we should not expect this role to be emphasized in a society that stresses liberty as much as we do.)

The Cognitive Incapacity Argument

The biologist Robert Morison (1967) has written a very strong statement of this point of view, attacking the family both as a breeding unit and as a place for training the newborn child. He argues that the family is no longer capable of teaching the child current knowledge; totally new ways must be created to teach them about twentieth-century science. If anything, the family tends to isolate children from modern social and scientific advances.

As public respect for formal education rises, Morison argues, the prestige and influence of the family must inevitably decline. The reasons are threefold: (1) the family may be perfectly adequate for transmitting conventional wisdom to children in a relatively static society, but it is disastrous for teaching new knowledge in a rapidly changing world; (2) our current understanding of population problems and of human genetics weakens the prestige of the family as the basic unit for human reproduction; and (3) we now know that children are incredibly teachable and, to ensure equal opportunity for all children, we have to invade the sanctity of the home in the early years.

Morison is not so foolish as to advocate abolition of the family, but he does argue that certain of its functions need to be taken over by other social agencies. This is a more critical and a more activist position than that of

William Ogburn, who simply calls attention to the loss or transfer of functions of the family but does not ask for a speed-up of the process.

Morison feels that the low estate of American parents, especially fathers,
can be traced to the fact that immigrants from Europe could not be very
helpful to their children in adjusting to the New World. He considers it
astonishing that the decline in respect for fathers, mothers, and priests as
sources of expert scientific knowledge has not been accompanied by a corresponding decline in respect for their moral influence. The old morality was
exhortative and dogmatic in nature; the new morality surges from facts and
theories. To cite an example, Morison suspects that the Surgeon General's
report on the harmful effects of tobacco contains far more and far better
reasons for not smoking than all the admonitions of parents and the Epworth
League (a Methodist youth organization) put together.

He contends that our current understanding of the plasticity of the human
development clearly shows that equal opportunity for all children is unlikely
as long as they are abandoned solely to their families during their most impressionable early years. The evidence is now overwhelming, he adds, that
this custom is primarily responsible for the fact that poverty is so hard to
eliminate. It is simply impossible for a highly complex society to rely on the
haphazard training given at home during the most teachable years of life,
the first six. In fact, Margaret Mead (1969) argues that modern society is so
completely different from anything preceding it in history that the new role
of parents is simply to take care of their children until they are old enough
to help their parents catch up!

Morison says that good parents in today's world are very careful, almost
reluctant. They take their family planning seriously and see to it that they
do not have too many children. After all, the father of a large family can no
longer take much pride in his brood; he is more likely to be embarrassed by
it. With our new knowledge of genetics, Morison says that we may have to
abandon the concept of the family as the prime unit of reproduction in order
to use theoretically superior models from animal husbandry. (You may very
well gasp in horror. Morison would probably say that, unfortunately, you
were brought up in a conventional family and therefore you find it hard to
think like a modern scientist.) Reputable geneticists claim that it may soon
be possible to eliminate hereditary defects and to produce heretofore un-
imaginable virtues by tinkering with the genetic code itself.

With due caution, Morison doubts that people will abandon traditional
childbearing methods without great controversy and intense anxiety. But he
does contend that scientific progress inevitably causes a gap between all the
conditions associated with sexual attraction and reproduction per se. Erotic
sex as the basis for reproduction has already become a social problem, especially by leading to unplanned or unwanted pregnancies. He foresees a future

when almost everyone will have fewer children, and an increasing number of people, for good genetic reasons, will have none at all.

Furthermore, Morison predicts that society will take a much larger share of responsibility for the care of infants and children. More and more people will be deprived of the pride of parenthood, and their sense of personal worth may suffer—temporarily at least. The family will have to be modified, perhaps only gradually and in relatively unnoticed ways. Artificial insemination, for instance, has come into use almost unmentioned in the mass media. It is still poorly understood by the public at large.

The father's role is most directly threatened. Morison grants that certain things, like a stable emotional atmosphere for children, can only be provided for the time being by the family as we have traditionally known it. He admits that the child needs a more or less constant mother figure to cling to, but he sees no comparable need for a father. In the future it may only be the unusual man who will feel very strongly about the children conceived by his wife, since they will often be the products of artificial insemination.

Betty Friedan (1963) has carried this general idea a step further. She argues that the day may come when only certain women will become mothers, and then only if they feel a particularly strong desire or show some special aptitude for it. In a sense, they will be "professional mothers." Oscar Eggers (1960) calls attention to the fact that the parent-serving professions are now getting established and that the "professionalization of parenting" would not be so inconsistent with other recent developments in career training. But Friedan pushes the idea of professional parenting much further than most contemporary agencies have in mind. According to her, mothering is already a distasteful chore to a great many women, although she recognizes that it is difficult for them to admit it. Data collected by Helena Lopata (1965), on the other hand, suggest that most women still consider mothering to be their most important and satisfying social role.

Morison believes that the greatest difficulties in the future will be finding ways to compensate people for loss of their parental roles. It is usually in the advanced societies—where the problems of immediate survival have largely been solved—that people are least confident that life has any real point. Lacking any real hazards in our own lives, many of us find a genuine feeling of significance in caring for children. The time is rapidly approaching when parents may need children more than children need parents. If Morison is right, society will need to develop new ways to give people basic rewards and satisfactions, and it will need new means to bind them together in small groups. Still, he clings to his argument—that it is unworkable for parents to keep their position as moral authorities for children while their authority in other areas is drained away. A dualism between the family and modern knowledge simply cannot last.

FAMILY BONDS IN A TECHNICALLY ADVANCED SOCIETY

Many people, however, would argue that the family can—and must—last. Although it is not responsible for modern science and may even inhibit it, one may wonder what the point of science might be in a society where family loyalties do not exist. And although science does indeed generate its own morality, as Morison claims, it cannot produce a flawless or total product. Science helps to resolve man's problems one at a time, but the moral framework for life is much larger and fuzzier than that part for which science gives us clear-cut answers. It is in the broad area of moral uncertainty that the ethical functions of the family flourish.

Thus, Morison is quite correct when he suggests that it is ridiculous to argue that parents should, through their right to veto the fluoridation of water, be allowed to decide whether or not their children's teeth will decay. But it does not follow that parents should have no rights at all in managing their children. Science and its morality are not yet wise enough to replace the home, wrong-headed as it sometimes is.

We should not infer from this that the family is good simply because it supplies needed services to the larger community. The values of familism are, in fact, ends in themselves (as well as means to other ends). People do find pleasure in family experiences; what is more, they take pleasure in the very *symbolism* of family life. For example, women do not simply enjoy their own weddings, they like weddings in general. These ceremonies make life seem complete. They give a feeling that the affairs of the community are as they ought to be.

And yet it remains true that modern family obligations have to compete with many other personal commitments. Are there ways to encourage familism and at the same time liberate the most progressive forces in society? Can we have two worlds: the special world of the family and another one where different, more rational and creative rules apply? Of course these two separate spheres already exist, in a mutually threatening cold war. The tension between them cannot be resolved in this book, but its general nature can be explored, and some of the means by which familism remains strong can be examined.

ROMANCE IN AMERICA

The dilemma of the value of family life shows up with exceptional clarity in the way we handle romance in America. For example, many writers have tried to explain why "love" is stressed so much in American courtship and marriage. It is not nearly as popular in most other societies, especially those less developed industrially (Goode 1959). Almost everyone agrees that love is a highly emotional and irrational force, and therefore one might expect it to be strongest in "backward" societies—those which are not highly developed in terms of science and modern education. Yet just the opposite holds true. People seem to be more anxious to "fall in love," to read, hear stories, and sing songs about love in places like the United States than in primitive or peasant societies. Why is that?

Sidney Greenfield (1965) has offered a very interesting theory on the subject. He claims that love as the basis for marriage is just as irrational as people say it is, but its irrational nature makes it all the more attractive in a highly organized, materialistic society like our own. As children grow up, they are urged to be rational and calculating. Competitiveness is impressed upon boys in particular, he argues; they are taught to look out for themselves—no one else will—and to recognize that they will be judged very largely by how much money they make. They should try to earn as much as possible and then spend their earnings in ways that show how successful they are.

Women and children can hardly be expected to compete in such a society, Greenfield claims, but if that is the case, how will they be taken care of? He argues that from a strictly rational point of view American men would be better off if they did not marry, but then women and children would be in trouble. By not marrying, men could devote themselves more completely to their careers, and they would have all the money they make for themselves, cars, clothes, and the high life. So why do they marry?

Part of the answer, according to Greenfield, is that they are thoroughly drenched in romantic ideas as they grow up. While they are learning a series of rational approaches to life, they also learn certain irrational ones. By idealizing love and marriage we create an image of life with more to offer than just material benefits; love is that "something more." Hence, men fall in love—an irrational experience—and they do precisely what their better judgment tells them they should not do: They get married.

From the point of view of society this irrational act is absolutely essential. It assures that women and children will be taken care of and therefore that *everybody* can busily consume the products turned out by a highly efficient economic system. In less productive societies men need women—and perhaps even children—to satisfy the essential requirements for survival. But as productivity through rational principles advances, women are needed less. So romantic love is stressed more and more to guarantee a high marriage rate.

You may very well object to Greenfield's theory. Certainly I do. You may even be enraged by it. For one thing, men need companionship now as much as ever, and what is the use of making a big, impressive salary if you have no one to share it with? In fact, men who earn the highest incomes also happen to have the highest marriage rates. And if they should make so much money that they cannot even spend it all on their families—as with millionaires—they set up foundations for the purpose of giving it away. Furthermore, if marriage lures men into sharing their wealth with women, why are modern women rebelling against marriage as never before in history? They claim that it is a trap for them, not for men. The women's liberation movement will see Greenfield's theory as another example of male treachery.

There may be many other loopholes in his argument, but it does raise an extremely important point. In fact, it is the main theme of this book: How does the family survive in modern society, a society that not only creates unprecedented problems for family life, but offers a variety of substitutes for it? What are the functions of today's family—in keeping social order, in organizing relationships between the sexes and the generations—and how well are they being met? How can the contemporary person decide what family course he or she should take?

SUMMARY

The popular appeal of the family is both direct and symbolic, since people ordinarily find home life enjoyable, and they take pleasure in the repeated references to it wherever they go. The family also enjoys a professional appeal, but that follows an entirely different line. Scholarly study of the family emerged with the growth of modern social science; it has been concerned with solving family problems and also with the more abstract question of the family's basic social purpose. Since "the family" is found in all cultures, it has long been considered essential, and writers have attempted to explain why. The most frequent approach is that it serves necessary human functions in relatively effective and economic ways. No other social arrangement can satisfy the complex combination of biological, psychological, and social needs so well. (Each of these will be discussed later.)

But the family faces exceptional problems with the rise of industrial nations, and it has received its share of criticism. It has rarely been challenged before, but the attack now has momentum—not always out in the open, but in ways of accomplished subtlety. Bernard Farber (1964) claims that the contemporary family ought to serve the individual, not the other way around, and that for this reason the new marriage philosophy is "permanent availability"—ideally, each person keeps himself ready for new marriage opportunities, much as employees keep an eye out for new and better job opportunities. Clearly this poses a challenge to traditional forms of familism.

Probably the most common argument of the past quarter century is that the family is losing many of its traditional functions or that these can be handled better by other social arrangements. We also hear that the family is very conservative, standing as an obstacle to progress or that it stifles individual freedom. In its very nature familism represents a particular way of life, and it exacts certain personal sacrifices from the people who subscribe to it. Robert Morison contends that the family no longer provides the best arrangement for human reproduction, nor is it any longer effective in transmitting our rapidly expanding knowledge to children.

This very broad problem has been posed: How can familism be preserved and bolstered even as the most progressive cultural forces available to modern man are liberated? The task of this book is to explore familism historically, cross-culturally, and in terms of the life cycle of the individual. In a sense, two cultures exist side by side in industrial society: One centers on the long-standing commitment to family life, the other on nonfamily pleasures and responsibilities. There is a lingering tension between the two, although they need not be considered mortal enemies. As key facts and theories about the family are discussed, an effort will be made to clarify the essential nature of this tension and to help the student find his own, personal way.

SELECTED READINGS

BOWMAN, CLAUDE C. "The Family and the Nuclear Arms Race," *Social Problems,* Vol. 11 (Summer 1963), pp. 29–34.

GOODE, WILLIAM J. "The Role of the Family in Industrialization," in Robert F. Winch and Louis Wolf Goodman (eds.), *Selected Studies in Marriage and the Family.* New York: Holt, Rinehart and Winston, 1968, pp. 64–70.

HOBART, CHARLES W. "Commitment, Value Conflict and the Future of the American Family," *Marriage and Family Living,* Vol. 25 (November 1963), pp. 405–412.

MORISON, ROBERT S. "Where Is Biology Taking Us?" *Science,* Vol. 155 (January 1967), pp. 429–433.

OGBURN, WILLIAM F. "The Changing Family," *The Family,* Vol. 19 (July 1938), pp. 139–143.

ZIMMERMAN, CARLE C. *Family and Civilization,* New York: Harper, 1947.

PART TWO

Anticipation of Marriage

CHAPTER 3

The Childhood Years

People pick up an incredible variety of impressions in childhood, on every conceivable subject. They learn particularly, though certainly not exclusively, about the family. They spend about as much time with peers as with parents and relatives, and they may learn almost as much from both sources. But their lives are anchored at home. Each household has its own style which, to children, seems "normal." In effect, this is an *ascribed status*, since the child is influenced by it whether he likes it or not. At home he will learn attitudes about politics, religion, and jobs, but these attitudes are temporary compared to the deeper influence of family style itself.

Only in modern society, however, has the family been so highly concentrated in its own little sphere. Prior to the twentieth century the child's introduction to family affairs covered the entire range of human training, so that political, religious, and occupational beliefs were implicit in the very existence of the family. Now a large part of our training is handled by the schools, while the family tends to specialize in close, interpersonal relations. One set of rules applies at home, where members receive according to their needs; another applies outside, where they compete for almost everything.

THREE STAGES LEADING TO MARRIAGE

In order to place this and the four chapters that follow in proper perspective, it is useful to distinguish three stages in childhood. In the first, lasting until the age of thirteen or fourteen, the child acquires a huge collection of information about family matters. Virtually all of it is colored by the structure and emotional make-up of his own household. Many things are learned, but knowledge is actually less important in most cases than the person's *style of life*, which determines the way his knowledge will be used and is the most important thing taught by the family. It will determine the underlying sensibilities of the person, influencing how he copes with family problems, how he makes personal decisions, and how he relates to others in intimate social settings. The present chapter is devoted to this stage.

The second stage is the dating or near-dating period, occurring in early to middle adolescence. At this time the heterosexual, pairing-off pattern takes over, but we will come back to that in the next chapter. Perhaps it should be noted that dating is not found in preindustrial societies to any great extent, so its function as preparation for marriage is new and unique. Being such a recent historical development, its full impact on the family has perhaps not even been realized.

The third stage is the period of courtship, when pairing-off is directed toward finding a marriage partner. It is more intimate and less stereotyped than dating and will be discussed in Chapter 7.

FIRST FAMILY EXPERIENCES

Ideally, early family life serves as the basis for a lifelong family commitment. The child hears thousands of references to the family, the overwhelming majority of which associate it with warmth, care, and happiness. Moreover, it is mentioned in ways that subtly suggest that he *ought* to respect it; morally, he has no choice. Anybody can be outraged by his family, but it takes many and frequent hard knocks to completely alienate most people.

Ernest Burgess (1926) once said that the family is a "unity of interacting personalities." Each family has its own unique manner, since every member brings a unique personal style to the relationship. Some sort of transformation occurs when people live together; over a period of time they develop a stable, even predictable, pattern. It is difficult, perhaps impossible, to tell just what this pattern will be by knowing only the mother or father, or even by knowing all members of the family as individuals. The pattern becomes clear only by observing the family together in their home, and even then only when they are not on their best behavior.

But how often do we have a chance to see the interior of other people's families when they are not on "company manners"? You may think you know what life is like across the street, but the people there will usually go to great lengths to keep you from discovering the truth. Most of us *really* know only our own families. And this is unfortunate because an awareness of alternative possibilities is always the key to personal and family improvement. Nevertheless, it is each home's spontaneous *unity of interacting personalities* that has the deepest impact on the child, and it is this unity that stamps the child with a particular brand of familism.

Family interaction occurs on three levels, each influencing the other two: the *sensory*, the *emotional*, and the *intellectual*. This trio was suggested by Harry Stack Sullivan (1953) in his influential work *The Interpersonal Theory of Psychiatry*. The sensory level, as the name suggests, occurs when family members have close physical contact—when they touch each other, disrobe together (while the children are young), see each other as they are rarely seen in public (before taking a bath rather than after), share the germs and contagious illnesses that family members bring home, and make less effort than usual to cover up natural body odors.

The possibilities for sensory interaction are unique within the family. Away from home, for example, people usually make every effort to keep from touching one another—except in highly stereotyped ways (Felipe and Sommer 1966). For example, in the college classroom, no matter how crowded, students almost always avoid body contact. If somebody so much as touches your elbow, you will inch away and become somewhat alarmed if he repeats this invasion of your physical privacy.

Within the family, body intimacy is taken for granted. Husband and wife enjoy almost total physical contact as newlyweds, and parents and children delight in cuddling and caressing when the kids are young. As they mature, touching, patting, and embracing become less common, which seems to be a normal, universal process. Husbands and wives also cut down on such things in the course of marriage, but if they begin to avoid any physical touching at all, their marriage is probably in trouble.

Emotional interaction within the family refers to the sharing of excitement. Children have thousands of exciting moments with their parents as they grow up. In fact, some of the more memorable ones may involve the complete range of human emotions, as when the family attends a funeral for one of the children's grandparents. Sorrow will be the predominant emotion, but elements of fear, humor, and (from the children's point of view) bewilderment will also occur. Almost all American families experience the excitement of acquiring a new car or a new home and of attending movies, circuses, and parades together. Excitement is also shared with nonfamily members, but an inventory of life's most stirring moments would probably show that most of them occur with the family.

The one stage in life when this is least true is adolescence, which is undoubtedly one reason that the teen years are ones of conflict between parents and children. This is also the period when youth have more intimate physical contact with nonfamily members than either before or after. Boys have their first intimacy with girls at this time, several years after they started keeping distance between themselves and their mothers. When they are little, boys enjoy very close physical contact with women (that is, with their mothers).

In the elementary-school years this is greatly reduced, and it may be elim-inated altogether in preadolescence or the early teen years. When boys start going out with girls they obviously like the body contact—some can hardly get enough. Girls like it, too, although they have somewhat different body contact experiences before adolescence. Father-daughter contacts appear to be less abruptly cut off in the middle stages of childhood than are those between mothers and sons, for example, and girls have less rough-and-tumble physical relations with one another than boys do. Daughters probably enjoy closer physical relations with both parents than sons do (good night kisses and other expressive acts), perhaps in part to compensate for the fact that parents tend to discourage physical intimacies by their daughters away from home. The dangers for daughters outside the home are usually per-ceived to be greater than for sons.

Primate studies show that young monkeys can derive a certain security simply from having body contact with a soft, pleasant object. The object has much the same effect as a mother when she cuddles and feeds her young (Harlow 1958). When the monkeys are frightened, they run to their mothers, or to doll-like substitutes for mothers. If these are soft and cuddly, the monkeys will soon move away to explore their surroundings. The ones that have been given wiry, uncomfortable mothers go to them when they are frightened, too, but find no relief. They cannot get the reassurance needed to make a fresh start.

Without suggesting that people are just like monkeys, which they cer-tainly are not, most human mothers have had somewhat similar experiences. The child may have been bruised in the backyard, for example. He comes inside, puts his arms around his mother's legs, or perhaps just stands close to her; in a very short while the tears disappear and the child returns to his play.

A combination of sensory and emotional interaction may occur, for ex-ample, in the midst of an electrical storm, when members of the family often cluster together. Fear is much easier to manage when you are physically close to a familiar person. Robert Douglas (1968) suggests that dinner time is par-ticularly representative of family interaction. This refers to the primary meal of the day, usually in the evening, when all (or most) members of the family gather together. Key attitudes of the family are expressed at this time, in the midst of sensory and emotional interaction.

Intellectual interaction refers to the sharing of ideas and abstractions. Although it undoubtedly occurs in all families (and some homes are very intellectual), most of them are much better at sensory and emotional inter-action. Obviously small children are not the best conversationalists, even though they do ask hundreds of questions and can sometimes handle ideas that utterly bewilder their parents. But more often they do not fully under-stand the routine ideas that parents take for granted. When father talks about politics, for example, the children will usually be more impressed by the level of excitement and concern he shows than by the brilliance of his argument, and they will judge what he is saying by his emotional intensity rather than by his logic.

Thus, sensory and emotional interaction ordinarily determine the family's special style. In terms of Charles Horton Cooley's (1902) classic description of the "looking-glass self process," the family provides the basic school for human nature. It is here that the child learns to be human and acquires his first meaningful conception of himself. No doubt children who grow up in intellectual homes will themselves acquire intellectual interests, but there are other sources for these. The child who has a secure home life can do quite well in school and retain respect for his parents even as he moves away from them in academic pursuits. But the child who is emotionally isolated at home is not likely to find intimate companionship on the outside.

Broadly speaking, family patterns experienced by the child will be the kinds that he will try to re-create in his own family later on. This is a major factor in mate selection—we are attracted to people who are very much like ourselves and who have had similar family experiences in childhood. In countless situations we learn what to expect at home; we get an image of the range and form that family life *ought* to take. As crises are met, for example, children watch their parents, although not consciously of course (if either parent is so inconspicuous that he is not even noticed, his actions are no less significant). Not only will the parents meet crises more successfully as they gain experience in facing them, the children ordinarily benefit, too, and may be able to handle emergencies better a generation or so later in their own families. It has long been known that persons whose parents have a successful marriage are more likely to succeed in marriage themselves.

Furthermore, life in the community at large usually reinforces these patterns. For example, although each middle-class family has its own unique style in certain respects, it will also have much in common with other middle-class families in the community. At the very heart of community life is a system of *social stratification,* whereby families are ranked (largely in terms of wealth, determined by the occupation of the "head" of the household). Middle-class families cluster together in the city, and economic and social pressures combine to make them very similar in family habits.

In this way social pressures assure that family life will remain similar from one generation to the next. While the child learns to prefer the kinds of family experiences he had as a child, he also learns at school and in the neighborhood the things he will need to know in order to have the same social status his parents had. Society manages to re-create itself as each new generation comes of age. As Charles Horton Cooley put it, "self and society are twin born."

THE ATTRACTION TO MARRIAGE

Although the elementary school years are often considered years of *sexual latency*, when the child has little or no interest in sex, research in recent years proves otherwise. Certainly the current theories of sex development do not ignore the preadolescent period (Broderick and Fowler 1961). One strong reason that children become interested in the idea of marriage is their growing curiosity about sex and their mounting excitement about having a love partner.

While the attraction to marriage becomes stronger, the family may lose out. Interest in family affairs at home tends to decline as the child becomes more involved in peer groups at school. The family's position as the main source of affection is challenged, and ties with parents often become tense and brittle. Charles Bowerman and John Kinch (1959) have found that the shift from family to peer attachments is continuous from about the fourth to the tenth grade; the pace tends to pick up in each succeeding year with only trivial exceptions. Carlfred Broderick and George Rowe (1968) have offered compelling evidence that there is a sequence of stages in the pre-adolescent period, most notably in the ten-to-twelve age span, that creates a powerful disposition in favor of marriage. The stages build upon one another so that each ascending step is dependent upon the successful completion of the previous one.

The first stage occurs in elementary school when children get a clear idea of the heterosexual nature of marriage for the first time. This is closely followed by a personal realization that marriage will probably occur in one's own future and that it will be a wonderful thing. Broderick and Rowe argue that this is a fundamental step in sexual as well as family development. Until it is achieved the child will be seriously handicapped in relations with the opposite sex (although difficulties at this time can sometimes be overcome in later adolescence).

Commitment to the idea that marriage is desirable leads in turn to the next stage, in which some member of the opposite sex is singled out as particularly attractive and placed in the special category of "boyfriend" or "girl-friend." This first attraction will probably occur in the 10 to 12 age range, but it is not likely to be reciprocal at this time (Broderick 1966). In fact, the object of affection may not have the slightest idea that anyone has a crush on him. Nevertheless, this kind of imaginary relationship is taken very seriously by the person involved. Although he may have endless daydreams on the subject, he is not anxious to share his thoughts with other people—neither friends nor parents. If accused of having a crush on someone, he will probably deny it or simply show signs of embarrassment. The majority of children studied by Broderick and Rowe described themselves as having been "in love" during this stage (using the term loosely, of course; the fact that it is not "true" love is beside the point for the moment.)

Having been in love leads to the next stage: wanting to be with a member of the opposite sex, especially for such things as parties or going to the movies. Youth who have never been in love prefer to go to movies alone or only with others of their own sex. Wanting a companion of the opposite sex precedes the next big step, which is going out on the first full-fledged date.

This sequence is not the least bit surprising, but it does show that basic heterosexual attitudes develop even before adolescence. A general growth pattern leads from simple recognition of the heterosexual nature of marriage to the more concrete pairing-off of a particular couple. The idea of being married at some future time (to the child it seems like a long way off) gradually gains a sense of inevitability, and it becomes even more real as detailed information about the nature of matrimony is added. The process begins in a fantasy-like relationship with some member of the opposite sex (who might even be an older male or female) and is gradually molded and shaped by the pressures of reality.

Actually, Broderick and Rowe did not find this sequence among all the children they studied. It did not show up among lower-class boys, for example. As we shall see, growing up in poverty produces a family outlook different in certain fundamental respects from the one found in middle-class America. Quite obviously, attitudes about family life will take a different course where children live in tense, brutal, or impoverished homes. All three of these qualities may go together in some families, but that is not necessarily the case.

Impoverishment is found by definition in the lower social classes, but brutality can occur in homes of middle or high status. Tension and unkindness can also occur in families of high status, although several studies indicate that they tend to be associated with impoverishment. Stephen Richter (1968), discussing the economics of child rearing, argues that lower-class parents lack the resources needed to keep control of their children, so they often resort to physical threats. Middle-class parents have more leverage because they can give and withhold economic privileges. Having less to offer, lower-class parents are tempted to overwhelm their children, but that works only when they are too little to fight back.

Thus, family life for the poor often includes serious handicaps in addition to the sheer fact of poverty. But even in these homes an attraction to marriage and familism is maintained in most cases. Children, knowing no other life, usually find pleasure, perhaps even enchantment, in what they have. Certainly most parents try to enchant their children, and they often succeed despite their handicaps. (Growing up poor is discussed in greater detail later in this chapter.)

BOY-GIRL DIFFERENCES IN FAMILY ATTITUDES

Family attitudes differ from one group to the next—by social class, ethnic status, religion, race, and possibly even region of the country—but the most thoroughly studied differences occur in connection with sex. Girls learn things about the family that seem strange or even silly to boys, and these are among the most important and most basic differences separating the sexes.

For example, when girls are still very young they are told that they will someday be mothers, often in dramatic ways even before they enter school. They watch what their mothers do, how they talk, and especially what they worry about. An eight-year-old girl may be overheard telling her little brother: "Look at you, dirty already. Really!"—a word-for-word imitation of her mother. Most girls can be counted on to have an interest in babies and to make a fuss over them whenever the chance appears. Boys pass infants in a hallway or on the street without any notice whatever, and some will remain indifferent as long as they live. A surprising number of teen-age boys have never had any contact with little children (except when they were little themselves) and are uneasy in their presence or actually afraid of them (Osborne 1961).

Boys spend less time in family activities than girls, and they usually have fewer chances to get involved. Very few boys help in child care or disciplinary matters, for example (Johannis 1957). Most of them stay out of family economic affairs, such as shopping, saving, paying bills, and financial planning, and they have very little voice in making household decisions (Johannis and Rollins 1959), except those directly affecting themselves. If they do any work at home it will probably be in the yard or emptying the garbage—not very important family duties. Girls are much more likely to have daily chores in the house (Francis 1963), and of course they are often used as babysitters. Boys are given freedom from their parents earlier than girls and are usually allowed more independence and privacy in personal affairs. Boys even ask for advice from their parents less often than girls do (Earle 1967).

Furthermore, the typical high-school boy spends very little time with his parents *away* from home and less time with them *at home* than his sister (Duvall 1961). Girls stand in an apprentice relationship with their mothers to a much greater extent than boys do with their fathers. The father may be a fairly visible model for his son, and he does put pressure on the boy to "grow up" and "behave," but mothers, by comparison, oversee almost everything their daughters do. As a result, girls can hardly escape becoming more sensitive than boys to almost every aspect of family life.

This does not mean that girls become just like their mothers; in many cases they live in constant conflict, perhaps *because* they are so close. In fact, boys seem to have child-rearing values more similar to their mothers than girls (Kell and Aldous 1960). One reason for this is simply that boys give so little thought to such things. Father's attitudes on the subject are often rather vague (in the United States), and he is away from home during the day, including the afternoons when the children come home from school. Mother reaches her son at least as much as father does. She is usually home after school, for example, and may help her son change clothes and fix him a snack. Because boys rarely think about parenthood in their teens, the most important years for daydreaming, they almost inevitably remain more "childish" in their approach to parenthood. They are left with uncritical memories about what mother did or said. Girls spend a much larger part of their time thinking on the subject and therefore have a better chance to develop their own point of view. But Alice Rossi (1968) argues that neither girls nor boys are adequately prepared for parenthood in the United States, largely because there are few useful guidelines to successful parenthood in this society. Shirley Angrist (1969) suggests that girls in particular develop a "contingency orientation" to the parent role; they are taught that they ought to marry and become housewives and mothers, but they also learn that they might not marry, that they can have careers and may have to support their families, that they will have to adjust to the special characteristics of their husbands (whom they do not even know during their formative years), and so on. Girls are probably more aware of the contingencies they may face in marriage than boys.

What boys think about marriage also seems to be more dependent upon the *quality* of their home life than is true for girls. According to a study by Paul Wallin (1954), for example, girls often look forward to marriage with eager anticipation even if their parents' marriage ends in divorce. Wallin found that girls in general had a more favorable attitude toward marriage than boys, no matter how happy their parents' marriage might have been. But boys who thought their parents' marriage was happy had stronger and more positive feelings toward marriage than other males. Wallin concluded that girls see marriage as the basic framework for their adult lives, so they have a good reason to view it in a favorable light. Compared to boys, they more quickly reject any unhappy thoughts about it and look for hopeful, optimistic signs in stories, movies, and on television.

To the girl's early attraction to family affairs another positive factor is added; she is much more likely to receive formal training for the family— in fact, almost twice as likely as her brother (Dyer 1963; Rosenstiel and Smith 1963). Boys get very little schooling for the role of husband, and they receive even less for the role of father (LeMasters 1957). In a survey of the enrollment in high-school family courses in Indiana, girls outnumbered boys by about three to one (Dager, Harper, and Whitehurst 1962).

Most of the teachers were women, and they had received their college preparation in home economics for the most part, an almost exclusively female specialty.

Even the play of girls tends to revolve around household activities. It is conducted in small groups where interaction is largely "expressive," a style rather like that which girls are expected to follow when they become wives, mothers, and housekeepers. Doll play also falls in this category, although in recent years it has become more concerned with courtship and relatively less with marriage and parenthood (Ball 1967). The play of girls is usually supervised by mothers and other women who can hardly fail to show their concern for problems of motherhood and housekeeping. Helping mother is sometimes work for the girl, but it may also be play, as when she makes fudge or other dishes that are considered "fun."

The play of boys is another matter. It takes two forms in particular that show the lack of male interest in familism. One is the boys' attraction to team sports; the other revolves around "the chicken game" (to be explained in a moment). While girls are playing in small, expressive groups, under the fairly close supervision of mothers, boys are more likely to be involved in athletics, where they are constantly challenging one another. While girls are *talking* with each other, boys are *competing* according to the rules of baseball, football, or basketball (and many other games, but none as popular as the big three). Of course, girls are not totally excluded from athletics, but they participate less than boys and are probably less likely to daydream about being an athletic hero.

Team sports may have something to do with family life, but the connection is not very obvious. Mainly, it is a world apart; even the weekend afternoons that boys (and men) spend watching football or baseball on television are, from mother's point of view, periods of escape from household chores, and they interfere with other things that the family might possibly be doing together. The key to success in team sports is competence and the will to win, and almost all boys are encouraged to try to make good in this way. They are driven to practice in sports in ways that can rarely be achieved in other fields. "The game" binds males together in exciting activities away from home, away from mother, away from girls. Fathers may be used as coaches, of course, but only one boy's father can do that job. Parents may also attend the games, making them family affairs in a sense, but even then it is not unusual for mothers to complain that their dinner schedules are upset, or their bedtime plans ruined. (In all fairness it must be added that mothers may help out at the refreshment stands, keep score, and so on. In some cases the *whole* family is involved, and the game is the highlight of the family's week.)

"The chicken game" is also part of this male ritual. It refers to the way boys constantly challenge each other and then respond to the challenge in the most "manly" way they know. There are two parts to it—the *dare* and the *manly response*—and it seems to occur in every country in the world, leading to physical contact, the risk of bodily harm, and an infinite variety of crouch-and-spring maneuvers. Girls spend almost no time at all in this way, apparently because it has no place in the affairs of adult women. In fact, girls are continually reminded not to have any part of it. They have very little feminine status to gain by being rowdy and physically overbearing. For boys, success in this sport is the essence of masculine status. It is related indirectly, if not directly, to the constant pressures of challenge and response among adult men.

The chicken game seems to be a human version of the pattern found among almost all mammals, setting up a male pecking order—a ranking system of power and prestige. Although the hierarchy is quite stable, it *is* occasionally challenged, and boys are probably more active than adult men in this regard. But men, in turn, are more active than adult males of any other animal species. Men of low social status rarely challenge those near the top, but contests among men of similar standing never seem to cease.

The main point of all this is to suggest that girls are involved in play or recreational activities that lead in a very logical way to their future roles as wives and mothers; boys are caught up in a pattern that seems to have no direct connection to their future roles as husbands and fathers. That does not mean that boys will turn against the family, of course, although it is certainly true that fathers are generally less dependable than mothers. In fact, the competition fostered by sports and other boyish activities is actually quite relevant to men's adult roles, because as *breadwinners* they are expected to compete with one another. Those who are successful share their earnings with their wives and children and thereby achieve at least one major basis for fatherly success.

If boys become alienated from the family it is probably mainly because of attitudes they develop toward girls and women (but we must be careful not to exaggerate this point). During the elementary-school years boys pretend to dislike girls, but there is hardly any counterpart for this kind of thinking in girls' attitudes toward boys. If anything, girls encourage one another to act as if they like boys, whether they do or not. Boys urge each other to stand aloof. They obviously prefer to be together in their own groups (which girls do, too), and they are gradually taught the off-color stories and jargon used by men and older boys to describe women. Gershon Legman (1968) contends that almost all dirty jokes are dreamed-up by males, with women bearing the brunt of most of them. His theory is that smutty stories are used by men to express their aggressive feelings toward the highly disturbing opposite sex. He may exaggerate this Freudian view, but there is a kind of smugness combined with aggression and fear in most male groups, often beginning even before adolescence.

It was noted earlier that the doll play of girls stresses dating and court-ship, apparently even more now than in the past. Clearly, girls in the ele-mentary years are interested in boys and are anxious to win their favor. But we do not have to rely on doll play to prove this; it is apparent in direct interviews with girls or simply by listening to their conversations. The fact that girls serve as cheerleaders for boys' activities is symptomatic of the gen-eral pattern. While boys are talking aggressively or in a deprecating way about girls, or just ignoring them as they work at their athletics and shock tactics, the girls are taking an almost opposite point of view.

The relationship between attitudes toward girls and attitudes toward the family may be self-evident. If boys are suspicious of girls, they almost have to be suspicious of marriage. But if this attitude occurs in the preadolescent period, extending into the early teens, then obviously boys must change their point of view somehow if they are going to settle down. For girls, the attraction to marriage is already there; it has developed with hardly any background of suspicion of either boys or family life. The teen-age period is the time when they must try to get boys as interested in marriage as they have been all along.

Boys' attitudes toward girls in the elementary years may be related to the fact that they have conflicting feelings toward their mothers at this time, a kind of conflict that girls rarely have to worry about. (As yet this theory has not been proved.) Both boys and girls are very dependent upon their mothers in the first few years of life, and they show complete, undiluted affection for them at this time. But two things happen during the elemen-tary years that makes boys rebel—at a time when they still *need* their mothers very badly. One is the incest taboo. As the boy matures it becomes more and more difficult for mother to cuddle and caress him as she did when he was small, and almost all physical contacts become more self-conscious. Boys begin to be awkward in mother's presence, a reaction that is extended to women at large, certainly to women of mother's age.

The second element in the boy's feeling occurs when he learns that men are supposed to be dominant in relations with women, at least not sub-ordinate or dependent. Nevertheless, he must be submissive to his mother for a number of years even after he realizes that this is *not* the standard male-female relationship. Not only does a difficult relationship develop between mothers and sons, female teachers are drawn in, too. Boys have to be subordinate under circumstances in which they are vaguely aware that they are not supposed to be. A certain resentment toward female authority is not too surprising under the circumstances. (Girls are not burdened by this, which is probably one reason that they do better than boys in the early years of school.) John Earle (1967) found that boys who feel close to both their parents are more likely to turn to father for advice than mother, ap-parently because men are less threatening to their sense of masculine independence. Most boys begin to outperform girls in the classroom only when male teachers take over in the later stages of the school system.

It would certainly seem that the first strong attraction to familism occurs among girls, not boys, and it begins in the elementary years. If there is ever a genuine breakdown in family life in our culture, the forewarning should show up in attitudes of young girls. Perhaps we are already witnessing a slight trend in this direction. The real turning point will be at hand when girls, like boys, show a positive distaste for housekeeping and child care. Although that is not yet the case for most of them, it does affect a growing number in college. But they usually reconsider—when tempting opportunities for marriage show up or when competition for the most demanding careers becomes particularly stiff.

A SPECIAL CASE: GROWING UP POOR

Children who live in poverty are not likely to find family life very romantic, but even they usually set up families much like they knew as children. Most of them, especially the girls, will find domestic matters at the center of their personal affairs as long as they live. Though they may be employed throughout much of their lives, they rarely think of "careers" in the middle-class sense of the term because the job opportunities open to them are so limited and unappealing. Their problems, which are worth special attention, are further aggravated among low-income blacks because of the continuing conditions of race prejudice and discrimination.

Lee Rainwater (1965) has described in detail the problems faced by low-income black children. (Bear in mind, of course, that all low-income families, regardless of race, have much in common, and that millions of blacks have middle-class status.) First, the poor family (white or black) tends to be larger than average because couples with limited income and education rarely use contraceptives or practice family planning. They therefore have children they may not want, do not plan for, and are not financially able to handle. The infant death rate is relatively high in such groups, but the fact remains that most unplanned children do not die. They may have greater-than-average health problems throughout life, but they survive, and hence the family becomes large. In fact, it is not uncommon for the family to have relatives living in, adding to the total number of persons in the household.

Although the size of the family is larger than average, the home itself is usually smaller. Rooms are below average in size; there are fewer of them; and the house or apartment is not very attractive. If a window breaks or a heater needs repairs, there may be a long wait before repairs are made. Not only is the house smaller than average, but all of the houses in the neighborhood are crowded close together. In the very nature of our system of *residential segregation,* lower-class families are usually clustered together in certain parts of town. With large families in small houses that are crowded together, it is obvious that children will not have places to play that are designed specifically for that purpose. They will still play, of course, but in places intended for some other use. This inevitably means that the children become greater nuisances to their parents and to adults in general than in middle-class families. (Children in even moderately affluent American families, on the other hand, are likely to have swings in their backyards and a room of their own in the house.)

Since children in the lower classes are potentially greater nuisances in the eyes of their parents, the latter spend less time in *character development* and more time simply trying to keep the children out of their hair. This happens because fewer concessions can be made to immaturity. The lower-class father, in particular, tends to assume an authoritarian bearing, but his children are likely to think he is just "crabby." He may also stay away from home for long stretches of time, and a much larger percentage of families at this level are therefore headed by mothers than in the middle classes. Up to one-half may be run by women at any particular time in some lower-class neighborhoods, and perhaps as many as two-thirds will fall in this category over a period of time. There has been much justified criticism of the notion that most black families are mother-headed (Billingsley, 1968). Here we refer only to lower-class families, black or white, living in poverty in our big cities. It is not that the men are completely missing, but rather that they come and go in ways that put an extra burden on mothers. A large number of lower-class men seem to disappear during their mature years, living in flop houses and spending time in institutions. The census data persistently understate their numbers. Lack of a stable father in the household unquestionably leads to a certain loss of family control within the lower-class community—not only affecting boys, but girls, too. One reason that the fathers are often away is because they are not anxious to take responsibility for their offspring; as children, they had few models for a life style of social responsibility, and the pattern passes from one generation to the next.

Rainwater notes that black women of very low income often become pregnant at an early age, even before marriage. When the baby is born it may be cared for by the grandmother (who is likely to be in her forties) rather than the new mother. While the grandmother may take pleasure in caring for the child, the young mother is rather indifferent to her role. She may marry, but relations with her husband are often strained. He will probably have difficulty holding a job, so he cannot consistently earn enough to care for his family. His wife treats him with very little respect when he is not working and often feels that he has little or no right to the customary household privileges if he is not earning a paycheck.

By comparison, middle-class wives are less likely to face the problem of having an unemployed husband on their hands. If that problem should arise, the husband in most cases will have built up enough good will to get his wife's sympathy, and she can help him through this ego-crushing period. This kind of support is much less likely in the lower classes.

After the lower-class woman marries and has children, and her husband has proved to be less than a steady provider, she frequently takes lovers. This happens often enough to be recognized and accepted within the community. Women are usually the "stars" in this system; men have to settle for a back seat. A particularly successful man can become a neighborhood favorite, of course, standing out above the women, but women are generally much more likely to be the center of attention for small children. Rainwater tells of a common situation in which the women sit around talking and telling jokes while the men play supporting roles, mainly as listeners, or are treated in a condescending way.

Both neighborhood and household conversation in this situation place a great deal of emphasis on personal criticism—the "put-down." Whether this is generally true of the lower classes is not known, but it probably is. The child grows up among people who have relatively little to brag about, but of course we all want to be noticed and looked up to, so the problem is not *whether* to "blow your own horn," but how to get away with it. Rainwater argues that in the lower classes much time is spent in the "unmasking of incompetence" in commonplace social relations. Few people are in a position to brag very long before others set the record straight, and it seems that males in particular take a beating.

It is likely that "boyfriends," who appear on "mothers' day" when the checks for aid to families with dependent children arrive, get no more opportunity to build up their egos than husbands who are out of work. The upshot is that masculinity itself is put down, and the pattern is not lost on children. Urie Bronfenbrenner (1967) argues that the exaggerated toughness, aggressiveness, and cruelty found in delinquent gangs reflect the desperate effort of boys in lower-class neighborhoods to strike back at their ego-depressing, womanized environment—and to find a masculine identity in the process.

There is a tight pattern to all this. Houses and neighborhoods are crowded, so children have few places reserved for play. The father is a relatively weak figure. Children spend more time with one another, less with parents or teachers, boy scout leaders, and so on than in the middle classes. Strong pressures are exerted upon boys to become part of a close, masculine peer group and upon girls to turn to groups of their own sex. Of much more than passing interest is the fact that members of these groups have constant contact with youths who are a few years older than themselves and who represent the "cool, high life." They do not serve as supervisors or protectors, but as models for a distinct style of life, one which is often in conflict with adult wishes. A contrast can be drawn between this and the middle-class pattern, where, for example, twelve-year-old boys have relatively little contact with sixteen-, seventeen-, and eighteen-year-old boys. The contacts they have with older people more often involve adults who act as advisers, coaches, and teachers.

The result is that lower-class youth are trained to a very considerable extent by people who are only a little older and a little more experienced than themselves, which certainly does not turn them in the direction of strong family values. The male peer culture usually has an exaggerated and perverse attitude toward girls, who become, above all, targets for seduction. The boy learns that he can get an enviable reputation if he can "make out" —have sexual relations—with as many girls as possible.

Meanwhile, the girls' reaction is to assume an attitude toward sex that is considerably more liberal than the one found in the middle classes. Their main object is to keep intercourse to a minimum, but not necessarily to eliminate it altogether (which may seem almost impossible). The girl can get a good reputation by being able to string the boys along, but she cannot keep it by denying them altogether.

Pregnancy before marriage is regarded as unfortunate, but no great tragedy. As was noted earlier, if pregnancy does occur, the girl's mother will probably care for the child (while in the middle classes the infant will more likely be put up for adoption [Jeffery 1962]). Then the girl can marry, after which she is considered a grownup and is given much more freedom than she ever had before. Rainwater contends that the first pregnancy is often treated as a mark of maturity for the girl—a sign of liberation, even when it occurs before marriage. Fewer pressures are put on her to get married than in the middle classes.

Clearly, attitudes toward marriage are implicit in this overall pattern. Neither boys nor girls are particularly anxious to marry or to even get excited about it, mainly because they do not have high hopes that it will work out. Carlfred Broderick (1965) found that from the ages of ten to thirteen, white children follow the traditional pattern: Girls are far more romantically inclined than boys. Black boys, however, show a relatively high level of interest in girls and romance at this time. Whereas white males become somewhat more willing to marry as they progress through the teens, the reverse is true for blacks, who become progressively disenchanted.

These differences no doubt show the relative commitment of the two racial groups to middle-class family norms and also their unequal opportunities within the predominantly white middle-class community. The black woman realizes that her man may have trouble providing for his family, and the man fears he will be embarrassed by his wife's infidelity. It is a strange fact that the men develop a strong impulse toward seduction in relations with women, but they still stand ready to be humiliated by an unfaithful spouse.

Although these conditions do not lead to a powerful urge to marry, expediency pushes couples toward marriage anyway. The marriage rate in lower-income groups is especially high among teen-agers. The husband becomes a poor provider just as his wife expected him to be. She has to work to help take care of the family, and her income is often more dependable than his. The couple may have two incomes, but the wife regards hers as her own to use as she pleases, especially in caring for the children, while the man's is for joint use to meet family needs. But since the man is not strongly tied to the family, he often holds out some of his money, and he is inclined to feel that the children are his wife's responsibility. The man's reluctance to share all that he earns stems not only from a fear that his wife will not respect him, but also from the deflated male ego caused by poverty.

This family pattern is most certainly the product of attitudes learned in childhood. It is perpetuated because the children who learn it proceed to rear a new generation with the same outlook. It is reinforced by a class system in the community at large, and it is aggravated by patterns of race prejudice and discrimination.

SUMMARY

Family attitudes are learned in childhood, and they last a lifetime for most people. Disillusionment and cynicism may chip away at them, but familism seems to have almost infinite resources at its disposal. In childhood the appeal of the family occurs mainly at the physical and emotional levels. Family members enjoy very close personal contacts with one another and share the entire range of human emotions. Each family has its own style—a configuration of attitudes and sensibilities suited to its own members—but patterns are also shared in larger groupings, such as ethnic groups and social classes. The child learns to prefer certain family practices, and later he is usually able to find someone of the opposite sex whose taste is very much like his own.

At an early age children find out about the basic, heterosexual nature of marriage. They learn that they will someday marry. Most of them are then attracted to one member of the opposite sex (who may not reciprocate the feeling) and have their first superficial feeling of "love." This usually follows an orderly pattern and establishes a strong disposition or readiness for marriage.

But the pattern is considerably different for girls than for boys. Above all, girls are more totally excited by the idea of getting married and having a family of their own, and their excitement begins earlier in life. High hopes for marriage among girls seem to be less dependent upon their parents' happiness. Perhaps this is because they spend more time in small friendship groups, and they are so much closer to their mothers than boys. Even girls' play—with dolls, for example—leads to an interest in the family. Boys spend more time in team sports and constant competition with one another. These activities provide no direct interest in family life and certainly do not idealize it. In fact, boys usually develop some hostility toward girls and toward family life in the elementary and preadolescent years, partly because of the divided feelings they have toward mothers and female teachers who supervise them. Girls have no comparable reason for hostility toward either boys, men, or the family. (Other reasons for the masculine attitude toward girls and women are discussed in Chapter 5, where premarital sex patterns are reviewed.)

In a sense, boys have to be "re-housebroken" during the adolescent years, after they have drifted away in preadolescence. But if the family is ever to lose its basic attraction, we should expect the early warning signs to show up in the attitudes of young girls. No widespread disenchantment has yet appeared.

The appeal of the family is relatively weak in the lower social classes or in any group where boys have special problems in finding masculine self-respect. That is usually the case where they have little chance to learn the skills needed to become stable breadwinners. Perhaps the comment about the need to attract girls to familism should be balanced by an equally important consideration: For optimum family life, boys need to have reasonably strong male self-concepts, and they need an opportunity to learn how to provide for their families. Otherwise marriage becomes an unstable and unappealing pattern.

SELECTED READINGS

ANGRIST, SHIRLEY S. "The Study of Sex Roles," *Journal of Social Issues*, Vol. 25 (January 1969), pp. 215–232.

BRODERICK, CARLFRED, AND GEORGE ROWE. "A Scale of Preadolescent Heterosexual Development," *Journal of Marriage and the Family*, Vol. 30 (February 1968), pp. 97–101.

BURGESS, ERNEST W. "The Family as a Unity of Interacting Personalities," *Family*, Vol. 7 (March 1926), pp. 3–6.

COOLEY, CHARLES HORTON. *Human Nature and the Social Order*. New York: Charles Scribner's Sons, 1902.

HARLOW, HARRY F. "The Nature of Love," *The American Psychologist*, Vol. 13 (December 1958), pp. 673–685.

HARTLEY, RUTH E. "Some Implications of Current Changes in Sex-Role Patterns," *Merrill-Palmer Quarterly*, Vol. 6 (April 1960), pp. 153–164.

RAINWATER, LEE. "Crucible of Identity: The Negro Lower-Class Family," *Daedalus*, Vol. 95 (Winter, 1965), pp. 172–216.

CHAPTER 4

The Dating Stage

In the twentieth century, for the first time in history, dating has become an established, conventional pattern. Although it is nothing new for young people to pair off before marriage for sex relations, and in some cases they have gone together simply for companionship, never before has *dating* been recognized and expected by the community at large. In the United States dating is practiced over a period of from five to ten years (or even more) for the majority of youth, under circumstances where couples can share close personal feelings but still have only minimal obligations to one another. Even these obligations apply only within the rules of the dating game itself, policed by youth who, for the most part, set their own standards and supervise their own activities.

Willard Waller (1951) once defined dating as "aim-inhibited activity." He meant that couples spend many hours together trying to have as much fun as possible without pledging themselves to any long-term responsibilities. Geoffrey Gorer (1948) regarded American dating as a kind of competitive sport taken up by youth with time on their hands. The object of the game is to attract the most desirable member of the opposite sex, then act out a light-hearted charade of pretended love. In this sense, dating is clearly a stage preceding the more serious business of courtship.

Dating and *courtship* become two relatively distinct phases in life, each operating according to its own special set of rules. But they overlap and blend together; the clearest contrast occurs only when both are in mid-stage. Youth in the later stages of the dating period, from about ages seventeen through twenty, move into the courtship phase without fully realizing it. And of course some seventeen- or eighteen-year-olds who are only dating may suddenly decide to marry, never knowing exactly when it was that they shifted to the more future-oriented world of courtship.

THE SOCIAL CONTEXT OF DATING

Dating as a special social realm was created by a whole series of new social conditions. All of them were associated with industrial development, which provided affluence to a large part of the population. Four new conditions stand out: (1) the growth of an *adolescent youth culture,* (2) the general *stress on love* in contemporary society, (3) the decline of traditional patterns of male and female separation—*sex equality,* and (4) *voluntarism* in mate selection. These four developments, each to be explained, unleashed a need for dating. Furthermore, the economic developments that "caused" modern adolescence also created the ability to support hundreds of thousands of youth in millions of hours of amorous dalliance.

Youth Culture

The foundation for dating was fixed by the growth of an advanced economic system. This not only supports a large middle class with a rising standard of living, but it requires a certain "middle-class life style," stressing educational achievement and consumer-oriented households, to keep the system going. Such a society has little use for the work-power of adolescents. It frees them from conventional labor and also from the kind of subservience that is almost always associated with physical work. It has use only for adults—people who have spent years in school to fill its managerial, professional, and skilled positions.

In this respect the new economic order *creates* adolescence. It creates a society in which youth have to go to school full time until they are seventeen or eighteen, and even then an increasing number spend four or more years in college. They spend much more time with each other than with adults, and their primary social interests are with others of approximately their own age. John and Virginia Demos (1969) claim that adolescence, as generally understood, did not exist before the last two decades of the nineteenth century. It was, in a sense, an American social invention. The word "adolescence" had been used before, but only very rarely. Thus, industrial growth generates an entirely new life style for the modern teenager. With neither planning nor forewarning it breeds a "youth culture" (sometimes called a "subculture" because it is really only part of the larger American society).

This new culture came into being along with modern adolescence, but even social scientists failed to spot it at first. They became convinced that adolescence was a novel and trouble-filled stage of life several decades before realizing that the most important new thing about it was the youth culture itself (Coleman 1962). Indeed, the concept of a special youth society remains controversial in sociology, and one point of view will not yet admit that such a society really exists (Elkins and Westley 1955). But the main body of current opinion does hold that an exceptional set of activities, with appropriate attitudes to support them, has appeared among adolescents and that they form the essence of the youth culture. It stresses dating, fads in clothing, music and dancing, and a variety of leisure interests for young people who wish to be with others of their age rather than with children or adults. Teen-agers live together according to their own codes, which they perpetuate and enforce in groups of their own choice.

The main objection to this point of view involves two arguments. The first is that, although the interests of adolescents are undoubtedly different from those of adults, they are different in only superficial ways; most adults share—and feel completely comfortable with—the underlying values held by teen-agers. For example, clothing and hair styles may differ between the two groups, teen-age dancing may seem a little strange from the adult point of view, and necking and petting are suited primarily to teen-age tastes and circumstances; but all these activities rest on fundamental values that youth share with their parents. The latter may wear clothes cut along different lines but, like their children, they are anxious to dress according to current fashions, and they usually want their children to be well-liked by being in style. The use of drugs by adolescents poses a more difficult problem, but even this does not necessarily violate basic community values in a society where pills, tobacco, and alcohol are used so extensively. Sex may also arouse concern among parents, but they still want their teen-agers to pair off. They are certainly appalled by homosexuality and suspicious of masturbation. It is not really surprising that adolescents work out ways to have heterosexual affairs—if only petting—during the period before they marry (which, for some, may last as many as fifteen years). For boys these are the most erotic years of their lives.

The second argument against the existenec of a youth culture is that adolescents are not sufficiently independent of their parents to have a genuine culture of their own. They live in their parents' homes, are fed and clothed by them, and receive constant parental advice and guidance. The social world they create is basically an imitation of parental customs. In a way, the adolescent style of life is an effort to establish some semblance of independence from adults even as they attempt to please their parents and become like them.

Contemporary adolescents have money to spend, and scores of large corporations spend time and money to exploit this teen-age market. They actually set standards of behavior for their young customers, which means that youth are manipulated as often as not. From a commercial point of view teen-agers are by no means independent; they are influenced by advertising, television programs, and movies. They become what they are taught to become, so their culture is not their own.

Although I side with those who see the adolescent society as a "Coney Island mirror image" of adult society and hence not *basically* different (Berger 1963), just how unique and independent it may be is not of critical importance right now. The main point is that a big part—in some ways *the* most important part—of the youth culture is the dating complex. Almost all aspects of life connected with adolescence touch in one way or another upon the activity of dating. It is for this reason that we can say that dating was created in the twentieth century—with the emergence of adolescence and its own special set of folkways. (But there are youth in some lower-income groups who have virtually no conception of dating as it occurs in the middle classes [Rosenberg and Bensman 1968].)

It is the dating complex that allows the middle stages of adolescence to serve as an important bridge between the potential freedom (and rebelliousness) of youth and the family commitments of adults. But once again we run into controversy. Robert Whitehurst (1968), for example, suggests that deep involvement in the peer group before marriage may be beneficial for nonfamily affairs, but it can actually be detrimental to marriage adjustment later on. His reasoning is that in the city family life tends to be divorced from nonfamily affairs, and the training of children for urban adjustment now occurs largely outside the home. When the modern teenager goes to school, not only is classwork unlike family life, but even the peer group operates from a different set of premises. Schooling is very useful, but it specializes in nonfamily rather than family matters.

Love and Dating

More will be said in the next chapter about the general relationship between love and dating in modern society. For now it is perhaps enough to say that love emerged as the primary reason for marriage even before dating became widespread, but it seems obvious that dating helps in finding a love partner. More than that, it conditions young people to the idea that they are supposed to find such a person before they marry. Love as the basis for marriage cannot really take over in any society until dating for teen-agers is widely accepted.

Sex Equality

The fact that boys and girls are attracted to family life in different ways was noted in the previous chapter. This difference demonstrates that the two sexes are still not treated exactly alike as they grow up. The trend, however, is toward greater equality, and it has been speeded up enough in recent years to suggest that the rate of change is connected with the rise of dating.

The most important new development is that boys and girls have more time together in small groups while they are young. The time is often spent in easygoing friendship and cooperation, not in relations that stress sex differences and masculine dominance. For dating to become an established pattern it is important that the sexes spend time together *before* the teen years—before dating begins. This sets the stage for the kinds of mutual understanding necessary for smooth heterosexual relations in adolescence. Dating *can* occur between boys and girls who have never had anything to do with each other before, and perhaps it can even be a workable arrangement in places where virtually all boys and all girls are separated before the teen years, but it will usually involve fewer anxieties and less awkwardness if they have a few years to associate with each other first.

It was said that economic development reached a stage in the twentieth century permitting widespread dating among teen-agers. In fact, we can go even further and say that recent historical developments have actually made dating necessary. That is, dating now helps people to cope with problems that did not come up in the old style of heterosexual relations. One important function of dating, for example, is to draw males toward girls in adolescence—under circumstances that lead inevitably to marriage and the assumption of family responsibilities (Greenfield 1965). Girls, on the other hand, are attracted to boys and marriage much earlier. Dating is certainly enjoyed by the modern girl, but it is in no way *needed* for the elementary purpose of getting her interested in marriage. In fact, trends in this regard seem to work in opposite directions for boys and girls: Whereas dating usually has the effect of luring boys toward marriage for the first time in their lives, it seems to be a liberating experience for many girls. Through dating, girls often become interested in sexual opportunities and the sheer freedom available away from home. Their interest in getting married may actually decline.

Carlfred Broderick and Jean Weaver's (1968) data suggest that romantic attraction between boys and girls tends to become stronger between the ages of ten and seventeen, while hostile relations decline; the reduced hostility probably occurs primarily among boys. David Knox, Jr., and Michael Sporakowski (1968) found that once males have had the experience of "being in love" they become considerably more romantic than girls. They concluded that the love experience in dating simply has greater impact on males than females. Robert Coombs and William Kenkel (1966) also found that boys are more likely to feel an emotional attraction to their partners after a first date. Boys are more excited, more satisfied, and more anxious to have another date. Thus, the dating process seems to push the male toward deeper and deeper romantic involvements. By comparison, its effect upon the girl is mild (but only by comparison).

Freedom in Mate Selection

The main reason dating is more necessary for boys now than in the past is that marriage has become a voluntary matter. Previously it was something over which they had very little control; it was an unquestioned family obligation. In many respects the male had little choice in deciding even whom he would marry. He was never given much freedom, and he was constantly supervised by elders, usually kinsmen. The contemporary boy still meets social pressures to marry from his family and increasingly (as he grows older) from the peer group itself. But he can also opt out of the marriage market, and he gets plenty of support for this choice from contemporary movies and magazines.

Another prod that influenced boys to marry in the past was the fact that they could be strong authorities as husbands and fathers. The power granted "the man of the household" was something boys could look forward to, since it was the key to the whole patriarchal value system. For many boys, becoming married also meant greater power and control over family property. Thus, with good reason young men moved automatically toward marriage.

The pattern is not as clearly structured today. And so dating itself, which the boy may have to be pushed into at first, leads him to marriage, replacing some of the older forces that accomplished this same purpose. Dating lures the boy into close association with girls and makes it likely that he will acquire a *need* for just this kind of relationship. He could once look forward to a position of esteem as head of a household; now he wants companionship and romance. Even his attitude toward children is changed. Although he may give very little thought to fatherhood before marrying, what thought he does give will probably dwell on the pleasures it can bring and the companionship possibilities, rather than on his role as a model or taskmaster for his children.

Another closely related need created by modern society is for children to learn to work and play as equals with members of the opposite sex. Historically, a "male-bonding" pattern has existed almost everywhere, starting even before adolescence, as Lionel Tiger (1967; 1969) has shown with unusual insight. He cites political parties, armies, occupational specialties, and secret societies as illustrations of his argument that the bonding process is a unique male phenomenon. Female bonding has occurred, too, but less notably and less self-consciously. Tiger argues that male bonding is a pro-

pensity deeply embedded in the male psyche, totally unlike anything female, but that is extremely questionable. He traces it back to the higher
primates in evolutionary history, especially to the early experience of men
as hunters. Men have had secret societies and exclusive access to the most
prestigeful kinds of work for centuries, and they have kept to themselves a
variety of social, political, and religious powers in the community.

Boys have also banded together, excluding girls, to learn things appropriate to manhood, and they are encouraged in this not only by older men
but by women as well. Small boys are cared for by women, but gradually
they turn to older males for coaching, advice, and initiation into what
really excites men. Traditionally, girls are kept under the tutelage of women
and are only rarely coached by men. When they marry they are traditionally released from control by father (who is a rather distant figure by comparison with the adult women in their lives) to control by husband (who
is also a rather distant figure by comparison with husband in the modern
romantic marriage).

Under these traditional conditions it is not necessary that boys and girls
have much to do with each other while they are growing up. Their relations
will be rather formal throughout life, and they will hardly ever need to work
and play together as equals. They will have to cooperate, of course, and
even work together in close alliance on certain projects, but the things they
do will be sharply differentiated by sex. Cooperation between men and
women is therefore more or less automatic or mechanical. As for playing
together, that has rarely happened in the past.

Now the pattern has changed enormously. Modern marriage requires
constant interplay between partners—to resolve differences of opinion and
to make decisions. Most of these differences cannot be resolved on the basis
of any clear-cut tradition or precedent. The couple will have no choice but
to talk the issue through and reach "an understanding." Although the wife
may have a special point of view because of her female training, and the
husband may have a "masculine" approach, in many respects their decisions
will not be determined by sex at all. Sex-linked opinions can occur often
enough to complicate matters, and we still tend to dismiss husband-wife
disputes as "normal man-woman differences," but that is unfortunate.

The role that dating plays in this connection is obvious enough. It builds
on the relatively close relations that the sexes had during the elementary
years—call it an advance form of sensitivity training, basically heterosexual.
Because bonding among adult men is now weaker and less crucial for cooperation at work, males have a greater need for female *ego support* even in
adolescence, and dating helps to meet this need. It provides an opportunity
for young couples to enjoy close relations, rapport, and empathy, thereby
enhancing their ability to get along with whomever they may later marry.

It is not necessary that a young man marry the particular girl with whom he has spent a great deal of time on dates. The important thing is that he marry someone who is *like* the girls he has learned about in dating.

In this connection dating also plays a role in the person's discovery of himself—the process by which his sense of personal identity is formed. This is an important new part of the "looking-glass self process." With the decline of same-sex bonding, we find it necessary to define ourselves to a much greater extent in terms of relationships with the opposite sex. Since both elementary-school children and adolescents now spend more time in heterosexual relations, the average boy learns to think about himself partly in terms of the way girls react to him, certainly more so than in the past. But he still gets his main sense of *male* identity before reaching adolescence in interaction with other boys. It is only as he enters the dating stage that he is likely to take careful notice of what girls his own age think of him, and it is at this time that he will probably make a real effort, on his own, to become more likable in terms of whatever qualities they use to judge boys.

Thus, the rise of dating is based on new developments in relations between the sexes, the decline of same-sex bonding, the emergence of a youth culture, voluntarism in marriage, and the greater need for *personal* selection of a mate. Dating made its appearance in the twentieth century because the economy could support it and because there were important functions it could serve.

DATING PROBLEMS

As noted earlier, dating can be distinguished from courtship in that it is not, strictly speaking, concerned with finding a mate. Although it may give useful training for marriage and adult life in general, the very fact that couples seek pleasure without long-run commitments means that certain problems will inevitably show up. This inevitability does not apply to each individual, of course, but rather to a sizable percentage of the population. When hundreds of thousands of young males and females are engrossed in such an emotional activity, some are bound to be hurt.

Perhaps the most obvious problem is sex. Margaret Mead (1953) once argued that dating is an unfortunate, perhaps malignant, twentieth-century growth. The more successful adolescents are in adjusting to it, she said, the less prepared they will be to meet the problems of sex adjustment in marriage. Her view was extreme, and she has tempered it on many occasions, but it does point up the fact that sex on dates is a different kind of sex altogether from sex in marriage. Willard Waller (1937), taking an even more extreme position, argued that dating is but one aspect of the decay of traditional morality and that it leads to thrill seeking and exploitation.

Although the view presented in this text is in almost total conflict with Waller's, it must be recognized that sex (short of intercourse) is now an accepted part of dating and that it does lead to soul-searching and can easily get out of hand. The attempt to find sexual pleasure in a context of only short-term commitments must be tension-producing, at least in a society that has historically linked sex to family obligations. This problem will be taken up in the following chapter, which deals specifically with problems of premarital sex.

Status Seeking

Related to the sex dilemma is one that comes up because teen-agers are usually not very sophisticated on dates. In fact, they can be uncomfortably awkward in situations requiring two people of the opposite sex to carry on a conversation for any extended period of time. Awkwardness leads teen-agers to act in stereotyped ways, to hide their true feelings, and to do things that literally encourage others to misjudge them. Part of this problem is eased by dating only when the couple can be with a crowd, keeping the time spent alone to a minimum. But this itself becomes a problem, because daters try so hard to impress the whole group as well as each other.

Dating thus becomes a "status-conferring act," a popularity game whose object is to date a person who can add points to your standing or at least one who will not take them away. This may operate even at the college level; social rank on the campus often reflects the class status of parents, and dating frequently follows class lines (Reiss 1965). Some students may feel a vague sense of phoniness about the whole business, but they find it hard to understand their own feelings because the group so clearly defines pairing off and dating as desirable. Even so, some persons will simply not be able to go along with it.

One of the more hopeful possibilities is that the rating-and-dating pattern is dying out, for reasons suggested earlier (Blood 1956). Boys now spend more time with girls in the elementary-school years, and hence the sexes are less awkward together. Dating developed first among adolescents who had not had the benefit of friendly heterosexual relations in childhood. Boys were clumsy with girls because all they knew was the "boy culture." More than anything else, they had learned that girls were targets for seduction. But the need to master girls and to "make out" has apparently declined, at least among middle-class boys. If this is true (supporting evidence remains largely impressionistic), couples in the dating period are now more anxious to develop genuine companionship than was the case just a few decades ago. Girls are not quite so compulsive in wanting dates to prove their popularity and to build up their inner self-esteem, and boys have less need for a lady-killer reputation in order to protect their masculine image.

This also suggests that dating serves one of its key functions better than before—that of providing an opportunity to learn how to work as well as play with members of the opposite sex.

The Double Standard

On reason why some girls no longer have to worry so much about being popular with boys is that they can now have careers of their own. They therefore are not so dependent upon the career prospects of their boy-friends, and they do not have to tailor their appearance—even their basic style of life—to the requirements of dating success. This is probably not the most common pattern, however. David Riesman (1964) argues that most modern college women, even the brightest ones, are not career-oriented. They want a "nice guy" and a family in the suburbs, and yet they also want jobs—before marriage, before the children are born, and after the children have grown. The work they have in mind is not really a career; it is viewed rather as a source of supplementary family income or simply as a personal "interest" (Turner 1964). The full impact of the women's liberation movement upon girls now coming of age remains unclear. The marriage rate has actually gone up in the last few years, but the average age at marriage has moved slightly upward, too. Elizabeth Almquist and Shirley Angrist (1970a) have collected evidence that does not completely reject the notion that girls who are highly career-oriented are different from other girls in dating, extra-curricular activities, relations with parents, and work values, but their data give that point of view only weak support. It seems that girls who have strong career interests may increasingly find support at school and in the peer group, and their interests may not be considered at all unusual.

For many decades girls in the United States have done very well in schoolwork during the elementary years, but when the time for dating begins, things change. They drop any strong interests in the more competitive areas of academic work. Data collected by Clyde McDaniel, Jr. (1969), for example, show that girls change their point of view as they move through the dating and courtship sequence. At the beginning they are often aggressive, or at least they regard themselves as equal to boys in rights, power, and authority. But as they progress to steady dating and start looking for a mate in earnest, they become subdued—to say that they are docile would be over-doing it—in relations with males. It seems that this deferential manner is a product of the girl's growing seriousness about marriage. It gets a boost from her need to conform to "helpmate femininity." Men tend to prefer women who are not too forward, and girls become increasingly anxious to please as their aim in life turns to matrimony. And yet they do well in high school and make even better grades than boys on the average, a situation which continues through the undergraduate years in college. Then, at the crucial moment, they usually choose not to go into graduate work (other than in school teaching). Many drop out of college in order to marry even if they happen to be good students. Career preparation is regarded mainly as insurance against not getting married. All of this means that the girl must put her primary hopes in finding a good man, and an early indication of success is the ability to get dates. This dilemma may be slowly changing, and perhaps an increasing number of girls do not rely first and foremost on marriage, but the number is still relatively small.

The fact remains that girls who can compete with boys for careers have greater freedom to act as they please on dates. They are also in a better position to ignore traditional sex codes. They may also be able to hold out on sex because they are not so jittery about pleasing boys. They are in the enviable position of being able to be themselves, but many girls are not so lucky.

Steady Dating

The competitive nature of dating poses another problem. Competition for dates is inevitable, since dating is a status-conferring activity. It is bound to promote rivalries and a certain sense of insecurity, especially among those who are at a disadvantage in the competition. Boys who want to date but are unsure of themselves must suffer an agonizing inner debate as they build up enough courage to ask a girl out, and the girls who are not so pretty must live in torment while they wait to see if they are going to be asked.

When the dating pattern first appeared, it was competitive in this sense. The date book for each weekend was arranged almost from scratch, all boys competing against all other boys for the most desirable girls. But as dating became established, the trend quickly moved toward steady dating and away from open competition. The insecurities of the latter were eased a great deal in the process. But going steady met with disfavor from parents at first and is still a sensitive issue. Gerald Schnepp (1960) found that over one-fourth of the twelfth graders in his sample were going steady, whereas less than one out of twelve parents approved of the practice.

The sequence of concern on this issue was very much like the sequence of dating itself. At first parents raised the question whether it should be permitted at all. When they realized it was inevitable, they turned to the question of when it should start—that is, at what age? William Goode (1963) has shown that conflict on this point exists in almost all Western countries, especially between parents and daughters. Nevertheless, both sexes have gained greater independence all over the Western world, and they increasingly have chances to meet in places where no element of family supervision can be conveniently arranged. But strong objections to going steady are still raised, such as the worry that it will allow the couple to become "too intimate too soon," leading either to premarital pregnancy or to a premature marriage. It gives some of the privileges of the traditional engagement, but without the responsibilities. Another fear is that it may cause the teen-ager to become overly dependent on one other person; if the relationship should break up, she (or he) may find it difficult to get back into circulation.

It seems very clear, however, that steady dating does reduce the anxieties of playing the field and that its benefits outweigh its disadvantages for most youth. In fact, for many of them there is never a period of open-field dating. Almost from the beginning they go steady—more or less—especially in the lower social classes (Bayer 1968). One writer says that there is an almost imperceptible transition from casual dating, dating "steadily" (which is not quite as intimate as going steady), through steady dating, thinking seriously about engagement, and finally becoming engaged (Delora 1963). "Pinning" occurs almost exclusively among college students and is associated with the declining fraternity-sorority pattern. It is usually a prelude to engagement rather than part of the more casual high-school dating culture. In each of these succeeding stages the couples are drawn together more securely, with only a thin line separating the dating phase from courtship.

Perhaps this fact, too, poses a problem. The teen-ager gets involved in dating in a rather casual way, but before he knows it he may find that he is in pretty deep. Part of the problem is simply not realizing what he is getting into. And yet there seems to be some inner logic to the quick transition from short-term fun to the search for assurance that the fun will last. If a couple find good times together they will want to keep on having them. Becoming engaged and getting married give at least the appearance of such a guarantee.

Of course couples do not always move blindly from dating to courtship without realizing what is happening. Furthermore, they may *fail* to make the transition just as blindly as others make it. James Skipper, Jr., and Gilbert Nass (1966) claim that dating can serve at least four important functions for the individual—recreation, socialization, status achievement, and courtship—but that any two daters may use it for conflicting reasons. For example, a girl may date a rich guy who drives an expensive sports car mainly for the status she gains, but he may be dating her just to learn about girls. Or a boy may date an attractive girl purely for sex, while the girl sees the boy as a potential husband. Skipper and Nass studied dating in a sample of girls in nurses' training and found that their boyfriends typically approached dating as recreation. But in most cases the girls were seriously looking for husbands. Under these circumstances the males usually held the upper hand because they had less to lose if relations broke off. The girls were forced to make concessions—meaning they were more permissive in sex than they normally would have been—in order to keep their affairs going. This caused them much distress to say the least, especially since giving in did not necessarily pay off in marriage. As Robert Coombs and William Kenkel (1966) have noted, a girl can spare herself a lot of disappointment if she holds back just a little on a date or, better yet, if she can convince herself that the matter of a later date is not important. Tradition gives the boy the upper hand because he is the one who gets to take the initiative. He is in a much better position to pursue only those girls who intrigue him.

And Parents?

The efforts of parents to control or influence their children's dating habits can complicate matters. Parents, of course, are enormously interested in their children's activities, and dating is easily as important to them as anything else. However, by its very nature it is a highly emotional and subjective experience. How can parents and youth hope to communicate on the subject? The problem has been described as one in which parents try to "control" or "influence" their children, but in actual fact many parents are satisfied just to be kept informed.

Difficulties in this connection are aggravated by a basic conflict that is symptomatic of the modern era: The influence of parents over children has been in a process of long-term decline at the very time in history that parents have become most emotionally involved with their children. This pattern has been building up for half a century, but its roots go back even further than that. Modern parents have fewer children to keep track of— and they are probably planned, which means that parents started making decisions in their behalf even before they were born. Beyond that, parents now keep elaborate records on their children as they grow up. Philippe Aries (1965) notes that the practice of keeping portraits of children first appeared in the sixteenth century, but it was not until the twentieth that a virtual explosion of new possibilities came on the scene. The careful collection of scrapbooks and snapshots has been elaborated by the new techniques of movies and tape recordings. Not only do parents keep much closer accounts on fewer children and attach a considerable part of their own egos to their children's yearly progress, they now look forward to a longer life during which they can follow every hint of accomplishment by their children.

And yet at the very time that this has occurred, children themselves have gained new opportunities to be different and apart from their parents. Teachers, for example, can be striking models for new life styles, and the peer group itself is much more powerful than it once was. This simply means that parents have become enormously interested in the dating activities of their children under circumstances in which they cannot have, and perhaps are not supposed to have, a deciding influence. We should expect these parents to try to get information from their offspring in indirect and roundabout ways. They will no doubt try to exercise a measure of influence, too, but their success will depend on the subtlety and tactfulness of their efforts.

We might also expect to find a certain amount of *patterned evasion* in this process, that is, certain facts or information may be ignored by all concerned because calling attention to them would only lead to embarrassment. Thus, for example, parents want to know whom their children have been out with and what they have done—up to a point. If a girl comes home from a dance after midnight and finds her mother waiting nonchalantly at the door in a houserobe, both the girl and her mother may be satisfied to share certain essential facts: The dance was a lot of fun, certain other couples were there, they dropped by a popular hangout for a hamburger and a Coke on the way home, and the boy asked the girl to go with him to the dance next month. Mother may calculate that a certain period of time was not fully accounted for in this recital of the evening's events, during which it is possible that some heavy petting occurred, but she would probably be wise not to press for further information on the point. In all her joy and excitement, the girl gives no hint that sex might have been a part—perhaps a major part—of the evening's fun. (The term "petting" refers to mutual fondling by the couple, including touching and caressing the genital areas and the female breasts. It does not include sexual intercourse but may lead to that and can lead to orgasm without intercourse.)

Actually it would appear that the general problem area we have been discussing is resolved reasonably well in the United States. In Chapter 8 it will become apparent that marital choice in America is strongly homogamous, meaning that most young people marry persons who are very much like themselves and therefore quite acceptable to their parents. Although parents have their troubles in advising offspring, the children still usually manage to date people who are acceptable, and the mate-selection pattern follows a nonrevolutionary course.

Nondating

One final problem is worth noting, however—nondating. This is not necessarily a problem, of course, but it can be. As we have already seen, dating is a status-conferring activity to some extent, and hence there must be "winners" who earn enviable status by their success, and "losers" who gain very little esteem or none at all. Apparently girls are more often left out than boys, because they play the waiting role, unable to take the initiative in getting dates. One study concluded that one-fourth of the males and one-third of the females felt that they were failures in dating (Williams 1949). We must remember that it is a little more necessary for the girl to fulfill a stereotyped image of prettiness in order to be asked; boys are more concerned about having a "good-looking" partner than girls are (Coombs and Kenkel 1966).

But not all nondaters are losers, since many of them manage to maintain self-esteem in other ways. Dating is a basic activity in most high schools, and adolescents who are highly committed to the school's extracurricular customs will find nondating either an embarrassment or a nagging source of frustration. But not all teen-agers are deeply involved in the youth culture, and there is at least one variation on the general theme which stresses other things—academic work and a variety of disciplined interests (Riley, Riley, and Moore 1961).

It is interesting to note that although dating behavior is stereotyped and organized in many ways in the United States, efforts to rationalize date-getting have made very little headway. Dating bureaus on college campuses rarely work out, and they are even less popular in the high schools. The aura of modern technology has added a new twist to their appeal, so that computerized introduction services have sprouted all over the country, but getting a date on one's own is still the ideal way to go about it. The most attractive girls do not subscribe to dating services, and hence male subscribers always outnumber the females in overwhelming proportions. One can guess that a real change in our dating patterns will occur only when girls turn to organized dating services as willingly as boys.

Blind dates arranged by go-betweens represent a rather special case. They are much less acceptable than dates arranged directly by the parties involved, but blind dating is considered perfectly all right when it would be difficult or impossible for either party to arrange the date for himself. This would be the case, for example, when visiting out of town or in an unfamiliar neighborhood. Among adults in the courtship stage of life, on the other hand, blind dates are almost always considered appropriate. It is assumed that high-school students have plenty of chances to meet members of the opposite sex and to compete for dates; people in their mid-twenties have fewer opportunities even in big cities, but they are still reluctant (especially the females) to try introduction agencies. Therefore a blind date may be just the thing.

TRENDS IN DATING

Nothing has happened to suggest big or sudden changes in dating in the foreseeable future. It has become thoroughly respectable to all but a few rather isolated groups, and the question worrying parents (as we have seen) is not whether to allow it, but at what age to let it start. Parents feel a variety of pressures to give in at earlier ages; in fact, persuasive forces push both children and their parents to want it to start sooner.

The trouble is that early dating is associated with early marriage, and a strong relationship between early marriage and poor marital adjustment has been demonstrated consistently in research (Burchinal 1960). Early dating has also been condemned on the grounds that it robs young people of their childhood, forcing them to grow up too soon. And yet early dating is prevalent among youth from the higher socioeconomic classes where marital success is actually most likely to occur. Samuel H. Lowrie (1961), for example, has shown that adolescents of more recent foreign origin, of limited education, of lower socioeconomic status, and from large families tend to begin dating later than those from affluent families that are more completely "Americanized"; they start dating later, but they tend to marry sooner.

Alan E. Bayer (1968) has offered a plausible explanation for this apparent inconsistency. He contends that the age when dating starts is not by itself an important factor in marital adjustment. What is important is the length of the person's dating experience before marriage—generally speaking, the longer, the better. Bayer's theory is consistent with the fact that youth in the lower classes begin dating later than those from higher status backgrounds, but spend less time in dating before they marry. The theory is also consistent with the current professional view of dating (which has lasted for a quarter of a century now—a relatively long time in a rapidly changing field) that it is a useful educational experience for most teen-agers. Skills that come in handy in choosing a mate are learned, and personal growth essential for marriage ordinarily occurs (Lowrie 1951).

The trend toward earlier dating seems to be related to the generally greater freedom of modern youth and to the fact that they pick up certain kinds of sophistication at ever earlier ages. Their free-spiritedness does not show up in psychological ways alone; the very social structure of childhood gives them greater leverage in dealing with parents. For example, they own more things, which gives a sense of substance and ego strength that sets them apart from children of past times—our reverence for private property guarantees that reaction. Not only do they have plenty of toys, clothes, bicycles, instruments, and sporting equipment, which they are encouraged to regard as their own personal property, they even have bank accounts and stock certificates. It becomes normal for the child to be sensitive about his personal status and his rights as an individual long before he gains true independence from his parents and the school system.

In addition, the peer group has become progressively more powerful—in its relations with adults (although militancy in youth groups occurs primarily among college undergraduates) and also in its ability to command the obedience of youth themselves. All of this speeds up the release of youngsters from adult controls and frees the dating system in the process.

It was noted that trends favor greater career-consciousness among girls, especially in the early and middle years of adolescence, the very years when this can have its greatest effect on dating attitudes. The result seems to be that girls are allowed to approach boys with less apprehension and subservience, which is to say that they need boys less than they used to. In fact, males tend to become even more important within the family as middle- and working-class women, for the first time in history, turn their attention away from the home. Women rely on men less as they work away from home more, but it follows that the family must rely on men all the more to fill the role abandoned by women.

Perhaps the most important trends in dating spring from the decline in its status-conferring role and the decline of seduction as a theme among males. Both of these are linked to the underlying drift toward greater equality between the sexes. Dating tends to become a more friendly relationship, developing quite logically out of closer ties between the sexes in the elementary years. Sex is still an inescapable part of dating, but it seems to get less self-conscious attention now than in the past. Because of this change of attitudes, the sexes now have less need to exploit each other to meet the demands of their two separate social worlds—girls no longer need to be liked by boys in order to be the genuine "feminine type," and boys no longer need to make out with girls in order to have the complete image of masculinity.

But all this leaves one or two important questions unanswered. If dating is moving in the direction described, thus giving better preparation for marriage and bringing adult men and women closer together, why do so many marriages fail? Aren't the couples in most cases "graduates" of the dating system? These are legitimate questions, and they are certainly not easy to answer. But we must remember that dating in America is just coming of age. It is very new in a historical sense, and a truly mature dating system may just be appearing. We must also bear in mind that contemporary marriages are subject to pressures that hardly even existed in the past. For example, in an engaging theory of *permanent availability* Bernard Farber (1964) contends that adults in contemporary society are expected—even encouraged—to be critical of their married life. The traditional stress on stability and self-denying family relations has been greatly relaxed, if not turned upside down. No wonder many couples are dissatisfied with their home life and eager for something better. In turn, people face a constant pressure to be attractive in social affairs if they expect to be eligible in the perennial marriage market. When personal choice is stressed in mate selection, anything that can build self-confidence and good judgment should be welcomed, and dating seems to fall into this category.

SUMMARY

Dating has emerged in the twentieth century as a major part of adolescent life. It can be distinguished from courtship because it is devoted to the fun of pairing-off without requiring long-term family obligations. Teen-agers are now freed from occupational drudgery and the need to earn a living. They are subsidized as they attend school, and they have time and money to engage in relaxed dating affairs. A youth culture has evolved, giving substance and continuity to the adolescent stage in life, with dating at the very center of attention. The fact that marriage has become a voluntary affair, rather than a kinship obligation, has undermined almost all opposition to the dating pattern. But this new arrangement would be incomplete if it were not for the breakdown of *sexual separatism* which had always characterized relations between the sexes in the past. Boys and girls now play together before adolescence, which leads to smoother relations in dating itself.

Just as new social conditions have opened the way for dating, they have also created a need for it. Lacking the lure of patriarchal privileges and pressures from kinsmen, boys are attracted to girls through dating which, in a spirit of sex and romance, does indeed accomplish its purpose: Boys fall in love (even more rapidly than girls it would seem) and ask the girls to marry them. Dating also offers teen-agers an opportunity to learn about members of the opposite sex, building upon the closer heterosexual relations of the elementary-school years. This *sensitivity training* contributes not only to better mate selection but also to closer work and play relations between the sexes throughout life. Boys now have less need to be masculine types in the traditional sense, because the pattern of male bonding seems to be less necessary in adult work. The contemporary man needs a personality flexible enough to deal with both males and females. Therefore dating in the adolescent period can add an important dimension to the training of urban youth.

Many of the problems of dating revolve around the fact that it is an aim-inhibited activity, stressing pleasure rather than family commitment. Sex is the most obvious problem and it will be discussed in the following chapter. Dating is a status-conferring activity and as such it invites snobbery and a tendency to act in stereotyped ways. The competitiveness of "playing the field" has been resolved to some extent by the rise of steady dating, and conflicts between parents and teen-agers have changed in the process. At first many parents opposed dating as such, but their concern has slowly turned to the question of when it should start and whether *steady* dating should be discouraged.

The entire problem of communication between adults and youth is complicated by the fact that modern parents have become emotionally involved in their children's affairs at the very time in history that teen-agers have gained extensive freedom from home controls. Although parents are terribly curious and frequently anxious about dating, they are limited in what they can do to influence it.

The fact that there is a trend toward earlier dating creates a problem, because it is statistically associated with early marriage, which in turn is correlated with marriage failure. However, dating at an early age seems to be characteristic of youth from the middle and upper classes who actually have higher rates of success in marriage. Apparently the age when dating starts is not as crucial for marital success as we first thought; the important thing is the total length of the dating experience. Children in higher status levels start dating early, but they also keep at it for an extended period of time. It is more typical of the lower classes and of youth whose parents arrived only recently in the United States to begin dating at a later age but to marry relatively soon after their first date.

Early dating is actually associated with earlier and greater sophistication among contemporary children. Not only do they know more about the world in general, they have had more frequent relations with members of the opposite sex. It also seems that dating is now approached with more concern for the *human* relationships involved. Boys are a little less interested in "making out"; girls are a little less interested in presenting themselves as pretty things that, above all, are anxious to please boys. Sexual intimacies may be greater than ever before, but only because they are taken for granted, not because of any greater obsession with sex per se. Many authorities contend that modern youth are actually less interested in sex than young people have been in the past—they have by no means *lost* interest, but other things are beginning to loom relatively larger.

If "graduates" of the dating pattern do not always succeed in marriage (and their failures have been notable in the twentieth century), it is probably not because dating gives only meager preparation for marriage, but because marriage is a more demanding relationship than it was in the past. Even courtship is more demanding, as we shall see. Youth now have opportunities to choose mates from a greater variety of people, which poses new problems and changes the courting game in a fundamental way.

SELECTED READINGS

COOMBS, ROBERT H., AND WILLIAM F. KENKEL. "Sex Differences in Dating Aspirations and Satisfaction with Computer-Selected Partners," *Journal of Marriage and the Family*, Vol. 28 (February 1966), pp. 62–66.

KNOX, DAVID H., JR., AND MICHAEL J. SPORAKOWSKI. "Attitudes of College Students Toward Love," *Journal of Marriage and the Family*, Vol. 30 (November 1968), pp. 638–642.

LOWRIE, SAMUEL H. "Dating Theories and Student Responses," *American Sociological Review*, Vol. 16 (June 1951), pp. 334–340.

MCDANIEL, CLYDE, JR. "Dating Roles and Reasons for Dating," *Journal of Marriage and the Family*, Vol. 31 (February 1969), pp. 97–107.

SKIPPER, JAMES, JR., AND GILBERT NASS. "Dating Behavior: A Framework for Analysis and an Illustration," *Journal of Marriage and the Family*, Vol. 28 (November 1966), pp. 412–420.

WALLER, WILLARD. "The Rating-Dating Complex," *American Journal of Sociology*, Vol. 2 (October 1937), pp. 727–734.

CHAPTER 5

Sex and Restraint

Sex for Homo sapiens knows no bounds; man is limited only by his imagination—and self-imposed taboos. The dilemma is that sex gives more intense physical and psychological pleasure than almost anything else, but it must not be allowed to interfere with certain other matters that are much less thrilling, though still essential.

Sex for other species poses no particular problem, mainly because of the automatic, natural restraints on their sexual appetites. Among most mammals, for example, the female is totally indifferent to sex except at certain times during her *oestrus cycle*. She is completely unresponsive until then, and the male has virtually no interest in her during these sterile periods. Rape never occurs.

Furthermore, a *dominance hierarchy* usually serves to organize the males. Those of lower rank stand back; they rarely challenge the system. This solves the problem of deciding who will have sex relations when the female is receptive and several males are close by. Human males are organized, too, but in entirely different ways—and they are much more likely to have rivalries, tension, and even bloodshed over sex. Most other species are not driven to murder because of sex jealousy, though fights to the death among contending males do occur on rare occasions.

In fact, sex among the "lower" mammals seems to be an almost trivial part of their lives, taking very little time and involving no anticipation of the event nor any prolonged memory after it is over. Learning about sex does occur, and perhaps individual members of each mammalian species develop slightly unique sex preferences. But what clearly distinguishes man's sex life from the other mammals is the fact that man alone magnifies erotic behavior into an infinitely variable world of symbols and fantasies. The human child starts learning about it at an early age, and by preadolescence he has elaborate daydreams on the subject. By this time he will also begin to dwell on his more exciting or troubling past experiences.

Therefore sex can be very distracting, drawing the person's attention away from other matters. The problems may not stop at this point, however, since thoughts and obsessions about sex apparently can cloud a person's mental life to such an extent he cannot even see things as other people do. You do not have to adopt everything in the Freudian point of view to recognize that sex "hang-ups" can greatly alter a person's ability to cope with life. The problem for man becomes one of fulfilling his sexual needs without undermining other important human relationships—nor family life itself.

EROTICISM AND FAMILISM

The fact that boys and girls are drawn into family commitments in different ways was discussed in Chapter 3, but the fact that their introduction to sex differs was only briefly mentioned. The most important consideration for girls is that they start committing themselves to family life even before sex becomes a strong interest. In fact, the traditional family concerns of girls, especially imagery related to motherhood, seem to stress sex restraint more than the sex drive can ever detract from their sense of familism. (That may be a little too strong; *some* women are very highly sexed, enough in fact to cause domestic problems.) For boys, fascination with sex is usually established before they start thinking much about the family, and their basic sex orientation tends to cause distraction. But it is also true that the sex lure girls hold for them in the early stages of adolescence is one major reason they ultimately take on family obligations.

Body Reactions

In tracing the development of erotic differences between the sexes a good place to begin is with the fact that boys and girls do not react to their bodies in the same way. In part this is because they are taught to respond differently, a fact that sociologists correctly stress. But their bodies are also different in ways that make distinctive male and female responses almost inevitable. The literature on this point has grown to impressive proportions.

Nevertheless, controversy and dogma continue to cloud the general picture. Joseph Rheingold (1964), for example, claims that no woman can transcend her body. He firmly contends that the female physiology sets inevitable limits to what women can do or be. Sigmund Freud (1956) once wrote that a woman is not what she is—a woman—but a man without a penis. The statements of both Rheingold and Freud reflect the persistent masculine bias found among many orthodox followers of Freud, but they can be grossly misleading in the study of sex differences. We would all do well to avoid the Freudian error that regards "anatomy as destiny," thereby explaining human behavior as a kind of instinctual reaction to the body. There is a mass of evidence showing that people, individually and collectively, can perceive their bodies in many ways and can act out their biological nature just as variably.

And yet it is also a good idea to avoid the position that Alfred Kinsey (1953) took when he concluded that there are no anatomical, no physiological, no neurological, and only slight hormonal differences between males and females that can account for differences in their sex behavior. Biological differences by themselves cannot explain the diversity of human sex life, but they do make a difference when placed (as they must be) in a social context.

The reproductive role that women play in all cultures, for example, without reference to how they may react to their sex organs, must be considered a universal part of the female sex style. Because of the complementary nature of male and female sex behavior, the reproductive role of women must also be a critical factor in the sex style of men. The fact that adult women become pregnant and give birth to infants has to affect the way young girls learn to think of themselves. Indirectly it will also affect the way boys view both femininity and masculinity. (Of course this also means that the current revolution in biological science, which forecasts entirely new ways of human reproduction, could radically change human sex life.)

But boys cannot react to their bodies exactly as girls do in any case. The fact that the boy has an external penis, which is plainly visible to the smallest child and which repeatedly hardens into erection, is an unavoidable, primary fact in his daily life. This hardening, or *tumescence*, occurs before the boy learns to talk, not once but hundreds, perhaps thousands, of times. Henry Halverson (1940) took the trouble to observe nine baby boys, all less than twenty weeks old, for ten consecutive days and reported an average of over two erections per hour per infant, caused by a wide variety of agitants and stimulations.

The boy attaches no particular importance to these genital erections at first, but he can hardly ignore them altogether. He will gradually learn the specifically sexual meanings as well as the ribald vocabulary associated with them. He will find that gratification, even a sense of security, can be gained by touching, holding, and exciting his penis, though no ejaculation occurs.

The male sex organ thus invites stimulation and provides incalculable pleasure long before puberty and long before its full erotic significance is ever known.

Nothing quite like this happens in the girl's experience with her body, although the literature of psychoanalysis is full of controversy on this point. Karen Horney (1967), for example, says that the vagina is excited unintentionally in any number of ways and plays its own proper part in the sex training of girls. But she also admits that they discover neither the vagina nor the clitoris very quickly as a rule. There is even a tendency to deny the vagina's existence, although girls have at least an unconscious awareness of it, especially as a "receiving" organ. Horney observes that the penis usually seems less vulnerable to boys than the vagina does to girls because its "intactness" can be checked so easily. Therefore she regards castration anxiety among boys, which Freud stressed, as a relatively unimportant matter. Although Horney is also skeptical about the significance that Freud gave to penis envy among girls, she seems to agree that the penis is a much more active and positive agent in the boy's sex development than the comparable female organ (the clitoris) in the girl's.

Largely because of pleasure associated with the penis and social reactions to it, the timetable for boys' interest in sex follows a different pattern than that for girls. Both the nature of their interest and the things that arouse it differ. Frank Shuttleworth (1959) has summarized the development of sexuality in males in this way: Infant boys have erections in response to a great variety of situations, rarely sexual in nature. A nonerotic form of masturbation frequently occurs from ages three to five, after which it disappears. Genital response to almost *any* kind of emotional situation reaches a peak at about age six or seven, whereas responsiveness to talk about sex and the nakedness of other boys seems to reach its highest point three or four years later. Homosexual reactions reach a peak at about age twelve and then diminish. The frequency of truly erotic masturbation rises to a peak around the age of fifteen and then declines. Arousal in response to female nudity, daydreaming, and dancing increases until the late teens and then recedes. Frequencies of nocturnal sex dreams also increase until the late teens or early twenties after which they decline sharply. The pleasures of petting usually increase into the early twenties, while active heterosexual relations begin in the teens, peak in the early twenties, and taper off gradually in the course of the mature years.

This sequence has to be considered tentative until much more information is carefully gathered and studied, but, as Shuttleworth has shown, the pattern for boys is unquestionably different from that for girls. The sex life of the average preadolescent male, for example, is considerably more active than the comparable female's. This is true for each of the stages mentioned above, although according to Alfred Kinsey and his associates (1948; 1953), eagerness for sex among women may rise in adulthood even as it falls for men. Furthermore, genital arousal among boys in the preadolescent period, as in infancy, can happen in a variety of nonerotic situations brought on by fear, anger, tension, and other strong emotions. Sexual arousal rarely occurs among girls in situations that have no sexual or romantic implications (Ramsey 1943). And yet sex stimulation itself is almost always considered a pleasant experience by boys, whereas it is often filled with ambiguity and guilt for girls.

Ejaculation and Menarche

In adolescence the fact of ejaculation (and the pleasure and release it gives) becomes the most exciting sex expression for boys. Once again the difference between the sexes is not trivial. Orgasm for boys is clearly defined; for the girl it is not so clear, although it is not as vague as we used to think (Masters and Johnson 1966). On evolutionary grounds alone, the male's capacity for orgasm is more certain than the girl's. For thousands of years the father of every boy must have been able to ejaculate in order to cause conception, which means that he probably passed this ability on to his son. Mother does not always reach a climax at the time of conception—she certainly does not have to—and survival of the species does not require that she pass the genetic basis for orgasm on to her daughter. But there is no completely valid basis for linking orgasm capacity to hereditary factors at the present time, and the Masters-Johnson (1966) research suggests that women may have even greater orgasm capacity than men, if it is not inhibited in some way.

Perhaps it should also be noted that the boy's first ejaculation can be a profound and disturbing experience. It often occurs in the form of a *wet dream*, leaving the boy puzzled and embarrassed. Gordon Shipman (1968) says that boys are bothered enough by the *"primus ejaculatus,"* as he calls it, to warrant much more study than it has yet received. But it is also quite apparent that later ejaculations are immensely pleasurable to most boys, even though they may lead to secrecy (and some suspicion) in relations with parents. This fact is important. In orgasm the boy discovers a pleasant sensation of considerably more than passing importance, but it is one that he cannot easily discuss with members of his family. If it can be discussed with anybody, the male peer group is the most likely place; the conversation will probably reflect the naïveté and swagger characteristic of boys in their early and mid-teens.

The girl's *menarche* (her first menstrual period) is the analogue of the boy's first ejaculation. The contrast in social and personal meanings of these two events sharply divides the sexes. Both the daughter and her mother look forward to the girl's menarche as its time approaches. They will often discuss the upcoming event at some length, and for many girls it is one of life's most notable experiences. But it is discussed mainly in terms of implications for pregnancy and childbirth; the erotic significance will probably be played down.

By contrast, the sexual coming of age of boys is charged with erotic significance and strong "underground" possibilities. It is not a subject of conversation within the family, and its impact upon the boy may not be shared with anybody. The overwhelming likelihood is that its implications for the family will be completely overlooked. However, Charles Bowerman and John Kinch (1959) found that puberty for girls is often greeted with new restrictions, causing some of them to turn toward peers and away from the family. This creates even bigger differences between themselves and their more conservative parents.

Boys mature in a growing intensity of genital gratification—a very specific kind of pleasure. It is not surprising that girls more often react with surprise and disbelief when they first learn about sexual intercourse (Shipman 1968). And they are also more likely to consider it vulgar and shocking. To boys, sex seems rather natural and acceptable, and they are usually happy to learn more about it (although they may be slow to admit that they do not already know everything).

Heterosexuality

Boys frequently learn to masturbate only from other boys; girls are much less likely to learn from other girls (Ramsey 1943; Kinsey, Pomeroy, Martin, and Gebhard 1953). Genital play for the girl is more easily hidden, just as the female genitals themselves are less prominent, but this kind of play is also less frequent in their lives. The fact that the boy often learns masturbation from other boys (instead of discovering it for himself) suggests a strange combination of biological and cultural pressures. He is attracted to masturbation more than girls are and is even encouraged by other boys to engage in it, but due to the strong taboo against it, he is also threatened by mysterious consequences if he yields to temptation. Although boys are usually given more opportunities to be alone and to have privacy than girls, they receive hardly any encouragement to become sexually self-sufficient.

Once again, a crucial difference between males and females shows up. The girl is drawn to heterosexuality by a combination of forces, and traditional mores stress the idea that girls who plan to be wives and mothers should inhibit all sexual activities not related to family roles. Sexual intercourse poses a problem mainly because of the girl's need to restrain herself before marriage. Boys are given more freedom, and they need not fear premarital pregnancy. They can think relatively more about genital release, and masturbation therefore is very tempting. They do not have to worry so much about guilt in sex relations with a girl (although many of them have few opportunities to test themselves). The point is that the boy's sex life is governed less by an interest in heterosexuality than by his interest in genital pleasure per se. This can be controlled in part through masturbation (despite the continuing taboo against it), but it is constantly being stirred up by pretty girls, pornography, jokes, and other erotic experiences. Boys not only take an erotic view of boy-girl relations, but, as Christopher Jencks (1964) says, they get exaggerated ideas about the pleasures of sex and of their chances to make out. (*Playboy* magazine and scores of other stimulants keep the male imagination excited.) In a sense, boys mislead each other in their swaggering talk, but they apparently take their sex curiosity quite seriously.

Deryck Calderwood (1963) reported that ninth-grade girls, in a situation in which they were genuinely free to inquire about sex and to ask questions that troubled them most, had fewer questions than boys, and, in strong contrast to males, raised no questions about their own sex organs, none about masturbation among girls, and few about the meaning of slang terms concerning sex. Their questions about intercourse were usually related to birth control. More than anything else, girls want to learn about boys in order to be able to cope with them—to get dates, to make boys like them, even be able, in alliance with mother, to control dad. Boys simply want to learn about sex. In spite of the boy's avid interest, however, he gets virtually no information or effective direction from his father and very little from mother (Kronhausen and Kronhausen 1960; Ramsey 1943). By far the most common source of information for boys, and the second most common source for girls, is other children. In one study three-fourths of the boys and half of the girls said they would never, or only sometimes, turn to either a parent or a school counselor for information when troubled about sex (Sliepcevich 1965).

Even homosexuality among males poses different problems from those facing girls. For boys and men it is usually an intensely erotic activity; for girls and women it carries a much greater social or expressive significance. In fact, the pleasure associated with masturbation among males is usually much stronger than any they can get from homosexuality, and therefore the sex tensions of young men separated from women can usually (not always, of course) be relieved short of turning to homosexuality.

Masturbation apparently does not serve women nearly so well. Lesbianism in women's prisons, for example, greatly exceeds the comparable rate in prisons for men—because women suffer more from the loss of intimate personal relationships. David Ward and Gene Kassebaum (1965), studying female prisoners, found their overriding need is to have a relationship with some other person that can bring love, support, and a sense of status. Sex per se is not enough. Unlike the pattern in male prisons, where sex tends to be a private matter (although it is always a popular topic of discussion, with erotic references to "sexy broads" on the outside), homosexual behavior is the key to social organization among female inmates and an important basis for personal security. Basically, female homosexuals are very much like other women. Sex for them is part of an interpersonal pattern, and the lesbian community includes a high proportion of women who keep relatively stable homosexual relationships—ones that are not built around sex alone (Simon and Gagnon 1967a).

Of perhaps more significance than anything else is the fact that boys acquire a rich, stirring vocabulary about sex as they grow up. Girls learn many of the scatological meanings found in the "boy culture" (although not all of them—they will learn them from their boyfriends and husbands later on), but the free-flowing use of four-letter words is the property of older boys and men (Lerman 1967). As Mark Twain once said of his wife's swearing, "She has the words but not the tune." Even some boys may be forever inhibited by the efforts of clean-speech advocates—mostly women— to keep their language pure.

The Need To Be Physically Appealing

Girls are under great pressure to be physically attractive to boys. The need that the sexes have for each other may be roughly equal, all things considered, but not in this particular regard. Ordinarily the boy has no intense need to be physically desirable, nor can his urge to have girls like him be satisfied by appearance alone. It is not surprising, then, that women have different body concepts from men, that they draw finer distinctions about their appearance, and that their self-awareness in this regard begins at an earlier age. They are more conscious of their distinguishing characteristics and perceive them in much greater detail (Kurtz 1968). The American girl learns at an early age that her physical image is the basic token of her sexuality, and throughout her life she will attach greater significance to the features of her face, her hair, and (above all) her figure than the boy does to his.

Efforts to teach boys how to manage their body image and posture are remarkably lax compared to the careful instruction of girls. Boys are permitted, although perhaps not encouraged, to slouch with almost no regard for appearance. Almost all of them have trouble sitting still in elementary school, and nagging rarely helps. They are spared the necessity of keeping their legs close together (as girls are taught to do in order to be ladylike and to protect, symbolically, their genitals).

Although boys, by contrast with girls, are rather timid in discussing how their appearance might be altered or improved (Frazier and Lisonbee 1953), they are not reluctant to discuss the appearance of girls. They speak of girls' bodies in a candid way, to put it mildly, and have a devastating collection of names to call girls they consider ugly (and to refer to "undesirables" in general). The vocabulary of girls is not nearly as inventive in this regard, nor as humiliating. Boys have a set of lewd terms to describe even the attractive girls, which they usually try to conceal from adults. In fact, girls are not sexy by themselves—not in terms of their own feelings or conceptions of themselves—but only as objects in the minds of boys (and men). Girls are usually quite content to encourage this illusion, without realizing the full extent of the lasciviousness they create.

As Erik Erikson (1968) has put it, boys learn to "make out" in "phallic-intrusive" ways; girls by teasing, provoking, and the minor forms of "snaring"—by making themselves tempting and seductive. At the same time, the girl must neither be nor appear to be promiscuous. The moral dilemma of the conventional American girl is that she must appear physically attractive even as she tries to hold back in sex (Bell 1966). Gary Schwartz and Don Merten (1967) have shown that the problem of the "good" girl is to make out (that is, to be liked and to be sexually attractive) without being "made," and her resolution of this dilemma becomes an important basis for her self-image. Geoffrey Gorer (1948) made a similar point with less supporting evidence twenty years earlier. The payoff for the correct handling of this problem is presumed to be a favorable and successful marriage.

The boy's sex problem is not quite so important for his self-image. He too must harness his sex drive, but homosexuality, not premarital sex and pregnancy, is the prime sin he is supposed to avoid (Gorer 1948). He is under pressure to try to succeed with girls because, if he does not, he runs the risk of being considered a homosexual. William Simon and John Gagnon (1967) point out that two spinsters can live together without suspicion, and their reputations can even survive a public display of affection, but the idea of two adult men living together will almost certainly suggest homosexuality. The Kinsey researchers (1953) traced the legal record in America from 1696 to 1952 and could not find a single conviction of a female for homosexual activity. They report data for New York City from 1930 to 1939 showing 700 convictions of males on homosexual charges.

Monogamy and Love

The intense desire on the part of most girls to get married, accompanied by a strong monogamous ideal, stirs the romantic drive as they go through the teen years. William Kephart (1967) argues that commitment to monogamy is much weaker among males, even in modern America. Girls, for example, tend to remember only those things about past romantic affairs that are consistent with monogamy; males are more eccentric in this regard and are more often in conflict with the family ideals of the community. They are certainly less captivated by the strictly social aspects of boy-girl relations, as Winston Ehrmann (1959) has shown, and their romantic yearnings are only weakly anchored in any social sense. The process of getting married and the state of marriage itself ordinarily do not enchant them.

But, as we have seen, boys also spend their elementary-school years in the midst of much greater genital activity than girls. Much of this is not, strictly speaking, erotic. It is preerotic, and yet it does set up a powerful basis for later sex interest. Boys develop an initial desire for genital release per se, and concern for mate-getting is superimposed on this more fundamental pattern. For girls, training in love precedes training in sexuality. As a result, sex for males has greater autonomy from any other interest or commitment and it can be enjoyed with relative detachment from other areas of life. For example, it is more independent of religious interests than for girls, for whom church activities apparently can compensate somewhat for lack of sexual gratification (Wallin 1957).

Ira Reiss (1968) suggests that one reason girls stress love more than boys is because they are taught to feel guilty about sex. If they have a premarital affair, the belief that they are in love can help relieve the guilt. For most women, however, the pursuit of sex pleasure as something separate from emotional or romantic involvement is not very attractive. For many it is simply impossible (Simon and Gagnon 1967).

Related to this is the fact that males are not ordinarily under any pressure to give sex favors on dates. They do not have the feeling of *self-disavowal* that is hard to avoid when you put your body at another's disposal; feeling a need to do this is a fact of life for many girls. Some girls (not most) learn to merely endure the sex act. The very fact that the girl is taught to think of herself as a sex object, and yet not a passionate one, leads to the conventional *service orientation* in sex relations.

Any sign of inhibition by the girl—that is, constant control of her impulses—is seen as a sign of self-control. *Inhibition* is the traditional and still vital key to female morality. Sex restraint and general restraint tend to go together, and becoming a woman is therefore a restricting process to approximately the same degree that girls are reared to think that respectability means being a virgin. The girl learns to take pride in holding her impulses in check, thereby proving that she is "good." She will earn the full rewards of womanhood if she can keep a clean and trouble-free record. In a sense, girls are *sexualized* whereas boys are not, since the former are urged to follow special female standards. The sex assertiveness of males can take many unconventional turns, but the woman is expected to conform to a rather narrow feminine stereotype.

She is also asked to be a helpmate, which is part of the traditional role of wife and mother. This is a self-denying role in its very nature, so that teaching girls to subdue the sex urge is basic training for the many other burdens of femininity. (This is true primarily in places where the size and strength advantages of men have been overcome by modern technology. Virginity has not been prized in many preliterate groups, but women are restrained relative to men anyway because the male's superior strength has much greater importance in preindustrial societies.)

Even in modern society it is easier to teach girls to suppress their sexual and competitive impulses than boys, partly because boys have more freedom as they grow up—more life space to explore—and partly because of the continuing assumption that boys simply cannot control their "boyish" energies. The assumption may be false, but it is nonetheless compelling; there is no similar folklore about "girlish" unmanageability. Not that boys are totally uninhibited, of course—they are at least as guarded as girls when it comes to trying new foods, for example. But they are almost totally exempt from the need to protect their virginity. Because "good" girls are presumed to be able to control the sex drive (Schwartz and Merten 1967), and they have so much more to lose if they fail to, drawing the line in sex relations becomes a female duty. Even "good" boys are expected to try to make out with girls—to cross whatever line the girls set up.

THE SOCIAL CONTROL OF SEX

Sex is a powerful force that can either strengthen family bonds or lead to alienation—more likely a combination of the two. And yet the dogma that sex must be brought under control deserves careful study. It is at least possible that we try too hard to control it—that our effort to make sex restraint a virtue is overdone. Actually, we face strong counterpressures on this point. Although we often assume that sex is dangerous and has to be carefully controlled, we also recognize that tensions build up when it is too harshly restricted and that these bottled-up pressures can be disastrous when they are finally, often suddenly, released.

The most basic control over sex—the incest taboo—is discussed in Chapter 16. Sex is always guarded within the family, partly to protect marriage, but also to preserve the parents' authority over their children. Many authorities believe that children in the elementary-school years need to be more or less free from thoughts of sex in order to learn a thousand lessons that can only be learned at this time. Sex play is therefore inhibited. It is a moot question, however, whether the elementary-school period is one of *sexual latency* because adults have kept children from thinking about sex or because children are too immature at these ages to think much about it anyway. In many nonliterate societies adults make no effort to censor the subject. They may even be amused when the children try sex experiments, tell off-color jokes, or sing raunchy songs. It was not uncommon in medieval Europe for adults to egg children on in these activities.

But it is also true that childhood has historically been very short; there was no need for prolonged schooling in the past. Only in modern industrial society do the elementary-school years become crucial. It was probably no accident that efforts were made to suppress sex among children when the system of formal education first developed. We are a little more relaxed in the United States today, and it is felt that children *should* learn about sex in an orderly way during the elementary-school years. The current argument in favor of early and continual sex education is not that children should be sexually stimulated—quite the opposite. The theory is that children who are informed about sex on all levels—biological, psychological, and social—will not be distracted by the opinions and misinformation that are spread by other chidren. In theory, modern sex training is designed to help keep sex under control.

But we have seen that in pre- and early adolescence boys usually have much stronger sex drives than girls (although the Masters-Johnson research suggests that women may be capable of far stronger sex drives than either they or men previously realized).

In fact, the problem of handling the male sex drive is presumed to be beyond the powers of all but the staunchest females, and so they are given various kinds of help (which reinforces the assumption that they need it). Even in college, girls are surrounded by regulations which have specific sexual implications, most obviously in the case of dormitory curfews. The curfews are being lifted almost everywhere now, but the fact remains that night represents excitement for males and danger for females. Boys are permitted to prowl until the very late hours; girls should be in their rooms where they are safe. John Finley Scott (1965) has shown that sororities at large universities spend a large part of their time regulating (or trying to regulate) members—to see that they date the "right" boys and make progress toward an appropriate marriage. Furthermore, older women keep surprisingly close control over most of these groups.

Fraternities supervise courtship among members, too, but not as much, and their usefulness to boys goes far beyond this "family" function. Older men have hardly any direct control over them. The greater range of fraternity affairs (compared to sororities) reflects basic, long-standing differences between the sexes. They persist for many reasons, but differences in the way people react to their bodies lie at the heart of the matter. Boys are expected to seek new stimulations, and their personal experiences with sex will keep the search going. Perhaps it is no longer scandalous for some girls to do likewise, but the encouragement they get will come mainly from predatory males, the very people they are warned to mistrust. Even in Sweden, where premarital sex between engaged couples is considered almost normal, the double standard lingers on. According to one study, the majority of men have had as many as five sex partners; most women are limited to one or two (Zetterberg 1969).

Although sex stimulation hits boys from all sides, the overall impact does not necessarily support familism, and it certainly does not lead to positive attitudes about fatherhood (Benson 1968). In the course of dating and courtship the sex drives of boys are usually brought closer into line with leading family values. But only after they are married, perhaps only after their wives become pregnant, do they begin to think very seriously about being fathers.

Girls, on the other hand, generally become truly erotic only as they start having closer ties with boys. Then they are introduced in a very direct way to the male approach. Winston Ehrmann (1959) in particular has tried to show that girls are introduced to a romantic view of sex before they have had a chance to learn about its more sensual possibilities. The acceptance of prolonged sex play—petting—as a part of dating undoubtedly pushes girls toward greater sexual arousal, which probably also pulls them away from their earlier family outlook. When dating is viewed in broad perspective, girls have certainly *needed* a liberating influence. The fact that they are now a little more expressive in sex means that they can be psychologically closer to their boyfriends and to their husbands later on. At the same time, sex play in modern dating helps to satisfy the man's sex desire even as it draws him into stable heterosexual relations and marriage.

One other problem in the social control of sex is keeping it in place *after* marriage—the problem of adultery. Since this chapter is concerned with premarital sex, adultery will be taken up later (in the chapter on marriage adjustment). Nevertheless, we can note here that the greater the variety of sex partners a person has before marriage, the more varied his sex fare is likely to be afterward. Premarital sex and the forces associated with it are by no means isolated from sex in marriage itself.

PROBLEM AREAS

Four problem areas in the social control of sex deserve individual attention: masturbation, homosexuality, premarital intercourse, and prostitution. Each poses problems in virtually all societies, and each has important implications for family life.

Masturbation

Masturbation is a common practice in all cultures, and efforts are usually made to keep it under control. But reaction to it varies greatly, from horrified concern to a kind of stoic tolerance, depending especially upon the age groups involved. The *societal* problem it presumably poses is that it could, if allowed to flourish without ridicule, drain vital sex energies from marriage, undermining the sex bond between couples. We cannot be sure, however, that this assumption is valid. Its biggest flaw is that there is no known way to measure the impact of masturbation on marriage, and we have no reliable information about masturbation rates in different societies.

Earlier in this chapter we discussed the special place of masturbation in the sex development of boys. According to Kinsey *et al.* (1948) about nine out of ten males take up active masturbation at some time in their lives. Ages fourteen and fifteen are the peak years, and rates seem to be especially high when the boys have conflict with their parents. Although the practice occurs less among girls, it is by no means uncommon even for them.

Some boys find out about masturbation on their own; many learn only from other boys. A much higher percentage of boys observe their friends in masturbation than do girls of similar ages (Masters and Johnson 1966). A few girls discover the practice on their own; some are introduced to it by other girls; and some learn about it from boys. It seems to be much less likely, however, that boys will get their first information from girls.

Almost all boys are reminded in one way or another that it is "bad," and until quite recently they were told that the practice could lead to some dreaded disease, insanity, or even worse. The literature on this subject now shows signs of merciful relaxation. In Wardell Pomeroy's (1968) lively book *Boys and Sex*, for example, the discussion of masturbation is devoted largely to refuting myths about its dire consequences. And yet Masters and Johnson (1966) contend that the superstition of physical or mental deterioration resulting from excessive masturbation is still firmly entrenched in our culture. It does seem that we are relatively more concerned about homosexuality now, and the boy may find some justification for self-play simply because it seems a lesser evil.

The fact that masturbation is such a concentrated act of genital gratification (accompanied of course by sexual fantasy) tends to make it less appealing to girls, apparently because of their greater interest in the social aspects of sex. Hence, homosexuality is relatively more acceptable to them. When women masturbate, concentrating only on their own sex demands without the psychic distractions of a partner, they may have repeated orgasms without resolving the original tension; Masters and Johnson (1966) say that possibly only physical exhaustion can bring the session to an end.

Heterosexuality is stressed so often and so impressively in later adolescence that masturbation usually declines at this time. But the pattern differs between middle- and lower-class youth. Kinsey noted that petting is regarded as a kind of perverted activity in the working classes, among whom heterosexual intercourse is more acceptable. Furthermore, Kinsey found that masturbation was subject to less fear and hostility in the middle than in the lower classes. It seems likely that, despite their stress on dating, the widespread acceptance of petting in the middle class may lead to relatively high rates of masturbation, especially after a long, torrid petting session. The excitement caused by petting gets another boost by the many sexually stimulating magazines and movies now shown. Furthermore, modern youth in the middle classes have considerable privacy. They often have rooms of their own at home, for example. It is possible that opportunities for masturbation and freedom from guilt are greater in contemporary American suburbs than they have ever been in history.

The big problem is this: To what extent is masturbation phased out of the person's life after marriage? Of course heterosexuality among adult married couples is universally preferred, and the practice of masturbation is scorned almost everywhere. But the habit does persist among adolescent males; the extent to which it does *not* disappear after adolescence is an aspect of sexuality that has never been adequately described, as William Styron (1968) has observed. Masters and Johnson (1966) say that automanipulation occurs with "some regularity" among adults, and they also guardedly allow that it can be as exciting and perhaps even as fulfilling as sexual intercourse. But we have no evidence about its effect on marriage.

The problem, of course, is that masturbation may serve as a substitute for heterosexual relations, and when it does, the bonding effect of sex is presumably lost. Suppose a certain wife does not find much pleasure in coitus with her husband. When he wants to have sex relations on a particular evening, the wife may squelch the subject with a plausible excuse, perhaps simply by saying that she has had a very rough day. This may happen not once, but fairly often. She may even anticipate her husband's wishes on any given day and head him off; the minute he gets home she may report how terribly weary she is. Since the husband probably engaged in masturbation in adolescence, maybe regularly up until the time of marriage, he is obviously tempted to try it again. Sooner or later he may succumb, and a whole new pattern develops. On some occasions he finds that sex with his wife is difficult because he is already drained, and the pattern feeds upon itself. Masturbation becomes more frequent, intercourse less, and sex for the married couple proves to be a problem that gets worse, not better.

But if we assume that the bonding effect of sex in marriage is only one element in a much larger pattern, then masturbation may not be such a disaster after all. The practice may actually make adjustment possible where sex relations are not otherwise satisfactory. For men who have the problem of premature ejaculation—reaching climax much sooner than their wives—masturbation by the wife prior to sex relations can contribute to better sex relations. Or, to take a different kind of example, masturbation may serve as a substitute for another woman when the husband is away on a business trip. Although social conventions (as well as the wife back home) would probably prefer that the man abstain altogether, masturbation is probably preferable to "an affair."

The object of this brief discussion is not to encourage masturbation, nor to condemn it, but to call attention to the fact that it does exist on a wide scale. Its full impact on family life remains largely unknown.

Homosexuality

Homosexuality is comparable to masturbation in that if it were allowed to flourish without opposition or if people openly encouraged it, it could draw sex away from marriage, and family cohesion would presumably suffer. But homosexuality, like masturbation, is found in all countries. Each has its own way of coping with it, although in some places the role of the homosexual may not exist, not in the sense that there is any clear-cut social stereotype of "a homosexual" (McIntosh 1968).

Every society evolves a system encouraging durable sex relations between men and women. In order to do this it cannot give equal encouragement to both heterosexual and homosexual affairs. At most, it can tolerate the latter in certain special cases. George P. Murdock (1949) surveyed scores of societies and concluded that all of them attempt to confine marriage and sex to persons of opposite sexes. Some permit homosexuality under carefully defined conditions, but only a tiny minority allow much freedom in this respect. The most commonly permitted practice is *transvestitism*, the practice of dressing and acting like a member of the opposite sex (usually a man dressing like a woman). In some European countries all homosexual acts by males are legally punishable, while in others only certain kinds are. The idea that the ancient Greeks idealized homosexuality (Licht 1932) has gained popularity, but the practice there occurred mainly among the literati who were actually very few in number and even they were subject to persecution and accused of corrupting the youth.

The most general technique used to control homosexuality is simply to convey to children the idea that it is disgusting beyond words. American boys in elementary school, for example, learn about the derogatory term "queer" sooner or later. At first most of them do not know what it means, but they get a clear enough impression that whatever it is, it is not good. Thus, they are actually taught to abhor the practice before they know what it is. Many people of both sexes are never quite sure precisely what homosexuals do. The subject remains vague in their minds, and it is the object of comparatively little fantasy. Probably the first impressions are negative or abominable enough to make it difficult even to try to carry the act through in their imagination. By contrast, most people have given quite a bit of thought to how heterosexual intercourse might be carried out before they actually try it (although the misconceptions are bizarre even here).

Thus, the overwhelming majority of people become completely hostile toward homosexuality, and they never find any reason to change their first impressions. They will not usually be approached by a homosexual, so their initial hostility is coupled with the fact that they have very few chances to see how they would act if an actual homosexual opportunity should come up.

How, then, do people get involved? The most compelling psychological theories are grounded in a Freudian approach, stressing the roots of homosexuality in pathological relationships between parents and children. These can take many forms, but the general pattern is believed to be one in which the child becomes overattached to his parent of the opposite sex, causing him to reject sex relations with other members of that sex. Case studies can be cited to support this view, but it is difficult to identify specific pathologies in parent-child relations that inevitably or even usually lead to homosexuality.

The most acceptable *social* theory is that homosexual groups exist in most of the world's cultures and, although they are composed of a tiny minority in almost every instance, they still manage to replenish themselves with new members in each new generation. They rarely conspire to corrupt innocent youth, but they do attract uninitiated people occasionally. The actual way that recruits are brought in is not fully known, although the general outline is reasonably clear. The same pattern operates as for other social practices limited to a small part of the population. The key is *differential association*, leading to *differential identification*. Through differential association, one has greater opportunities to meet certain kinds of people than others. A person may happen to sit next to a homosexual in school, for example, or to meet one in his neighborhood. Anther person may never have this experience. Chance factors are involved, but the activities one engages in and where one lives also raise the likelihood of meeting certain kinds of people rather than others. Once friendships have been made, it becomes possible to identify with them and to develop a preference for the activities they enjoy.

People learn about homosexuality in a process involving *acquaintance*, *persuasion*, and *example* (Davis 1966). In prisons, for example, persuasion of new inmates ranges from subtle inducement to outright compulsion (Ward and Kassebaum 1965). Male prostitutes are usually lower-class, adolescent boys who find it an easy way to make money. They are drawn to this form of hustling by older boys from whom they learn how to make contacts, how the victims can be handled, and just what rules to follow to keep from getting caught. For some the pattern becomes one of "queer-baiting"—attacking the homosexual for his money; he is almost never in a position to press charges (Albert Reiss 1960).

Because confirmed homosexuals represent a small group (and it is often quite loosely knit, with no clear dividing line between who is "in" and who is "out"), they reach only a small proportion of people who are at a vulnerable stage in their personal development when they might go along. Still, some people—even those who have strong objections but little real knowledge—meet homosexuals under circumstances leading to friendship, mutual trust, and finally to sex attraction.

The novice is usually attracted in a setting that can disarm, or perhaps overwhelm, his previous objections (which is not meant to suggest that it was planned that way, in a conspiracy to seduce). Differential association gradually becomes differential identification. The person who has an opportunity to learn of homosexuality under favorable circumstances becomes at ease with the practice and may at some later time introduce another novice to the inner world. Obviously not all who have the opportunity succumb to it or stay with it, but we have no idea what the entrance and dropout rates are.

The latter is undoubtedly high, however, because homosexuals are at best tolerated by the nonhomosexual community, and at worst, persecuted. The few individuals who become confirmed homosexuals often do so because they find it difficult or impossible to make conventional adjustments in life (Davis 1966). By assuming a feminine role, for example, a man can escape the aggressive and often uncompromising struggle among men. On the other hand, the dominant male homosexual has no need to assume the taxing relations with women that heterosexual adjustment requires. Donald Cory (1961) argues that such a man is actually less attracted to males than he is in flight from females.

Be wary of easy explanations of homosexuality, however, especially those that say, in effect, that the homosexual is not as "good" as the rest of us. Putting homosexuality down is one thing; explaining it is another. According to William Simon and John Gagnon (1967), homosexuals do conform to social expectations in most of their behavior. Homosexuality takes up a relatively small part of their time and attention.

But once homosexuality has become a confirmed pattern it is not easy to return to conventional family life (English and Finch 1954), and it is not easy to have a stable homosexual life, either. Homosexual pairs often act as if they are "married," setting up housekeeping and expecting mutual fidelity. They also distinguish themselves according to who is the dominant and who the subordinate partner. But they will almost inevitably break up, since their relationship is vulnerable to scores of undermining influences to which heterosexuals are immune (although female homosexuals are much less vulnerable than men, as noted earlier). Conventional marriage, of course, has the initial advantage of being a legal arrangement; formal obstacles are designed to keep it from breaking up. In addition, countless pressures combine to keep married couples trying to make their marriages work. The homosexual couple will face pressures that frustrate their best efforts. No good data exist on the average life span of homosexual marriage, but one that can last an entire year would have to be considered a rather successful affair.

Kingsley Davis argues that homosexuality can survive on a broad scale only if it has unusually strong social supports—through the establishment of legal rights for homosexual partners, protection of children against exploitation, and a licensing system to identify and clarify standards of acceptable behavior. In effect, this would be a system for governing and protecting homosexual rights like the one now used for conventional marriage. Lars Ullerstam (1966) claims that homosexuals even now are the most privileged of the erotic minorities, because they are the only ones who have created clubs and organizations for their own protection.

But it certainly seems that homosexuality can become widespread only where people are cut off from conventional society or from members of the opposite sex. For example, prisoners, soldiers far from home, and students at all-girl or all-boy colleges geographically isolated from the opposite sex are especially susceptible. People traveling in certain social circles also have high rates—strippers, for example, are subject to social and psychological pressures that lead many of them to lesbianism (McCaghy and Skipper 1969). We have already seen that homosexuality in women's prisons seems to be a key to social life there—more than in men's prisons. Apparently in some prisons homosexuality is allowed to flourish; in others an effort is made to crush it. It would be useful to know just what happens to inmates after they are released, especially from prisons where homosexuality is rife. A study by Alan Davis (1968) suggests that in some prisons homosexuality is part of a cruel "masculinity ritual," and it virtually cripples its victims.

The army has had long experience in keeping homosexuality under control. Its success varies, but apparently American soldiers do not ordinarily have high rates. Selective factors operate to some extent, so that men recruited into military service are strongly opposed to the practice (although latent, hidden interests may be more common than we know). When civilians are drafted, however, men who had never been tempted before face a new challenge. For this reason the military, with civilian support, tries to promote heterosexuality among the troops. Pinup pictures are not only tolerated but encouraged, and movies starring pretty girls are enormously popular. No matter where the boys go, the image of sexy, leggy, buxom girls follows. Rather than homosexuality, the boys in most cases either pine away for their girls back home, or combine heterosexual longings with pickups and masturbation.

It should be apparent that homosexuality involves a variety of activities. Mary McIntosh (1968) is correct when she argues that it is a social role or a set of them and not necessarily a special psychological condition within the individual. This discussion has been almost exclusively about people who take it up in the context of a homosexual subculture or where normal heterosexual relations are not possible. But homosexuality also occurs among people who, without being in such groups, have an isolated affair or one repeated very rarely. Kinsey (1948) found that 37 percent of his white male sample had had an overt homosexual experience at one time or another, but only 4 percent had been exclusively homosexual. Among his white females the two percentages were 13 and 1 respectively (Kinsey *et al.* 1953). At first Kinsey was skeptical of his own figures, but each new group he studied followed essentially the same pattern. Occasional homosexual encounters, however, do not seem to be of any general importance so far as family commitments are concerned.

Seward Hiltner (1953), a theologian, has outlined four basic considerations for a socially responsible attitude toward homosexuality: (1) recognition of the difference between one-shot affairs in the person's youth and an exclusive homosexual pattern in adulthood; (2) careful concern to give all possible help to people who have homosexual tendencies *that they want to change*; (3) recognition of the distinction between homosexuals who are predatory (especially toward children and adolescents) and those who are socially responsible despite their homosexuality; and (4) clarification for both homosexuals and others of the nature, meaning, and social significance of this unconventional behavior. The Wolfenden report in Britain in 1957 —still a landmark—recommends that mature homosexuals who do not otherwise pose problems for the community should simply be left alone.

By way of conclusion, most children develop a bias against homosexuality before they even know what it is. A few may still meet people who accept the practice, and some turn to it in a continuing way. But they will find no peace; homosexuality receives very little social or legal support, and it is the target of enormous ill will. It is suppressed all over the world—which may explain why it does not ordinarily constitute a serious threat to the standard family pattern. It may even, on balance, strengthen marriage, because the very existence of a few homosexuals creates a sense of moral integrity among people who condemn the practice. Homosexuality becomes the deviant pattern which defines what is good; only because it exists as an evil can heterosexuals take pride in being normal.

Premarital Sex

The family problems posed by premarital sex take many forms. The subject encompasses two kinds of sex—petting and intercourse—and each has an impact on marriage. As individuals, the course we take depends on what we consider important. One fact no one can avoid, however, is that sex before marriage is not isolated from marriage—it does make a difference.

It is strange that a relatively liberal attitude toward premarital intercourse developed in the twentieth century even before the one for petting. Following the lead of Alfred Kinsey, Ira Reiss (1967) contends that an *institutional gap* between dating and courtship on the one hand and the family on the other reached its peak in the 1920s. By that time, courtship was well on its way toward freedom from parental control. Power had shifted to the courting couples themselves, who had been reared under an essentially different system from their parents. Many studies show that rates of premarital intercourse increased rather sharply at this time. There is little evidence of changing intercourse rates since then, except among college students (Simon, Gagnon, and Carns 1968) who make up an increasing part of the population. Important changes have also occurred in other areas—especially in petting.

Conflict between parents and youth over sex has become less and less evident, mainly because the big changes lie in the past. In fact, most parents who went through courtship in the late 1940s engaged in sex practices very much like those their offspring are having today according to Ira Reiss (1967), although this does not seem to take increased college attendance and its impact fully into account. In both the early intercourse revolution and the later, milder petting revolution, white females, particularly from the middle and upper-middle classes, have shown the greatest change toward greater sexual permissiveness.

Males in the Western world have always had more freedom than females; the major new development for middle-class men is the fact that the women with whom they first have sex relations are no longer prostitutes or "easy" girls from the lower classes. They are girlfriends and fiancées of their own social level. The male has simply had to adjust to a new type of sex partner before marriage—one he is much more likely to marry. (Nobody can say for sure, but it is possible that premarital sex gives more pleasure to men under these circumstances. Certainly it does for women.)

Reiss (1967) has outlined the developmental pattern for most contemporary youth. The child gets his basic set of values from parents, friends, and other people he happens to be exposed to. As dating begins he falls under the influence of the more permissive values popular among adolescents. There is a general tendency for the teen-ager to consider his parents' sex attitudes as the low point on a permissiveness scale and his peers' as the high point. He places himself a little closer to his peers, particularly to those he regards as his close friends (Mirande 1968).

Young people are increasingly knowledgeable, even sophisticated, about sex, and as their knowledge increases, their anxieties are relaxed. One important sex restraint operating in the past was fear based on ignorance, a kind of control that is now under constant attack. The biological sex drive is powerful during adolescence, of course, although even among American teen-agers—who may seem totally uninhibited by world standards—there are many self-imposed restrictions, particularly among girls. While allowing permissiveness, freedom does not ordinarily lead to promiscuity.

Nevertheless, for the majority of teen-agers the modern dating-courtship period is one of increased open-mindedness about sex. Adult-induced guilt feelings are not as strong as they used to be. Petting is not only condoned, it is taken for granted. If youth are given a chance to set their own standards, they push toward greater permissiveness on almost all issues. Though they are not considered adults, they want to be treated as full-fledged citizens and to have all the rights of adulthood they can get. According to Reiss, freedom for adolescents is an unintended consequence of the open, *participant-run* courtship system. Since parents generally approve of the system, there is little they can do about its permissive consequences.

Following marriage, however, most young couples quickly return to the influence of the adult-run family standards. They begin to express relatively austere opinions about sex, confirming the old mores against which liberal values are contrasted by each new crop of adolescents.

Petting, as we have seen, has the general effect of drawing boys into closer social and physical relations with girls; on balance it seems to strengthen family commitments in modern society. Not only does it pull the male toward marriage, it certainly seems to provide good training for the kind of marital sex that contemporary sex manuals call for. The male is urged to prolong sex play before intercourse to bring his wife to a more receptive mood (on the theory that women need more foreplay than men in order to feel relaxed and wanted—that is, in order to find sex enjoyable).

Sex is almost always more satisfying when both partners take an active role, not leaving it to one or the other. Historically men have been the aggressors perhaps because of their strong *genital orientation* discussed earlier. Furthermore, sex gives more pleasure when the lovers can communicate verbally; whatever improves general communication between males and females seems to increase erotic pleasure (Moskin 1969). The prolonged petting experiences in dating thus afford a training ground for more sensitive sex relations in marriage and more total enjoyment. The point of all this foreplay is to create a loving human relationship, not to bring the body, male or female, to some kind of mechanical ecstasy.

It is plausible, though not proved, that petting also leads women to accept a variety of sex activities that they would have considered taboo in an earlier time. In fact, data collected by Eugene Kanin and David Howard (1958) suggest that wives are likely to regard premarital intercourse as more beneficial in marriage than petting. They found that the more advanced the level of intimacy before marriage, the more likely women are to think it is helpful for early marital sex adjustment. William Reevy (1959), on the other hand, found that heavy petting among girls was not associated with the likelihood of success in marriage. The girls in his sample who were more active in petting were actually less favorably disposed to marital success. But it is still possible that the *general level* of petting in recent times is a good thing. The long-run effects of heavier-than-average petting should not be used to gauge the overall impact of current standards. Perhaps it is best to suspend final judgment on the long-term impact of petting. Only one thing seems certain: It is here to stay.

The premarital sex problem that receives the great bulk of attention is not petting, although that once was a truly controversial issue. The reason that petting is still a problem in many minds is not because parents consider it deplorable as such, but because they feel that it may get out of control. That may be true, but it is also true that thousands of teen-age daters do engage in heavy petting without taking the final step toward intercourse. Many of these couples apparently find sex play and body caressing pleasurable all by themselves.

What then are the problems of premarital intercourse? Three kinds appear: The first concerns its effect on traditional family values; the second, its impact on marriage; and the third, the fact that it may cause premarital pregnancy (which is related to the first two problems, of course, but it also poses a problem in its own right).

With regard to the first one, the issue turns on the fact that many people consider sex restraint before marriage "good." In particular, virginity for girls is prized, or has been, and premarital pregnancy is considered a crushing humiliation. The morality underlying these reactions is now subject to much criticism (it is often ridiculed by college students in my own classes), but it is still widely held among both youth and adults. Although this point of view is undoubtedly accepted by millions of people in our society, its open expression seems to have dropped remarkably in recent years; the most vocal contenders against premarital sex now rarely base their case on the virtues of virginity. And it is in this sense more than any other that we have had a sexual revolution.

Instead of claiming that the issue is one of preserving the family, or the value of chastity, traditionalists are more likely to argue that premarital sex leads to social and psychological consequences that most people—even those unimpressed by traditional beliefs—are anxious to avoid: guilt feelings, regrets, and recriminations. Some boys may use intercourse as an excuse for losing respect for a girl, for example, thereby breaking off the relationship. But if it lasts, difficulties may carry over into marriage itself, which leads to the second problem area: the impact of intercourse on subsequent marriage.

Does premarital sex cause problems that would not occur if the couple had abstained? Let us assume for the moment that a couple has sex relations before marriage (without causing pregnancy). What then? Is there some lasting tension? Do they regret the fact they did not wait? Is sex in marriage better or worse as a result?

As for tension, good information is simply not available. There are many ways that premarital sex *might* be a source of continuing trouble—perhaps nagging suspicion—between spouses, but we do not know how to measure its impact. The quality of marriage itself is extremely hard to determine. Undoubtedly couples who never had intercourse before marriage may take pride in that fact, and they do not ordinarily regret that they put it off. But couples who had sex before marriage do not ordinarily regret their past actions either. They may not even think about them. And if they do, they can choose one or another of several ways to convince themselves that what they did was justified. Furthermore, distressed couples who think that the roots of their failure in marriage go all the way back to sex before the wedding may be using this "indiscretion" as a scapegoat. Their problem is probably much more complicated than that.

Perhaps the biggest issue is a more specific one: the effect of premarital sex upon sex satisfaction in marriage. One might think that couples who have extensive sex play before marriage (and who are not forced into marriage by pregnancy) would have reasonably satisfactory sex relations afterward. If sex were not a pleasure they presumably would not have got married in the first place. But once again we do not have the kind of information needed to tell for sure. We simply do not know how many couples who fail in sex before marriage decide to break up the relationship for that reason. Furthermore, can the quality of sex before marriage even be compared with its quality after the wedding? *Courtship sex* occurs in a unique setting, usually more romantic and certainly different from that of marriage. Couples customarily see each other in the evening only after dressing up and getting ready for a special occasion. The increased tension often involved in courtship sex may, paradoxically, also add to the pleasure. It may very well be that any fun the couple has before marriage cannot possibly be duplicated later in a routine, workaday household.

We have been talking about married couples who have intercourse only with one another before marriage, not with third parties. Ira Reiss (1967) has shown that the main justification for premarital sex in recent years is that the persons have known each other for some time, feel they are in love, and plan to marry. There is no indication that sex before marriage is promiscuous for the great mass of young people. Even the courtship pattern surrounding premarital pregnancies is neither deviant nor exploitative in most cases (Vincent 1961; Pope 1967). But for persons, especially girls, who have sex relations with many different partners, rates of extramarital sex after marriage are also likely to be high.

It is possible that a more tolerant attitude toward adultery is developing in some parts of the population. But to whatever extent adultery is a source of tension and possibly divorce, the higher rate of premarital sex must be considered a possible source of this instability in marriage. This may not be true in Sweden, however. According to one study, 98 percent of the Swedish married population has had intercourse before marriage, but the overwhelming majority is appalled by promiscuity, and the incidence of extramarital sex is described as "remarkably low" (Zetterberg 1969).

In a study of American honeymoon behavior, Eugene Kanin and David Howard (1958) found that over 40 percent in their sample had engaged in premarital intercourse, roughly the same figure that Ernest Burgess and Paul Wallin had found earlier (1953). The percentage was even higher when the social-class background of husbands was higher than that of their wives. Women who had premarital experience actually had greater sex difficulties immediately after marriage than the others, but those who had reached orgasm, as compared to those who had intercourse without a climax, had much less difficulty. At the end of the first two weeks of marriage less than one woman out of twelve who had had premarital sex reported her sex life as unsatisfying, in contrast with approximately one out of four of the inexperienced women. Furthermore, experienced wives were much more likely to find sex on their wedding night generally satisfying even though they also reported more difficulties concerning the specific circumstances associated with the act. It is possible, of course, that the relationship between sex before and after marriage can be explained by the intensity of the sex drive. Women with a stronger drive are probably more likely to have sex before marriage, and they may also enjoy it more afterward.

Premarital pregnancies, however, change the nature of the problem altogether. The key *social* function of marriage has always been to legitimize parenthood, not sexuality; sex outside of marriage is not at all rare in many societies. But because marriage is the basis for parenthood, sex that can lead to pregnancy without even the possibility of marriage is almost universally condemned.

What happens, then, if there is pregnancy without even the likelihood of marriage? One possibility is abortion; its effect on later marriage patterns is unknown. (Opposition to abortion rarely stresses its implications for marriage. Even proponents of liberalized abortion laws usually ignore this angle.) Another possibility is that the baby will be put up for adoption, a likely occurrence in the middle classes. Although this may have no great impact upon ultimate marriage success, it can cause a terrible emotional setback for the girl involved.

Another possibility is that the baby will be kept by the girl or by her parents or kinsmen, which is a common way of handling the problem in the lower classes. This is known to be associated with family instability, especially where the male family figure is weak and unreliable, and it is not a random happening. Unmarried women who have kept their babies often have daughters who go through the same experience. This way of life almost qualifies as a subculture. However, premarital pregnancy per se does not cause the pattern; it is only one part of it, and more often a symptom than an explanation.

Still another possibility is that the premarital pregnancy will lead to marriage. (The original condition of our hypothesis was that marriage was very unlikely, but couples sometimes do in fact change their entire outlook when the girl becomes pregnant.) Some such marriages are altogether successful, but the prognosis is certainly not good. Quite obviously the male may be a reluctant groom, and he might take the first chance he gets to abandon his wife. Marriage success is strongly influenced by whether the pregnancy causes the couple to decide to marry; it has a much less disastrous effect if it simply leads to an earlier wedding than was originally planned. As a *cause* of marriage, pregnancy is decidedly not a good omen (Christensen 1960; 1963).

One final problem, charged with profound implications for familism, concerns the use of contraceptives by teen-age girls. Many of them are badly informed on the subject and hence have no way of protecting themselves (if they have intercourse). But there are plenty of girls (an increasing number) who are by no means ignorant. The strange fact is that they go unprotected anyway. A variety of pressures cause girls who know everything they need to know about all the latest contraceptive devices to shrug off their knowledge and even their own better judgment.

For example, almost every American girl is taught to avoid sex before marriage, a point of view she may take quite seriously *except* during the hour or so of heavy petting on a date. In a romantic setting, especially if her boyfriend shows genuine affection, the code can easily break down, or just seem no longer relevant. But it only happens in the most impulsive way, so that the girl's better judgment is overwhelmed.

Before she has the date she *could* prepare herself with contraceptives of one sort or another, but in order to do that she would have to admit to herself that she deliberately plans to violate the code. Her self-image may not be able to take that confession. Or, even if her self-image is flexible enough, she would still have to get up considerable courage to equip herself for the act. That simply cannot be done without making it obvious to someone that she is preparing for sex, and she may not be able to go through with such a commitment. (In some countries—Sweden, for example—contraceptives used by girls are readily available in stores and even from sidewalk machines. A girl can keep herself in pills for a dollar a month, but premarital pregnancies are still commonplace.)

The girl's easiest solution to the American dilemma is to suppress any thoughts about sex and, if conditions should happen to be right, surrender to her impulses. The only birth control used under these circumstances will be used by the boy. Thus, the condom is pressed into service. It is the most commonly used contraceptive among unmarried teen-agers (Furstenberg,

Jr., Gordis, and Markowitz 1969). It can be fairly safe if used properly and with care, but conditions make that rather unlikely. The boy, of course, does have access to a supply of "rubbers" even while he is on a date (since they are often available in men's rest rooms), and buying them will probably not lower his self-concept. It can even give him a sense of greater masculinity.

The boy who uses a condom may feel that he is absolved from responsibility for any pregnancy, since he has taken every precaution—more than the girl herself. Although unwed fathers are actually more concerned for the welfare of the girls than popular opinion realizes (Sauber 1966), they share the common belief among teen-age males that girls ought to bear the blame when they get "in trouble" (Vincent 1960; Moore and Holtzman 1965). And the evidence is very clear that girls do indeed suffer the most; boys get off relatively easily as a rule.

Prostitution

Like homosexuality and masturbation, prostitution occurs in all countries of any size, and it is almost always viewed as a threat (or potential threat) to the family. In addition, perhaps even more important, it is considered a vice, a corrupting indulgence of a base appetite that can serve no worthwhile purposes, and it raises the risk of venereal disease at the same time.

Although the practice may be tolerated with no misgivings whatsoever in certain limited cases, when it expands beyond these limits strong efforts will almost certainly be made to get it back in its place. Thus, "red-light" or "tenderloin" districts have existed in American cities where prostitution was known to flourish, but any effort to move the operation to respectable neighborhoods is quickly crushed. Prostitution sometimes thrives in upper-class residential areas, but only so long as it is kept quiet, discreet, and manageable. The "call-girl" business, patronized by upper-middle and upper-class men, quietly flourishes in virtually all major American cities, but it remains invisible to most local citizens. At the time of this writing, the morning paper has a report about the chief of the vice squad in Paris, who is waging a campaign to keep street-walking prostitutes out of a certain wealthy Paris neighborhood (but he complains that arrests are difficult to make because the prostitutes have a "sixth sense" about plain-clothes men).

Aside from the popular concern about vice, the fear is that prostitution will draw sex energies away from the family or that it will simply let these energies go unharnessed and wasted. Prostitution involves a high degree of promiscuity, and it promotes no useful social purpose. Not only does it flaunt sexual infidelity, it does so by selling sex in the marketplace to the highest bidder. It is attractive to the male for this very reason—it by-passes the difficult task of attracting a woman or perhaps becoming involved in courtship and marriage.

Perhaps there is also some worry that the very existence of prostitution can be a seductive provocation for girls, tempting them to leave a virtuous life in favor of the more profitable wages of sin. I doubt that this is taken very seriously, however. In fact, the existence of prostitution and the moral shame attached to it establishes a basis for the respectability of good wives, the ones who confine their sex to the honorable customs of the community. As Kingsley Davis (1966) argues, prostitution serves a useful purpose for this very reason: Without it there would be no solid grounds for identifying female virtue. Davis notes that the wages of the prostitute are not paid primarily for services rendered, since there is very little skill involved; they are the price the female must be paid to forgo the status and self-esteem of a "good woman." The prostitute is paid to be bad, and so she suffers the social ostracism that bad women must suffer.

In fact, the prostitute's wages are far above those found in ordinary women's work (Murtagh and Harris 1957). James Bryan (1966) has shown that certain skills are in fact needed by prostitutes, especially proficiency in getting down to business with men who sometimes prefer to dally, and in the essential matter of collecting the fee. It also helps if they can develop a skill in spotting plain-clothes men.

Whether prostitution is actually a threat to the family remains debatable. No critical test of its social impact has yet been devised. It seems that the most serious problems for marriage occur when prostitution reaches teenage boys. Contact with prostitutes conceivably could make it difficult for them to sustain stable sex relations in marriage at a later time. This pattern is most characteristic in places where the triple sex standard is strong (sharply segregating people into three categories: men, virtuous women, and fallen women). Such a pattern, where relations between the sexes are not intimate or equalitarian, is found in preindustrial and early industrial societies and is preserved to some extent in the lower classes in contemporary America. Boys and girls are sharply segregated as they grow up, and many boys learn about heterosexual relations in brief encounters with prostitutes or with girls who will soon join the profession. In this way prostitution reflects certain general features of society. These in turn determine the most basic kinds of relations between men and women.

A different picture occurs in the middle classes. Here boys are not very likely to have close contact with prostitutes in the early or middle years of adolescence. As seniors in high school they sometimes get up enough courage, in a group, to visit a place believed to house prostitutes and, overcoming the reluctance of the shyest members of the group, may actually enter the premises. Some of the boys may then be able to go through with the entire act—to have sex relations with a prostitute and perhaps even enjoy it. But some of them will find the affair altogether miserable.

Half of the teen-age boys studied by Lester Kirkendall (1960) expressed dissatisfaction with their fling with a prostitute, and about one-fourth of the rest had mixed feelings—or worse. (These boys were enrolled in college and were predominantly middle class in social background.) The entire episode was probably regarded as a lark and may have no important influence on their relations with middle-class girls. It survives as an out-of-place masculine ritual, a holdover from an earlier and different kind of society.

In my own survey* of 156 college men enrolled in sociology classes in 1970, 68 (or 43 percent) had had relations with a prostitute; 34 of them (exactly 50 percent of those with prostitute experience) had visited the prostitute's place with a group of boys. What was most surprising was that 43 of the total sample (29 percent) had been involved in a group sex affair (one girl—not necessarily a prostitute—and two or more boys, which they invariably called a "gang bang." The practice was called "pulling the train" among lower income Puerto Rican boys in New York studied by Bernard Rosenberg and Joseph Bensman [1968]). Although boys who had had this experience had also had one with a prostitute in almost every case, it does seem that the most callous relationship that middle-class, city boys have with girls is the gang type sex affair. This fairly common occurrence has rarely been studied. Hunter Thompson (1966) describes several instances of it among the "Hell's Angels" in California; according to his account the women become involved willingly, but if the incident gets public attention they usually claim they have been raped.

Prostitution has become thoroughly commercialized in modern times because of the generally higher status of all women. For one thing, as the general position of women goes up, prostitutes must be paid relatively more for their services. They are asked to forfeit more esteem when they give up whatever goes with female respectability. But perhaps even more important is the fact that the higher general status of women deprives high-class prostitutes of the nonsexual functions they often had in the past. *Courtesans* once provided men with entertainment and sometimes even intellectual companionship. But all kinds of companionship—intellectual, social, and sexual—are now available to most men from the ranks of women in general.

Middle-class boys are now more likely to have their first sex experience on dates, with mild intimacies gradually leading to sexual intercourse. Kinsey noted some time ago that as sex standards for men and women become more similar, the premarital sex that men used to have with prostitutes is replaced by affairs with their girlfriends. Under these conditions,

* This survey was conducted in association with Larry R. Kimsey, M.D., and John E. Meeks, M.D.

dating couples who will later marry learn about sex together to a very considerable extent. The boys are not initiated by "bad girls," and sex itself seems to get a better name in the process.

SUMMARY

Sex for Homo sapiens is both psychological and physiological, but it is the symbolism ascribed to it that sharply distinguishes man's sex life from that of the other animals. Since it is a creative and mythical force, sex enters almost all of his social and personal affairs in one form or another. And for this reason it can be a distracting, even paralyzing, element in human affairs.

Sexuality develops differently in boys and girls. In particular, the very existence of the male penis leads to repeated genital stimulation and to a greater range of sex interests among males than females. This seems to be characteristic of male-female differences throughout the world.

But almost all of the recent changes in sex behavior are linked to one central trend—toward less segregation and greater equality between the sexes. This is the same underlying trend that came up in our discussion of dating in the previous chapter. In the preadolescent period boys lose some of the hostility toward girls they used to act out. They are inclined to think of girls less as sex targets and more as romantic partners—persons with whom they can share intimate confidences and enjoy warm physical contact.

Purely physiological sex does occur in adolescence, of course, and it may even be more erotic than in the past, especially since petting can be very inventive and remarkably time-consuming—it can undoubtedly last much longer than conventional intercourse. But it is often matched by close relations of an affectionate and confidential nature that tend to make it *person-centered* rather than *body-centered* (Ira Reiss 1960).

It would appear that masturbation is accepted to a much greater extent than in the past; it may absorb some of the sex tensions built up in the course of petting. Homosexuality, too, has come out of hiding, but to say that it has gained popular acceptance would be far from accurate. Prostitution, on the other hand, has lost ground. In fact, it has almost disappeared as an important part of the sex life of the new middle classes (though, as noted, the call-girl business flourishes).

A major change in sex has been caused by the new outlook adopted by many women. Girls may be somewhat more concerned with career opportunities now and less obsessed with the need to please males. As they are liberated in the sex sphere, they are no longer constantly held back by the need to be "feminine"—nice, good, pure, and wholesome. They can have lives of their own, and be more creative in the broadest sense of the term (Straus and Straus 1968).

There is, in fact, a type of *contraceptive-minded, affection-oriented permissiveness* that has been developing among the new middle classes, particularly within professional groups (Reiss 1967). Women influenced by this trend can approach sex relations in a spirit of much greater equality with men than was possible before, a development that seems to be tied to the trend away from women's dependence on their husbands. It may help to explain why divorced women who have had training in graduate schools are less likely to remarry than women who have finished fewer years of college (Udry 1966). They can have lives of their own and need not forego a variety of relationships with men that would have been considered indiscreet in the past.

Although there may have been a sex revolution in the United States in recent times, there is very little evidence that girls are now encouraged to be truly hedonistic about sex. They are not ordinarily advised to try to get as much excitement from sex as possible by seeking promiscuous outlets, although books telling how to perk up sex between married couples are now easy to find (and can be checked out of most good libraries). Teen-age girls are still encouraged to believe that a part of their reputation is established —earned—by being restrained about sex. They have to draw the line rather than boys as a rule. Modern boys are probably not egged on to sex aggressiveness as much as they once were, however, and girls are spared the need to be as sexually inhibited as before.

If any conclusion emerges from this general discussion, it would have to be this: Sex is increasingly kept under control by the quality of relations between the sexes, not by fear and dogma. Ideally, sex is based on mutual respect, starting in childhood and coming of age during dating, courtship, and the early phases of marriage.

SELECTED READINGS

DAVIS, KINGSLEY. "Sexual Behavior," in Robert K. Merton and Robert A. Nisbet (eds.). *Contemporary Social Problems.* New York: Harcourt, Brace & World, 1966, pp. 322–372.

EHRMANN, WINSTON. *Premarital Dating Behavior.* New York: Holt, Rinehart and Winston, 1959.

KINSEY, ALFRED C., WARDELL B. POMEROY, AND CLYDE E. MARTIN. *Sexual Behavior in the Human Male.* Philadelphia: W. B. Saunders, 1948.

MCINTOSH, MARY. "The Homosexual Role," *Social Problems,* Vol. 16 (Summer, 1968), pp. 182–192.

MASTERS, WILLIAM, AND VIRGINIA JOHNSON. *Human Sexual Response.* Boston: Little, Brown, 1966.

REISS, IRA L. *The Social Context of Premarital Sexual Permissiveness*. New York: Holt, Rinehart and Winston, 1967.

SHUTTLEWORTH, FRANK K. "A Biosocial and Developmental Theory of Male and Female Sexuality," *Marriage and Family Living*, Vol. 21 (May 1959), pp. 163–170.

WARD, DAVID A., AND GENE G. KASSEBAUM. *Women's Prison: Sex and Social Structure*. Chicago: Aldine, 1965.

CHAPTER 6

Love: Myth and Reality

Of enormous significance for modern family life is the fact that love is now the main reason for marriage. It has replaced kinship obligations and tradition—even expediency to some extent—as the ideal reason for marriage. The very nature of marriage changes as love takes over, although perhaps not *because* of love. It is more likely that romance is idealized only *after* certain basic changes occur in the family. When people feel very strong ties to their kinsmen, marriage is merely an extension of the existing family, and the new couple take their place in the large kinship circle. When these ties are weakened, marriage becomes the start of a new and independent family, and romance can be unleashed. Falling in love becomes the bridge linking two very turbulent phases of life—dating and courtship.

Although romantic love may have existed throughout history, massive support for it has appeared only in modern industrial society. As other reasons are dropped, love becomes the only completely acceptable motive for starting a family. But it is by no means perfect; true love is hard to identify in the first place and even harder to keep up. In this chapter we are concerned with the conditions that have made love both necessary and troublesome. From the individual's point of view we ask: What should I know about love and what can I expect from it?

Viewed in broad perspective, all societies have to make sure that young people get married under appropriate circumstances—appropriate in the sense that they lead to family stability. So far as we can tell, there has never been a time when most girls were not eager to have families and rear children. The biggest problem has been getting boys to cooperate. But even this has not been very difficult, as long as men could be given status in the community and authority at home. When they cannot find a sense of esteem in their work, they usually cannot find it at home either. Their willingness to support a family then becomes a bad gamble. But at least love can now be counted on to make most of them want to try.

The situation in modern society is not basically different from earlier times. Men of means and rank still find family life more attractive than men who are poor. And it remains true that their social status is very important in determining whom they will marry. Men in the upper classes usually marry women of similar social background. The modern stress on love makes only one key difference: The man is *supposed* to marry a woman because he loves her, not because her social position is right.

Thus, the philosophy of love and romance is injected into more practical matters. It is given such strong and repeated emphasis that at least some people may reject practical considerations altogether. The modern problem is to get young people to fall in love and marry, hopefully in pairs that can work together and keep mutual respect, but also under circumstances in which they will meet their family obligations even if love—which is rarely perfect—dies.

Family obligations are rather minimal when there are no children, of course (and married couples with very different social backgrounds usually have fewer children than others). Even with children, however, family obligations do not rule out divorce as long as arrangements are made to protect the legitimate interests of all concerned. In a nation that relies heavily on love as the main reason for marriage, it seems necessary to provide not only for easy divorce, but also for ways to safeguard members of the broken family, especially children.

THEORIES OF LOVE

For any number of reasons, love is an almost disastrous subject for scientific study. Sex gets much more attention—witness the Kinsey studies, or those of Masters and Johnson (who have described the physiology of sex arousal and release in truly scientific detail—see Chapter 5). Considerably more is known about intercourse than about romantic attraction, and most theories of love are therefore underdeveloped and certainly undernourished by hard facts. For many people, love is too sacred to study; for others it is too sublime. Furthermore, it is a kind of activity that would seem to change in basic ways when put under close observation (which is true to a lesser extent of almost all human behavior). Hence, the folklore of love remains very powerful; it is almost all we have.

Nevertheless, a body of theory about love is beginning to take shape. The purpose of this section is to present and assess the leading theories, especially as they relate to the central problem of this book: How are family commitments maintained in contemporary society, and what do these commitments mean for the individual?

Romantic Love and Marriage

With more success than anyone else, William Goode (1959) has tried to outline the theoretical importance of love, noting its changing nature as society at large changes. Goode defines romantic love as "a strong emotional attachment, a cathexis, between adolescents or adults of opposite sexes, with at least the components of sex desire and tenderness." Couples in love tend to see only the best traits in one another; they experience strong emotional and physical attraction, evaluate each other more or less uncritically, and identify with one another to the extent that they *care*. Thus, romantic love includes *idealization, physical attraction,* and *sympathetic understanding*. It is, Goode argues, the most *projective* of the emotions, just as sex is the most projective of the human drives. It is therefore difficult for anyone to believe that the person he loves does not love back.

This definition is not altogether satisfactory (it rather arbitrarily rules out homosexual romance, for example), but a certain vagueness and arbitrariness is characteristic of all efforts to pin love down. We could overcome these difficulties by using a more detailed *operational definition*, such as saying that love exists whenever two people answer a series of questions about their relationship in a certain way, but then we would have to accept precision in method at the expense of intelligence in content.

The biggest controversy centers on the question of love's motivation—whether it must be selfless (Fromm 1956) or whether it is essentially motivated by self-gratification (Winch 1958). Selfless love is a noble ideal, but I think we must cling to the basic premise that people seek to fulfill personal needs through their romantic behavior (though they may not know or admit exactly what they are doing). Goode does distinguish between *romantic* and *conjugal* love; the latter refers to the rather sedate pattern of affection and understanding that may develop between a married couple, as distinguished from the more emotional (and demonstrative) romantic pattern.

Although Goode grants that romantic love is a universal possibility, he argues that it rarely occurs unless it gets strong social support, and this has rarely happened in history. Love as the basis for marriage has been very infrequent because it can lead to severe conflicts between married couples and their relatives. In most societies mutual obligations among kinsmen are vital for social stability. Love, therefore, which is no respecter of such obligations, is given little chance to develop. This is probably why anthropologists have paid hardly any attention to the subject in their field studies. They deal with societies where kin obligations are very strong, and where romanticism (as a basis for marriage) is considered foolish, if not subversive.

The point Goode makes was first developed by Max Gluckman (1955), whom Goode duly credits. Even where romantic love is strong as in modern America, Goode argues that it is rare for people to defy social pressures just for the sake of love. The psychological cost is far too high. A few courageous couples may brave community stigma, physical dangers, or the gods themselves, but nowhere is this kind of heroism common. Violent, self-sufficient love is always an exception to the general rule.

Since romantic love is at the very least a universal *possibility*, and it may even be based on a universal *tendency*, how have people managed to keep it under control for so many centuries? Goode says that love is by no means a modern discovery; it has always threatened to break out in extravagant proportions, disrupting kinship loyalties. It has failed to do so only because precautions are taken to keep that from happening. He calls attention to several ways this can be done. The best control of all is to keep love from occurring in the first place. Once a young couple think they are in love, outside efforts to kill the affair are awkward to say the least, and may simply be impossible.

One way of stopping love affairs even before they start is through child marriage, and this has in fact been used effectively in many places. It has several drawbacks, however (where death rates are high, for example), so that it is never truly foolproof. Another method is to carefully restrict the range of eligible partners, especially by setting up detailed kinship rules. If romance should then occur between a qualified pair, it will not disrupt anything—but under this system romance probably will not have a chance, as Linton C. Freeman (1968) has shown. Another technique is isolation, so that a person of marriageable age simply has no chance to meet anyone who is also of the right age *unless* that person meets certain kinship and status requirements. Isolation, however, is often expensive, since it requires exclusive living and recreational arrangements; only upper-class families can afford it. Still another technique is to provide close supervision over youth by chaperones or relatives, which makes romance between mismatched couples almost impossible. (It also stifles the kind of courting needed for intimate love even between eligibles.)

Goode argues that the full development, or institutionalization, of romantic love is almost always associated with the rise of a strong adolescent youth culture, such as the one we now have in the United States. Although other social controls also have to be developed, the peer group disciplines the way love-making should proceed and judges whether couples are properly paired off. Thus couples fall in love with the "right" members of the opposite sex because they face ridicule and ostracism if they do not.

John Finley Scott (1965), for example, has shown how the college sorority system polices its members (although this is apparently an exaggerated form of control, which is not simply peer-group control, since older women have unusual power over their younger sorority sisters). But the point to bear in mind is that, if romantic love as a reason for marriage is widely accepted, efforts will be made to see that young people do not make foolish choices ("foolish" according to conventional standards). Young people are advised to find someone of approximately their own status and social position; only when someone *suitable* comes along do they feel completely free to let love go to work.

Although the peer group has a big role in policing this process, parents also try to guide their offspring in the "right" direction (Sussman 1953). They can influence or control their children's choice of friends beginning in the earliest years, and (without even realizing it) mold their basic conception of who is likable—ultimately, of who is lovable. Parents move to neighborhoods considered appropriate for their status and automatically start their children playing with others like themselves. In the most general sense, parents act out a style of life that their children copy. The children are then almost inevitably attracted to people from similar families who have become accustomed to this same style.

Love poses a special problem for families of high social status, however, because here kin loyalties have a strong economic basis—there is money at stake. A new marriage at this level is an extension of an already-existing family. Wealth becomes the key to solidarity among several related families, and special efforts are made to supervise mate selection. Romantic love is fine—as long as it does not endanger the family fortune. It is in the upper classes that parents have the greatest leverage in controlling their children. They can keep them segregated from whoever is considered ineligible, and they control the money. But the children are taught an upper-class style of life in any case, and they usually prefer to date people who are relaxed and comfortable in this style.

By way of summary, Goode's theory holds that romantic love can be the basis for marriage only in urban, industrial societies, where the core family is rather independent of the larger kinship circle. Relatives can disregard the question of who marries whom only where property, power, lineage honor, and basic family relationships do not flow through kinship lines. Thus, the degree to which love is a usual and expected prelude to marriage is linked with the degree of freedom allowed in the choice of mates and the degree to which husband-wife closeness is the key to stability in the family. It is also linked to the growth of a youth culture which helps to control "the way love happens" among teen-agers. The very independence of young people from their relatives tends to create a social vacuum, but it is quickly filled by youth themselves. And romantic love is ideally suited to this arrangement because, as Goode implies, it is not just a *psychosocial* possibility—it stems from a very basic human tendency. Love is also particularly useful in a society where close relations exist between parents and children. It helps to pull the child away from his parents—from his dependency on them—toward marriage. Romantic love draws the couple together, propels them toward marriage, and holds them together long enough to build the basis for a reasonably stable marriage.

Can Love Last?

Ernest van den Haag (1962) offers a somewhat different theory, one that is a good deal less optimistic (although optimism is not the key to Goode's approach, either). He builds on the Freudian outlook (where love in adult life is believed to reflect our earlier relations with parents), and accepts Goode's idea that romantic love as a reason for marriage turned up only recently. Love, he claims, is based on the child's first feelings for his parents, the original source of *unconditional love*—love that is given freely, without any strings attached. The child usually has an idealized image of his mother or father, young and uniquely beautiful, not the real parent others see. This *love for an ideal* lingers on as an intense longing throughout life, yet parents in most cases will disappoint their children by the time they reach the mid-teens. Then comes courtship and marriage, during which the teen-ager searches for a replacement for the fallen parent ideal, but can find only an imperfect mate. After marriage the longing for an ideal love must either be abandoned or transformed into something more manageable.

The key to this approach is that the search for a love ideal can be a particularly powerful lure to marriage, but by its very nature it is not likely to give complete satisfaction after the ceremony. That is not to say that married couples cannot love one another, but the bond that they forge together will not ordinarily meet the requirements of romantic love. Unity in marriage will have to be based on conjugal love (mutual concern and understanding rather than an idealization of one another) if it is to be based on love at all. Romanticism is whipped up among people in the marriageable ages, assuring that they will think they are in love and should for that reason marry. Marriage, however, creates a whole new set of conditions and humdrum problems in which the requirements of romantic love are not likely to be met.

But ideally love is supposed to last in marriage, and many couples are undoubtedly disappointed that it does not. Almost all couples will try to keep the symbolism of romantic love alive to some extent, doing some of the same things they did in courtship—calling one another by endearing terms, caressing, and so on. The trappings of romantic love remain, but the subjective experiences are changed beyond recognition.

With perhaps more application to "puppy love" than to the full-blown romantic variety, James Folsom (1943) describes a pattern he calls "cardiac-respiratory love." This is a condition in which the body (mainly in the chest area) has a profound and exhilarating feeling, especially among persons having their first real crush. They feel a strange, rapturous sensation, almost like being intoxicated. But this cannot last long because the body eventually needs rest and some kind of long-term equilibrium. Rapturous love, Folsom argues, is simply not habit-resistant. The economy of the body cannot take it. He feels that where so much stress is placed on love, young couples may marry when all they have going for them is this cardiac-respiratory reaction. After marriage the exhilarating sensation disappears, and they are left with no binding resources. Clearly, more than a wildly exciting experience is needed for a lasting relationship. In marriage the couple will have to depend on this "something more."

Too Much Love?

Philip Slater (1963) has carried this approach even further. His main premise (like van den Haag's) is that romantic love must inevitably wither after marriage. It not only has to but *ought to* be replaced by other kinds of affection based on cooperation and mutual respect. Slater claims that it is imperative for the welfare of the larger community that love *not* be too intense between married couples. (His theory actually makes little or no use of the word "love." Instead, he refers to *libidinal energies*, as this term is used in the Freudian tradition—basic energies that can drive the individual toward particular goals. But it does no violence to his theory to say that when two individuals direct libidinal energies toward one another in a concentrated way, they are expressing love.)

Slater's point is that societies require people to scatter their energies in order to fulfill a variety of purposes. The more objects that people can direct their energies toward, the larger will be the number who can cooperate in joint endeavors. Slater argues that if husbands and wives could point all their thoughts and actions toward one another they might very well have less tension in marriage, but they would be of little use to other people. On the other hand, when a person spreads his interests around, he cannot expect to have perfect harmony with his love partner, but he *can* be counted on for collective work.

We must bear in mind of course that Slater's theory is unproved. It would be almost impossible to test it, although an ingenious solution may yet show up. But the idea is plausible enough, and it fits in with Goode's theory. Romantic love (a concentration of libidinal energies binding two individuals together) has the effect of isolating couples from other social efforts. It serves a useful purpose in getting them to leave home and enter marriage, but it would be overdoing its own usefulness if it kept them starry-eyed after they started working and rearing a family.

Van den Haag suggests that the conditions of marriage itself are enough to assure that romantic love will not remain very strong after the honeymoon. Still, we might also ask whether social pressures are somehow used to keep it in check. Possibly so, although it would certainly seem that they are insignificant compared to the stress on romance and to the repeated suggestions that couples *should* love each other as much as is humanly possible. I cannot help but think that romantic love subsides in marriage not because society tries to keep it down, but rather because the basic sources of love and the conditions of marriage make it almost impossible to sustain. This was van den Haag's argument.

Love as a Social Control

One last theory of love is found in many current discussions of the subject, and it is compatible with almost everything that has been said. It holds that love can be a powerful *social control*, particularly in the rather brief period just before marriage.

As the child grows up he is reminded in various ways that someday he will fall in love. He is intentionally led to believe that once he has found love he will live happily ever after. Almost all of us become disillusioned about this happy ending, of course, but we do learn that we are supposed to find a lifelong love mate.

Meanwhile, in a love-oriented society each of us is showered with tokens of love from our parents. We get so many that we are actually conditioned to *need* them, not only during childhood but throughout life. The word "love" is an extremely emotion-laden, almost sacred, word, with a wide range of semantic uses. It becomes verbal food; people grow up on it, are nourished by it, and will return to it over and over again in later intimate situations. Apparently it looms much larger for women than men. They use the word more often; men seem to be more skeptical of it, more awkward in using it, and perhaps a little afraid of it.

In fact, love is a major organizing theme in American life, as Geoffrey Gorer (1948) argues. If you find love, you will have discovered approximately half of what it takes to make a good life. Worldly success supplies the other half, says Gorer. The twin themes of love and success establish the core personal goals of most Americans. Other themes may be more important than Gorer realizes, but few observers would argue that love and success are only minor matters. They do indeed push Americans to extreme efforts.

The fact that the child looks forward eagerly to a romantic experience assures that some such experience will occur. A leading personal question in late adolescence or early maturity becomes: "Is this it? Is this the love I have been looking for?" Thus, love affairs occur because children have been reared to believe they must. When a person comes along who meets certain minimum expectations, there is an excellent chance that love will blossom.

Because people are conditioned to need love, most of them will make an effort to get it. Mother gives love freely, of course, independent of the child's behavior, especially in the very first years of life. But gradually even mother begins to pull back a little; she makes it clear that children are expected to meet certain minimum standards if they want people to like them, certainly if they expect love. But mothers are limited in their ability to deny their own flesh and blood, so children receive *mother love* almost unconditionally. Father will probably be harder to please, but he is usually a more distant figure, and the child may not try quite so hard to win his love—his respect perhaps, but not his love.

In adolescence, distance between children and their parents becomes greater, especially in modern society, and it is at this time that love as a social control has its greatest power. A boy, for example, who has not responded to his mother's efforts to teach table manners may show an amazing aptitude when he starts trying to impress his girlfriend. Why do teen-age athletes try so hard? Partly because they have learned the rules of the game, where winning is practically an end in itself. But the drive to win is also strengthened by the smiles and congratulations an athlete receives after a winning effort. In high school, the boy finds a whole new realm of admiration from potential girlfriends.

Whereas girls start molding their behavior to the "love market" in the elementary-school years, boys usually begin their efforts only in adolescence. Then, the knowledge that they are supposed to have a love affair becomes a powerful reason to do things that please girls. So romantic love not only draws boys toward marriage, it puts pressure on them to live up to the social codes of the community. Boys on dates can do some pretty unpleasant things, but they usually act better than boys of the same age in all-male groups.

The impact for girls follows a similar pattern, though less intense. The need for love makes them try to please boys—an inducement needed more now than in the past. After all, they are less obligated by family duties now, and they are liberated to some extent as new career opportunities open up. But romantic love stresses an aspect of family life that has not been given nearly as much attention before—close, even sexy, relations between spouses, along with distance from kinsmen.

The romantic bond also seems to stand as a challenge to the traditional obligations of motherhood. When wife becomes mother, she is forced to divert some of her love—certainly her attention—to the child. It is quite possible that the husband's opinion of her as a sex partner will change when she starts acting out the maternal role. Some men begin calling their wives "mother" after a while, and it seems very likely, because of the incest taboos, that they are taught to rule out any thought of "mother" as a sex partner. Modern women will probably play down the motherhood side of marriage as they stress its romantic possibilities more.

One further observation about this must be made. As romantic love declines in the course of marriage, it should be replaced by a new and deeper respect between the spouses. But if this fails to show up, the wife may find some consolation by turning her love to the children, perhaps in an exaggerated way. In fact, the more the husband has been taught to need love, the more likely he too will turn to the children if his marriage has no spark. (He could also turn toward his career, especially if he has a job that can draw his total energies; that is precisely what happens in some professional careers and even in some blue-collar occupations.)

Parents who need love from their children to make up for its absence in marriage may do foolish things; "overmothering" as well as permissive indulgence can create real problems. It is possible that the more parents turn to their children for love in a love-obsessed society, the more the children are taught to need love in turn, and the whole system feeds on itself. In short, love-starved parents can breed love-starved children. To blame parents would be missing the point, however. The intensity of the love theme has been building up over many generations. It does seem characteristic of modern industrial society to exaggerate romance—to set it up as absolutely essential for personal happiness. No doubt it can be a wonderful thing, but it becomes terribly easy to expect too much.

LOVE IN HISTORY

To fully understand this pattern we have to have some knowledge of the historical development of love in Western history. Scholars have dealt with this subject in different ways, but one of the most influential approaches is an outline developed by Hugo Beigel (1951). He contends that the first significant development of modern love occurred in the twelfth century, in a form commonly called *courtly love* (and sometimes *distant love*). Its growth was associated with the coming to complete power of a new ruling class, along with the full acceptance of knighthood. It was supposed to occur outside of marriage, but it did *not* involve sex relations, largely because of the strong Christian taboos. Unselfish service to a noble lady—a married woman of the ruling class—became a duty of the young knight. He was explicitly sworn to this duty in an oath taken at his dubbing ceremony. The rights of the woman's husband were safeguarded, however, because there was to be no sex in the affair—theoretically at least.

Beigel contends that courtly love was no whimsical thing; it sprang from vital needs of the time. It was part of a social-psychological process that tried to reconcile basic human needs with frustrating social conditions. In particular, medieval customs prevented the free choice of mates in marriage, and yet pressures for just such a liberation were appearing. (Freedom in mate selection would have to wait about 500 years, and its full development, another 200 years after that!)

Although sex fulfillment was taboo between mistress and lover in the courtly pattern, partial satisfaction of sex desires was allowed. The knight had the right to go with his lady to her bedchamber, to help her disrobe, even to put her to bed. Occasionally he could sleep with her, but tenderness alone was allowed, not "carnal knowledge." The knight could have symbolic unity with his beloved by tying her veil to his armor, or perhaps she would wear his blood-stained tunic.

Beigel argues that courtly love represented the refinement, or *aesthetization*, of uniquely adolescent feelings, and he says that this aspect of love has lasted all the way up to the twentieth century, although the specific content of teen-age customs has changed drastically. Knights themselves were usually in the middle or late adolescent stage of life; the married women they pledged themselves to were probably not much older in most cases, although their husbands most certainly were.

Courtly love introduced an idealization of the upper-class female (which was later extended to women of middle-class status, and still later to women in general). It also stressed voluntary fidelity, restraint, and the "magnanimous gentleness of the male" (Beigel's expression) to relations between the sexes. These were not believed to be essential or even possible in marriages based on the patriarchal ideals of the Middle Ages.

Beginning especially in the fourteenth century, the family was subject to a slow but continual stripping away of its earlier economic, religious, and political functions. The father's authority declined and the children were treated more tenderly by their mothers. This, together with the gradual loss of economic functions for children, led to an important change in personal styles, especially in the case of sons. In later centuries a host of romanticists rebelled against the new industrial order, particularly because it glorified machines, materialism, and rationalism. They sought escape from these unbending forces through freedom of the emotions. Thus, a romantic philosophy friendly to the concept of love was slowly coming into view.

Courtly love itself changed at the same time. Upper-class women were still loyal to their husbands, even when they professed love for their gallants, but the taboo on sex fulfillment was apparently relaxed. Love could be used to justify sex, but love between husband and wife was considered a rarity. Even in the seventeenth and eighteenth centuries the noblemen of Europe held to the belief that love and marriage were virtually incompatible. Thus, the lover's deeds were rewarded with sex favors, thereby uniting sex and romantic attraction—but not in marriage.

A great change was occurring among the new middle classes, however. For them, sex and love had to be combined within marriage itself. Religious and moral beliefs of the new middle classes were based on monogamy, with stress on mutual faithfulness between the husband and wife. Sex outside of marriage could only be considered sinful. Marriage was still largely arranged by parents and relatives, but the language of love—borrowed from the courtly period—had entered relations between the sexes. Here, too, fidelity was expected.

Actually, romance was not so much brought into marriage as into courtship before marriage. It was no longer an affair between a young nobleman and a married woman, but between a bourgeois suitor and a marriageable girl, usually younger than himself. The man was expected to "court" his girl and prove the genuineness of his love through conversation, gifts, and poetry (although poetry as a personal product quickly disappeared in favor of popular jingles and clichés). The new pattern raised middle-class women to a status previously occupied only by aristocratic ladies, and by the end of the nineteenth century this new approach to marriage had won its battle throughout the growing middle classes.

To Beigel, romanticism was an almost inevitable reaction to the unsentimental, bulldozing effect of industrialism. He credits the eighteenth-century English novelist Samuel Richardson as the first writer to champion love as a prerequisite for marriage. To Richardson (and other romanticists) love became an antidote to the insecurity created by all the disturbing social changes. This reaction was picked up by such literary figures as Schiller, Byron, Keats, Shelley, Coleridge, Wordsworth, and Scott, and it represented a new twist in social criticism.

A somewhat different approach to the history of love is that love became the ideal basis for marriage because of *declining family functions*, especially because the large family could no longer control the mate selection of youth, nor could it hold their loyalty after the new marriage was formed. Young couples wanted to have independent homes, budgets, and lives. The rise of the love cult was certainly associated with the rise of the romanticists, but it did not just *happen* to accompany changes in the place of the family in society; it *had* to accompany these changes.

Quite obviously romance in the twentieth century has been further democratized; it now has a powerful appeal in the working classes. But women are no longer idealized the way they once were. Today the girl must be alert to the possibilities of exploitation in courtship. She no longer has the respectability that the very existence of hard-core prostitution once guaranteed. Since she is more equal with her male lover in social status, she has no choice but to take some new risks.

Perhaps the most significant social development associated with romance in the twentieth century is its almost total commercialization. Because it is so undeniably popular, and everybody wants some, it is not surprising that alert businessmen have created a variety of industries to meet the demand. Movies, novels, stories, songs, love goddesses, glamour boys, perfume, flowers, cosmetics, diamond rings—almost anything that can possibly be linked to the love game is given a romantic twist, either to let people have a glimpse of love as performed by super-lovers or to improve their own attractiveness in the marketplace of romance.

LOVE AFFAIRS

Since love is a theme of such unusual importance in the United States—it is gaining popularity all over the world due to industrial growth and the American influence—it is not surprising that many people actively seek romantic affairs. Not just teen-agers are involved; the search occurs in the mature, already married population, too. This is seen in popular novels and movies, where it is apparent that pressures to find love can lead to some bizarre kinds of behavior.

The love affair can be considered a special kind of human behavior, worthy of study in its own right. It is not just a state of mind, but a series of events—an identifiable episode in the life of the individual. The subject raises many questions: What effect does the widespread search for it have on family life? What are your chances to have such an affair (or several), how will you handle them, and how will you react when an affair comes to an end?

To provide some order for this discussion, it will be approached from four different directions: (1) a review of the frequency of love affairs; (2) a discussion of the content of love stories; (3) a section on the lyrics of love songs; and (4) a look at the problem of neurotic love.

The Love Count

As an opening plunge, how many love affairs is the average person likely to have? (Kinsey counted "sex outlets" but ignored love.) G. V. Hamilton

(1929) reports a study whose subjects had an average of 6.8 affairs, including those both before and after marriage. There was no important difference between men and women, but only 15 percent of the 1,358 affairs reported by Hamilton led to marriage. In a casual study (based on detailed essays of seventy-five students over the age of thirty who had enrolled in my course on the family over a ten-year period) the average number of love affairs was 8.7—10.1 for males and 7.2 for females (653 affairs were mentioned in all). After surveying a sample of younger college students, William Kephart (1966) estimated that the average student will have about ten romantic episodes before marriage, and that a few of them will have affairs with two persons at the same time. A study of sex patterns in Sweden revealed that the average number of partners (not necessarily love partners) with whom men over thirty had had sexual intercourse was seven, but for those between twenty and thirty the average number was already eight (Zetterberg 1969).

In my study, two problems (in addition to the small sample) appeared: One was the fact that the students were often undecided whether to include an affair; they could not be certain in their own minds which ones qualified as bona-fide love episodes. They were encouraged to include all cases where "genuine affection existed between themselves and their partners," that is, those involving strong mutual attraction. Whether this is the sort of social fact that people exaggerate or underestimate remains unknown. The other problem was that some of the students in their early thirties, and perhaps even those in their forties and fifties, may have several more love affairs before they retire from the love game, so the figure cited is not necessarily a lifetime total.

In any case, a general pattern seemed to emerge. These people tended to have between seven and eight affairs on the average before marriage, and about one afterward (although the majority of those who were married— thirty-eight out of fifty-five—had no extramarital affairs at all; others had as many as five). The question was raised whether the most intense love affair was the one that led to marriage and, as expected, it was. And yet in about one-third of the sample—twenty-six out of seventy-five—that was not the case. The more intense affairs for a sizable minority ultimately broke up, but they were certainly not forgotten. Generally speaking, later affairs were more serious than earlier ones, which Kephart (1966) also noted. David Knox, Jr., and Michael Sporakowski (1968) collected data suggesting that American youth become more realistic in their attitudes toward love as they grow older, particularly during each successive year in college, which may help to explain the greater seriousness of the later affairs.

Winston Ehrmann (1959) once showed that dating teen-agers usually progress quickly to whatever level of sex relations they had reached in previous affairs. This is most characteristic of girls, since they usually set the limits. Boys may have gone considerably further with girls they are no longer dating than they are allowed to go with their current partners, but girls will usually go as far as they have ever gone. This *intimacy-readiness* probably also occurs in love affairs; people have a tendency to return to the level of romantic intensity reached at some time in the past.

This may not be quite so likely for love as for sex, however, because love is so totally psychological. For example, it may be impossible to ever again reach the intensity of your very first love affair. Willard Waller and Reuben Hill (1951) suggest that there may be a certain loss of capacity for love after unhappy experiences. The person develops various protective devices and collects "scar tissue" from romantic wounds, dulling his sensitivity. However, there is no strong evidence that this always or even usually happens.

Clifford Kirkpatrick (1945b; 1963) has reported a study in which persons were asked about their feelings at the outset of the affair—from dislike for one another through a neutral or indifferent attitude on up to love at first sight. Usually the affairs began in indifference, climbed toward a feeling of love, and then tailed off toward the initial indifference. Rarely did they end in hatred or hostility, and so Kirkpatrick concluded that the majority of love affairs just fade away.

Generally, people recall pleasant things about their past affairs rather than the painful parts, and it takes hardly any time at all for most of them to readjust after the breakup. Each one usually feels that he was more honest and straightforward than his partner. In a sample studied by Clifford Kirkpatrick and Theodore Caplow (1945), the men more often reported a feeling of love in dating episodes than women; they were also more likely to feel jilted after the affair had run its course.

Married students in my study were asked to give some indication of how helpful the love affairs were that preceded the one that led to marriage. Had they become wiser in some way, making them better able to judge the "validity" of later affairs? Most respondents agreed that the first affairs had served a useful purpose, as might have been expected. The results were overwhelmingly in favor of this proposition, but it should be added that people in the sample had considerable difficulty explaining just how their experience had helped. In most cases students could give only rather vague explanations, although in a few cases they were quite specific and negative —especially saying that they would certainly know enough never to "fall for a guy like that again." Apparently most people have several love affairs before they marry, and they are quite certain that their early experience gives them better judgment in mate selection. A disappointing or downright frustrating experience does not ordinarily leave the person vulnerable to a foolish rebound affair, although fifteen people did admit to that kind of reaction.

An interesting question comes up: Do people whose marriage lacks the companionship they had hoped for seek affairs outside marriage? (Let us assume for the moment that they remain married; the divorce and remarriage alternatives will be discussed in a later chapter.) The sample for the author's study is simply too small to provide a satisfactory answer to this question, although 32 percent of the males and 30 percent of the females admitted to having extramarital love affairs. Clearly these represent only one kind of reaction to a lack of love fulfillment in marriage. Disappointment occurred in a number of cases, but most people denied any thought of solving the problem by having an extramarital affair.

Kinsey and his associates (1953) found that 50 percent of the husbands and 26 percent of the wives in their sample admitted having extramarital intercourse, which is a higher percentage for men than the present sample reveals, but about the same for women. Of course *extramarital sex* is not necessarily the same as a *love affair* (although they probably go together in most people's minds). It may be difficult to see how a married person can have a love affair without sexual intercourse, but that does in fact happen. It is quite possible that extramarital sex involves love more often for women than for men. The stronger association between romance and premarital sex for women (noted in Chapter 5) points in this direction.

Love Stories

An entirely different way of studying love affairs is through analysis of popular love stories. Short stories, novels, movies, and television shows reflect people's opinions or their ideal images of love. They not only suggest rules to follow in having affairs, they are also sensitive to changing patterns of romance. A popular theme in the folklore of romance is that affairs start with love at first sight, while a perennial Hollywood theme has been hate at first sight. In movies using this approach, the couple meet in the story's first scene and immediately dislike each other; the rest of the movie, as all who have seen the plot know, is devoted to showing how the pair fall in love, marry, and are presumed to live happily ever after. Reality is tame and very unromantic by comparison.

R. W. England, Jr. (1960), compared a sample of love stories printed in the *Saturday Evening Post* and *Colliers* magazines from 1911 to 1915 with a sample of such stories in these same two magazines between 1951 and 1955, with very interesting results. His *content analysis* of the two samples led him to conclude that stories from the later period were not quite as realistic as the earlier ones. In particular, the protagonists were more often stereotyped in terms of physical appearance in the more recent era, and there were fewer references to any economic or financial complications. During the forty-year span the trend was toward more stories about love in the middle or upper-middle classes and relatively fewer in the working classes; the change in this regard was unmistakable.

In addition, the later stories more often involved people who were divorced or widowed, replacing the young, naïve, first-time lovers of the period from 1911 to 1915. As a result, affairs in the recent stories were more likely to lead to remarriage than to first marriage. The later stories often told of couples who had met without the traditional introductions or other conventional trappings. A decided trend was noted here, suggesting that readers in more recent times enjoy tales of love starting with exotic encounters—a more free-swinging, unsupervised type of love. Although the peer group may control the course of "true" love in various ways, as suggested by William Goode (1959), these fictional stories do not seem to recognize this fact. Many of us would probably rather have love proceed without any supervision by the crowd. In stories, at least, outside influence is almost always a threat to romance.

The later stories also showed a trend toward shorter courtships—the whirlwind type—and an increasing number did not lead to marriage at all. These were tales of unlucky lovers passing in the night, very brief affairs as a rule, ill-fated in the sense that neither person could afford to let the relationship develop and mature. They leave the melancholy impression that true love might occur much more often if not for one little fact: The principals have already committed themselves to a family that would be very difficult or painful to break up. Many people are not permanently available, and their family obligations disqualify them for affairs that might prove to be very dramatic.

England concludes that twentieth-century love affairs are not too closely tied to the conventions of marriage and family life. It seems that romantic love is more often considered something that can interfere with the family or that family obligations may interfere with love. This sounds like certain aspects of courtly love discussed earlier.

Song Lyrics

Like the love story, lyrics of love songs can be studied as a way of learning about love or about the way people view it. For example, Donald Horton (1957) did a very clever study of the popular American songs of 1955. He arranged them into a series of four dramatic acts, tracing lovers through almost all aspects of a love affair.

Horton shows that popular songs provide a simple language of love that can be used in dating and courtship. They express a narrow but intensely emotional range of human feelings. Of course lovers do not actually talk to each other in verse, and they rarely sing about their love. But they do murmur the lyrics of songs as they dance and will occasionally repeat lines or phrases from the big hits. Since the knack of talking about our highly personal feelings is not as widespread as the need for love, a popular love poetry comes in handy, and it may even be necessary. The language does not have to be used directly. All the lovers have to do is listen to a song together; the lyrics then serve as a vicarious conversation. In a way, the popular singer is a messenger of love to his audience, dramatizing the songs and the appropriate emotional expressions. He gives "stage directions" to young lovers, and that can be a very useful service.

As each person goes through adolescence he moves through successive stages of the drama, using the dialogue (or variations of it) heard in songs, while the lyrics for earlier stages already finished take on deeper and more personal meanings. Horton concludes that television, movies, and popular literature identify and dramatize roles for all phases of our romantic affairs, while popular songs provide the basic language of love.

Eleven years after Horton's study, James Carey (1969) found popular songs different in two key respects. For one thing, in the more recent lyrics personal freedom is stressed more often; the expression "falling in love," for example, is used much less. It implies a fatalistic approach, lacking in individual control, and the recent mood seems to rebel against that. There is also a more positive, welcoming acceptance of the aloneness that follows an affair. Isolation offers the possibility of exploring certain facts about life and self which is only possible when one is alone. In the earlier period isolation was more often regarded as a painful, almost excruciating condition.

The lyrics of popular songs may also be changing in ways that correspond to changes in love stories. It seems likely that songs of recent years are not tied in with marriage as much as before. Certainly there are now many examples of lyrics in which love interferes with schoolwork or with marriage itself. ("What would they do; what would they say? They think that we're in school all day, but we're making love.") It is doubtful that such songs existed (on popular records or in lyric reprints, at least) to any appreciable extent before the 1950s.

The Love Compulsion

There is still one other approach to the place of love in modern society. It begins with the idea that, whereas almost everyone reared in a country like the United States seeks love and hopes that it will lead to happiness, some people hunt for it much more compulsively than others. For a fairly large number, the search becomes an obsession. The love compulsion can begin in a variety of ways (presumably in childhood), but the more intense the case, the less likely it is that the individual will have personal qualities that are truly lovable. An *obsessive* need for love almost always remains unrequited.

Knowledge about the exaggerated need for love is inadequate—at least it is unsystematic. Some people undoubtedly marry and find nothing but frustration, followed by divorce, remarriage, and further frustration. Others may dwell on the unbearable fact that they have never found any real hint of love. Some of these people turn to "lonely hearts clubs," correspondence clubs, or any of the large variety of ads in magazines designed to tap this market. Lonely hearts clubs have been studied very little, but certain general facts are known about their clientele (Wallace 1959). Many more men than women sign up, especially in the young adult age bracket, which does not necessarily mean they are more obsessed by love than women. Our folklore suggests just the opposite. The fact that lovelorn men can be more aggressive in trying to fill the vacuum in their lives means only that the double sex standard lives on. Women may have one advantage, however; the very fact that they are given little opportunity to hunt men aggressively means that they are more likely to seek other ways to satisfy their romantic needs. The fact that men can be more adventuresome certainly does not assure greater success. It simply encourages them to keep at the difficult—in some cases impossible—task.

SUMMARY

Love has emerged in modern industrial society as the proper reason for marriage. It can be traced to courtly, extramarital love in the twelfth century, which was gradually transformed into the romantic love so familiar in recent Western history. The rise of love in courtship is associated with the decline of the large family system and seems to be a workable arrangement only in societies where new marriages constitute new families and are not considered appendages to already existing families.

But even in modern society love has to be kept under control. New social agencies have come into existence for this purpose, replacing the controls once exercised by parents and relatives. One such agency is the youth culture. It acts independently of parents to a considerable extent but disciplines its members according to values much like those of adults. Adolescent groups give extraordinary attention to proper mating procedures, although their values in the areas of sex are more permissive than those of their parents. Romantic love is almost universally experienced by individuals as a unique and unpremeditated event, yet it can usually be explained in terms of fairly predictable social patterns.

Love has become the proper basis for marriage, but that does not make it easy to sustain after the honeymoon. Some writers argue that love involves a search for an idealized parent figure, which can only lead to disillusionment. Others say that society itself devises ways to keep couples from being too romantic after marriage, since libidinal energies must not be too concentrated if people are going to be active in community affairs. It has also been argued that the practicalities of family life undermine love in marriage. The household may be a wonderful place for personal security, but it is not likely to give movie-style romance and excitement. Thus, love serves its most useful purpose simply by drawing couples together and pushing them toward marriage. The process is usually—not always—surrounded by forces that lead to conjugal love after the wedding.

Where love is stressed, children are reared to need it, and they are also taught that it is a reward for certain kinds of behavior. As a result, it can be a powerful social control. After learning that they must have it, they discipline themselves in order to get their share. For example, the dating period, with its emphasis on love, puts strong pressures on boys to please girls. They respond by striving to do things their parents could never get them interested in before.

Love affairs are dramatic episodes in love-oriented societies; they occur with remarkable frequency among youth before marriage, and are not altogether unknown afterward. Part of the fascination with the subject may be satisfied simply by reading about it, and so love stories are extremely popular. These seem to be less conventional and less familistic in recent years than they were earlier in the century. It is possible that the popular idea of love is gradually moving away from the traditional concern for family commitments, although perhaps only slightly.

Since love is so attractive, and yet the language of love is by no means easy to master, people are given various kinds of assistance. Love songs can be very helpful in this regard. The lyrics not only give couples a mental picture of events that are likely to occur in their love affairs, they also supply verbal expressions that can be used to carry them out. In this and many other ways the love-oriented society surrounds people, especially those in the dating and courtship stages of life, with high hopes of finding love.

SELECTED READINGS

BEIGEL, HUGO G. "Romantic Love," *American Sociological Review*, Vol. 16 (June 1951), pp. 326–334.

ENGLAND, R. W., JR. "Images of Love and Courtship in Family-Magazine Fiction," *Marriage and Family Living*, Vol. 22 (May 1960), pp. 162–165.

GOODE, WILLIAM J. "The Theoretical Importance of Love," *American Sociological Review*, Vol. 24 (February 1959), pp. 38–47.

HORTON, DONALD. "The Dialogue of Courtship in Popular Songs," *American Journal of Sociology*, Vol. 62 (May 1957), pp. 569–578.

KEPHART, WILLIAM M. "Some Correlates of Romantic Love," *Journal of Marriage and the Family*, Vol. 29 (August 1967), pp. 470–479.

KIRKPATRICK, CLIFFORD, AND THEODORE CAPLOW. "Emotional Trends in the

Courtship Experience of College Students as Expressed by Graphs, with Some Observations on Methodological Implications," *American Sociological Review*, Vol. 10 (October 1945), pp. 619–626.

SLATER, PHILIP E. "On Social Regression," *American Journal of Sociology*, Vol. 28 (June 1963), pp. 339–364.

VAN DEN HAAG, ERNEST. "Love or Marriage?" *Harper's Magazine*, Vol. 224 (May 1962), pp. 43–47.

CHAPTER 7

Courtship: Mate Selection and Engagement

Dating and courtship blend into one another, but dating, in its most characteristic form, is a gamelike activity; courtship is primarily concerned with mate selection. Most people have fun on dates—it is almost a youthful duty—but acquiring a spouse can be hard, tense work. If we are more self-conscious about it now than in the past, as some people say, just remember that many people still marry without knowing what they are getting into —with little real soul searching as to whether they have found the right person or picked the right time.

It does take *time* to find a mate, but there are terribly strong pressures to speed things up. The entire process has been glorified, and the freedom to look around extended, but for many youth the alternatives available are very poorly explored. Statistics available while this is being written show that the average at marriage is now going up, after declining little by little for decades. This is a hopeful sign.

THEORIES OF MATE SELECTION

Although pressures affecting our choices in courtship are numerous, most current knowledge on the subject can be explained by just three theories: the ecological theory, the theory of homogamy, and the theory of complementary needs. A good case can be made for each one, although the complementary needs approach has less research support than the other two, and all three together still leave some important questions unanswered.

The Ecological Theory

Ecology refers to the study of *the relationship between organisms and their environment* and has been most highly developed in biology. As it applies to mate selection, it is primarily concerned with the relationship between where people live and the mate choices they make. As expected, young people almost invariably marry individuals who live nearby.

Although there are now greater opportunities for roaming far from home, and even people in the late teens and early twenties have such opportunities, the fact remains that when people are ready to marry they will probably meet an eligible partner close at hand. Studies of residential patterns in mate selection have been made many times in the past quarter of a century, and they always come to the same conclusion: *Propinquity* is a powerful force (Katz and Hill 1958). Marvin Koller (1948) found it operating in times of peace and war and during both prosperity and depression. (Maybe the point should be stated in just the opposite way: It is not that propinquity is a powerful force, but that a strong counterforce is needed to overcome its inertia.)

Quite obviously a person cannot marry someone he has not met, and meeting a person from another city, state, or country at the marriageable time in life is not likely. If it does happen, the chances are that it will not be under circumstances that give courtship much of a chance. For example, males who are traveling away from home in their late teens and early twenties may be looking for women, but rarely for wives. Girls who are away are less likely to be looking for men just to have a good time (due to the nature of their training and the fact that sex holds greater dangers for them), but by the same token they are not likely to be very receptive even to a man who might have genuine courtship in mind.

What is most difficult to explain in the residential proximity studies is the fact that even within a given city the chances are surprisingly limited that anyone will marry a person from across town. It would appear that people are likely to find acceptable mates close to home and, this being true, there is no need and perhaps little opportunity to seek further. This is in line with Samuel Stouffer's (1940) *theory of intervening opportunities,* which holds that the number of persons who travel a given distance will be directly proportional to the number of intervening opportunities (that is, the number of opportunities that might come up along the way). Alvin Katz and Reuben Hill (1958) suggest a modification of this hypothesis, called the *interaction-time-cost theory.* A person will probably spend more time with others for whom the time and cost involved are minimal, and both the time and cost needed tend to increase as distance increases. People in the upper classes, however, can have friends farther from home because of their greater wealth (Harris 1935).

It is often argued that the rising rate of college attendance throws people together who have been reared in different cities or states, expanding the geographical boundaries of mate selection. (It may go without saying that colleges are places of intensive courtship, especially for girls. Sororities, for example, seem to serve primarily to direct courtship traffic for their members.) The long-run impact of the college boom will undoubtedly have this effect, but we must remember that most young people go to colleges not very far from home. The big jump in college attendance tends to cluster in community colleges and senior-level institutions of large cities. Rather than mixing students from far-off places, the college explosion more often mixes people who attended different high schools within the same city. The geographical basis for mate selection is wider, but still not as wide as one might think. The long-run effect of the growth in college attendance may be more dramatic, partly because persons whose parents have attended college tend to go to one farther from home than first-generation students. Even so, the college campus becomes the arena where mate selection occurs, and marriage between college students on the same campus still meets the propinquity test.

The Theory of Homogamy

The theory of homogamy does not conflict with the ecological approach and is in fact closely related to it. *Homogamy* occurs when people marry others very much like themselves in a broad range of traits, more so than if marriages were arranged by chance. The influence of residential propinquity is one good reason for homogamy, but that approach was covered separately because its dynamic feature is physical distance alone. The theory of homogamy suggests that people seek marriage partners who are socially and psychologically like themselves, and therefore one might be willing to travel some distance (if that were necessary) in order to find the right mate.

Evidence supporting homogamy is overwhelming. A persistent and popular belief that opposites attract has not begun to draw comparable factual support. August B. Hollingshead gathered a convincing array of supporting data in 1950, and later studies have not changed his report substantially (although not all of Hollingshead's conclusions about the relative importance of traits have held up). It has been argued that love is an exaggeration of the difference between one person and another; judging from the general similarity among spouses, it almost has to be.

Race was the strongest homogamous factor in Hollingshead's data, and it still has that distinction today. The prophecy is occasionally made that interracial marriages will become more common as race prejudice declines, but support is hard to find. David M. Heer (1965) contends that the most unpredictable element in black-white intermarriage is mating between black males and white females; the marriage rate between white males and black females has been rather constant (and very low) over the past fifty years.

He also tried to calculate the time required for a full fusion of blacks and whites in the United States. It would take thirteen generations, or approximately 351 years, for a complete amalgamation of the races according to the most liberal of his twelve sets of assumptions. (It is likely, however, that big changes in courtship habits will occur in the next 50 years. The next 350 years will be a period of such fantastic change in human society as to rule out *any* meaningful projections.)

Hollingshead found that *religion* was the most decisive homogamous factor after race. It is not as important today as it was at the time of his study, but it still carries weight. Catholic girls, for example, still prefer Catholic boys, other things being equal (of course other things are not always equal). However, religious information is recorded on marriage license applications in only one state, Iowa, and studies of the religious factor in marriage choice are rare. Church allegiance in the United States is relatively easy to change, so a tendency for couples to develop similar religious affiliations after marriage seems to occur with no great difficulty. Interreligious marriages are most frequent when couples are younger or older than average at the time of marriage, when they are remarrying, and when the religious group of one of the partners is underrepresented in the community compared to its typical representation in other communities. In the latter case, there are apparently fewer opportunities for the minority group member to find a mate within his own group, and he associates more with members of other groups. Couples who marry across religious lines quite often have different backgrounds in other respects, too (Christensen and Barber 1967).

Nationality background is a related factor, setting limits to the field of eligibles in marriage. Like religion, its influence tends to drop as each new generation of Americans is separated by time and experience from the Old World culture, but Glazer and Moynihan (1963) have shown that pressures still exist to marry along ethnic lines. This is true in spite of the fact that ethnic divisions today have little to do with the native cultures from which differences originally sprang. They feed on political, neighborhood, and religious loyalties that are rather unique in big American cities.

Social class is now probably the strongest influence on mate selection after race; we usually marry people of our own class background. Since families live in neighborhoods that are segregated by income and other social traits, class is closely related to the ecological factor mentioned earlier.

The most interesting variation on the theme of social-class homogamy is the fact that men are more likely than women to marry someone below their station in life; women have better chances to "marry up." *Hypergamy* refers to the situation where women marry men of higher status than themselves, whereas *hypogamy* is the opposite—where men marry women of higher rank. Hypergamy is also sometimes referred to as *the mating gradient,* and it has long been more common (or presumed to be) than hypogamy (Zelditch 1964; Burchinal 1964). In fiction the hero marries the boss's daughter, but the fact is that women have better opportunities to marry the boss's son.

In a recent study, however, Zick Rubin (1968) concluded that any overall tendency toward either hypergamy or hypogamy in the United States is negligible. He did find that daughters of white-collar workers have rather high rates of marriage to sons of professional and managerial workers, and that farmers' daughters tend to marry sons of white-collar workers more than their brothers marry white-collar daughters. Hypergamy was only slightly more common in his sample than hypogamy, but it was particularly characteristic of marriages between members of the two highest classes.

This suggests that upper-class women are handicapped in the marriage market, since they have to compete with women of lower status, who may be a little more willing to give in to men; John Finley Scott (1965) calls this the "Brahmin Problem," due to the aloofness of higher status women. To say that they are handicapped may be a mistake, however; they are more independent and in a better position to pass marriage by.

But if there is a group of women with low marriage rates, some men must also go without brides. What happens on the male side of the ledger? The answer, of course, is that a relatively large percentage of lower-class men are cut off from family life. There is a lack of symmetry here, with upper-class women and lower-class men having low marriage rates. Perhaps in both cases they learn how to adjust. In fact, lower-class men are probably unaware of their place in the overall community; upper-class women, on the other hand, have a much better chance to work out happy alternatives or at least satisfactory ones.

The case for *education,* with certain marginal differences, is similar to that for social class. Generally, men are expected to have a little more education than their wives, but the balance in education between couples varies by social class. In lower-class groups, for example, girls often stay in school longer than boys, and so they acquire more education than their husbands. In such situations family life is more often mother-centered, with the woman acting as head of the family.

In the middle classes, men usually finish more years of school than their wives, especially in the upper-middle classes, and here men have relatively more power at home. In the upper classes, too, men often stay in school longer, although not quite so much stress is placed on advanced degrees at this level. The bachelor's degree has been a standard upper-class achieve-

ment for some time for both sexes. But elite education is more often preparation for a style of life than for a specific vocation or profession. Since
male and female styles are a little different in the top social levels, and the
sexes often attend all-boy or all-girl schools, the amount of education is less
important than its quality or content. The point of all this is that husband-
wife equality in education is rarely perfect, but similarities are still greater
than would occur by chance. The differences that do occur reflect differences in social-class background.

Homogamy also extends to *intelligence, attitudes,* and even *physical
characteristics.* People who score high on intelligence tests tend to marry
others who score high; people with liberal attitudes in politics (as but one
example of an attitude measure) tend to marry others with liberal attitudes; and people who are tall tend to find tall mates. In many other ways
the physical characteristics of spouses are more similar than a random selection of mates can explain. Correlations in such areas are never perfect, but
they are impressive nonetheless. The one area where homogamy is difficult
to demonstrate concerns personality traits, so we have to look for some
other theory of mate selection here. (And we shall turn to that in a moment.)

Since the evidence in support of homogamy is so thoroughly established
(except with regard to personality types), the real problem is not to prove
that it exists, but to explain why. A variety of plausible theories have been
set forth, but three stand out above the rest. They do not conflict in essentials, and the validity of one cannot be construed to mean that the others
are invalid. In fact, they are complementary in nature.

First, as already implied, homogamy may simply be the product of ecology. People who live close together are usually similar in social and personal
traits, and they tend to meet at that time in life when courtship occurs.
According to this theory, persons with similar traits marry mainly because
they are likely to meet; and homogamy becomes little more than a consequence of residential proximity (Davis and Reeves 1939). But there are
too many varieties of homogamy for this approach to be convincing all by
itself. Furthermore, there is evidence that homogamy has occurred among
some groups—the Irish in New Haven, Connecticut, for example—even
when couples did not live close together before marriage (Kennedy 1943).

A plausible theory falling in the realm of social psychology is the *theory
of role reciprocity.* Its basic premise is that marriage consists of playing
roles. For that matter, most of our daily behavior involves doing what is
expected of us in the various roles we happen to be playing at the moment.
Role playing is reciprocal; each role has a counterrole without which neither
would have any meaning. In order to be a teacher you need students; to be
a friend you have to have a friend; in order to be a wife and mother you
must have a husband and children. Role playing works out more smoothly

if the person playing the reciprocal role has the same values as your own. It helps to be able to anticipate the moves of the other person and to sense the reasons for them. The theory of role reciprocity explains or accounts for homogamy by saying that people are attracted to others who act much as they would act in similar situations. This assures a high level of empathy and rapport.

Perhaps there are times when you might be attracted to a person precisely because he surprises you; people who are completely predictable can be terribly boring. But sooner or later surprises, though not boring, can be very exasperating. What first seems to be a charming discovery because it is so unanticipated becomes an intolerable distraction. Couples who are very dissimilar may marry and even have a wonderful marriage, but there are good reasons why they usually stay together only a short time before the adverse reaction hits. In any case, it seems likely that couples who are nonempathetic break up with greater frequency than others. At the same time, empathy and *communication efficiency* usually improve as couples spend more time together (Kirkpatrick and Hobart 1954; Goodman and Ofshe 1968).

A third explanation for homogamy is the *theory of persistent family satisfactions.* It is essentially this: In childhood most people become accustomed to certain family practices which give them pleasure. Since these are so basic to the person's sense of what is right, he continues to seek them, more or less unconsciously, throughout life. Children tend to resemble members of their family in physical ways; they often look like their parents, and brothers and sisters resemble one another. Family members also react to common cues when they make important decisions. They are alike in the greatest possible variety of ways. When people begin to think seriously about marriage, they quite naturally look forward to the kind of married life that is familiar, and they are attracted to persons who can meet these expectations—people who resemble members of their *family of orientation,* the family of their childhood.

This theory might be called a *parental image theory* (Kephart 1961), but there is more to it than that. It does not say that the individual seeks a person like his parent of the opposite sex, although there may be some tendency to do that (which is quite consistent with the theory of homogamy), but that he seeks a life after marriage that is meaningful in terms of his most important earlier experiences. The parent of the opposite sex may have been the key to these, but not necessarily. No matter whom a child has had close relations with—mother, father, sibling, even an uncle or grandparent—that person will probably be very much like himself. (For that matter, even the children he plays with in the neighborhood are likely to resemble him in both attitudes and physical appearance, more than children chosen at random from the whole community.)

This approach suggests that the more gratifying a person's experiences in childhood, the more homogamous his choice in courtship is likely to be. Although supporting evidence has to be considered shaky, there are strong indications that happiness in childhood is correlated with success in marriage (Burgess and Locke 1960). Perhaps the most important consequence of a secure childhood is a lack of confusion; the person who approaches courtship with a sense of self-confidence may automatically associate with people like himself and, in turn, be acceptable to them.

The Theory of Complementary Needs

The theory of complementary needs is one of the most stimulating theories about mate selection (or almost any aspect of family life) of the past quarter of a century. It was set forth initially by Robert R. Winch in 1954 and 1955 and has been put to a variety of tests since that time. Empirical support is weak at best (Udry 1967; Murstein 1967; Trost 1967), but the theory has so much intrinsic interest and plausibility that it just will not die. In fact, variations on it have appeared in the folklore of marriage for generations, and it is implicit in some of the most popular works in psychology—in that of Sigmund Freud, for example.

The theory is based on the premise that the personality of each individual determines not only how he copes with problems, but what kinds of problems he chooses to deal with. As such, it creates *needs* for the individual. A shy, retiring person, for example, manages his life in a particular way, and his style not only helps him solve some of his problems, it makes certain kinds of solutions very difficult. The theory of complementary needs holds that each person is attracted in courtship to somebody who can help him solve his personality-created problems (assuming, of course, that such a "somebody" exists—an assumption that cannot always be met).

Since people resolve their personal problems on a number of different levels—some do not stem from underlying personality traits at all, as in the case of many routine financial problems—it must also be assumed that courtship lasts long enough and is intense enough to expose our deeper selves. We are attracted to people who "complete" our personalities and enable us to cope more successfully with our underlying needs.

Two types of complementariness have been described in detail (Ktsanes and Ktsanes 1968). Type I occurs when the same need (such as the need for achievement) appears in both partners but at different levels of intensity. Type II occurs when altogether different needs are involved (one person may need to dominate, while the other needs to be dependent or subordinate). A third type may also occur when the needs of the couple are both identical *and* complementary. A person with a very strong sex drive would probably be better off with a spouse who is also sexually active, and two people with powerful needs for achievement might very well be able to help each other.

Winch (1967) himself has reviewed the research on his thesis and feels that the results so far are inconclusive. He argues that the importance of complementary needs in mate selection will vary, depending on the kind of society and the kind of family system involved. Clearly the theory has limited application where people have little or no choice concerning whom they marry. It is only likely to work where there is freedom in mate selection and a stress on love as the main reason for marrying; it becomes more important as kinship obligations are reduced and as the division of work in marriage becomes less stereotyped. If, for example, the role of husband and father is firmly fixed, as it tends to be in agricultural societies, then complementary needs may be beside the point. In this case it is more important that the man and wife be able to act out their roles according to social customs than that they be psychologically tailored to each other.

/ But Winch recognizes that even in modern society people cannot be attracted to each other on the basis of complementary needs until the forces of homogamy have been worked through. A filtering process occurs first, assuring that couples will have much in common. Then the dynamics of complementary needs *may* come into play, allowing the person to select someone who is psychologically different from himself, but in complementary ways / A shy, white, upper-middle-class Methodist college man may, after dating a variety of girls, finally find one who not only is white, upper-middle-class, Protestant, and going to college, but also has a certain assertiveness that can help him overcome some of his problems.

So far we have discussed this theory from a positive point of view, assuming that people are attracted to others who help them cope with life *more successfully* than they otherwise would. But it does not always work that way.

Snell and Gail Putney (1964) suggest that people may often seek marriage partners who reflect their own unique qualities or weaknesses—but in a favorable way. Two rebels, for example, may be drawn to each other because each is able to justify the other's rebellion. The Putneys call this *reciprocal rationalization*. Finding someone who reflects one's own personality characteristics can sometimes be a source of exciting self-discovery. The main pitfall, according to the Putneys, is that when we find someone who can help us release our own unused talents, we tend to become very possessive. The relationship can be stimulating while it lasts, but it contains within itself the seeds of discord, especially in the form of jealousy and dependency on the other person.

What if a person has some distinctly neurotic twist in his personality? For the purpose of illustration, let us say he has all the symptoms of a prealcoholic, his family background is a perfect textbook example of the psychosocial forces leading to alcoholism. What kind of woman is he attracted to? According to the theory of persistent family satisfactions, he will be drawn to one who can revive some of the happiness he had as a child or at least some of the most basic experiences he had at that time. His wife would then be someone like his mother or like the person who was most responsible for his underlying personality. The theory of complementary needs, however, says that he will be drawn to a woman who can help him contain or even defeat his weakness.

The evidence from psychiatric case records indicates stronger support for the first (pessimistic) approach than for the second. In fact, if the theory of complementary needs is given a negative twist, then it becomes possible that anybody with a basic personality problem may be drawn to someone who will aggravate his problem rather than help to correct it. Case records as well as folklore are replete with stories of men with alcoholic tendencies who marry women who can only make matters worse. They may divorce only to marry women just like the ones they married the first time. Unfortunately, evidence from counseling records and psychiatry must inevitably be negative on this point. If the prealcoholic man marries a women who helps him solve his problem, he will *not* go to a psychiatrist, and the story with a happy ending will never be told.

COURTSHIP ESCALATORS

Let us assume that a young couple have met the basic requirements of homogamy (meaning that they are alike in several important respects) and that they also have a few complementary traits going for them (in the positive sense). They have known each other for a month or two and are beginning to think seriously about marriage. What will tip the scales in favor of a firm decision to marry?

In a sense, almost all the decisions people make are made on impulse. We know this to be true of Americans as consumers and not just when they buy cheap things. Even the decision to buy a car or a house is often made on the spur of the moment. The decision to marry may boil down to a moment of reckless judgment: "What the hell—let's get married." (Impromptu marriage is certainly a popular dramatic theme.) But no matter how sudden the decision may seem to be, it occurs only under circumstances that a particular kind of couple manages to get into. Before the final decision, a series of steps are taken that reveal the deep roots of human character.

Charles Bolton (1961) has suggested the useful concept of *escalators* in courtship, which can help explain behavior that may seem to be sparked by sudden impulse. These are conditions that create momentum, drawing couples toward marriage and making their relationships progressively more binding. There are five in particular. (Bolton was the first to identify them, but their names and the description of each have been modified for present purposes.)

1. *Satisfaction escalators* are the most obvious ones. If two people find pleasure together, they will probably take steps to keep their relationship alive. This occurs in virtually all cases of successful courtship, but the most significant point is that it rarely operates all by itself. Other driving forces are needed to convince many couples. If our national marriage rate had to rely on satisfaction alone, we would have fewer weddings and very likely a national crisis.

In any case, satisfactions are not likely to be nicely divided between the two people involved. One is almost certain to like the arrangement better than the other, and will work harder to keep it going. A number of years ago Willard Waller (1937) called attention to the *principle of least interest* among couples: One is usually less interested in maintaining the relationship than the other, and he holds the upper hand as a result. He can say, in effect: "If you want this to last, do as I say." Waller's point calls attention to the fact that the very conditions that drive a couple toward marriage can also be a source of trouble after they get there. The person who is most anxious to maintain the relationship may consent to things during courtship that he will fiind hard to accept after marriage. He may even say to himself: "I'll take it now, but just you wait. . ." Thus, escalators in courtship can lead in predictable ways to trouble in marriage (to which we shall return in Chapter 9).

2. *Milieu escalators* are pressures to marry from close friends or from the couple's general surroundings. They suggest in no uncertain terms that being married is a better lot in life than not being married. Of course we start getting ideas about marriage long before a likely partner comes along —long before we even start dating.

Milieu escalators include the reminders and insinuations expressed by friends, but also pressures from the leading themes of society. They are acted out everywhere in the mass media as well as by real-life couples who seem to have found happiness in marriage and in all kinds of activities— having a home, babies, and so on—that marriage makes possible. (Marriageable girls usually see examples of domestic happiness all around them.)

But the people in one's own social circle are probably most crucial. If a girl has three best friends, for example, they are a *reference group* for her. In a sense, they comprise her "class," and just as she may graduate from high school or college with them, comparing her progress with theirs, she wants to keep up with them in marriage. Sooner or later one of them will have a wedding, then another, and with each one she feels greater pressure to keep up. If she meets a boy who is reasonably eligible, the temptation will be powerful to consider him an acceptable groom.

The milieu escalators for boys are not as strong as for girls. Girls are constantly reminded that the proper thing to be is married; boys are warned that sooner or later they will have to give up the freedom of bachelorhood, and the obvious inference is that the later they capitulate, the better. But the fact of the matter is that males, too, belong to little clusters of friendship groups, and as their friends marry, increasing pressure is put on them to join the domesticated crowd.

3. *Public commitment escalators* are a third kind. The longer two persons have been going together, the more they are defined as marriageable by people who know them, and the more difficult it will be for them to break up without giving some kind of embarrassing explanation. It may take real courage to call the affair off, because an element of failure or even immorality is involved. Each time the couple is seen together a kind of public announcement is made affirming that the relationship is a lasting one. This public record establishes the couple's obligations to each other and implies that they will take the next step. Taking that step—deciding to marry—may actually be easier than deciding not to.

There should be no misunderstanding on this point, however. Couples *do* overcome the momentum of their drift toward marriage, even after engagement (as we shall see). Nevertheless, many people reach a point where they *feel* trapped, particularly if they are part of a fairly close-knit social circle. They not only want to please their partners, but all their mutual friends as well. Engagement, of course, is the most public commitment of all. An engaged pair who have set their wedding date—perhaps the girl has already had showers and put her gifts on display—will find breaking the engagement an agonizing reappraisal, with crying mothers, grumbling fathers, embarrassed friends, and a lot of painful explaining to do.

On the other hand, people who live in a place where they have few mutual friends, perhaps no friends at all, will not have to worry about this. Perhaps the growth of cities and gigantic universities (which is where much contemporary courtship takes place) offer relief from just these pressures, and one traditional boost for marriage fades away. But it has no effect whatsoever on the overall marriage rate, which remains extremely high in the United States. The *quality* of courtship may be affected, though, freeing people to stress other things, particularly the satisfaction escalators.

4. *Familiarity escalators* (also called *fear of withdrawal*) are a fourth kind. They stem from the fact that the pair increasingly rely on one another as they spend more time together. Independent of the level of their mutual love, they will find it progressively more difficult to face the possible emptiness of no relationship at all. Clifford Kirkpatrick (1963) calls this

the *jackpot hypothesis*: When couples have invested a lot of time and energy in an affair, abandoning their investment becomes ever more difficult (just as slot machine players will often work a particular machine until they hit the jackpot—time and finances permitting. They do not want somebody else to hit it two minutes after they leave.)

This kind of pressure hits hardest at people who have very few opportunities to meet other eligible singles. In a sense, these are the people who are not really in a position to "select" a mate in the first place; having a choice obviously implies the existence of several possibilities. In actual fact, the chance to make a selection—"I'll take this man"—is given to very few women, and men have fewer alternatives than most women would guess. But even if you have no idea who the replacement for your present partner may be, you would do well to assume that this is by no means your last chance.

5. *Expediency escalators* refer to the possibility that marriage may solve some pressing problem for the couple (or for one of the partners) that is totally unrelated to their suitability for each other. The most obvious case is premarital pregnancy. Marriage can solve the immediate problem of legitimacy, but whether the two people are appropriately matched is another question altogether. In fact, pregnancy may cause the girl to marry someone other than the baby's father just to make things look "right" and to legitimize the infant. This apparently does not apply in Sweden, where almost half the brides are pregnant (Zetterberg 1969). Pregnancy in many Swedish cases occurs only *after* the couple has gotten engaged and started living together. The wedding is a legitimizing formality, of course, but it is not considered unusual. Nevertheless, pregnancy *is* a courtship escalator.

But expediency is a very inclusive motive. Marriage may help to resolve any number of problems, at least in the short run. A young woman who lives at home with her cranky mother may find marriage just the excuse she needs to get away. Or a restless college girl under pressure from home to make better grades—or just to stay in school—may welcome marriage because it gives her a good reason to drop out. Marriage may even be a means by which one of the partners can gain leverage in dealing with the other one. Marriage will change the nature of the relationship and at least open the way for a new distribution of power.

Considering all five of these escalators together, it becomes clear that any two individuals who manage to keep their affair going long enough are likely to feel strong pressures to take the final step. Of course they may go together for months—or even years—without making the decisive move, but the fact is that most couples are not so hard to break down. In courtship the prevailing pattern seems to be "get married or quit going together," and the decision is reached quickly as a rule.

Even indecision appears to work in favor of marriage; it allows the courtship to last long enough for two or three prodders to take effect, especially the public commitment factor and the familiarity escalator. It also gives the couple a chance to discover how marriage could be a useful expedient. Both of them can think of ways that marriage might make life better or more secure.

It is quite possible that some people enter any new affair at a particularly high level of marriage readiness—those who have been in the marriage market for several years, for example, and who may have almost married once or maybe several times. They are anxious to marry from the start and are willing to hurry through the preliminaries. Instead of waiting for a broad combination of proofs of their marriageability, one or two faint ones will do. (Remarriages often follow this pattern.) The actual decision to marry will seem impulsive, but the final jump is the product of years of personal development.

IDEALIZATION AND MUTUALIZATION

Two processes tied very closely to the escalators are *idealization* and *mutualization*. Each is unique enough to deserve special attention. Both of them, like the escalators, can lead to trouble after marriage and for similar reasons—the mutual attractions built up in courtship have to be sustained by different conditions after marriage, different from those that drew the couple together in the first place.

Idealization is the process by which people, beginning with dating, are prone to see the best qualities in one another and overlook the worst. It may not occur at first, although even in rather casual dating we usually want to see desirable qualities in our partners, not bad ones. And we tend to see what we look for. Certainly by the time we reach the courtship stage of life our wishes lean in this direction. By definition, courtship is the period when we are most self-conscious and most determined in the search for a mate. Anyone who is not capable of at least a little idealization, that is, anyone who sets unrealistically high standards and is very hard to please, is a candidate for either bachelorhood or spinsterhood.

Sidney Greenfield (1965) argues that idealization is the primary social function of romantic love. Without it, there are compelling reasons in a society that stresses rational decision making to forget about marriage, especially in the case of men. Idealization helps to persuade them to try family life; the romantic trappings of courtship assure that the lovers' faults will not be fully discovered before the wedding and that the nation's marriage rate will remain high.

In fact, evidence clearly suggests that men idealize their partners in courtship more than women. The beginnings of this curious state of affairs came with the rise of courtly love (see Chapter 6), when the idealization of women became fashionable under certain circumstances. The pattern has taken a more practical turn in the twentieth century, however. In an interesting study, William Kephart (1967) found that the contemporary girl's romantic striving is more adaptive than her boyfriend's. Women can control and manipulate their romantic feelings better, adjusting them to the particular courtship problems they happen to have. Only about one-fourth of the girls in Kephart's sample said they would *not* marry a fellow who had all the qualities they desired even if they had no love for him. But about two-thirds of the males claimed they could not marry a girl under such circumstances. (Most of the girls did not say they *would* marry the man; they simply did not want to rule him out.) The implication is that the girls in Kephart's sample took a more practical attitude toward love than did the boys.

Robert Coombs and William Kenkel (1966) have a plausible explanation for this. They reason that since the family's social status is largely determined by the husband's work (he is the breadwinner), a woman's status and life chances are largely determined by the man's career performance. In contrast, the wife's contribution to the status of the family is impossible to measure in most cases, and the male cannot judge his girlfriend by objective, performance standards. He is therefore highly susceptible to idealization. Very few men judge women in terms of the kind of breadwinners they may turn out to be—but things are changing.

Since so much depends on the husband's job future, the woman is likely to be more practical than her boyfriend about the entire matter of mate selection and to view courtship partners in the broader context of future security. Because it takes time to judge a man accurately, and since the girl cannot afford to make a mistake, she is more likely to be reserved in her emotional commitment. Coombs and Kenkel did indeed find that women are generally more skeptical after a first date than men and that their skepticism tends to continue in later dates. At first glance this may seem to be in conflict with the greater marriage-proneness of women, but not really. Women have both a greater urge to be married *and* a greater need to keep their idealization of men in check.

Through *mutualization* the man and woman acquire habits and routines that fuse their life patterns. Each gives up a little freedom and spends less time with third parties, and the two start taking one another into account in planning for the future—for the coming evening, the next day, the next weekend, or the next year. Rhona Rapoport (1962) refers to the early stages of marriage as the time of change from *self-orientation* to *mutuality*, but this process actually occurs in courtship, when the first commitment to a life of mutual concern has to be made. Mutualization needs to be fairly highly developed before the familiarity escalators can do their work.

If idealization and mutualization take hold in a normal manner, and two or three of the courtship escalators have their effect, the couple will decide to marry. They may choose to rush the wedding, allowing neither time to plan a big ceremony nor to ponder the living arrangements to follow, but most couples give themselves a few weeks—perhaps even a few months— after deciding to marry before the knot is tied.

THE ENGAGEMENT

A period of engagement before marriage is not required, but it is a pre-ferred custom. It is also a stable one, since the percentage of couples who get engaged before marrying does not fluctuate very much from year to year or from generation to generation. At one extreme is elopement; at the other is a long engagement, with formal announcements, showers for the bride, a series of parties, an elaborate wedding, and participation by a large circle of friends and family. Most engagements fall somewhere between the two extremes, leaning toward the elaborate side.

Engagement signifies different things to different people, but the basic premise is that the couple has decided to marry. The period of engagement allows time to make arrangements for the wedding and the honeymoon (if there is to be one) and to work out household plans. Above all, it gives a new perspective to the relationship. The couple are no longer trying to decide *whether* to marry, so they can turn to other matters.

A reasonable estimate is that about one-third of all engagements will be broken (Burgess and Locke 1960). The fact that the couple has settled the basic question forces them to see each other in a new light, which may help to account for the high rate of engagement failure in the United States. Apparently engagement is a very brittle relationship, but one which, once broken, does not ordinarily cause prolonged sorrow or any deep sense of bereavement. The nation is full of people who have survived broken en-gagements.

One major reason for the high failure rate is that couples begin taking one another for granted. Sooner or later one of them, or both, realize that they are no longer acting in that special way that made them think they were in love. After all, planning the wedding and preparing for the new house-hold can be very trying (although some couples may find this exciting, even romantic). The best argument to be made for engagements, especially in a society that places so much emphasis on romantic love, is that they usually strip some of the glamour from the affair; doomed marriages can then be detected and mercifully avoided. Ernest Burgess and Paul Wallin (1944; 1953) have contended that *engagement success* ranks among the best predictors of marital success, although just what constitutes engage-ment success is not altogether clear. Various studies have also suggested that the longer the engagement lasts (up to a point), the greater the likelihood of success in marriage.

The engagement is usually made public. It can be kept secret, but an important part of its function is totally lost if it is. After a public statement of intent, the couple receive feedback from friends and kinsmen, while in the preengagement stage they were largely on their own. Engagement opens the affair to a kind of community analysis, and the decision to marry can be reviewed by a greater variety of people. Not all of their opinions are passed on to the couple, of course, but presumably some do manage to get through, and they may have an effect. (Some couples are so excited they cannot hear or see anything.) Furthermore, there are all kinds of pressures on youth to pair off long before the engagement, and pressures to break the engagement can rarely be as strong. Couples who are not subject to pressures to marry from other people are possibly the ones who are *least* likely to go through a period of engagement before marriage, since both pressures of engagement and marriage are conventional practices.

Generally, women discuss their wedding plans more frequently and at greater length than men, and so the bride-to-be probably gets more feedback than her fiancé. She thinks about her marriage almost all the time, and although some of the advice she gets is welcome, some of it is not. Alan Bates (1942) asked a sample of young married persons whether their parents had attempted to influence courtship; 69 percent of the women said their fathers had tried, 97 percent said their mothers had. The corresponding percentages for men were only 49 and 79—considerably lower, but impressive just the same.

There is good reason to believe that the more the girl talks with others about sex and family roles, the more consistent her marriage and family attitudes become (Kammeyer 1964). Men, talking less, have less clear-cut and less consistent ideas about what is likely to happen after the wedding. Although the girl may have faced some disturbing questions, because she has thought so much about possible problems, she is inclined to go through with the wedding anyway, entering marriage with greater apprehension than men ordinarily experience. (This is in line with the studies by Kephart, Coombs, and Kenkel discussed earlier.) As a result, she is more completely prepared for the reality shocks of marriage.

Men, who often have reservations about marriage because they joke about it so much, are more likely to call the whole thing off if they become jittery or suspicious about what they are getting into. When it comes to breaking the engagement, they have the advantage, since girls cannot be as aggressive in approaching possible new partners; the man can look for another girl or simply wait for a better time.

For anybody who may be concerned about keeping the marriage rate high, it is probably a good thing that men do not discuss their courtship problems with one another any more than they do. If they did, a larger number might back out. On the other hand, if they discussed these things more, it is also possible that they, like women, would become more adjusted to mixed feelings about marriage and would be better prepared to cope with its inevitable troubles. Wives often complain that their husbands simply do not want to "talk about it." Husbands are less likely to complain about tight-lipped wives.

There is one special case for which engagement seems to be particularly useful—when a young man is called into military service about the time he decides to marry and he cannot be sure whether to marry quickly or settle for engagement. The latter seems to be the wisest solution in most cases, for reasons that are obvious enough in a calm, detached study of marriage, but which are not always so obvious to the eager young couple. Engagement supplies an emotional bond which may comfort the man while he is away from home. But if the two should drift apart (and the chances are pretty good that they will) the engagement can be broken fairly easily—much more easily than marriage and with fewer loose ends to settle.

COUNSELING AND PREDICTIONS OF MARITAL ADJUSTMENT

The first attempt to predict the chances of success in marriage for young couples was made by Katharine Davis (1929) in the 1920s, followed by several research projects along the same line in the early thirties. These first efforts were very limited, however, usually stressing only one or two premarital factors believed to be associated with marriage adjustment. It became apparent that further progress could only come from more ambitious projects. These would have to include a large number of facts about couples, combined into an *expectancy table* from which prediction scores for particular couples could be calculated. The work of Lewis Terman (1938) and Ernest Burgess and Leonard Cottrell (1936; 1939) did exactly this. Several efforts to refine their methods followed for a period of ten or fifteen years, most notably by Harvey Locke (1951), and then rather suddenly the subject seemed to lose its fascination. Many difficulties had been encountered, but some predictions were successfully made, and it is still possible to make certain kinds of useful marriage forecasts.

This entire effort seems to have been a unique American phenomenon, developed to meet special American needs and problems. It was stimulated in part by the data-oriented social research that has characterized the rise of all behavioral sciences in the United States. It was also inspired by the enormous American effort to develop scientific methods to predict the future—that is, by the effort to make social prophecy a science rather than an art and to work out standard procedures to plan for the foreseeable future.

On top of all this was the fact that love as the only acceptable reason for marriage had its greatest impact in the United States. It was here that teen-agers were first freed to engage in the prolonged game of dating, and it was here that variety in the population was so pronounced, throwing together young people with a hodgepodge of ethnic, religious, and racial backgrounds.

Homogamy is the general rule even in the United States, but the opportunities for mixed marriage are staggering by European standards. It is not surprising that American social scientists would convert the prosaic idea of homogamy into a general theory of mate selection. In most countries no widespread alternative to that pattern existed. But when alternatives are available, people do take advantage of them. This is of more than passing importance for the rapid rise of the American divorce rate in the past seventy-five years. The awareness of the upswing in divorce, duly reported by the new techniques for social scorekeeping, created a need to predict success in marriage, and American sociology and psychology led the search.

Perhaps the biggest difficulty, however, and the main reason for the recent loss of enthusiasm, is the problem of determining just what success in marriage consists of. That, too, becomes a tangled problem where variety is the order of the day. Is success the ability to stay married and keep out of divorce court? Is it a condition where both spouses say they are happily married? But if it is that, what objective conditions in the marriage cause the couple to say they are happy? Will all couples living under similar circumstances answer such a question in the same way?

Perhaps the best means of determining success is to state a series of conditions that describe exactly what it is, and then ask couples whether these conditions are met in their marriages. But even then can we be sure that they will answer the questions honestly? And if they do, what if there is disagreement among questionnaire makers over what constitutes marriage happiness? For example, does happiness require that couples never, or only rarely, quarrel? Some couples like to fight, and two writers, George Bach and Peter Wyden (1969), say that we all should—so long as we fight fairly —and they try to establish ground rules. Is it necessary that they kiss each other often and call each other by endearing terms? Some couples feel uncomfortable doing such things, but they still say that their marriage is a happy one. Peter Rossi (1965) says that happiness may be too personal and too subjective to be measured by the crude devices currently available. Edwin Lively (1969) is even more pessimistic. He says that use of the terms "marital adjustment," "marital success," and "marital happiness" in their present imprecise state of development may do more harm than good (at least insofar as scientific study of the family is concerned).

Not only do different couples look for different things in marriage, they develop different habits in describing such things. "Happiness" is a throw-away word to some people, in the sense that they have never seriously considered that they are anything but happy; they use the word very loosely. To others it is a term that must be very carefully earned; they are unwilling to call themselves happy unless they are absolutely sure.

William Goode (1964) argues that the measures of marriage adjustment used in current family literature may only discriminate between *conventional* couples and the rest of the population. People who are conventional will consistently answer marriage questionnaires in predictable ways, usually showing themselves to be well-adjusted. Unconventional people may be more truthful, but by the standards built into the questionnaires they will also be considered less well-adjusted.

Recognizing all these difficulties, let us assume for the moment (in order to proceed) that some agreement on the nature of success exists. That assumption is in fact often made, despite the misgivings. The next step in the construction of a prediction device is to find a sample of successful marriages and another sample of unsuccessful ones. Then we try to identify the important ways that these two samples were different *before* they married. The nature of the two groups, of course, will be determined by the standards used to identify success and nonsuccess. Let us assume that we have two such samples. Now the problem is to get accurate and relevant information about their premarriage lives.

Conditions of Marital Success

Many studies programmed along these essential lines have been reported, and the results are reasonably consistent (Burgess and Locke 1960). In general terms, four kinds of premarital conditions are linked to marital success. Some of them are undoubtedly more basic than others, although judging their relative importance is an extremely difficult task. Perhaps it is enough to say that consensus among the experts is less than complete. The four kinds of conditions or qualities are:

1. Significant Relationships with Other People in the Person's Background. Various studies suggest that the person who can honestly say that relations with both his mother and father were warm and satisfying has a good chance in marriage. It also helps if his parents were affectionate but firm and consistent, and if they were happily married. We have already noted that adjustment in engagement is a good clue to adjustment in marriage. It also seems to help if the couple have mutual friends of both sexes with whom they will continue to have close contacts after marriage (Ackerman 1963; Scanzoni 1965).
2. Environmental Conditions in the Person's Background. These conditions may be both social and physical, but it seems doubtful that the

latter *cause* success or failure in marriage. If the person claims to have had a happy childhood, has not grown up in poverty or in conditions of physical deterioration within the city, and has completed extensive formal education, his chances of success are relatively good. The socio-economic level of the husband's parents is apparently more significant than that of the wife's—it is more likely to determine the status level reached by the new family.

3. Particular Events in the Individual's Past or the Timing of These Events. Marriage at an early age is not favorable (Hart and Shields 1926; and many studies since); a whirlwind romance is not favorable; a premarital pregnancy is not favorable; but parental approval of the marriage *is* favorable. (This last factor might also come under point one above—warm and satisfying relations with parents.) If the young man has a good work record and has made effective plans to enter an occupation marked by a high degree of social control (where his career could be hurt by divorce), an absence of moving around, and job security, or an occupation that requires more than average education, his score will probably be high.

4. Psychological Attributes of the Individuals. The influence of these are most difficult to gauge, but they are undoubtedly important. They may also be products of the environmental qualities and social relationships mentioned under the first three points. The attitudes that are most crucial are those that have to do with familism itself; a person who has very little interest in family life or is only fitfully committed to it is not likely to make an all-out effort. The most promising arrangement usually occurs when the couple have similar views, but weak family commitment does not improve the couple's chances even if it is shared. It is beneficial, to say the least, if at least one of the partners has a strong drive to succeed in the family sphere of life. Undoubtedly many marriages have been preserved because of the extraordinary efforts of just one of the spouses. In fact, if marriage relations themselves have greater stability than the activities of either of the spouses considered separately, which may frequently occur, it is because marriage is by definition a joint affair that can be kept alive by a strong effort on the part of either spouse. Divorce may still occur after one of the partners has done all he can to avoid it, but when neither makes such an effort, there is not much hope.

Couples who fill out marriage prediction forms are assigned a score, and the score gives them some idea of their chance for success. The score, however, is probably less valid in its way than most intelligence test are in theirs; that is, it has no clear meaning for some couples. Blacks, for example, have different marriage problems from whites, and the upper-middle-classes have problems that never come up in the lower classes. Marriage prediction tests are not always keyed to the particular "risk group" the couple happens to belong to. A score of 150 might mean one thing to a black couple with very low income and an altogether different thing to an affluent white couple.

It is at this point that counseling can be helpful. The problem is not so much one of forecasting success or failure in marriage—after all, these are either–or concepts and are frightening in their finality. Marriage prediction tests are most helpful when used by skilled counselors to pinpoint probable trouble areas, not to predict utter bliss or total chaos. The primary goal of premarital counseling is to expose areas of stress and to work out ways to cope with them (Rutledge 1966). Members of the American Association of Marriage and Family Counselors are professionals with experience in precisely this area—no group has more.

But in many cases the couple's difficulties may be obvious enough. For those with low income the manifest problem is financial, and no counselor is needed to tell them that, nor can a marriage prediction test improve the diagnosis. But a counselor might call attention to the syndrome that usually comes up in such homes. The husband will have trouble making a living, and his wife will be quick to denounce him when he is out of work (Rainwater 1965). He will then react in predictable ways, all the more predictable the less he understands his predicament. Both he and his wife will follow a series of moves and countermoves that they only vaguely comprehend. Counseling could forearm them against this syndrome. (But it would be wrong to infer from this that marriage counseling is a cure for poverty.)

Of course couples living in poverty rarely visit counselors before they marry, and they are only a little more likely to do so afterward. Nor do middle-class couples seek counseling in most cases, although they are certainly *more* likely to. They are also more likely to have taken a marriage and family course in college, and they will usually have more insight into the troubles they can expect in marriage. If they have filled out a marriage prediction questionnaire and reviewed it with a competent counselor, they are all the more likely to have some notion of the problems their particular marriage can expect.

Why then is premarital counseling neglected in the United States? There are all too many reasons. Ask yourself: Would you get married without counseling? You probably would. You probably have never even considered it. And that is just the point. As yet there is no popular concern about premarital counseling—no commercials on television trying to sell it the way bad-breath killers are pushed and hundreds of other things are promoted to improve human relations. It has not yet become a priority issue in our national scale of values.

Courtship Warnings

Many marriage problems are implicit in the courtship escalators discussed earlier. Mutual satisfactions, for example, draw the couple toward marriage, but they can be altogether different from the kinds of pleasures the couple will have in marriage. The fun of courtship tends to center on leisure activities and sex; satisfaction in marriage simply cannot rely on these diversions alone. Clearly a wise couple will arrange to work as well as play together before they marry. A couple cannot rehearse the actual conditions of marriage, of course—very few people regard engagement as "trial marriage," although that point of view has advocates—but they can at least try to avoid a steady diet of fantasy.

The other forces that push couples toward marriage hold hidden dangers, too. Milieu escalators are not directly related to the suitability of the partners for one another, so the more they influence the decision to marry, the greater the danger. But this point should at least be qualified: Milieu pressures are most dangerous when the couple plans to live in an entirely different environment after marriage from the one that surrounded their courtship. Where they will be part of the social network that pushed them toward marriage, that environment should continue to operate in their favor.

This same general point applies to public commitment escalators. The more the decision to marry reflects commitments to people with whom the couple will associate after marriage, the more appropriate it is. If it is a matter of indifference or is even resented by people they will have to live with, or if it pleases a different crowd altogether, the marriage may be in trouble.

The expediency escalators are the most dangerous of all. In no sense are they likely to improve the couple's chances of success. They cause constant trouble in the modern city, and only by stretching a point do they have any redeeming virtues at all. Only one thing can be said in their favor: If people marry to escape from a truly intolerable situation, then the new one *may* be less intolerable.

SUMMARY

For some people the search for a mate is a highly self-conscious one. For others, it follows so effortlessly from the fun of dating that no conscious decisions are made at all. But even for the person who floats through courtship, mate selection operates according to fairly precise social rules. Three theories help to explain this process. One is an ecological approach based on the inescapable fact that most of us marry people who live close by. Not only are neighbors more likely to meet, the time and cost involved in mate hunting far from home is usually prohibitive. Only the rich can afford it.

The theory of homogamy holds that people are attracted to persons very much like themselves. Empirical support for this is about as strong as for the ecological theory. In fact, residential segregation is an important basis for homogamy. But it has also been noted that role playing in marriage is made much easier by homogamous mating. The couple will then respond in similar ways to a great range of social cues and will probably find one another comfortable and satisfying. What is more, this gives a strong assurance that the marriage will re-create the kind of family life both husband and wife learned to prefer when they were children.

The theory of complementary needs holds that we are attracted to people whose personality traits complement our own. They can help us cope with the kinds of personal problems we are most likely to have. Evidence in support of this theory is not very impressive, but it has a certain plausibility not easy to deny. Actually, complementary traits can have a negative as well as a positive twist; people with personality problems may be attracted to persons who aggravate their personal troubles rather than relieve them.

It is likely that most people go through a weeding-out period of differential association in courtship. They meet many people in casual ways, but are attracted to those who are similar to themselves in terms of a broad variety of personal and social qualities. This establishes the homogamous base for marriage. Then there may be an opportunity for complementary needs to come into play, but not if the pressures to marry are so strong that the person cannot take his time. Finding a person like oneself in terms of the major social classifications is not so difficult; finding an ideal personality blend is a first-class challenge, and it cannot be done overnight.

After people who are more or less suited to one another have met, courtship escalators propel them toward marriage. Five of these are: satisfaction, milieu, public commitment, familiarity, and expediency. Each holds a key to trouble after marriage, because the forces that draw us to the altar are often totally different from the ones we have to live with when we settle down.

After the decision has been made, the couple can rush the ceremony, have a prolonged engagement, or work out some compromise in between. Engagements in the United States are often broken, but they do serve an important function: They change the character of the relationship, letting the couple see one another and their life together in a new light.

Efforts to predict success in marriage have had a curious history in the United States, based on two things in particular—the rise of behavioral science and concern about the divorce rate. Several kinds of premarital traits are known to have a bearing on marriage adjustment: relationships with key people in the person's background, childhood environmental conditions, events or the timing of events in the person's premarital life, and the person's psychological make-up. It is helpful for young couples contemplating marriage to review their prospects in the company of a marriage counselor and to review the potential dangers inherent in the courtship escalators.

Courtship may very well be the most crucial stage in a person's life. The divorce rate is high, of course, but most people do in fact stick with the first (and only) person they marry. There are other decisions that are also "life-binding"—occupational choice, for example—but none is more important than mate selection. We need all the help we can get in making a wise and sensible decision.

SELECTED READINGS

BOLTON, CHARLES D. "Mate Selection as the Development of a Relationship," *Marriage and Family Living*, Vol. 23 (August 1961), pp. 234–240.

GREENFIELD, SIDNEY M. "Love and Marriage in Modern America: A Functional Analysis," *Sociological Quarterly*, Vol. 6 (Autumn, 1965), pp. 361–377.

HEER, DAVID M. "Negro-White Marriage in the United States," *New Society*, Vol. 6 (August 1965), pp. 7–9.

KATZ, ALVIN M., AND REUBEN HILL. "Residential Propinquity and Marital Selection: A Review of Theory, Method, and Fact," *Journal of Marriage and the Family*, Vol. 20 (February 1958), pp. 27–35.

RUTLEDGE, AARON L. *Pre-Marital Counseling*. Cambridge, Mass.: Schenkman, 1966.

WINCH, ROBERT F. "Another Look at the Theory of Complementary Needs in Mate-Selection," *Journal of Marriage and the Family*, Vol. 29 (November 1967), pp. 756–762.

CHAPTER 8

The Legalities of Marriage

Broadly speaking, the entire sweep of history has been toward more formal and legalistic ways of assuring social order. As a result, the family has become less and less self-sufficient. Samuel Mencher (1967) argues that the industrial era in particular has called for repeated intervention by government into the "sacred" affairs of the home. The general trend has been described in various ways, such as a trend from *status* to *contract* (Maine 1885) or from *mechanical solidarity*, where people are held together by their common experiences, to *organic solidarity*, where they are united in a complex division of labor even though they have few beliefs or experiences in common (Durkheim 1893). The family itself is always founded on shared values more than anything else, but some people must still serve as judges when vital family interests come into conflict.

Even in the simplest societies family rules can be extremely complicated. In fact, this is where they are most complex. Only in modern nations have elaborate kinship rules lost their power. But in mass society impartial judges who know the law become increasingly necessary, along with an even larger group of pleaders and defenders to represent people who have no legal training.

At the same time, social change often brings new problems for which there are no legal solutions. In fact, the vast majority of laws dealing with sex and marriage are almost impossible to enforce. Alfred Kinsey (1953) concluded that less than 1 percent of the people committing sex violations are apprehended, prosecuted, or convicted. Many laws still on the books have lost their relevance; the circumstances that made them meaningful have long since disappeared.

Although family laws often go unenforced, they do not always lag behind new social developments. Sometimes they are far ahead of their time. In India, for example, a Child Marriage Restraint Act was passed in 1929 setting the minimum age of marriage for girls at fourteen, but it was almost totally disregarded (Chekki 1969). Among girls between the ages of five and fourteen in the 1951 Indian census, over 6 million were divorced or widowed. The law was in conflict with popular social norms and it could not be enforced, especially among poor people.

More recently a variety of welfare acts and laws have been introduced, which attempt to give equal rights to Indian women. These rulings have led to almost frantic reactions. D. A. Chekki (1969) contends that these laws have resulted in fierce family conflicts, and that matters will probably get worse unless the laws are changed. New welfare programs usually affect the family, but they accomplish little when they stand in direct opposition to traditional kinship patterns. Most people in India still count heavily on the family for both daily support and help in crises.

The legalities of family life cover a very broad range, but they tend to fall into five main areas: (1) the requirements for marriage, (2) the requirements for dissolution of marriage, (3) the responsibilities of parents to their children, (4) the rights of parents with regard to their children (covering child custody rights, which cause the most poignant and the most vicious legal struggles in the entire realm of family litigation), and (5) the rights to property vested in members of the family.

In each of the five areas, the laws are controversial and their effectiveness is virtually impossible to assess. But this is an inherent problem of any legal system. Who can say whether punishments imposed by the law are as effective as they should be? Laws are made by men (usually men of high status) to protect the values they respect, but there is no sure way to tell how wise these laws are (Litwak 1956). Capital punishment, for example, has been debated for many years, but critical tests of its effects have appeared only in the last quarter century, and they are still rare.

The legal requirements for entering marriage constitute the primary subject matter for this chapter, which is why it has been placed immediately after discussions of dating, love, and courtship, and just before the discussion of marriage adjustment. (Divorce will be taken up in Chapter 13.) We have explored the processes by which couples discover one another and decide to marry; their only remaining task is to meet the legal technicalities (which are almost always minimal and which virtually all couples can meet).

Marriage is, of course, a contract between individuals. But it is a special kind of contract, in which society itself has an interest. The notion that marriage is a unique legal status has been handed down from the English common law, and it is unique in two ways: (1) The contract cannot be broken by mutual agreement between the couple involved; it can only be dissolved by an act of the state itself. (In most private contracts the parties can modify, restrict, enlarge, or entirely abandon the agreement whenever they want to.) (2) The *legal capacity* to enter marriage is also given a special meaning; people can marry, for example, before they are old enough to make a binding business contract. At the same time, the right to marry and the choice of a mate are restricted by law in various ways, as in the rule against marriage between parents and children or brothers and sisters.

Generally, legal codes waver between protection of rights for the *individual* (whether married or not) and protection of the *institution* of marriage. Although there are often material advantages to being married (as when the married man files a joint income tax return), there are also distinct disadvantages. If domestic relations laws had been written solely for the purpose of giving special privileges to married people, they would be much different from what they are.

But any legal system that attempts to protect individual rights will at times give an advantage to the single person. In folklore it has often been presumed (by men) that the single man gives up freedom when he marries, in both an informal and a legal sense. Thus marriage seems to protect womanhood; without the legal and social constraints of weddings men might be able to exploit women without mercy. And yet another idea repeatedly expressed in the past century is that marriage laws serve primarily to keep women down. Clearly the trend is to weed out all laws that can be construed as favoring one sex over the other.

LEGAL REQUIREMENTS FOR MARRIAGE

It would be possible to have very strict and exacting rules for marriage. Politically there is no chance, but theoretically it could be done. The rules could be as tough as tests given for drivers' licenses or as the selective service standards used by the United States Marines. Marriage requirements are, of course, easy to meet in every state in the United States. If laws for marriage reflect the will of the people, and they probably do, then clearly there is no popular demand to make marriage difficult. The chief function of the existing rules is probably to keep records for the important legal *consequences* of marriage.

Thus, marriage is easy to get into but not so easy to get out of, and once you are married a number of legal burdens appear that can be avoided only by people who have nothing of value to share with others. Thus, a man is legally accountable for the financial support of his family, but what can the law do if he is broke? His family can only press the issue for spite, not support.

All states have certain basic qualifications for marriage, but people who cannot meet them are free to travel to a nearby state where the laws are not as strict, and that often happens. All states consider marriages valid if they were lawful at the time granted. State laws usually prescribe that a license must be obtained for the marriage to be legal, and they describe the content of the application along with the procedures for getting one. The marriage license itself serves two primary purposes: It can be denied when couples do not meet the legal requirements, and it helps in recording certain marriage statistics (again, almost always minimal).

Age

What are the standard legal requirements? For one thing, the couple must be old enough to marry. Historically, the minimum age has been about the time of puberty, but the modern trend has been upward. Parents can use their own discretion for two or three years (between the ages of about sixteen and twenty-one, depending on the sex of the child), and then the responsibility shifts to the offspring themselves.

What the minimal age *ought* to be is a moot point, but in most states the male must be twenty-one (without parental consent—eighteen with consent) and the female must be eighteen (sixteen with parental consent). Men are slightly more likely than women to lie about their age on marriage licenses. Dale Womble (1966) says efforts to keep age falsification under control are surprisingly casual; there is also some evidence that states with stricter age laws have higher rates of age falsification.

Nevertheless, men *are* usually a year or two older than women at the time of marriage, whether they need to be or not. But several states make no legal sex distinction. The difference is impossible to justify on scientific grounds in any case; it is simply a tribute to tradition and popular belief. Since women outlive men, and can now look forward to ever longer periods of widowhood, the tradition is probably outmoded. (Are eighteen-year-old girls more ready to make wise decisions than twenty-year-old males?)

Recent statistics show that age differences between newlyweds are actually going down (Parke and Glick 1967), probably because of greater equality between the sexes—laws as such have nothing to do with it. Where the double standard is strong, men are usually much older than their brides; where it is not, newlyweds are more similar in almost every respect. At the heart of the matter is the fact that boys and girls now spend more time together in childhood and adolescence. This not only equalizes the sexes, it also gives boys a better chance to compete for girls of their own age.

The most obvious reason for parental consent laws is that youth are not presumed to be wise enough to make sensible decisions about marriage; parents, who are older, presumably can. Another traditional reason is much more questionable in modern society. It holds that the minor child has certain duties to his parents—to remain in their custody and to render certain services to them. Thus, the laws are designed to assert the rights of parents and to protect people who are believed to be too young to protect themselves. This reflects social patterns of an earlier time when parents were much more directly involved in managing their children and when dating and courtship as we know them today hardly even existed.

But David Gover and Dorothy Jones (1964) collected some data that suggest that parental consent laws have little influence on early marriages anyway. When young couples are determined to marry, they do. And when they no longer need their parents' consent, they are no more likely to marry than persons of the same age who live in states where parental consent is required. Ira Rosenwaike (1967) concludes that parental consent laws do not deter marriage so much as they cause young couples to head for another state. Brides are younger where age laws are more lenient, but apparently largely because they are drawn from out of state.

All age laws are extremely hard to enforce. In fact, underage marriages are not *void*; they are simply *voidable*, which means that legal action has to be taken to annul them. This can be contrasted with a bigamous marriage, for example, which is void on the face of it; it is null as soon as the woman discovers the man's true status, and no court action is usually called for. A voidable marriage is considered valid until it is nullified by an appropriate court proceeding (which must occur during the couple's lifetime).

Underage is by far the most common grounds for voiding marriages (but certainly not the only one). "Shotgun" grooms, husbands of frigid wives, and brides of homosexuals can usually get annulments. But in some states the distinction between void and voidable marriages has never been cleared up (by either the courts or the legislature) and that can mean bitter legal hassles.

Incest

Formal incest taboos are found wherever an established legal system exists, but their enforcement has very little to do with laws. As noted in Chapter 2, children learn to abhor incest at an early age, law or no law, and they reject any thought of marriage to parents or siblings. Cousins are another matter. They are preferred for marriage in many societies, and second or third cousins are still sometimes preferred in our own upper classes—where kinship obligations remain relatively strong. Nonliterate societies can have extremely complicated incest taboos, but no formal legal system at all. This complexity reflects the social importance attached to incest. The most general rule seems to be this: The more complex the kinship structure in a society, the more complex its incest rules, but people who are closely related are also more often eligible to marry where the rules are intricate.

In America the laws vary from state to state. All states prohibit marriage to one's son or daughter, mother or father, grandmother or grandfather, sister or brother, aunt or uncle, niece or nephew, and over half of the states ban the marriage of first cousins. The old "affinity" law (prohibiting marriage to a former spouse's blood kin) has been dropped almost everywhere in the country.

Mental Retardation and Mental Health

Several states have laws specifically prohibiting marriage for the mentally retarded, but in the absence of any generally accepted definition of mental retardation, the pattern is very uneven. The fact is that many people marry who are mentally retarded by some authority's definition.

Most states also have laws against marriage for people who are mentally ill, or "insane," but experts do not agree on the legal definitions of these terms either. Presumably, anybody who is seriously mentally ill is incapable of giving genuine consent in marriage, so the marriage is at least voidable. Furthermore, a person who suffers to the point of insanity would probably create severe problems for all concerned, especially children. The whole question of *personality prerequisites* for marriage will probably receive extensive legal review as the fields of psychology and psychiatry mature in years to come.

Race

Laws restricting interracial marriages were passed at one time or another in almost every state, but they have all been declared unconstitutional. No one can be prohibited by law from marrying the person of his choice for racial reasons. But, just as the avoidance of incest is almost totally independent of legal action on the subject, it is doubtful that laws have much effect on interracial courtship. *Miscegenation* is policed informally by all the forces of homogamy discussed earlier.

Still, rates of interracial marriage might possibly increase as prejudice, segregation, and discrimination decline, especially between black males and white females (Heer 1965). That is the combination that has always been most frequent. Perhaps, as David Heer suggests, this is because males usually take the initiative in proposing marriage in the United States and, due to traditional patterns of racial bias, black males have more self-esteem to gain by marrying white women than white males have to gain by marrying black women. But as this paragraph is being written it is quite apparent that the perception of color differences is in flux among both blacks and whites. For one thing, an intense reaction has set in to the old bias favoring lighter skin color within the black community itself. The "black is beautiful" point of view may have long-term implications for racial intermarriage, but whether it results in higher or lower rates remains to be seen.

Health

Efforts to set health standards for marriage have waxed and waned in the twentieth century, although interest has never run very strong. The most recent concern turns to genetic traits, due to some rather startling scientific breakthroughs in genetics. But these have had hardly any impact on the law as yet. Suffice it to say that there is ample room for reform with regard to medical examinations before marriage.

The requirement of a blood or serological test to screen people for venereal diseases became popular in the 1930s. This started in the midst of national anxiety about syphilis and gonorrhea; public concern seems to have cooled off, but the threat of venereal disease is probably as great as ever. Tests to spot venereal disease are now common in the United States, despite their serious shortcomings (Clarke 1957). In some states, for example, women do not have to take them, and the inspections are often handled in a very superficial, if not sloppy way. Some places do an excellent job, but some are not so careful.

Rarely are health examinations required beyond the blood test, although such tests can be used to identify other problems than venereal disease if they are done properly. In a few states the time required to process the blood sample may amount to little more than a waiting period before marriage. (Of course this would be true only where a waiting period is not specifically set by law.) In any case, unusually strict laws can be dodged through out-of-state marriage.

Waiting Periods

Legal waiting periods exist in many states. They vary, usually from one to five days, hardly ever more, and can take several forms. The most common procedure is simply to set a mandatory interval between the date of application for a license and the time it can be issued. In some states a period of time must elapse after the license is conferred before the marriage can take place; it is also possible to have a waiting period before the license is issued and then another waiting period after it has been granted.

Studies in this area are scarce and as yet inconclusive, but at least some evidence indicates that the longer the waiting period, the greater the number of couples who will break up in the interim and never marry. One study showed that some couples, when they had to register and then return later to pick up the marriage license, never came back; the couples who did not return seemed to be the ones who were the poorest risks in marriage (Shipmen and Tien 1965). Almost any obstacle standing in the way of marriage seems to discourage some people. Presumably these are the ones who are only weakly committed to marry or for whom the thrill of one romantic moment may not last for even a day or two. Most of these couples are probably relieved, in retrospect, that they dropped out.

The Ceremony

Some sort of ceremony is legally required in all states; but the formal demands are very loose, so the wedding ritual can be extremely variable. The legal essentials are met by four conditions in virtually all states: (1) having a marriage license, (2) stating assent to the marriage at a ceremony presided over by a qualified official—when clergymen perform the ceremony they serve as civil officials in addition to the religious symbolism they supply, (3) having witnesses, and (4) giving a properly completed marriage certificate to the appropriate recording official. The wording of the ceremony can include almost anything at all, so long as statements of agreement to the marriage are included. Many ministers, especially on college campuses, now encourage the young couple to write their own wedding script. And the ceremony can be held in almost any conceivable setting. Weddings have been performed in parks, on beaches and mountaintops, underwater in a fish tank with diving gear, and in the nude (*Time*, July 4, 1969, p. 57.). The ceremony will come up again in the next chapter.

Breach of Promise

One kind of action that has almost disappeared is the breach of promise or "heart balm" suit, where a woman (it is virtually always a woman) sues her reluctant suitor, claiming that he said he would marry her and that she has suffered from his broken promise. Support for such suits once existed, but they conflict with current thinking about courtship and its purpose. One function of the engagement is to give the couple a last chance to find out if they are truly suited to one another; if there is reason for doubt, then the engagement *should* be broken.

Like all legal actions, this kind of suit has a long history. It can be traced all the way back to the "precontract" phase of marriage among the ancient Hebrews. Now it is outlawed in most states, and most people take it for granted that the legal obligations of marriage do not begin until the wedding vows. Until that time a promise is worth what the character of the individual who makes it is worth, no more.

In fact, suspicion of breach of promise suits is hardly new. They have been used by women to harass or blackmail wealthy men and have rarely been available to men at all. Awards were sometimes outrageous, and, where blackmail was not at the root of the matter, the publicity itself could be extremely damaging (Clarke 1957). But broken engagements still cause an occasional legal skirmish. Lawsuits over the engagement ring are sometimes filed, for example. Who does it belong to when the couple break up? Most girls are happy enough to give it back, but not necessarily. The weight of authority is that she must return it, on the grounds that it is unfair for a person to keep the fruit of a broken promise (Goldstein and Katz, 1965, pp. 568–570).

Common-Law Marriage

Common-law marriage occurs where couples live together as man and wife, with or without children, by-passing the marriage license, the wedding ceremony, and the marriage certificate. Although it can happen under a great variety of circumstances, it is most likely to occur where people are only weakly bound and protected by the legal customs of the community. (A new problem has come up recently in establishing the legal status of communal families. Fourteen persons living together in two "voluntary" families in Palo Alto, California, brought suit claiming the same legal protection as other families; the judge ruled against them on the grounds that membership in the groups fluctuated and that members had no legal obligations of support or cohabitation [*Time* Magazine, 1971].)

Common-law marriage seemed understandable in the American past in situations where nobody was available to perform the ceremony, but that rarely occurs now. It was not objectionable for the couple to live together rather than endure a prolonged and perhaps tense delay. The couple could legitimize their marriage when they got the chance, although circumstances sometimes changed, or they may never have gotten around to it. These marriages were valid as long as the couple were legally marriageable—that is, if they met all the eligibility requirements for marriage—and lived together as husband and wife, presenting themselves to others in the community as a married pair (Goldstein and Katz, 1965, pp. 584–585).

Common-law marriages assume an entirely different meaning in countries where large numbers of people simply do not use formal legal procedures.

This is true of places where relatively few people are rich and the bulk of the population live in poverty (or very close to the poverty line). A study by Hyman Rodman (1961) in Trinidad, for example, tells about two alternatives to the standard marriage pattern: *friending*, and simple cohabitation. In the case of friending, the man visits his woman at intervals for sex relations and may help to support any children they have. The children are given his surname, but he can disown or neglect them with virtual impunity. Another possibility is for the couple simply to live together. But they are not legally married and may be independent of one another in important ways—in money matters, for example. These alternatives are more common than marriage itself in Trinidad because marriage means heavy economic obligations for men under circumstances where poverty is standard.

The culture of poverty is most characteristic of peasant societies, although we have it in America, too. For people of higher status, formal marriage is almost always followed. Rich people carry on their affairs in a context of legality and propriety, at least in most spheres of life, but the legal system applies to poor people only in the sense that they can get into trouble through violence or theft. Under these circumstances many couples live together without benefit of a formal wedding, a fact which is rarely a matter of alarmed public concern. Poor people in the United States live outside the mainstream of middle-class (or even working-class) life. Here we find fear, hostility, and sheer ignorance concerning many routine legal matters, and the formal trappings of marriage are not always taken very seriously. Enforcing marriage laws is not easy, to say the least, but forgoing use of certificates and other formalities can still create some serious problems. Records of vital statistics cannot be as accurate as we would like, for example, although this is a general problem in the lower socioeconomic levels; the collection of personal and family information for various purposes is almost impossible wherever the culture of poverty exists. This means that common-law marriage hampers efforts to improve family life by either government or private agencies. Some people may be against such efforts in the first place, but they are in fact made, and interference with personal freedom is rarely (if ever) their intention.

Common-law marriages also create confusion over inheritance and property rights and the legitimacy of children. If one of the parties says he had no *intention* to marry—which is required to make a common-law marriage valid—there can be serious and lengthy legal tangles. But once again these matters are of much greater concern in the middle classes than in the lower classes. Inheritance is not likely to be a problem for poor people. Conflicts over property rights would cause much greater problems than they do if it were not for the fact that claims are usually settled informally. The woman, for example, is usually ensconced in the household; her husband is often gone precisely because he did not make very much money and had no property to defend. Since children stay with the mother and are probably considered "hers," it is easy to see who keeps most of the property.

All of this does not mean that common-law marriage is nothing to be concerned about. But the fact remains that where income is high, property is extensive, and illegitimacy is considered a terrible humiliation (and illegitimate children are usually put up for adoption), people are almost certain to live by the laws and fill out all the forms. That is the best way to protect their personal as well as family interests. Where people have low status and nothing to gain, they simply do not go to very much trouble. Sometimes considerable hardship and expense is required; the really significant question, in fact, is why they bother to meet legal requirements as often as they do.

Love and the Law

One final observation is in order concerning the fact that there is virtually no way to exercise legal controls over love. As we all know, the stress on love as the basis for marriage is no trivial matter. The search for a love partner or simply for love assumes great importance in America. We should not only expect people to be very sensitive about their personal romantic needs, but that a profitable industry would spring up to meet the demand. It has indeed. We should also expect some people to be inept in their search, more than a little frustrated as a result, and easy prey to exploitation by unscrupulous people. That is where the law could conceivably step in, but it is precisely at this point that it is sadly helpless.

In Chapter 6 we talked about William Goode's (1959) idea that the romantic basis for marriage has, until fairly recent times, been systematically suppressed. It had to be restrained because marriages based on love threaten the solidarity of kinship groups. Only where kinship ties are weak can love be unleashed. Goode's point seems to be essentially correct, but decisions based on a *need* for love can be very irrational in any kind of society, and they do not always promote the best interests of the people involved. Since kinship controls are now so weak, two kinds of protection are left. One is legal control, but, as we have seen, that cannot be of much help. The other possibility is the person's own knowledge and resourcefulness. Since we acquire a need for love as we grow up, we also need—for the sake of balance—equal training in how to handle it. The solution to this dilemma can only be found in child rearing or education, not in the courts. Maybe it is only wishful thinking, but it does seem that the *interpersonal competence* acquired by children in contemporary society in the normal course of peer group interaction often includes powers of self-protection in just this area.

THE LAW AFTER MARRIAGE

After marriage the law turns to the couple's rights and responsibilities, and the latter get a good deal more attention than the former. Before they have children, the couple's main obligation is simply to remain married but, failing that, to meet all the technicalities of divorce before marrying again. (Divorce laws will be reviewed in Chapter 13.) Property rights and obligations take effect as soon as the marriage is official, and various public and private agencies are needed just to keep the records straight.

When children are born, the couple assume legal responsibilities as parents. (Laws even include responsibilities for the prenatal period now, and we can foresee the day when birth planning will be subject to tough legal controls.) Though a hodgepodge of laws exists describing the obligations of parents to children and children to parents, they are among the least enforceable ones we have. Any attempts to give them force are inevitably challenged by defenders of the sanctity of the home.

As a parent, I was alarmed at the power I had over my children when they were young (and in their most impressionable years). Whereas I cannot hit another person without instant censure, I am free to swat my children—and there are those who will say I am shirking my duty if I do not. Laws to protect children from the battering of angry or disturbed parents exist, of course, but only for outbursts reaching a state of hysteria. In fact, the greatest violence parents do to their children is probably not covered by law at all. *Psychological violence* to the developing self-image, to the child's basic sense of identity and security, is not subject to any legal control.

Abortion Laws

Laws restricting abortion affect young women before marriage, but they apply to married couples as well. Most abortions are in fact arranged for married women, especially those in their third, fourth, and later pregnancies. Having failed to use effective contraceptives, but not wanting the child, they resort to abortion (Crawley *et al.* 1964). Until very recently the laws have virtually forced women in such cases to have an illegal operation, since abortion laws have been very strict. The only alternative was to have the baby.

In recent years a number of states have liberalized laws for abortion, so that four kinds now exist. First is the spontaneous abortion (or miscarriage), which occurs naturally and without being induced. It is the body's way of bringing an abnormal pregnancy to an end. Efforts to cause miscarriages by pounding the abdomen, falling, or taking exotic potions virtually never work.

Second is the illegal abortion, induced contrary to state laws. It may be handled by a licensed physician, but then again it may not. These are more dangerous than they need to be, partly because of the possible inferior qualifications of the practitioner, but also because of the need to take shortcuts and maintain secrecy. (Under the most favorable circumstances abortions in the first three months of pregnancy can be reasonably safe, although there is always some danger.) Estimates of the number of illegal abortions in the United States range as high as 2 million a year, but accurate statistics are nonexistent.

The third kind of abortion is the therapeutic variety, where the life of the expectant mother may be endangered by childbirth. Usually a panel of doctors is appointed to decide whether the woman qualifies, and each doctor has the power to veto the request. Therapeutic abortions granted under strict medical controls are far too infrequent to handle the great demand for abortions now existing in the United States.

Social status is a factor in this pattern, because women of higher economic position are apparently more likely to qualify for therapeutic abortions in the private hospitals to which they go. Women of lower economic status more often use public health facilities, where such abortions are performed less often.

A fourth kind of abortion is now permissible in a few states. It is one where the woman simply makes arrangements with a doctor to perform the operation; it has no therapeutic implications. Pressures to legalize this kind of abortion are based on the assumption that each woman has a right to decide if she wants to have the baby. They also assume that no baby should be born that is not wanted.

It seems obvious that abortion usually represents an action taken only after the failure to use effective contraceptives. Some women may prefer occasional abortions to the use of pregnancy prevention techniques, but the great majority seem to prefer the latter. Efforts to improve family planning before pregnancy will help to reduce the need for abortions. In the meantime, abortions—illegal, therapeutic, or by legal choice—will remain frequent, with a strong trend toward the third category: personal choice without violation of law.

AVENUES OF REFORM

Many of the laws governing marriage and family life are controversial. Defenders are numerous, but critics are just as easy to find. It would seem that almost everybody has some pet reform he would enact if given a chance, and some people would settle for no less than an overhaul of the whole system. Possible reforms concerning requirements for marriage will be discussed here, leaving the subject of reform in other areas to the chapter on divorce and to the concluding chapter of the text.

One kind of change that seems to be welcome is the drift toward more uniform laws across state boundaries. Hardly anyone still argues that the states have marriage problems so different from one another as to require fifty special codes, although some writers do caution against destroying the rich diversity in American society (Cohen and Connery 1967). The growth of the middle classes, with a predominantly suburban orientation to life, creates a strong pressure toward uniformity. If five days is a reasonable waiting period in Florida, it is probably reasonable in Oregon, too.

If anything, the trend toward uniformity is moving too slowly. Pressure for quicker adoption of certain laws is evident, such as for those that make the weddings of runaway minors voidable. But the actual process of unifying marriage codes can only follow an exasperatingly slow timetable. Lawmakers in any given state are not impressed by the argument that they should change a law just to make it similar to one in some other state—unless by not doing so they lose business, tourists, or tax revenues. Rarely do marriage laws have a powerful impact on business, although it is true that in some states—such as Nevada—they seem to tie in very well with the tourist trade. Still, the fact that marriage laws vary from one state to another rarely causes hardships that can stir up the voters. Efforts to overhaul family laws have been made in many states, but usually less to revise than to clarify or to make them more consistent with one another.

One desirable reform would simply be better recordkeeping. We live in a record-keeping society, in which the amount of data on file about each citizen is enormous by past standards. But better ways to tabulate the statistics have long been sought by family professionals. Reliable information is needed to evaluate almost any change that might be proposed—and also to defend current practices that are under attack. Better records would be invaluable to a great many people whose status is in legal limbo for lack of accurate information.

The legal requirements for marriage could certainly be made more exacting, as many people have argued, and for at least two reasons: (1) to put the legal status of marriage on a level commensurate with its social importance, and (2) to protect individuals from themselves more than is now encouraged by the law. Our divorce laws are relatively strict, presumably for this very reason—to give couples a chance to think seriously before taking the final step. The argument for a longer waiting period before marriage is usually proposed in just this context. (But if this change is made in only one state, many couples will simply cross the border to marry in another—as they already do at a time when no state has a truly long waiting requirement.) It might also be noted that the laws for re-marriage need not be the same as those for first marriages, since the cir-cumstances, including the presence of children, are often much different (Kargman 1969).

Another reform would be to require more complete medical checkups, especially in the light of modern genetics. H. Bentley Glass, for example, argues that each couple should have to visit a genetic clinic before mar-riage, to be forewarned if genetic factors are present that could hurt the health of a child. The requirement of a general health checkup for young couples is not an unreasonable one; its purpose is not necessarily to protect unborn children, but rather to inform the couple about themselves in what is surely an important aspect of life.

Couples in the upper-middle classes already have fairly thorough health examinations before marriage as a rule. Extending this practice to the lower classes could be done, but it would take more than a new law; it would have to be accompanied by cheap or free medical facilities. This might be considered a luxury that our nation cannot afford, but upgrading marriage in the lower classes is certainly not a worthless frill. The peace-time welfare potential of America has by no means been realized in the twentieth century.

Perhaps even premarital counseling could be incorporated into the legal framework of marriage. All couples would not have to have it—although that might be advisable—but rather it would simply be available to them as a matter of course, a service financed by the community itself (no doubt with federal assistance, since almost any service getting more than mini-mal economic support now receives federal aid). Couples seeking a mar-riage license could be given information about the nature of services avail-able and exactly where and how these can be used. Ideally the couple would have to make a decision *not* to have counseling (if that was their preference) rather than the current pattern where couples must make a positive effort, going to some trouble and expense, to get it. The present system guarantees that some people will be left out; facilities must be more than simply *available* to poor people: they must be actively *delivered*, be-cause people in poverty are cut off from the mainstream of community life (Andrew 1968).

Premarital counseling could easily be linked to facilities for physical ex-aminations. We could have an impressive building, housing the various agencies concerned with marriage, including a section for premarital coun-seling. Even attractive civil marriage ceremonies could be made more generally available. Most (more than three out of four) American wed-dings are held in churches; their elaborateness varies, although it seems safe to say that the majority are quite dramatic. Many are staged in a church because the religious site represents the popular image of a proper wedding, independent of the religious sentiments of the couples involved. Lawful weddings can be held almost anywhere, of course, and they certainly are, as already noted. Nevertheless, handsome places for marriages could be arranged to meet the needs of people who want nonchurch weddings but lack the facilities. The community building set aside for family services might be rented at modest cost. Secular "marriage palaces" have been available in Moscow for some time, complete with waiting rooms, banquet halls, flower gardens, souvenir shops, courtyards, registration rooms, and wedding parlors (Gribov 1960). Secular facilities also exist in America in such places as Reno and Las Vegas, but church weddings seem to serve well enough in most parts of the country. When the need for different arrangements becomes strong, Americans will probably find a way.

It is not the purpose of this chapter to argue for any particular reform, but rather to call attention to some of the alternative possibilities. Basically, Americans are committed to a legalistic approach to many sensitive family problems. Furthermore, the *status function* of the family, whereby children are ascribed the status of their parents, is deeply entrenched in our legal system, as it is in every other Western nation. The wealth of parents is vested in themselves and their offspring, and there is more to this than law alone; the present system is considered moral and just. Certain difficulties exist in passing wealth from parents to children in highly socialized nations, but even there the family is still status bound enough to assure that what parents have, their children tend to get. The family system as mankind has known it so far seems to be inherently conservative. It takes care of its own, and laws either assist in the process or only minimally interfere with it. In the nonsocialist nations laws almost always reinforce a key function of the family: to preserve the broad outlines of the class system. Control of wealth by the family is the cornerstone of this system. At the same time, these laws assert the individual's obligations to his family, such as the father's legal responsibilities to his children, and the other side of the coin—the rights of parents as legal guardians. Is it possible to conceive of a legal system that consistently tries to make it difficult for family members to pass their status, their style, their money, and their possessions to children? That may seem rather doubtful, and perhaps subversive beyond all sound reason, but this point will come up again in the final chapter of the book.

SUMMARY

Laws affecting the family, especially those stating the qualifications for marriage, are minimal. Almost all laws affecting the family are hard to enforce, and the reasons given to justify them are not always convincing. But there seems to be little public sentiment to make marriage hard to enter into. By and large, a high marriage rate is considered a sign of community health, and laws waver between protecting the rights of individuals and the institution of marriage.

Age requirements are specified in all states, and fairly serious efforts are made to enforce them. But they are policed mainly by the family itself, and the couple's friends. Underage marriages are most likely to occur in the lower classes where taboos against them are not so strong. They are least likely to be annulled at this level, too.

Laws against incest are found in all states, and yet incest is controlled almost completely by teaching children to abhor it. Efforts to prevent marriage among the mentally ill or mentally retarded, on the other hand, are much more difficult, largely because of ambiguities in definition. Interracial marriages have been and continue to be infrequent because of racial segregation, prejudice, and the general tendency toward homogamy, but laws designed to forbid interracial marriage are clearly unconstitutional.

Health requirements for marriage are minimal, as are legal waiting periods. Usually only a few days' delay is required after application before the marriage license is issued, at which time the couple is free to marry in most states. The ceremony itself can take almost any form, requiring only an appropriate presiding official, assent to marriage by the couple, witnesses, and a completed marriage certificate.

Once the couple have married, the law becomes more demanding. Property in particular is carefully watched, since laws are by no means indifferent to rights and claims of a material nature. After children are born, the couple take on the legal responsibilities of parents, and they are given extremely broad powers over their children. The law is much more concerned with property than with the rights of children.

Many legal reforms have been proposed in the twentieth century. Most observers wish we could have more uniformity in the different states and a better system of family record keeping. The legal requirements for marriage itself could be more demanding, or minimum qualifications for parenthood could be introduced. Any couple eligible to marry is now automatically qualified to have children, but this pattern will probably face growing criticism in years to come. There are also good reasons for making premarital counseling more available to young couples. Even attractive civil marriage facilities might be made more widely available.

Perhaps the most important fact underlying this entire discussion is that the family serves a status-conferring function, one which is deeply rooted in our legal system. Not only *can* the wealth of parents be passed on to their children, the law encourages it to be (as do the mores). In this basic way the family is an essentially conservative institution. It keeps wealth in the family line and places children in the same relative status position as their parents.

SELECTED READINGS

AMERICAN SOCIOLOGICAL ASSOCIATION COMMITTEE ON MARRIAGE AND DIVORCE STATISTICS. "The Need for Nationwide Marriage and Divorce Statistics," *American Sociological Review*, Vol. 23 (June 1958), pp. 306–312.

CLARKE, HELEN I. *Social Legislation.* New York: Appleton-Century-Crofts, 1957.

COHEN, NATHAN E., AND MAURICE F. CONNERY. "Government Policy and the Family," *Journal of Marriage and the Family*, Vol. 29 (February 1967), pp. 6–17.

GOLDSTEIN, JOSEPH, AND JAY KATZ. *The Family and the Law.* New York: The Free Press, 1965.

HEDRICK, A. W., AND CHARLOTTE SILVERMAN. "Should the Premarital Blood Test Be Compulsory?" *American Journal of Public Health*, Vol. 254 (February 1958), pp. 125–132.

LITWAK, EUGENE. "Three Ways in Which Law Acts as a Means of Social Control: Punishment, Therapy, and Education," *Social Forces*, Vol. 34 (March 1956), pp. 217–223.

MENCHER, SAMUEL. "Social Authority and the Family," *Journal of Marriage and the Family*, Vol. 29 (February 1967), pp. 164–192.

PART THREE

Married Life: Adjustment and Change

CHAPTER 9

Beginnings: The Wedding, Honeymoon, and Early Adjustment

Family life covers four very broad processes: anticipation, formation, accommodation, and dissolution. Anticipations of marriage were discussed in Part II of this book, particularly in Chapter 3. The formation of marriage was also discussed in Part II, in Chapters 7 and 8 on mate selection, engagement, and the legal requirements for marriage. In this and the next three chapters we turn to accommodation. When that breaks down, dissolution is the result, and that will be taken up later.

As family adjustment is discussed, we should bear in mind that although the breakup of a family is traumatic precisely because we set our hopes so high, it must occur sooner or later. It is all the more inevitable where people put their trust in the small, nuclear family. The large family system approaches immortality—it can last for generations, perhaps even centuries, as a recognizable social unit. Any nuclear family that can keep its identity for two or more generations is an unusual one indeed. An important factor in our current unease is a growing awareness of just how brittle the family is. People can no longer depend on it as their one social certainty, as they could in the past.

Problems within the family are made more acute as its existence becomes more uncertain. And the very conditions that undermine the large family system increase the possibilities for trouble in the small family. As people live longer, for example, they have a greater variety of problems to adjust to in the course of the normal lifetime. They must adjust to the stage in marriage before children are born, to the rearing of infants and small children, to new developments when the children enter adolescence (there is probably just as much storm and stress for parents as for teen-agers), to the period of active maturity after the children leave home, to the period of retirement and high rates of widowhood from ages sixty-five to seventy-five, and to the period of chronic health problems and chilling *disengagement* after that. Not only has old age been extended, so has middle age, especially in the sense that more people manage to survive until the time of retirement. But adjustment to youthful maturity comes first. Let us start at the beginning—with the wedding.

THE WEDDING

The significance of the wedding ceremony to the couple and to society at large depends on the general place of ritual in the community. The United States is not a particularly ritualistic society, although much depends on what is meant by the word "ritual." It usually refers to a specific event where traditional roles are acted out in highly stylized ways. Thus, most weddings are rituals, and they are viewed as such by members of the community. Someone might argue that workers who line up to receive their pay checks are acting out a ritual or that when the United States delegate to the United Nations denounces communism he is simply performing a ritual act, but these are very loose usages of the term. Most people do not interpret such acts that way. In the narrow, technical sense of the term "ritual," the United States is not a ritualistic nation. Indeed, even in the broadest sense of the term Americans are usually described as nonritualistic by comparison with European nations and most other cultures in the world. We have been so regarded ever since Alexis de Tocqueville's (1956) remarkable essays on American democracy were first published in the 1830s.

Since potent rituals are so few in America, the ones that remain are probably made more dramatic than they would otherwise be. The critical situations that have a sense of inexpressible sanctity are the crises of marriage and death, and the most stirring ceremonies are used to dramatize these events: weddings and funerals. Both serve the key function of cere-monialism—of unifying people in their common commitments (above and beyond the specific uses they may have for the individuals most immedi-ately involved). Even these rites may seem empty in a society crowded with headline-making events and a steady diet of television. Still, when people attend a wedding or funeral they are almost certain to be struck by a sense of realism that the mass media can rarely capture. These are indeed significant occasions in people's lives.

They ease the transition for all concerned by allowing the full expression of their personal and social feelings (Gluckman 1963). Arnold van Gennep

(1909) argues that marriage is basically "the incorporation of strangers into groups"; newlyweds are dramatically welcomed into the clan. As the couple's social position changes, so does their image of themselves, their behavior, and their expectations of others. But the wedding is a concern not only of the bride and groom. It is an affair of the larger community to which they belong (Rapoport 1962). This is true even in the United States where the separateness of the couple is stressed more than in most countries. Philip Slater (1963) suggests that the pranks played on honeymooners reflect our worry that they will become too detached.

In the last chapter it was noted that three-fourths of the marriages in the United States occur in churches. This provides a religious setting for many couples who are otherwise only weakly attached to any organized church. Apparently church weddings are important for both the church and our image of marriage. Without them the generally favorable, even sacred, image of organized religion would probably not be quite so strong. Marriage has not always been considered a religious affair, however, and in early colonial times there was strong sentiment *against* church authorities having anything to do with weddings. (Anticlerical feeling ran high at that time in many other ways as well.) But since that early American experience the sentiment has shifted radically; the idea that marriage is, or ought to be, a religious affair has taken over on a very broad front. It is certainly possible that the sacredness attached to marriage has helped to balance the debunking and secularizing trends in our society, which could have made marriage an even weaker institution than it already is.

Unfortunately, the range of feelings that people hold about marriage as a sacred event has never been studied. Some people undoubtedly think of it more unconditionally in this way than others, and some attach no sense of sacredness to it at all. It seems likely that if people were asked whether they had given any thought to the possibility of divorce *before* they married (that is, if all attempts to make marriage work failed, would they get a divorce?), we would discover that many had indeed considered the possibility. Willingness to think of marriage as a temporary arrangement is probably most prevalent among non-Catholics and among people not affiliated with any church.

Having a church wedding is mildly associated with success in marriage, although no causal connection has been shown to exist between the two. Some critics claim that the marital success of people who have church weddings may simply mean that they are conservative and conventional— the church ceremony is the most conventional wedding a couple can have, and the people who choose it are also the most conservative. But conventional people are not only less likely to seek divorce (independent of how effective their marriages may be), they are more likely to answer marriage adjustment questionnaires in conventional ways, thus giving the appearance of greater happiness than may actually be the case (Ellis 1948; Edmonds 1967). People who are married in a church are also more often part of a conforming neighborhood—a supporting milieu—which helps to stabilize the marriage. Any rift between the couple will probably lead to reactions by friends and kinsmen, all under the traditional influence of the church. Hence, rifts are either healed or covered over.

THEORIES OF THE WEDDING

Why do some groups or cultures have more elaborate wedding ceremonies than others? One possible reason is that those cultures that give a religious or transcendental meaning to marriage are more likely to have elaborate rituals, tying them in with their guiding myths and religious themes. Perhaps where weddings are highly ritualistic, ritual in general is stressed. But that does not seem to be true in modern America. Nor for that matter does there seem to be any necessary connection between the significance attached to weddings and how elaborate they are.

A *family obligations theory* of the wedding is another possibility: Couples who are expected to assume heavy family responsibilities after marriage have the most elaborate weddings. The wedding becomes a social occasion to dramatize marriage responsibilities; the greater they are, the more impressive the wedding. If this is true, elaborateness would most likely occur where the large kinship group is stressed. But there are too many troubling exceptions to this rule. The Old Order Amish in America, for example, are extremely familistic but have weddings noted for their simplicity. The Amish may be merely an exception, but it is tempting to think that the degree to which kinship is stressed may be beside the point. In our own society married couples often have extensive obligations after marriage, but not necessarily to relatives. They can be socially obligated to friends, business associates, fellow church members, and so on, and it would seem that the more the couple is part of a large social circle, kinship or not, the more likely they are to have a big wedding. People in their circle attend the wedding and convey their hope that the marriage will succeed. In effect, they admonish the couple to try to *make* it succeed.

A *potlatch theory* of the wedding provides still another possibility. It holds that there is an element of conspicuous display and waste in weddings, comparable to the "potlatches" once held among Indian tribesmen of the American Northwest. During potlatch rituals wealth (in the form of furs, blankets, copper shields, carved dishes, and other property) was garishly destroyed or given away as a means of gaining social status. In this view, weddings symbolize the social position not only of the bride and groom but of the people who attend. This is underscored by the gifts given, the dowry provided, or the bride price paid.

We now have commercial advisers in the United States for almost every facet of the wedding—gowns, photographs, attendants, the staging of the ceremony, and so on. In most cases they openly suggest that parents of the bride spend as much as they can possibly afford. The potlatch angle also suggests that elaborate weddings will be characteristic of societies where some families have more wealth than they know what to do with; one way of publicly proving this enviable fact is to stage grand, expensive weddings. This helps to explain why some families and some cultures have more elaborate weddings than others. However, if a tribe or nation had strong inhibitions against the ostentatious display of wealth and cultivated an apollonian style of subtlety and grace, the weddings of upper-class couples would more likely be meticulously correct than big and overpowering.

One last theory deserves mention: the *family precariousness theory*. It proposes that the greater the general instability or precariousness of family life in a society, the more elaborate its weddings will be. It certainly seems plausible that where the chances for marriage success are not high, a way to improve the odds would be to dramatize the wedding (as suggested also in the family obligations theory).

But the opposite actually seems to occur; couples who have the greatest chance for success (no matter what kind of wedding they have) are the ones who have the most impressive ceremonies. But surely the ceremony does not cause stability; it is merely a symptom of it, one small part of the total configuration. Both marriage stability and the big wedding, in this case, are linked to a favorable social and economic inheritance. The more wealth the family can pass on to the new generation, the more ornate a wedding they will have and the more substantial social supports the marriage will have.

By way of summary, we can predict with some confidence which couples within a particular society are likely to have the most elaborate weddings— they come from families of higher status, ones with wealth both to spend and to transmit to their children. Such families place great importance on marriage and stress strong social obligations for the newlyweds. No good theory can explain why some societies stress the wedding ceremony more than others, although it is apparent that weddings will be exceptionally elaborate where there are few taboos against the conspicuous display of wealth or where people actually admire ostentatious social exhibitions.

THE HONEYMOON

After the wedding some couples return immediately to their daily routines, but the majority postpone reality for a few days at the very least. Of the sample studied by Theodore Johannis (1959a), 84 percent took honeymoons, as did 95 percent of a sample studied by August Hollingshead

(1952). The median length was seven days in Johannis' group; nine in that of Hollingshead. In a sense it is expected behavior, but the idea of having a vacation from humdrum routine after marriage is so widespread in the world as to suggest that there is an immediately recognizable need for it—especially when the wedding has been an elaborate one. (This last point is important, and we shall return to it later.)

Post-wedding activities take many forms and can be traumatic as well as fun. Anthropologists have been impressed with the profusion of symbolic practices immediately following marriage. Reports call attention to such rites as the display of the bride's hymeneal blood, ordeals for the bride or groom or both, ritual defloration, and seclusion of one or both partners (Westermarck 1891). Rhona and Robert Rapoport (1964) contend that only in fairly rich countries can the newlyweds get away from their customary social obligations for very long. In fact, many American couples in this small study were anxious to get back home by the time their honeymoon ended, and some of them returned ahead of schedule.

The Rapoports found three kinds of honeymoons in the United States: (1) In the *lovers' nest* variety, newlyweds converge on popular honeymoon resorts, such as Niagara Falls or Bermuda. This is a peculiar North American taste; it astonishes Europeans, who have absolutely no interest in honeymooning in a crowd of honeymooners. (2) In the *perpetuum mobile* honeymoon the couple simply get in a car and go, without plans, reservations, schedule, or itinerary—with nothing but money and a probable date of return. (3) The *vacation* honeymoon is just that, and it follows the same conventions that apply to a vacation. Whatever the couple enjoy—whether it is camping or night life—that is what they do on their honeymoon.

The honeymoon is commonly thought of as a period when the couple can enjoy physical intimacies away from ordinary work activities, but its social and psychological importance extends beyond this. Its very persistence suggests that it may serve a marriage-strengthening role, although no body of research can be cited to substantiate this point. It is at least possible that in more cases than not honeymooning couples discover things about one another, or about their relationship, that cannot possibly do any good. But obviously that is not the honeymoon's purpose.

Viewing it in a positive light, the honeymoon affords the. couple a period of relaxation to adjust to their new status. It can help them ease into the reality shocks of marriage, which are especially troubling to people marrying for the first time. Remarriages usually involve less ritual than first marriages and are followed by shorter honeymoons or none at all (Hollingshead 1952). There are fewer showers for the bride, fewer bachelor's parties, a less formal wedding, fewer persons in the bridal assemblage, fewer wedding guests, a smaller reception, a shorter wedding trip, and the bride's family is less likely to pay for the wedding. Remarriages are also more often kept secret (Ricards 1960). Presumably people who marry for the second or third time have less need for an elaborate wedding and also less need for social procedures to protect them against their own inexperience. Consistent with this point of view, Kanin and Howard (1958) found that couples who had not had premarital intercourse were much more likely to take a honeymoon than those who had already experimented with sex.

If one important function of the wedding ritual and the series of events preceding it is to divert the couple's attention from possible flaws in their marriage plans, holding them in a state of sheer excitement during this difficult period in life, then perhaps the honeymoon can be viewed as simply an extension of the overall ritual. During it the couple is distracted from the deeper problems involved in their life together. It may be best to shield them from "real life" for a short while after marriage, and the honeymoon guarantees that they will not have to face up to the facts of life right away.

Along this same line of thought, the honeymoon *may* strengthen the marriage simply by adding an intensely pleasurable event to the couple's collection of memories about their relationship together. The *pleasant memories hypothesis* springs from the assumption that anything that adds to the store of cheerful recollections for the couple can help them weather stormy periods later on. The honeymoon presumably enlarges the couple's stock of memory resources, if it is indeed a pleasant experience, not a clumsy failure.

Most of the married women in Stanley Brav's (1947) early study of this subject looked back on their honeymoons with great satisfaction, and they also seemed to have rather detailed recollections of what had happened. About three-fourths of his subjects rated their honeymoon as a "complete success," but disappointment was the verdict of others—20 percent said the affair was far from ideal, and over half said troubling difficulties arose. (Some in the latter category considered their honyemoons *highly* successful anyway.) Apparently many of these women had expected too much in the first place. Undoubtedly the honeymoon is glorified in America, and as such it may, in itself, confront the couple with a reality shock.

At least three reasons help to explain why honeymoon expectations are often unreasonably high. One concerns sex. If neither the bride nor the groom has had sex experience before the wedding night, that night may prove unsettling to say the least; one or both will probably not reach climax, which will bother them in direct proportion to their sexual naïveté. If both should manage to reach orgasm, they still probably will not have it at exactly the same time, and yet the synchronized climax is clearly the ideal in our sexual folklore. The ability to reach orgasm together often takes time, perhaps years, and may never be achieved at all. The bride in particular will probably be inexperienced (although the chances that she will have had some heterosexual experience are increasing), and the honeymoon can be a major emotional crisis for the virginal woman. Perhaps the most critical fact is this: Sex adjustment in marriage usually takes time—much more than the honeymoon allows. If sexual bliss is what a couple expects, disappointment is what they will probably get.

Nevertheless, less than 8 percent of the women studied by Eugene Kanin and David Howard (1958) could trace any long-term sexual difficulties to problems of the first two weeks of marriage. (Out of 177 respondents, 4 did say that wedding night confessions of prior sexual indiscretions were still plaguing their marriages.) Kanin and Howard conclude that there is little evidence to suggest that sexual problems in the earliest stages of marriage are likely to carry over into later years. While the very first sex episode was considered unsatisfying or worse by almost two-fifths of the women, considerably less than half this number rated the total sexual experience of the first two weeks of marriage as disappointing. Even for the virginal wives, a high degree of sex adjustment was reported to have occurred within a short span of time, despite uncounted difficulties on the wedding night itself.

Kanin and Howard could find no connection between the strenuousness of wedding preparations, the length of wedding receptions, or the tiresomeness of honeymoon trips on the one hand and the degree of satisfaction with the first sex experience in marriage on the other. Nor could they find any relationship between the "artificiality" of the honeymoon and sexual maladjustment.

In balance, vacations (whether honeymoons or some other kind of vacation experience) are usually fun and rewarding, and the vacationers are glad they went where they did. But certainly not always. One major complaint registered by the wives in Stanley Brav's (1947) study was with the site picked for the honeymoon. Maybe in some cases the location was used as a scapegoat, taking the blame for a disappointing interpersonal experience. As a matter of fact, the first troubles that young couples have in marriage will often be blamed on external conditions; only gradually do they realize that most of their problems are their own making—they are *relationship problems*, and the surroundings are not to blame.

Financial complications can also upset honeymooners. Before marriage they keep their money matters separate as a rule, but marriage abruptly changes that. The groom no longer spends his personal money, he spends the *couple's* money. Thus one of the very first marriage adjustments involves joint decision making in the use of limited wealth. Brav has shown that this can be an irritant of more than trivial proportions on the honeymoon, and the wives in Theodore Johannis' (1959a) study seemed to agree.

Another way of looking at the honeymoon is to see it as simply the closing phase of the total wedding episode. As such it is but a subphase in the critical role transition of getting married (Rapoport and Rapoport 1964). The peak of emotional intensity for the entire episode is reached during the wedding: it begins to subside during the reception, but even then a very high level of exhilaration is maintained. This is followed by the emotionally charged wedding night. The implication should be clear; after the couple—especially the bride—have been lifted to an intense state of excitement, it simply does not seem right for them to return to work the very next day. That would not be *ceremonially adequate.* In this light, the honeymoon is an essential extension of the overall wedding ritual, rounding it out and letting the couple ease back into their daily routine. The more elaborate the wedding, the longer the build-up for it and the longer and more becalming the honeymoon should be.

At the same time, the honeymoon is a more sharply defined ritual break from the past than the wedding itself. The wedding is a *rite of passage* for the couple involved. It is a dramatic public announcement that their status has changed; no longer are they single; they are suddenly entitled to all the rights and burdened by all the obligations of a married pair. But the honeymoon, as a ritual break from the past, actually takes them out of circulation for a brief period of time. It enables not only the couple but all concerned to adjust to their new status.

ADJUSTMENT IN THE EARLY STAGES OF MARRIAGE

We have accompanied the typical young couple through dating and courtship, the engagement period, the legalities of marriage itself, the wedding, and finally the honeymoon. The newlyweds are now ready to move into their new living quarters. The accommodation they make will not be determined solely by events following the marriage; patterns of family commitment were forged long ago, when the couple were still children. Their sexual development was started at this time, and the ultimate nature of their marriage adjustment was partially molded through peer and dating relations in adolescence. The mate-finding process that followed was one of attraction and elimination based largely on the principles of homogamy and was accompanied by the still rather mysterious processes of personality screening.

Ideally, the couple returning from the honeymoon are better able to make a go of it in marriage than if they had been matched in any other way. Obviously this ideal is not always realized, but it *tends* to be fulfilled if our theory of mate selection has any valid basis at all. There is no possible way for each of us to search the world over for the one person (maybe a hundred virtually perfect substitutes could be found) who is absolutely our best possible match (but some people do keep searching—even after marriage—and the geographical range for mate selection grows wider all the time).

Since the married person must make at least a temporary peace with whomever he happens to marry, certain problems between the husband and wife exist at the very beginning. *Accommodation* is probably the best term to use, although *adjustment* is used more frequently. Accommodation conveys most literally the idea that people have to adapt in marriage to something less than total perfection. Adjustment, on the other hand, often implies that couples can completely resolve their differences, which is not very likely. (In order to avoid a tiresome repetition of the word accommodation, however, adjustment will be used interchangeably with it.)

Favorable marriage accommodation occurs when each spouse not only changes his behavior to some extent to adapt to characteristics of the other, but accepts, without prolonged resentment, the fact that his spouse is not everything one could possibly ask for. The most promising accommodation consists of changing what can be changed and accepting gracefully whatever cannot.

Needless to say, it is much easier to make a graceful accommodation to some men or women than to others. But if the mate-selection process works well, most people find mates with whom a just and lasting peace can be negotiated, and some couples will find peace and happiness beyond understanding. The exact specifications for adjustment remain unknown and are subject to only haphazard study. Clark Vincent (1967) contends that the study, diagnosis, and treatment of "marital health" should be a bona-fide professional health specialty in its own right, but that day is not yet at hand.

One very general approach to marriage adjustment is the *developmental tasks* approach. The idea was first introduced by Robert Havighurst (1950; 1953) to apply to child development and only later extended to the processes of accommodation in marriage. It holds that adjustment occurs in stages, each one posing a challenge or task for the couple which they may or may not resolve adequately. Furthermore, there is a sequence to these stages, so that certain tasks ordinarily are faced before others. If the first one is managed successfully, then the couple is in a better position to master the next one, and if that is taken in stride they are even better prepared to tackle the next one, and so on.

Success in the early stages creates a disposition toward success later, although no early success can guarantee total victory. Conversely, failure to meet the early tasks in an effective way sets the stage for failures later on. This second, negative approach is probably more valid than the positive one; early failures assure later failures with greater certainty than early resourcefulness can guarantee later success. Marriage adjustment is probably as difficult as any other kind of adjustment, but with hard work, it can be achieved.

The developmental tasks theory, plausible as it may sound, is not easy to translate into an actual sequence of marriage problems, where the later ones clearly and logically build upon those that have gone before (Rodgers 1964; Magrabi and Marshall 1965). Which problems come first? Does sex adjustment have to be resolved before learning how to cooperate in spending the family income, or vice versa? Or are these problems interdependent, operating without any necessary time sequence at all?

If we take a commonsense approach, certain problems obviously do come before others. The honeymoon, for example, comes before the couple move into their new home, and usually they have to adjust to one another as husband and wife before they face the roles of father and mother. Furthermore, they will probably have to make out with a limited budget before they can luxuriate in a thoroughly adequate one (if that day ever comes), and they will have to adjust to youthful maturity before middle age, middle age before old age, and usually all of these before they face retirement and widowhood. Clearly marriage follows a life cycle, and it poses a sequence of predictable events each requiring its own mode of adjustment. Success in the earlier phases would lead any observer to predict success in later ones.

It is also safe to assume that people will meet new crises more or less as they have met them before. Couples as well as individuals develop characteristic ways of handling their problems. This is consistent with the developmental tasks theory in the sense that each new crisis poses a problem for the couple, and the way that they solve the early ones will condition their later efforts. But it also poses a challenge to the theory because the *crisis style* of a couple may actually change, grow, and improve as the spouses mature. We all know individuals who had nothing but failure in their youth but who later showed remarkable resourcefulness. Such a pattern may be an exception to the general rule—it probably is—but this particular kind of exception is an important one; similar ones can be found in the area of marriage adjustment.

The developmental tasks approach raises some interesting questions about the changing quality of marriage during the course of the complete marriage cycle (lasting from courtship all the way through widowhood and death). If resolution of the earliest crises prepares the couple for later ones, then these early efforts are both more important and more difficult simply because they come first. The only couples for whom the early problems are easier than later ones are those who mismanage them, thus making the later ones that much more difficult.

In the light of this fact it would seem that couples are likely to try harder in the early years. They must if they have a clear grasp of their overall situation in life. They face problems for which they have relatively little preparation, and they have just emerged from the intense emotional experiences of courtship. They assume the most challenging task they will ever have (although they may *not* realize it). Still, newlyweds usually give more thought to their marriage, recognizing a need to make adjustments, than they ever will again—unless at some later stage they decide to quit and start over.

If couples fail miserably at their domestic challenge in the early years, they usually seek a second chance, which may account for the peak divorce rates in the first years of marriage. Then the couple is spared the need to wage an uphill battle, which is the unpromising assignment given them by the developmental tasks approach. If they succeed only moderately well, they will probably do only moratey well (at best) all along the way—or turn to other matters. A wife, for example, who has made little headway with her husband may not throw over her marriage, but may give prime attention to the children.

If, on the other hand, the couple succeed handsomely in the early years, they may have little need to extend themselves later on. They will have established a way of living that makes new situations progressively easier to handle. The fact that their marriage is so satisfying may mean that they will not become too deeply engaged away from home. And they can remain genuinely attracted to one another in the middle and later years precisely because they did not withdraw in the course of early difficulties.

Of course tasks may be altogether different for couples whose circumstances differ. Even the perception of problems can vary. Earl Koos (1950) found that lower-class couples perceived *fewer* marriage crises than middle-class couples, although the actual conditions of their lives made it seem that they would have more. This puzzle is resolved when we realize that lower-class couples have such unrelenting problems that they find it difficult to recognize the purely *marital* ones. They have crises, but these often seem to be the inevitable problems of life, not marriage.

In the middle classes critical problems are less frequent, but they are also more visible. Couples perceive them more clearly and apparently can resolve many of them. They may even benefit (socially and psychologically) from their brush with adversity. Lower-class couples cope less effectively with their troubles at least in part because they are less able to identify them. In terms of the developmental tasks theory, later troubles will be that much worse because of lack of sensitivity in the early years.

One final question is raised by the developmental tasks approach: Does the sequence of problems differ for men and women? Are the burdens roughly equal? Or are there distinctly male and female patterns calling for different kinds of adjustments, with different implications for success or failure in marriage?

Much of our theory about the sexes, for example, seems to say that women are taught from childhood to organize their lives around the home. They are given much less room than men to move freely in the nonfamily world. Learning masculinity, on the other hand, involves two somewhat conflicting pressures: The boy is supposed to prepare for the breadwinner role, which has clear familistic overtones, but to be highly successful as a breadwinner he must enter the world of male competition where narrow family loyalties are usually discouraged. He is taught to be a provider, but he is also taught that some of the time that might be spent with his family may have to be sacrificed in order to be successful. Active men often face a dilemma in deciding whether or not to take a more demanding job (which can cut into family time), but the male code of success states that they ought to take the more demanding job anyway. Our codes for femininity have advised women against that course of action in the past, but current trends suggest women should have the same career options as men.

If the woman's prime commitment is to her home, while the man has a dual commitment to home and career, the task of family adjustment seems to be greater for the wife. The man's work creates a special set of demands and his developmental tasks are therefore career-centered (or at least partly so). The hard reality of the man's career also establishes certain demands upon his family to which the wife has to adjust. She finds herself adjusting to both the man and his work routine (and soon to the demands of her children). It looks as though male and female marriage tasks are both different and unequal. The woman is more completely challenged by domestic problems and is more defenseless against their pressures.

It is interesting that when the newly married person first sees something in his (or her) spouse that goes against his expectations, he usually takes a "wait and see" attitude. If the offense is repeated, sooner or later some kind of direct effort will be made to cope with it. Beverly Cutler and William Dyer (1965) collected data suggesting that wives in particular tend to change their own behavior in response to their husband's reactions. If there are greater marital problems in the United States now than in the past (which is not necessarily the case, but it seems to be) then we might infer that something has happened to the way women respond.

This point of view develops as women are liberated from the old pattern in which they were explicitly trained to accommodate. George Levinger (1965), for example, contends that the modern wife's feelings are more important than her husband's in creating divorce proneness, and the wife's tolerance for her husband's behavior in marriage, especially any actions on his part that deviate from community ideals, is a crucial factor in the decision to break up.

The one balancing factor, noted earlier in discussions of dating, sex, love, and courtship, is that contemporary men are themselves more often reared to adjust to women, at least to a greater extent than has ever been true before. And it is precisely in social circles where they are not trained for this task that marital instability is most pronounced: at the lower educational, occupational, and income levels.

SUMMARY

Of the four broad processes in family life—anticipation, formation, accommodation, and dissolution—this chapter has been concerned with the final acts of formation and the early patterns of accommodation. The wedding is an emotional high point in life and is celebrated as a rite of passage in virtually all cultures. The ceremony itself takes many forms, differing from one society to the next. American practices are enormously varied, although most couples follow a predictable pattern. The more affluent they are and the more deeply entrenched in a web of social activities, the more elaborate their wedding is likely to be. The wedding as such probably has little to do with success or failure in marriage, but it is closely associated with other matters that do bear on the outcome. Couples who are active in a supporting social circle are likely to have a stable family. They will also be treated to an impressive wedding as a rule.

The honeymoon is a subphase in the overall process of getting married, during which the couple's membership in the larger group and their separateness from that group are delicately balanced. The conflict between social obligation and individual rights seems to be particularly strong in the United States. In many societies there is virtually no wish to separate the life of the couple from the larger group, and hence the honeymoon— that is, the post-marriage ritual—is more likely to stress the couple's social duties. In America the honeymoon affords a ritual break from almost all responsibilities. It gives a sense of ceremonial adequacy after the intense emotions building up to the wedding. Where premarital chastity is stressed, it gives the couple time to make their first attempts at sex adjustment.

The reality shocks of marriage probably begin during the honeymoon, although we think of that as a temporary reprieve from just such things. In any case, trouble spots begin to appear soon after marriage, and they seem to pile up rapidly during the first three to six months. In courtship the partners probably acquire an ideal image of one another; joint living arrangements almost always lead to at least some reconsideration. After the initial awakening, couples begin to see faults that were hidden before. Thus, a very important task for each partner is to come to grips with this new reality, to work it through and—hopefully—to make the marriage work.

SELECTED READINGS

BLOOD, ROBERT O., JR., AND DONALD M. WOLFE. *Husbands and Wives.* New York: The Free Press, 1960.

CUTLER, BEVERLY R., AND WILLIAM G. DYER. "Initial Adjustment Processes in Young Married Couples," *Social Forces,* Vol. 44 (December 1965), pp. 195–201.

KANIN, EUGENE J., AND DAVID H. HOWARD. "Postmarital Consequences of Premarital Sex Adjustments," *American Sociological Review,* Vol. 23 (October 1958), pp. 556–562.

KOMAROVSKY, MIRRA. *Blue-Collar Marriage.* New York: Random House, 1964.

LEVINGER, GEORGE. "Marital Cohesiveness and Dissolution: An Integrative Review," *Journal of Marriage and the Family,* Vol. 27 (February 1965), pp. 19–28.

RAPOPORT, RHONA, AND ROBERT N. RAPOPORT. "New Light on the Honeymoon," *Human Relations,* Vol. 17 (February 1964), pp. 33–56.

CHAPTER 10

Patterns of Adjustment

This chapter is divided into four main topics: the kinds of adjustment spouses make to one another, the special case of sex adjustment, the general problem of birth planning, and the adjustment to parenthood (before the children reach adolescence).

COUPLE ADJUSTMENT

Serious troubles can come up on the honeymoon, and one or the other spouse may have had premonitions of disaster even earlier, but the first burden of marriage is usually the discovery of a string of new facts about the couple's basic relationship and about the unavoidable realities of male-female living arrangements. These realizations are, to varying degrees, "shocking," in that they involve the most intimate aspects of living. Young men, for example, may have many different images of women, but they tend to think of them as being neater, prettier, and less messy or slipshod in their personal habits than the fellows they lockered with in high school or perhaps roomed with in a dorm at college. And yet a young husband may find his bride, who was indeed the very image of prettiness and feminine order on dates, to be another sort of person altogether around the house. Unfortunately, our knowledge about the revelations of the first weeks and months of marriage is very inadequate; novelists have probably shaped the sociological imagination in this area. But it would certainly seem that the conditions at issue are discovered at home more than anywhere else. In fact, they turn up most often in certain places in the home, three in particular: the dinner table, the bedroom, and the bathroom.

Home is the place of shocking discovery mainly because the one thing that the couple (or at least most couples) could not do before marriage was live together. If they obeyed convention, they engaged in recreational activities, largely away from home. They probably contrived to be in a good mood, on their best behavior, and dressed in their most attractive clothes. When they start living together—getting ready for bed together, eating together, being totally fatigued together (which does not breed romantic togetherness under any circumstances), and facing the morning coffee together, an entirely new set of sensibilities takes over. In a matter of weeks these new sensibilities will govern how they see each other.

Earlier it was noted that idealization in courtship is a *mis*perception process in many respects. Couples need to think of one another as being at least a little exceptional to convince themsleves that they are in love, and the romantic trappings of courtship help them to keep this idealized image. This does not mean that they enter marriage starry-eyed or in some kind of romantic trance—evidence to the contrary is abundant enough. Paul Hilsdale (1962) found that neither men nor women ordinarily have unduly romantic images of one another. But they do have a naïve faith in their ability to work out their problems, mainly because they feel they will be able to talk calmly and reasonably with each other. They have, he says, an "almost infantile confidence in the medicinal powers of mere communication." The man may have no greater faith in communication than the woman, but he is more prone to think, mistakenly, that interpersonal problems in marriage are easily solved. This is a rather unconscious transfer of the spirit of engineering—a male specialty—to family life.

After marriage, however, the ideal images of courtship are remolded by daily routines. Spouses may not see each other in proper perspective even after marriage, but their perspective is certainly different. Traits that loomed large become indistinct and may even disappear. Physical appearance, for example, tends to "wash out" in the course of daily interaction. Beauty protects the individual less, and homeliness is no longer such a disadvantage. Idealization is often based on a *halo effect*, where one outstanding trait distracts attention from a score of faults. In marriage the faults surface; a very impressive virtue may still carry the day, but it will have a much heavier load to bear than before.

A second process associated with courtship is mutualization, and this, too, must inevitably change after marriage. In courtship, the couple's identity as a twosome is not based on common residence, a common budget, nor the need to coordinate their affairs on a virtually uninterrupted basis. In marriage, the husband may be asked to sit still and think about a great many things in the presence of his wife that he never thought about or showed interest in before. The wife will face this problem, too, and she may also find her daily routine subject to a critical scrutiny that she never bargained for.

Mutualization after marriage is inherently more difficult than in courtship. The key to the difference is that in courtship the couple *played* during most of their time together, often under circumstances when any lull in the conversation could be filled by other young couples, all part of the gay, courtship setting. The couple may have *overengaged*—done things that neither was particularly interested in but that, as part of the courtship excitement, helped ease the relationship along. In marriage, couples play less and work more, and they are also alone together much more often. They may find work and privacy more fulfilling than anything they knew in courtship, but the odds do not favor that. The main point here is that the couple were attracted to one another in the midst of one set of activities, and they have to live together in the midst of another.

Most couples still manage to make some sort of accommodation to the aspects of marriage that are not completely satisfying. This is adjustment to reality—to some measure of disillusionment—and it does not occur only in marriage. If it did, successful marriage adjustment would be much less common than it is. All of us learn to face up to disillusionment in childhood and the teen years; adjustment to marital disappointment is just a special case of reaction to the irksome facts of life.

But trouble in marriage can be terribly distressing, and the alternative to a private truce is *marital deterioration*. Failure to compromise differences and work them through turns the two processes of idealization and mutualization on their heads. Idealization becomes *alienation,* and the spouses begin to see only the worst qualities in one another. Mutualization becomes *disengagement,* and they begin to pull apart rather than become closer together.

Even the most basic attraction to marriage may suffer; enchantment becomes *disenchantment* (although the allure of marriage as an institution is usually not lost, judging by the high remarriage rate). Nevertheless, hope for the present marriage is destroyed. The three forms of deterioration—disengagement, alienation, and disenchantment—work together as a more general process of marital devolution (Pineo 1961). We will return to this when divorce is taken up in Chapter 13.

INSTRUMENTAL AND EXPRESSIVE ADJUSTMENT

For very general purposes human behavior can be divided into two types—*instrumental* and *expressive*—each posing certain special problems for marriage. Instrumental behavior occurs when we try to solve specific problems or to achieve certain goals. In its very nature, it calls for self-discipline by the individual and cooperation in groups. It thrives on emotional restraint and a desire for accomplishment. Sometimes it means making harsh, unpopular decisions. Feelings may be hurt, but the goal can be reached no other way.

Expressiveness, on the other hand, is characterized by a basic desire to please others—to respond to them in kind and sympathetic ways in order to get pleasant responses in return. When friends get together, for example, they are expressive, and they enjoy the simple act of being with one another. They try to be congenial and talk about things of mutual interest. In this way pleasant relationships become ends in themselves. They are not "investments" leading to long-run goals (as, for instance, in the case of the first visit by an insurance salesman). Their main objective is to give satisfaction right now.

A large body of literature suggests that girls are schooled in expressiveness as they grow up; boys are pushed more often in the direction of instrumentalism (Benson 1968). The two kinds of behavior are not mutually exclusive; everyone has to learn both because we all relate to other people for sheer pleasure at times, and at other times we cope with the many practical problems of life. Most of us try to be a little of each most of the time.

But for a variety of reasons it is useful for girls to cultivate expressive talents—they will be rewarded if they do, and their conceptions of themselves as girls (and as aspiring women) will usually be more comfortable. Boys are urged to develop the instrumental manner to a greater extent for two overriding reasons. One is that they have to compete in tough, disciplined ways with other boys (especially for athletic honors, although quite obviously not all can be winners). The second is that they are reminded in countless ways that they must someday be breadwinners and that their success will depend on how they make out in competition for jobs. The boy must learn to cooperate with others, but he must also learn to compete with them, to win if at all possible, and to move on from each victory to greater things until he reaches his limit (or possibly one rank beyond since, according to the "peter principle," people tend to be promoted beyond their competence).

Accommodation in marriage occurs on both the instrumental and expressive levels. In the developmental tasks approach, expressive adjustments come first since the couple were probably drawn to each other in basically expressive ways. In marriage they will have to handle daily problems reasonably well; expressiveness alone will not get the job done. Thus, instrumentalism becomes a more pronounced problem after the honeymoon is over.

Robert Winch (1967) suggests that a happy combination of expressive and instrumental abilities may bring the couple together, and that either the male or the female may be the more expressive (or instrumental) partner, but after marriage it is much better if the traits follow cultural stereotypes. In the United States—and almost everywhere—the marriage will therefore run more smoothly if the husband is the instrumental spouse and his wife is more expressive. The wife will then be proud of the fact that her husband is a model "man," and he will be reassured if his wife can act out the image of expressive femininity. Instrumentalism is also very useful to the husband, since it helps him to be a good provider.

But the expressive-instrumental balance shifts in the course of marriage, and hence problems of adjustment must inevitably change. Elaine Cumming (1963), for example, argues that the instrumental style may carry a man through his early and middle years, but it may actually be a handicap in old age. The most severe crises for men occur at the time of retirement, when the work orientation suddenly loses its moorings. The comparable period for women strikes in the middle years when their children leave home and the most significant instrumental role in their lives—child rearing—abruptly ends. They may pick up careers or other pursuits at this time, with variable success, but in old age their essential expressive style can come in very handy.

SEX ADJUSTMENT

In America sex is highly glorified. Boys learn to expect great things from it, and sentiment increasingly favors the idea that women should share the pleasure equally. (Motherhood is downgraded in the process, since it traditionally stands for sacrifice and sex-restraint.) In dating, couples can prolong sex at great length in the form of petting, but the time given to it in marriage is greatly reduced. Other pleasures—or obligations—must be substituted to keep the couple returning to each other for social and psychological support.

The glorification of sex takes many forms. One example is the popular idea that sex adjustment is the key to marital success. In this view, marriage can hardly fail if the partners are sexually suited; if they are not, the marriage has no chance of success. The roots of this idea are deep in our national history, fed in recent times by popularizations of Freud and Kinsey. The careful literature on this point, however, raises serious doubts. It suggests that sex is but one part of marriage among many, although it does loom larger than the rest because of the special symbolism attached to it. Couples with marital troubles usually have complaints about sex, and hence sex satisfaction is a fairly sensitive *index* of marital adjustment, but it is not necessarily the *cause*. When William Masters and Virginia Johnson (1970) counsel couples who have problems of sexual inadequacy—and they may know more about this subject than anyone else—they treat the *marriage relationship,* not just sex per se. For example, if a man feels that his wife is undermining his self-confidence in any aspect of life, it can become very difficult for him to sustain an erection. This is true even if he cannot put his feelings into words (perhaps especially then). The wife in turn sees his impotence as further proof of his masculine incompetence, and it becomes progressively more difficult for the man to find anything but numb frustration at home.

Masters and Johnson contend that over half of the married couples in America suffer from sexual inadequacy and that in virtually all of these cases their ability to approach one another either verbally or physically concerning sex has broken down. It is hardly surprising that "unhappy" couples say that sex is a devitalizing force in marriage and that happy couples see it as a strengthening factor. They are telling the truth. But the fact remains that sex is only a prominent symptom, not the total condition of marital happiness. *Mutual ego support,* not mutual orgasm, is the key to marriage success. What counts is how well couples manage to support each other's sense of personal worth. The ego is the part of the psyche that needs constant care in marriage, not the id.

The popular ideal, of course, is overnight sex adjustment. This may be realized in some cases, but the greater likelihood is that sex fulfillment will take time, and for some undisclosed number of couples it will never come at all. Fervor in sex relations almost inevitably subsides as the couple become thoroughly accustomed to each other and as the pattern of their sex life becomes a surprise-free routine. Frequency of intercourse declines, and yet there is usually no commensurate drop in the perception of sex adjustment, especially for women (Pineo 1961). Apparently men more often than women feel that the full promise of sex in marriage has not been realized, but for both sexes the image of the spouse as a sex partner tends to fade. The new image can be favorable or unfavorable, but in any case it relies less and less on sex.

In Chapter 3 attention focused on differences between males and females in the development of attitudes. The twin processes of feminization and masculinization refer to the different social and psychological influences upon maturing girls and boys, leading to different sex styles at every stage in life; these differences are especially strong in the area of erotic behavior. For one thing, males usually react more quickly to sex cues in their environment, so they are more easily aroused than females. (This difference is not necessarily biological, however. Boys are trained to respond to a greater variety of sex stimuli than girls.)

Men are also more frequently confronted by sex symbols than are women. A partially clad female striking a mildly provocative pose, for instance, is seen much more often in ads and commercials than whatever the comparable stimulant for women might be. Even the lingerie ads in newspapers and magazines create a strong *background sex stimulus* for men; such images show up on any given day and guarantee a steady sex charge for almost all males in the population. There is no comparable background level of sex stimulation for women, since their arousal is more dependent on romantic settings, which usually call for a particular pattern of interpersonal relations.

Generally speaking, the timing of arousal also differs for the sexes. Since men tend to live at a fairly high level of sexual excitement, they are in a state of greater readiness for arousal—specifically, for genital erection. In an older terminology, *tumescence* (which may be either readiness for erection or the erection itself) for the male is a quicker, more frequent, and more predictable process than arousal for the female, and the sex tension it creates is also more quickly satisfied.

What this means, of course, is that the husband should proceed rather slowly with his wife so that she can reach the peak of feminine excitement, and he should try to keep emotional contact with her for a while after the peak is reached. The contemporary manuals on sex invariably tell males all about this, but just how widely they heed the advice nobody knows. It is safe to say that men are probably satisfying their wives more fully than they used to.

Traditionally, women have complained that sex often becomes a chore, a service they submissively render to their husbands. Mirra Komarovsky (1964) found that most of the women in her sample of working-class wives felt that wives do sometimes submit to intercourse when they do not really want to, but only women with the very least education agreed that it is the wife's *duty* to do so. It seems that equality in marital sex occurs more often in upper than in lower social classes. Most of the women in Professor Komarovsky's sample felt that, ideally, wives should get as much pleasure from sex as their husbands, but that women must also adjust to reality. The great majority were convinced that men are more highly sexed than women and that it is fitting for women to yield to this fact.

Fortunately, changing conditions may ease women's dilemma in this regard. New technology gives new possibilities for equality. For example, cheap, effective, and convenient contraceptives make it easier for wives to let themselves go in sex relations; the fear of pregnancy, or perhaps simply an underlying concern about it, has long interfered with their ability to concentrate on sex. Men in many cases can approach it without guilt, or at least with very little, freeing them for both physical pleasures and erotic fantasies.

Not only does sex hold implications for the woman's future, making it harder for her to act as if it had only passing importance, but most women have grown up being constantly reminded that their basic purpose in life is the dual role of wife and mother. Almost all of the imagery of motherhood tends to stifle a sensuous erotic approach to life. Even the imagery of "the good wife" leans in this direction; since she is expected to be a faithful helpmate to her husband, she is not supposed to develop any tastes that might lead to promiscuity or adultery.

Sex for the woman thus tends to be a highly moral act, posing the constant possibility of guilt. Once again, the contemporary manuals not only attempt to reassure women, but advise men that their handling of sex can reduce the guilt that wives have traditionally had to bear. Contraceptives can also help; they are used most often now by the very women who have traditionally had the greatest restraint—women in the middle classes. Lower-class women are much less likely to use contraceptives in their first sexual experiences, such as on the honeymoon (Kanin and Howard 1958), and this often becomes a continuing pattern in marriage.

IMPOTENCE AND FRIGIDITY

Two special problems in the area of sex adjustment deserve at least brief mention. They are called "special," although they are not in fact limited to a small part of the married population. Sooner or later each of them touches the sex experience of almost all marriages, though not necessarily as a chronic problem.

The first is *impotence* in men. It is a relative matter, not "either–or" as it is often presumed to be, and it can take two forms. One is the inability to reach orgasm (ejaculation); the other is the inability even to achieve an erection. Of the two, the latter is almost always more painful to the male ego. Organic reasons can sometimes explain either reaction, but in both cases the condition is more likely caused by psychological trouble in the marriage—by feelings of guilt about sex (which men as well as women can have) or by some personal setback for the male. Almost all men occasionally have an embarrassing struggle to reach orgasm or to get up an erection; only when the problem persists does the label "impotence" apply. Yet many more couples have fears and anxieties in this regard than ever seek counseling or medical treatment. Perhaps many of them are wise enough to suspect the social and psychological reasons for their trouble. Unfortunately, many are not. Masters and Johnson (1970) claim that most women "overexpect" of men. They think normal men can always perform, which simply is not true.

The comparable problem for women is *frigidity*, which also takes two forms. The first is inability to reach orgasm, as in the male, and the second is simply lack of erotic response—no spark at all. In the case of the male the latter is localized in his penis (the man is usually bewildered and maddened by his unresponsive, "dead" organ). A certain lack of specific physiological response occurs in the female, too, as Masters and Johnson have shown, but for her the pattern is considerably less localized. Hence her "lack" is more easily recognized as psychosomatic.

For the male, the penis often seems to have a life of its own (which is a fallacy), and yet in the folklore its performance is the mark of the man. Male sex heroes have giant organs capable of encore after encore. The anti-hero may look virile, but his organ simply does not live up to the man's outer appearance. And yet the size of a man's penis has no direct bearing on either his potency or his virility. Lack of erotic response for the female, on the other hand, is taken by many—both men and women—as a kind of natural feminine condition; no sense of shame need be felt about it. The woman does not have to be erotically aroused to satisfy the man and, as noted earlier, many wives (in the working classes in particular) feel that it is occasionally their duty to have sex relations even when they can do no more than passively receive.

It seems likely that as women gain equal rights, frigidity may become a more serious embarrassment, comparable to the ego loss caused by male impotence. The one significant and inevitable difference, however, is the fact that women can conceal frigidity so much more successfully than men can hide impotence. This is not only true of erotic arousal, but of orgasm itself. The woman cannot always be sure even in her own mind that she has made it; she is in a better position to know whether the man reached orgasm than he is to tell if she did. Thus, women have at least one basic sex advantage over men: They are endowed with greater ability to discover their husbands' impotence than men are to discover their wives' frigidity. The wife may tease or even ridicule her husband after such a discovery, but she may also try to help him. However, some women may blame themselves for their husband's frustration.

ADULTERY

Adultery is another special problem, and it, too, affects a great many couples. Alfred Kinsey's data, still holding up remarkably well in the light of more recent studies, indicate that about half of the men and a quarter of the women in the United States sooner or later become involved in adultery.

Sex relations outside of marriage do not *necessarily* constitute a problem, however, although they can confuse the issue of paternity and in some small percentage of cases lead to venereal disease. The more important difficulty, which is not inherent in extramarital sex itself, is posed by the high value placed upon marital fidelity. This has long been equated with sex fidelity, almost as if the latter constituted, by itself, the entire issue of marital trust.

Faithfulness is more than sexual inhibition, and with the rise of love as the basis for marriage, along with the slow (and still fuzzy) growth of a love-centered sex philosophy, the concept of fidelity now tends to encompass *love* relatively more and *sex* per se relatively less. Thus, in the romantic ideal a couple is expected to be constant in their love for each other; but it is at least possible for them to have extramarital sex relations without violating this essential constancy. Furthermore, to the extent that love is the key to conjugal devotion, a marriage without it (but still retained for practical reasons) would not necessarily place a high value on sexual loyalty. John Cuber and Peggy Harroff (1965), after interviewing 437 upper-middle-class Americans, concluded that most of them firmly believed in monogamous marriage, but many of them also condoned extramarital sex. A few did so quite openly, but most tried to conceal their affairs with a variety of pretenses. Several authorities speaking at the annual meetings of the American Psychiatric Association in 1969 argued that guilt associated with adultery has all but disappeared among some groups in the United States, but their percentage in the population remains unknown. In *Adultery for Adults*, Joyce Peterson and Marilyn Mercer (1969) call adultery "horizontal enrichment" and say that it strengthens marriage in several ways: It keeps the spouses alert and alive, opens new vistas for couples to share, improves their grooming, is good for their general health, and is a civil right of women. Obviously these ladies offer reassurance to the people who have adultery without guilt.

Nevertheless, the idea that sex fidelity is proof of marital loyalty is still strong, and adultery continues to be a major domestic problem (especially if it cannot be kept secret). A husband who has been cuckolded is expected to make an issue of it—to confront his wife and her lover, perhaps even kill the man (although he has to do it quickly, in a state of uncontrolled passion), and seek divorce. Exposed adultery is supposed to create a family crisis by the very nature of its cultural definition.

The question of greatest interest is not why adultery leads to marital strife, but why it may very well *not* have that effect. It is quite apparent, for example, that a great deal of adultery is "absorbed" in the United States; it does not necessarily ruin marriages that are otherwise reasonably successful. This would seem to be an area where patterned evasion can be useful—a married woman, for example, may prefer not to learn about her husband's extramarital affairs, which she could discover easily enough by being only normally curious about certain suspicious behavior on his part (such as when a sudden change occurs in his established evening routine). She may look the other way as long as his performance as husband and father is acceptable in other respects and as long as he handles his affairs in a discreet way. This has been a workable arrangement in the upper classes for centuries, but immoral to middle-class eyes. It is too soon to say whether a majority in the middle classes are ready to go along.

Kinsey argues that religion gives the best clue to differences in adultery among women—the more active they are in the church, the less likely they are to engage in extramarital affairs. However, the religious factor proves to be of little use in explaining adultery for men. The key for them is education—the more years of schooling completed, the less likely they are to get involved, although the differences reported by Kinsey are not pronounced. More important than frequency is the age at which adultery occurs. Men with less education tend to reach a peak in their twenties, while the more educated men approach maximum rates in their late thirties and early forties. Women reach peak rates in their thirties and early forties, too, according to Kinsey, but there are no strong differences among them in terms of educational attainment. People often assume that the extramarital affairs of middle-aged men take a spurt when they start brooding over sagging sex powers and fading personal attractiveness, but this fails to explain the sharp educational differences.

Opportunities for extramarital sex undoubtedly vary with education, although the educational factor by itself is probably not a direct cause of this. It is symptomatic of different life styles—and of corresponding differences in life chances. Men with little education, for example, not only reach a peak in extramarital sex earlier, they reach their limits in earning power and overall life involvement sooner.

It is also possible—indeed quite likely in terms of the evidence given in Chapters 4 and 5—that men of limited education are generally more hostile to women; they find it more difficult to establish intimate, friendly relations with them and are not as strongly committed to most kinds of family obligations. They are also more likely to view women as sex targets. It is not surprising, then, that these men would be more quickly disillusioned in marriage and that they might start looking for outside sex opportunities sooner. Of course disillusionment can hit men of higher status, too, but not quite so soon (in part simply because they marry later).

High frequencies of premarital sex are also more common in the lower classes, and rates of premarital sex are correlated with extramarital affairs. In fact, sex is *generally* less restricted to marriage in the lower-income brackets. If men of lower social status have relatively fewer illicit affairs in their late thirties and early forties than other men, it is partly a reflection of declining sex activity as implied earlier, but it is also because they have a shorter span of active social involvement. This is generally true of people in careers limited to a low level of achievement.

Men of low status also have relatively low marriage rates, and their opportunities do not improve with age; opportunities for men of greater success *do* improve as they grow older. (In a sense, all older men have relatively better chances simply because younger women outnumber them at this time. But the really big advantage goes to men of high status.)

Implicit in this pattern is a highly plausible proposition: The rise and fall of a man's occupational career is a sensitive indicator of his involvement in all sorts of things—even extramarital sex. Full proof for this awaits further research, but evidence currently available is one-sided in its favor.

BIRTH PLANNING

A strategic task facing the couple early in marriage is planning for children, and the first question raised is *when* to have them. Ordinarily the question of "how many" is no pressing matter until the couple has already had two, since having no children or only one is rarely considered ideal (although a small percentage of couples may be almost belligerently opposed to having any at all). Birth planning is going on implicitly even when the young couple make decisions about other matters, such as deciding to buy a home or to save money; it comes up in countless ways not directly related to the question of childbirth.

Generally speaking, men and women have similar opinions about the ideal number of children to have (Christensen 1961). Due to the processes of homogamy in mate selection, the attitudes of spouses on this point are more similar before they even begin to talk about it than if they had been matched in some random fashion. Furthermore, strong differences in the desire for boys or girls only rarely occur in the United States (although boys have usually been preferred in preindustrial societies). In fact, the sex of the child is ordinarily a secondary matter insofar as planning is concerned, but it may affect the decision to have a third or more children, especially due to the common wish to have children of both sexes (Freedman, Freedman, and Whelpton 1960). Thus, the couple might feel that two is the ideal number, but if their first two are girls they may plan for a third in hopes of adding a boy.

Harold Christensen (1968) suggests that although marital success is influenced by the number and spacing of children, the crucial factor is whether the couple manage to get what they want. Five children born one after another are not too many if that is what the couple wanted, but three spaced well apart *are* too many if that is not what they had in mind. Furthermore, it is now clear that planned children are more likely to get a warm and confident reception from their parents than unplanned children; at least this is the drift in recent history. But it is also true that seven children may be an impossible number for a low-income couple even if they are eager to have that many, because it takes money to raise children in the modern city; good intentions are not enough.

The quality of marriage is also at stake. John Hurley and Donna Palonen (1967) claim that there is an inverse relationship between the number of children per household and the satisfaction with marriage (when the length of marriage is held constant). They call the ratio of children to years of marriage *child density* and suggest that the greater the density, the lower the level of marital satisfaction. Their limited data, from a sample of parents attending college, tend to support the theory. (It is possible, of course, that child density is a rather special problem for couples who are college trained.)

It is amazing how rapidly birth planning has progressed in the United States since the 1920s. Margaret Sanger, a nurse who had been reared with nine brothers and sisters in a very poor family, was one of the earliest champions of the cause; she spent a brief period in jail about the time of World War I for creating what was then considered a "public nuisance." Mrs. Sanger persisted, gained supporters as the years passed, and in 1968 the two living past presidents of the United States—Harry Truman and Dwight Eisenhower—served as honorary cochairmen of the Planned Parenthood Federation.

And yet reservations about contraceptives are still widespread, especially before the wife's first pregnancy (Potter, Sagi, and Westoff 1962). A study of women in Sweden, where family planning is very broadly accepted, revealed that only 56 percent of those under thirty used contraceptives during their first sex experience (Zetterberg 1969). Many couples are indifferent to birth control until they have their second child or get close to the birth limit set for themselves. Then their control of fertility improves sharply (Westoff, Potter, and Sagi 1963).

But new techniques are changing reproduction patterns. Development of the oral contraceptive ("the pill") in the 1960s led to its rapid adoption by young married women—especially those with a college education. The pill can be used effectively not only to control the *number* of children couples have, but also *when* they have them (Ryder and Westoff 1966). (However, concern for the possible side effects of the pill caused many women to stop using it in 1969 and 1970, at least temporarily, upsetting their birth control plans in a number of cases.)

The use of contraceptives is bound up with patterns and frequencies of sex relations in a complex way. For example, a wife may use her fear of pregnancy as an excuse for avoiding sex, but still refuse to take responsibility for contraception. In the general confusion she does not have to go through the sex act as often as her husband would like. In this arrangement, the couple may have more than the average number of children but less than the average amount of sex. Or, if the woman has a strong sex drive, she may willingly assume responsibility for contraception so that her husband can feel uninhibited (Rodgers and Ziegler 1968).

In the lower classes in the United States a lack of interest in family planning persists, and it does lead to problems. The feeling that nothing can be done about pregnancy—that it is simply "natural"—is fairly common. Such an attitude is the primary reason for the higher birth rate among poor people (the reason is not that they *want* more children).

The fact that planning per se (not just birth planning) is only a fringe concern in the lower classes has been described exceptionally well by Lee Rainwater and Karol Weinstein (1960). To the person reared in poverty the world usually seems chaotic and unpredictable—controlled by fate, chance, and callous big shots. Naïveté pervades whatever sense of order exists, and the very self-image that people acquire tends to reflect this fact. They do not consider themselves capable of effective planning, especially for long-term goals. Since they have rarely learned how to plan and have not been very successful in the management of their personal lives, planning in the area of family affairs does not come easily, and planned *nonparenthood* is out of the question. It is rarely considered, but even when it is, it seems like an artificial idea—an effort that runs against nature.

Therefore, not having children when they are not wanted becomes a matter of luck for women and married couples and a matter of cunning for single men. If contraceptives are used at all by the lower classes, the least effective ones are picked—the condom in particular. (This is also the technique most often used by young unmarried couples. Boys can get "rubbers" fairly easily, and using them does not hurt their self-image. Girls face considerably greater obstacles in getting and using female birth-control devices. Even in marriage condoms are widely used in the lower class, mainly because of ignorance and lack of planning. But unmarried middle-class girls can foolishly become pregnant despite their general commitment to planning; one thing many of them find difficult to arrange *before* marriage is the use of contraceptives.)

Lack of birth planning in the lower classes is part of a larger pattern of confusion with regard to children in general. The whole pattern can be traced to circumstances before marriage, even to childhood in the unplanned family of the previous generation. It begins to show up in visible ways just before marriage. Courtship is characterized by little or no discussion of future family matters and virtually no mention of contraception itself (Rainwater and Weinstein 1960).

Wives have trouble carrying on conversations with men in nonplanning marriages, and the couple share fewer mutual interests. Apparently these men are harder to approach than middle-class men and are less intimately involved in almost all kinds of family relations. This sense of separateness from wives and children contrasts sharply with the emphasis on confidential relations projected in the middle classes (Rainwater 1962; Komarovsky 1964). Half of the women in a low-income Puerto Rican sample studied by J. Mayone Stycos (1955) reported a virtual absence of activities with their husbands outside the home, and many of the remaining women reported only infrequent or limited mutual interests. Oscar Lewis (1951) found the same pattern in Tepoztlan, Mexico. Spouses in that community participated in relatively closed and separate circles, giving each a rather independent sense of stability and continuity in life.

In lower-class Puerto Rican marriages the man may be a hard worker but a casual husband and father—a thorough *macho*, the traditional he-man of Puerto Rican society. The *macho* believes that women belong in the home; the place for men is in the street where they can prove their masculinity with other men—and chase women (Rogler 1965). American working-class males are also prone to see domestic affairs and child rearing as the responsibility of the female side of the household (Kohn and Carroll 1960; Komarovsky 1964). This segregation of marriage roles causes communication problems for husbands and wives on almost all matters that are not unmistakably defined by tradition (Hill, Stycos, and Back 1959).

Under these circumstances, the man may pride himself on the number of children he has but be almost completely indifferent to the *quality* of his performance as a father. In a questionable combination of values, men who do not plan the size of their families often have a greater desire to become fathers than those who do, and they take more satisfaction in the social esteem of fatherhood per se, yet they are low in family dependability and slow to assume family obligations. Among Puerto Ricans, the position of the Catholic Church with regard to birth control further inhibits the use of contraceptives.

Wives in this setting find it hard to talk to their husbands about family goals, and the need to limit children to accomplish such goals may never even come up. As a result, they have no choice but to struggle with large families, although in a literal sense *choice* has nothing to do with it; the underlying processes that have been described either influence or actually determine the choices people make.

Birth planning among the lower classes is not altogether hopeless, however, especially due to efforts by women. They are ordinarily more concerned and more knowledgeable about fertility than their husbands. The men have trouble putting their concern into words and may even abandon the family rather than try to deal directly with it. About half of the men studied by Rainwater and Weinstein had no clear idea of what is involved in controlling the reproductive process. Women scored much better in this regard, but their knowledge is also more crucial than their husbands'. Women are more likely to bring up the subject, and their concern is therefore the key to the couple's joint planning effort.

Before leaving this subject it is worth noting that pressures on couples to have children are changing pretty rapidly. Having them continues to be an important basis for marriage (so most single women are still very squeamish about getting pregnant), but the *need* to become a parent is not nearly as strong as it once was. In fact, pressures tend to run in the opposite direction now, although a childless couple may be urged (in subtle ways by friends and relatives) to have at least one, and a couple with only one child may sense some disapproval from people who fear for "only children." But a couple can stop at two without any sense of guilt; in earlier times this would not have been so easy to manage.

Of course, there is now virtually no danger that we will fail to reproduce ourselves, and we no longer think of reproduction as a religious deed calling for special foods and stimulants when the man's sex powers begin to sag (which was only recently the pattern among Moslems [Beck 1957]). Keeping the human race going is no longer a fertility problem; fertility magic has been replaced by scientific birth control and the fear of overcrowding or maybe nuclear extinction.

It is a safe bet that we will have still fewer children per marriage in the future and that an increasing number of people, in response to genetic counseling, will have none at all. Robert Morison (1967) sees the day when adults may feel as pleased with themselves for *not* having children as they now feel in having them. There may even be legal restrictions on the right to bear them. Nevertheless, the freedom to have babies is one of the least interfered with freedoms we have; should the question of legal limits become a live issue, as it very well may before long, we may find that people are more concerned about how to judge the social and psychological aptitudes of young couples than about their genetic strengths and weaknesses.

In any case, the average urban male does not regard the siring of children as a central life interest. He no longer has the urge to propagate in great numbers, and he is not obsessed with the desire for a son to continue his name and family line. Less concern for boy babies is part of a complicated chain of events; it has brought about an upgrading of the status of women along with the need for fewer pregnancies to maintain any population level. The rise of science, modern medicine, public health efforts, and effective birth control make community survival possible through a low birth rate and long life expectancy. These conditions, where the problems of immediate survival are largely solved, cause parents to stress the *quality* of their children rather than their *quantity*.

BIRTH CONTROL TECHNIQUES

Many kinds of birth control are currently being used. And many people now believe that *no* couple should engage in sex relations without first making this decision: Are they willing and able to accept responsibility for a baby? If not, then they should either skip sex altogether or use an effective means of preventing pregnancy. This is not merely a personal matter— it is a social obligation.

Currently, the most effective contraceptives are the *intrauterine device* (commonly called IUD) and the pill or *oral contraceptive*. The IUD is a plastic, spiral-shaped device that is fitted into the woman's uterus by a doctor. It prevents the zygote (a fertilized ovum) from lodging in the uterus, and thus prevents pregnancy. This is most often used by women who have already had a pregnancy, and its effectiveness is virtually 100 percent. (*Virtually* 100 percent is still not perfect; there are more than a few American women who have found that even the IUD can fail to do the job.) The device is fitted to stay in place indefinitely, but the woman should check with her physician periodically to make sure that it has not been dislodged.

The pill is also close to 100 percent effective if used properly. The woman must take one each day for twenty consecutive days during her menstrual cycle, with the supervision of her doctor. It causes a hormonal reaction preventing ovulation, but it has no effect on her interest in sex or her ability to reach orgasm. New and better pills will be developed—hopefully more convenient ones, with fewer side effects, and ones for use by the male as well as the female.

A number of other techniques are only partially effective. The *condom* (or "rubber") is used by approximately 30 percent of the married couples in America and is even more popular among young, unmarried couples. It is a thin sheath of rubber that slips over the erect penis, keeping the male sperm from being released in the woman's vagina. Condoms are quite dependable if used properly (they rarely leak), but there are many reasons why they are likely to be misused through fumbling and carelessness in the course of sexual arousal, after the male erection. About 20 percent of the couples relying on them report pregnancies, which is too high to afford complacency. (Failure rates for contraceptives are extremely hard to determine; we should consider them only as plausible estimates.)

The *diaphragm* is another contraceptive that is popular in the United States. It is a round, thin piece of rubber with a flexible but hard rim that is fitted by a doctor and is inserted in the roof of the vagina. It covers the cervix at the back of the vagina, thereby keeping male sperm from reaching the female ovum. The Masters and Johnson (1966) study reveals that it is not as effective as we used to think because it can slip out of place during sexual intercourse when the vagina expands, becoming much larger than its normal diameter. It is usually used with spermaticides, without which it might be even less reliable.

Spermaticides include a variety of jellies, foam sprays, suppositories, and creams that destroy or immobilize the male sperm as they are released in the woman's vagina during ejaculation. Though the reasons are somewhat obscure, these are not as effective as they should be to give sex partners peace of mind. The failure rate approaches 50 percent when spermaticides are used by themselves.

The one technique currently approved without reservation by the

Catholic Church is the *rhythm method*. Only for the brief period of about four days before ovulation (when the mature ovum is formed in the female) and one day afterward can conception occur during the woman's menstrual cycle. If the timing of ovulation can be accurately predicted, and the couple refrain from sex relations during this five-day period, they will not conceive. For some women the prediction of ovulation can be determined with accuracy and dependability; for others it is not so easy. Even the more predictable women will occasionally ovulate off schedule because of special strains or circumstances in their lives. Therefore the rhythm method is not perfect, and its failure rate appears to be at least 20 percent. Another problem it poses, however, is the need to abstain during the five-day period, which can create tension just before, during, and perhaps immediately after this stage of the menstrual cycle.

A rarely used method is *withdrawal* (or coitus reservatus), whereby the male withdraws his penis immediately before ejaculation so that no sperm can enter the vagina. This is neither easy nor popular. In fact, preejaculation fluids are released which can carry sperm, so the technique is not foolproof even if the man follows directions.

Popular in Europe is the *douche*, a flushing of the vagina right after ejaculation with water or some other liquid. It is an old technique, often used as a kind of feminine hygiene as well as for contraceptive purposes. As a means of birth control it is not at all effective—to be so it would have to be done *immediately* after ejaculation; every second counts. In some cases it can even *help* the sperm reach the female ovum.

There are two other birth-control techniques that are highly effective, but they involve surgery. These are forms of sterilization, about which there is much public ignorance. Neither is illegal, and neither reduces the person's ability to have or to enjoy sex relations. About 2 million Americans have been voluntarily sterilized (according to the Association for Voluntary Sterilization, Inc.), although many hospitals require that a staff committee give approval. For the male, a *vasectomy* is a very simple operation clipping the tube carrying sperm from the testicles. This tube (the *vas deferens*) is readily accessible to the surgeon's scalpel. The man remains just as potent in sex relations as before, but his ejaculate will not carry sperm. There are no hormonal changes, the sperm is reabsorbed by the body, and if the man has no misconceptions about the operation, he should have no emotional reactions. This procedure can be performed in a doctor's office quickly and with local anaesthesia, but realigning and rejoining the tubes is not so easy. The operation is therefore hard to reverse should the man ever want to reproduce again at a later time. A new technique is being tested in which a thread is inserted in the tube, blocking sperm passage. The thread can be removed with no great trouble, "unsterilizing" the man.

The most comparable operation for the female is a *salpingectomy*, which involves cutting and tying the woman's Fallopian tubes, thereby making it impossible for the male's sperm to reach her ovum. This, however, is a major operation, and so it is not quite comparable to the male vasectomy. It is usually performed on women having babies by Caesarean section or soon after a normal childbirth. Any effort to reverse the process would also be a major operation, which in effect means that it is extremely unlikely to be reversed. New techniques for reaching and severing the Fallopian tubes without making a long incision are currently being tried. The vasectomy would ordinarily be preferred over salpingectomy as a birth-control method for the couple—provided that the woman restricts sex relations to her husband.

PARENTHOOD

In most cases, young couples have about a year after the honeymoon before the first child arrives. During this period the couple can explore each other's abilities and limitations very closely—and much differently from the way that parents, teachers, peers, and employers have been evaluating them. But usually the couple will not be too hard on each other at first. Alice Rossi (1968) suggests that the first pregnancy marks the end of this *psychic honeymoon* (it often lasts through pregnancy until the baby is born). Not all couples are so fortunate, of course; a period of marriage accommodation before parenthood may be by-passed altogether due to premarital pregnancy. When this happens the developmental tasks sequence is overloaded from the start, which is certainly no good omen.

If we can consider the birth of the first baby as a crisis for the couple, then the sooner it occurs, the more likely will it aggravate the problems of early marriage adjustment. Rhona and Robert Rapoport (1965) point out that whenever two critical changes in life occur at the same time, the *crisis effect* of each will probably be greater. This would seem to be what happens when a person marries about the same time that he graduates from high school or at the same time that he becomes a parent. And Alice Rossi (1968) argues that neither sex is adequately prepared for parenthood as a rule, since clear guidelines for mothering and fathering simply do not exist in our society.

Pregnancy

It is not surprising, then, that early pregnancies usually lead to greater-than-average marriage troubles. For example, couples who have children very soon after the wedding will probably have special money problems, and these are all the more difficult if they married at an early age. They will not find it easy to gather the basic capital for family life, and they often become discouraged about ever coping effectively with life's problems (Freedman and Coombs 1967). This seems to be part of a larger divorce-prone syndrome (Christensen and Rubenstein 1956). In fact, premarital pregnancies are statistically associated with younger ages at marriage, ignorance of contraceptive devices, lower social status, brief premarital acquaintance, mixed religions, below average educational levels, and minority racial status (Lowrie 1965), all of which are also associated with high rates of marriage failure. Among groups that are not fully part of the middle-class pattern, however, premarital pregnancies are also less likely to lead to marriage in the first place (Pope 1967).

Of course, some marriages that come after pregnancy were never meant to last; the purpose of the ceremony was simply to legitimize the baby. Hurried marriages such as these are most likely to occur precisely where premarital pregnancies are most highly condemned (Christensen 1963). And yet where pressures for a quick marriage are strongest—in the middle classes, for example—the pregnancy will have the most harmful effects. Harold Christensen (1960) found that the most liberal nations, such as Denmark, have the highest levels of premarital pregnancy, but also the least harmful consequences. Clark Vincent (1959) concluded from his own studies that mutual ego involvement accompanies sex relations in the middle classes to a greater extent than in the lower classes. He suggests, therefore, that lack of any deep personal relationship may account for the *relatively* low incidence of divorce among couples of low status whose marriages follow pregnancy.

Pregnancy before marriage can cause problems because of the very nature of the couple's conceptions of each other—where the man, for example, is suspicious of his wife for having allowed herself to become pregnant, and the woman resents the fact that her husband "caused" the pregnancy. There may be no end to this underlying lack of confidence. Since a major basis for adjustment in marriage is the couple's ability to give mutual ego support, starting out with doubts makes adjustment all the more difficult.

Couples who *delay* marriage after a prenuptial pregnancy have the most trouble of all. This observation may seem strange or untrue at first glance, but it is explained by the fact that couples who do not delay were probably planning marriage anyway (Christensen and Meissner 1953). In a hurried marriage, the couple rushes the *decision* to marry; moving the ceremony forward is not as disastrous as making a decision to marry under pressure.

If, as is usually and ideally the case, the first baby is born a year or so after marrying, then the pregnancy can probably be taken in stride; at least it is not so likely to be a traumatic experience. If the couple has trouble working out a comfortable sex pattern, the pregnancy can be delayed for a while, although many couples are anxious to have children no matter how well their marriage is going. The pregnancy *is* likely to bring the couple closer together—for a while at least. This certainly does not mean that a couple on the brink of divorce will be "saved" by having a baby, although that sort of thing can occur. Good data on this point are lacking, but couples having trouble who are also planners usually have fewer children than other couples.

After pregnancy the husband almost certainly will begin to see his wife in a new light, and that is probably the most significant consequence of the pregnancy for him. The expectant mother, on the other hand, begins to think much more about herself, her physical condition, the child she will soon have, and the things that are in store for her. In fact, she becomes a mother psychologically even before the baby is born, especially when the fetus begins to show life.

But she is not likely to change her mental image of her husband as much as he changes his image of her—a difference in reactions with much more than passing significance. The man is virtually the same man he was, to himself and to his wife—no *image transformation* takes place. He may give fleeting thoughts to his approaching role as father, but little more. Men apparently have great difficulty putting themselves into family roles that they have not already experienced, largely because they do not discuss such matters with each other while they are growing up, and they discuss such things less than women throughout life. For the woman, reveries about her impending role as mother are deeply felt. They are extensions of a personal interest that she started developing as a child.

In the very last stages of pregnancy the couple usually become particularly close, and the husband can grasp even more clearly the fact that he not only has a role to play at the time of birth (seeing that his wife gets to the hospital on time, for example, and worrying through the tense moments that will occur there) but that after the baby is born his own daily routine cannot remain totally unaffected. The fullness of this realization is probably stronger in the modern small family than it was in the past, since the new mother will not be surrounded by older women who once shouldered much of the burden. The contemporary mother has to rely more on her husband, and on child-rearing and pediatric experts (such as Dr. Spock). It is quite possible, in fact, that an underlying connection exists between the declining aid of older female relatives in caring for infants and the decline of the birth rate.

Apparently there is no widespread modern counterpart for the *couvade* (found among some nonliterate people), where fathers have severe reactions at childbirth, even more than mothers. But many men do suffer psychosomatic ailments during their wives' pregnancies, and they have been known to do strange things at the time of delivery (Wainwright

1964). In addition to nausea, dizziness, absent-mindedness, and various signs of acute nervousness, they have been known to suddenly develop symptoms of mental illness. In fact, women are often more willing than their husbands to have another child despite the fact it means more work and greater physiological hardships for them (Rose 1951).

Parent-Child and Mother-Father Relationships

The birth of the first child under the best of circumstances can be a crisis in the life of the couple, although this point has run into some controversy. E. E. LeMasters (1957) collected data suggesting that becoming a parent is quite often a crisis, and Everett Dyer (1963) added further evidence of its traumatic nature. Later, however, Daniel Hobbs (1965) studied the subject and concluded that "crisis" is probably too strong a term; couples regard their introduction to parenthood as a period of considerable strain to be sure, but ordinarily they keep a good sense of balance unless the child has unusual health problems.

Hobbs, at the suggestion of Harold Feldman, carries this point even further, suggesting that there may be a "baby honeymoon" of one or two months after the infant is born. He admits that parents are expected to be elated with their first baby, and so it may not be easy to spot all the negative feelings that are suppressed. Still, the people in Hobbs' sample most often felt "happy, wonderful, and lucky" after childbirth, and later they said that parenthood had made them "more mature." (It has long been claimed that parenthood is a maturing experience, or at least a chastening one. Hobbs' respondents admitted—or is this bragging?—that being conscientious parents requires a great deal of just plain work.)

LeMasters reported that fathers were generally more disenchanted at the birth of the first child than mothers, but the fathers in Hobbs' study were even more likely than mothers to think that their marriages had improved. Dyer found that new fathers were especially disturbed by loss of sleep and the fact that their routines were disrupted, whereas the fathers studied by Hobbs seemed to be more concerned about financial complications. Hobbs makes a strong and convincing case in this regard; he suggests that parenthood is a crisis primarily for men of low income, and that, as time passes, the economic responsibilities of fatherhood get worse, not better.

Stephen Richter (1968) has added depth to this point. He says that children make heavier demands on the family's pocketbook as they grow older; unless the father's income goes up, he loses an important kind of leverage with his children—that of being the source of financial patronage. This is in complete harmony with evidence from many sources concerning other aspects of marriage and family commitments in the lower classes.

Problems of fatherhood are aggravated for lower-class fathers in at least two ways. Not only do they often react negatively to the presence of children—at least when compared to men of higher status—but the very childhood background leading to low earning power also leads to weaker commitment to family obligations.

The evidence also suggests that fathers, much more than mothers, view their relationship with children in economic terms, and they seem to become more upset by parent responsibilities as they are drawn into them more deeply. If they seem less disturbed than their wives, it is probably because they find more escape from the many daily problems that mothers cannot avoid—partly because of their work away from home, but also because men are usually given greater freedom from household chores even when they are at home. Most books written specifically for fathers give suggestions about how to prepare for the first baby (Corbin 1944; Genné 1956; Schaefer and Zisowitz 1964), and yet this is not necessarily the time of their greatest need. As the children grow older, fathers become more involved, and they become progressively less able to dodge or repress the problems of relating to their children.

A pattern emerges in which the reactions of mothers and fathers are determined by different expectations, by a different set of roles to play and by a different combination of worries. The woman is most completely in charge of infants and little children and, despite the fact that her work can hardly be called easy, she will probably accept it more willingly than the father can accept his. As the children grow older the father is drawn in more, at the very time that economic demands become greater and problems between the generations also become more strained.

The mother establishes her essential relationship with the children before they develop a truly critical perspective. She ordinarily does not lose her strong identification with the children as they grow older, and she usually retains her style of mothering in the most basic sense of the term —that is, as if she still had little children who needed her constant attention. Father becomes the more demanding parent and is characteristically more willing to throw the child on his own resources. It is the traditional male—or breadwinner—disposition to prefer people who can stand as separate, independent egos. The mother is the parent who, in the traditional image of love and nurturing, will often attempt to do things for her children that they might be able to do for themselves.

The arrival of the first child can strengthen relations between the couple, but, as with sex, the initial bond may not last. How the couple play their roles of mother and father will lead to either cooperation or lasting conflict. In fact, conflict over child-rearing methods (especially over discipline) can become a terribly abrasive force in their life together (Peterson 1969). Once again, the key to marital accommodation is mutual ego support. The main way the father can undermine the couple's relationship is to imply in context after context that his wife is bungling her mother role—in effect, that she is a failure.

The corollary, of course, is the mother's reaction to the father, but with less impact as a rule. Being a failure as a father is not very damaging to the ego of many men. Mother can get to his ego more quickly by casting slurs at his powers as a breadwinner. Men have an advantage because their wives rarely have an opportunity to observe them at work (although they do see the pay check). Her own performance is embarrassingly visible. She may complain that her husband is not earning enough, which is a common enough refrain, but she is not in a position to snipe at his daily performance on the job.

In this discussion two aspects of parenthood have been stressed. One concerns the way the spouses become parents and react to their new roles. The other concerns the way parenthood affects their marriage. Women are relatively better prepared to tackle the role of mother because they have rehearsed it in their minds for years while growing up. Fatherhood is a less carefully rehearsed role, and men (in the middle classes in particular) tend to be caught up in preparation for their careers instead. These differences in parental training are institutionalized—they are built into social roles that we start learning in childhood and that are reinforced almost everywhere.

But there is much less preparation and guidance for the interaction of the couple as parents. The girl, for example, rehearses motherhood making certain assumptions about her husband's behavior, but the man she marries may or may not live up to her expectations. As we have seen, the husband has probably given little thought to either parenthood or husband-wife relations before the very last stages of courtship, and even then the subject may not capture his imagination. His most vivid images of women in childhood were probably of his mother and other motherlike women. He discovers girls in adolescence, mainly because of their prettiness and erotic attraction and the fact that one of them seems to care about him. The need to cooperate in the rearing of children at some time in the future simply does not come up. It is not surprising that the most difficult task couples face with regard to parenthood is often not child rearing per se, but the task of helping each other as parents—of reinforcing their parental confidence. This fact can go unnoticed by many couples; it is not always stressed in the literature on marriage adjustment.

SUMMARY

The developmental tasks approach to marriage calls attention to several stages of adjustment. This entire text is organized in terms of a sequence of tasks for children, teen-agers, young couples, parents, middle-aged couples, and then the elderly. One stage leads inevitably to the next, and developments in each cannot help but influence succeeding stages.

First, the couple must adjust to one another. Every kind of human ingenuity will come in handy, but the key in modern America is mutual ego support. The urban family is rarely a work unit; it is consumer-oriented and companionship-centered, and new talents are required to make it successful. The ability to help one's partner have a healthy ego in practical, not merely sentimental, ways is the object—but there is no magic formula for accomplishing this. Only one thing is fairly certain: Every put-down by one spouse will almost surely lead to retaliation by the other. A benevolent cycle of compliments is the ideal, but one compliment does not lead as certainly to another as one disparaging remark will lead to reprisals.

Though sex is often considered the single most important aspect of marriage, it poses many problems and its role is easily exaggerated. Sexual inadequacy is not uncommon; overnight solutions do not exist. Men and women learn different cues for sex arousal and performance, leading to inhibitions and unequal sex needs. But trends show declining inhibition among women, perhaps less self-centeredness among men, and greater willingness to open the problems of both sexes to intelligent discussion.

Ideally, birth planning is a serious concern of the young couple, and it has become a standard part of the truly contemporary marriage. It is not fully used in lower-class homes, however, and its absence is symbolic of a wide range of family difficulties. Even middle- and upper-class planning efforts will probably show greater sophistication in years to come as our knowledge of how it should be done improves.

The great majority of couples have not completed their adjustment to one another before the first baby arrives, so reactions to the baby are in fact a key part of early marriage adjustment. As in the case of birth planning, the greatest problems occur in the lower classes where men often have a life style that makes fatherhood awkward and in some cases unbearable.

Only a fuzzy line separates the couple's adjustment to marriage from their adjustment to family life. The problems of one blend imperceptibly into the other. Very soon after marriage husband and wife become father and mother; then they start reacting to each other in terms of how they act as parents. But the overriding consideration is still the same. The prime obligation of the couple as a married pair is to give mutual ego support, first in their roles as companions, then as cooperating parents.

SELECTED READINGS

BENSON, LEONARD. *Fatherhood: A Sociological Perspective.* New York: Random House, 1968.

CHRISTENSEN, HAROLD T. "Children in the Family: Relationship of Number and Spacing to Marital Success," *Journal of Marriage and the Family*, Vol. 30 (May 1968), pp. 283–289.

CUBER, JOHN F., AND PEGGY B. HARROFF. *The Significant Americans: A Study of Sexual Behavior Among the Affluent.* New York: Appleton-Century, 1965.

HOBBS, DANIEL F., JR. "Parenthood as Crisis: A Third Study," *Journal of Marriage and the Family*, Vol. 27 (August 1965), pp. 367–372.

KOMAROVSKY, MIRRA. *Blue-Collar Marriage.* New York: Random House, 1964.

MASTERS, WILLIAM H., AND VIRGINIA E. JOHNSON. *Human Sexual Inadequacy.* Boston: Little, Brown, 1970.

PINEO, PETER C. "Disenchantment in the Later Years of Marriage," *Marriage and Family Living*, Vol. 23 (February 1961), pp. 3–11.

ROSSI, ALICE S. "Transition to Parenthood," *Journal of Marriage and the Family*, Vol. 30 (February 1968), pp. 26–39.

CHAPTER 11

The Middle Years of Marriage

Who is middle-aged? Most of us would prefer to be young—or perhaps simply "mature." Let us say that middle age begins in about the mid-thirties for the majority of people and lasts until about their mid-sixties. In terms of its social symptoms, rather than chronological age alone, it is associated with having teen-age children, seeing them leave home and set up households of their own, learning to live as a couple again, and becoming grandparents.

For the couple, middle age is a period of redefinition of their married life together and of their hopes and plans for the family. For the individual, middle age is a time of change in five key roles, each holding important implications for the family.

1. The *parent* role is modified as children approach and reach maturity.
2. The *spouse* role changes in subtle ways as parenthood takes a new course.
3. The role of *offspring* is altered as the middle-aged person's parents grow old. This tests the resources of the elderly, of course, but the middle-aged generation does not escape responsibility. In fact, this is a critical period for all three generations: elderly, middle-aged, and children (Chilman 1968). Problems for the middle-aged couple change as they take on the status of "generation in the middle."
4. The man's *career* has now reached its peak, or it may be opening up

as never before, but in either case he usually has a new perspective on both his past and his future. The middle-class male in particular may became even more absorbed in his work and its routines, including travel and association with cronies. The record of his performance is now tentatively in, and chances are slim that he will make any truly significant achievement that is not already well on its way. He can conduct a measured view of himself—in an achievement-oriented society, people are supposed to take stock of themselves at this time. It also seems that achievements come relatively early in life in modern society; but peaking out too early may complicate adjustment in the middle years.

5. The man's role as a healthy (or not so healthy) person—as a *biological specimen*—is also likely to be subject to much greater self-scrutiny. By now he may have lived through a period of serious worry about his health, or he may be carrying an increasing load of guilt for not having that health checkup he knows he should schedule. Perhaps his doctor has warned him to cut down here and there, or he may simply become very touchy about the fact that he is no longer a young man, as signs of age begin to show up.

The five key role changes are phrased from the man's point of view, but each one applies to women, too (although the sexes respond to them differently as we shall see). The last two (job and health) are not *necessarily* related to the family, but indirectly they have almost as much to do with it as the obvious family roles of spouse, parent, and offspring.

OPTIMISM AND EMPTINESS

In current commentary on middle age, peace and serenity are often contrasted with turbulence and conflict (Gravatt 1953). Actually, either can occur, but at different stages in the long mature phase of family life. Catherine Chilman (1968), for example, suggests that people experience a *latency stage* between about ages twenty-five and forty and once again between the ages of fifty and sixty-five. These are relatively calm periods when the upheavals of earlier years can be resolved. Then the person is ready to move on to the next stage in his developmental spiral. If Chilman is correct, the most critical phase of middle age for most people comes between the ages of about forty and fifty. It is at this time that familism can give life a sense of meaning and accomplishment or make it seem empty beyond hope.

We must keep in mind certain special circumstances of the American small family system, since the nuclear family faces a basic change in mid-life, when the children enter the later stages of adolescence and begin to leave home. James Bossard and Eleanor Boll (1955) claim that the late forties and early fifties are particularly critical years for women, not only because their children can now take care of themselves (much more than mother would like to admit), but also because their husbands are now often inadequate as sex mates, and the menopause casts its ominous shadow.

And yet many good reasons for a sense of fulfillment can occur at this time: The family home is about as attractive as it will ever be, considerable family capital has been accumulated, and most fathers are now reaching their peak earning power. Families are likely to have their heaviest family expenses during the decade from age forty to fifty, but far greater financial ease is achieved after the last child leaves home and before retirement, especially for professional and managerial groups whose income continues to rise during this period. The household routines have now been worked out; they may be imperfect and not completely satisfying, but by now they can at least be taken for granted. The couple no longer have any delusions about getting rid of *all* tension. They may have become a little cynical, but a dash of stoicism is probably present too. Thus, the life style of the family is firmly established. There is an awakening excitement as the children come of age and near the time for college and marriage. Whatever achievements they are capable of will soon be posted.

But there is also an awareness that the children will be gone and their return may be very infrequent. The house will have empty rooms. Parents start thinking about what will happen when they are left alone. A common expectation—or overexpectation—is that the children will come home more frequently than they in fact do, and that they will confide in their parents more often than they are actually willing to. In fact, intimations of this begin to appear in the teen years. The way parents react can determine how complete their children's break from the family will be.

The Husband and Father

The middle-aged father is no longer a patriarch—he is not even very dignified by historical standards—but ideally he is still a man of substance, especially in economic ways. It helps if he has money to dispense to his wife and children because *largess* is still an important source of personal pride to many men. Success in this gratifying aspect of fatherhood is based on some degree of personal achievement (unless the man inherited wealth), and hence the middle years combine career reflections with self-appraisal.

The man may judge himself in many ways. He may be obsessed with the amount of money he makes, comparing his salary with that of other men in some kind of accounting system where people are judged solely by earning power. Or he may think of the skill or progress he has achieved in his own line of work or, if his ambitions are higher, he may compare himself with the most successful and accomplished men of his era. In each case he measures himself against other men *as individuals,* not as fathers or as family men.

But he may also take stock of himself as a provider—that is, of his ability to supply a home with all or most of the domestic conveniences— and in this line the great majority of fathers in the United States do quite well. After all, we do live in an affluent society. Although some families have more material wealth than others, differences in the great range of middle-class homes are drawn not so much between those who have and those who have not, but between those who have very expensive furnishings and those who have essentially the same things, but cheaper. A subtle gradation of status ranges from very high to very low with the great mass of people in the comfortable middle area.

Very little scientific information is available to tell us how men assess their careers in mid-life or how they relate these thoughts to family matters. Much probably depends on the aspirations they set for themselves when they were younger. A majority of the fathers in Leland Axelson's (1960) study of middle-aged couples reported improvements in such areas as activities with wife, career interests, and financial worries after their children started high school. There seems to be little reason to doubt that a powerful source of satisfaction for the middle-aged male ego is the sense of having provided for his family or of having served as the economic supporter of a family with a respected community identity.

You may doubt whether most families can have a respected community identity in the modern metropolis—it is too big, too anonymous, and too crowded. And yet such an identity is not really so hard to achieve. The important thing is to have a few friends and relatives, a steady job and bank account, a reasonably clean slate of paid bills, and a feeling of being part of the community at the time of its most enjoyable celebrations— during the Christmas season, for example. Perhaps it is in this spirit that the entrepreneurial manner is kept alive in a highly bureaucratic society. Maintaining a home and family becomes a business enterprise where father is chairman of the board. He maintains that rank, however, only if he does consistently well as a breadwinner.

Some readers may object, arguing that this stress on the male breadwinner role is overdone. It suggests a bias against the economic status of both women in general and lower-class men. The man's earning power may very well be stressed too much in the United States, but for the moment we are interested in the way things are, not in what they could or ought to be. New possibilities for the future will be discussed in Chapter 17.

In the past, even in the absence of material affluence, men have usually managed to wield authority at home, backed by community traditions and a stable neighborhood life. Farm life and the small town assured most fathers of respect, often in spite of economic hardships. Children had little choice but to respond in a dutiful way to father's pressures (although they have not always liked it, and American youth have always had greater opportunities to leave home than children in the Old World).

Now these conditions are only a nostalgic memory. It has become much more appropriate for fathers (like mothers) to be agreeable objects of affection rather than distant figures of authority for their children. And it is no accident that the new emphasis on warmth and love in parent-child relations has occurred at about the same time as the appearance of an exaggerated "gap" between the generations. Teen-agers are far less demanding *physically* than younger children, but they put heavier pressures on their parents' *psychological* reserves. The middle-class father's dilemma in contemporary society is that he can now hand out greater economic largess than ever before, but he also is a less respected figure in his own home. He may attempt to purchase the admiration of members of his family only to learn that they would much rather admire him for his personal qualities. Perhaps the most essential quality is a sincere and consistent interest in their individual lives. Thus, as father's breadwinner role gets easier, and material success becomes commonplace, more is asked of the man himself.

Conclusive data are not easy to come by, but all indications suggest that the contemporary father (not including the man living in or near poverty) is more likely to find himself lacking as a *person* than as a *provider*. And the key to his self-doubt is the empty feeling that his generation has nothing to say to its replacement—it can learn more than it can teach. The situation is not one of any particular father's making; it is the collective response of youth as well as fathers to the spirit of the times.

The one element of hope is that the later stages of middle age may see a much more comfortable set of relations between the generations. Wayne Thompson and Gordon Streib (1961), for example, contend that particularly in the period of early retirement (which is customarily considered the first part of old age rather than the last part of middle age) the *content* of parent-child relationships changes rather drastically, becoming much more friendly in nature and less characterized by hollow constraints and stereotyped obligations. The interchange between parents and offspring at this time is more likely to be regarded as meaningful *in and of itself* than at any time since the period of greatest enchantment—when the children were little.

The Wife and Mother

The middle years for the wife are in some respects harder than for the husband. But this has not always been so. Keep in mind that we are talking about the new economy with its high level of industrial development. One reason for the modern woman's troubles is the recent stress on emancipation for children. Children are now expected to leave home, to set up independent households, and to lead lives of their own.

The problem for women actually begins before the children move out. By the time of adolescence mothering in the traditional, "nurturant" sense is a dwindling part of the woman's life (or should be). In the past, children did not leave home as they do now (at least not so completely), but they mastered the basic skills of life even earlier. Mother faced a transition when her children were big enough to manage most of their personal affairs, but she usually kept close working relations with them anyway, especially with her daughter (or daughter-in-law). She had a continuing role to play in giving advice and assistance and in keeping up a steady stream of daily contacts with the offspring. The father, too, had continual contacts with his sons, which is true in most places where the father's work status is transmitted directly to his son.

Dorrian Apple Sweetser (1966) has shown that the mother becomes the key figure in kinship relations when families move to the cities, where ties between the nuclear family and the wife's parents are usually closer than those with her husband's parents. But if the mother has a more strategic place than the father in dealing with relatives in modern society, why is her status in the middle years so often more upsetting than the father's? Both she and her husband are victims of the generation gap; both have to give up control over children to a greater extent than before. Mother actually has more power now as the pivotal figure in contacts between the parent and offspring generations. The plight of the middle-aged mother can only be explained in terms of rapidly changing family values and work patterns. The fact of overriding significance is that motherhood has been overwhelmed by so many new competing opportunities.

Caring for little children still has its attractions, but it is accompanied by an institutionalized effort to eliminate all the hard work. The modern mother diapers her babies with disposable diapers and bottle-feeds them with disposable bottles (if she uses bottles; breast feeding is the latest trend, but women do not breast feed their infants for as many months as women used to). She uses a babysitter, and in countless other ways she is invited to escape from the chores of motherhood. These were once patiently endured; there was simply no relief.

The contemporary mother, for the first time in history, seems to be entering an era when her mothering role is reduced to its elementary function, that of providing love and warm comfort to the child through direct body contact. As the child grows, the love and contact is supplanted, or overlaid, with ego support and a barrage of advice. Hopefully, the love and ego support will forever be appreciated, but opportunities for body contact almost disappear after the early years and may become a troublesome issue later (especially with boys). The advice becomes a genuine problem in contemporary society. Even though the woman may have become the key figure in kinship relations, she finds that her advice should be easygoing and friendly or it will not be welcome. But this means that her chief *responsibility* in life (by traditional standards) becomes less substantial.

Until recently the central work role for women has been mothering itself, whereas the comparable role for father is his job away from home. As the children prepare to leave, and do in fact go, the man still has his work to perform. The woman's mother role is stripped of its traditional meaning, and her dilemma is: How can she fill the vacuum in her life? (The analogous problem for men is retirement, which comes twenty or twenty-five years later. That is when men face a genuine role vacuum, and we will come back to it later.)

The mother's dilemma has been popularized in the past quarter of a century, providing material for a steady stream of essays and professional advice. The woman can seek employment, or become a volunteer worker, or join clubs. What she does with her personal sense of emptiness will depend on the kind of talents she has, her willingness and that of her family to let her use them, and the local demand for paid and volunteer workers. Participation by wives in the labor force shows a marked upsurge from age forty into the fifties.

Nevertheless, the potential skills and aptitudes of middle-aged women are probably the second greatest untapped resource in America. (Number one would surely be the abilities of lower-class boys, which are so often forfeited by our failure to make the nation's public school system work for them.) Many women who did well at school—perhaps better than their husbands—know no way to find work that can make full use of their abilities, and they are reluctant to take low-paying jobs requiring little skill. The problem of middle-aged women will be discussed again in the concluding chapter of this book. It seems certain that something will be done about the present dilemma, and the steps taken will probably be linked to broad changes in the family's role in postindustrial society.

The Middle-Aged Couple

The postparental phase of life is new in a sense, a stage most people experience (Cavan 1963), and its overall effect is one of radical change. The modern couple now live almost as many years *without* children in the home as they do with them there—a consequence of greater longevity coupled with a decline in the average number of children for each married couple.

But what is the effect of this stage of life on marriage? This is one area where the evidence is reassuring, at least in part. (But conclusive data are lacking and the definitive study of middle-aged marriage has not yet been made.) The overwhelming majority of postparenthood couples in Irwin Deutscher's (1964) sample—a small one—considered their marriages satisfactory, although upper-middle-class couples had a more favorable outlook than couples of lower status. Lewis Terman (1938) once suggested that marriage happiness scores begin to decline shortly after marriage, reaching low points in the seventh and sixteenth years; after about the sixteenth year they usually begin to go up again, but never reach the levels attained in the early months. Leland Axelson (1960) found that the intensity and intimacy of marriage tend to decline over the years.

The wives in Deutscher's study tended to be most extreme in their reaction. Of the men and women who judged this period favorably, the women judged it more favorably than the men; and of those who judged it less favorably, the women again were more extreme. Deutscher suggests that men are simply less expressive with regard to the quality of marriage than women, but he also says that the postparental period may be more critical for women. It represents a kind of retirement for them—from mothering—and hence they are forced into a more intensive and often painful self-scrutiny. The husband still has his career.

Gertrude Gass (1959), however, concluded that the women in her sample found greater contentment in the middle years of life after the child-rearing stage, not less. In a similar vein, Robert Blood and Donald Wolfe (1960) concluded that middle-aged couples whose children had left home had higher levels of marital satisfaction than those who still had children to manage. Sons and daughters bring much adverse pressure to bear on marriage, they claim, and the pressure mounts as they grow older. Infants may bring couples closer together, but older children and teenagers are not usually so helpful. After the "launching stage," many marriages take a turn for the better.

It is probably best to suspend judgment on the question of whether middle-aged couples make better or worse overall adjustments than couples in earlier and later stages of life. Certainly their problems are different, but many of these differences seem to be caused by general changes in our society, not in the marriage itself.

Take the movement of families to the cities, for example. We think of the modern family as a consumers' rather than a producers' unit, mainly because of the switch from the family farm (where there was work for all members of the family) to the city household (where each family member usually looks after his own affairs during the day and returns home for relaxation in the evening). The farm family was a hard-working survival unit, and it continued in this capacity even after the children grew up. The contemporary city family, by contrast, is more an expressive, ego-supporting group throughout its cycle, but especially when the children move away from home. (Some people argue that the only justification for marriage in modern society is to have children, but if that is the case, what happens when the job is done?)

Until this phase of marriage the parents have been busy rearing children and pointing a large part of their expressive energies toward them; these energies obviously have to be redirected. Helen Lopata (1965) has shown that women—even modern women—are often more interested in their mother role than the role of wife, a preference that simply has to change when the children leave home. If we can assume that the expressive needs of parents have been met reasonably well (by a combination of relations with each other, with their children, and with other people in the community), then releasing the children almost inevitably upsets the achieved equilibrium. It is perhaps with this in mind that Erik Erikson (1963) proposed that the general reaction to the middle-aged period is "generativity"—reaching out in a giving and supporting attitude toward the larger community as opposed to the tendency toward self-absorption earlier in life.

But another reaction to personal loss is for the middle-aged couple to move closer together. They were probably extremely close in the early stages of marriage, before children came along (although the first child is often born before the couple have completed a single year together). The children probably forged a new bond between them, but one that may have been misleading since it turned them away from themselves. While playing their parental roles they could slip off together occasionally to be alone, but they may have cut down on such holidays as the years went by. Figures are not available, but studies do suggest that couples tend to disengage over the years (Axelson 1960; Pineo 1961), each spouse acquiring a few interests of his own and a few separate friends. As a consequence, reforging the relationship is not always easy—partly because the couple may have let their marriage slide, but also because it calls for a new set of sensitivities and expectations. Apparently wives grasp the nature of the problem first (Thompson and Chen 1966).

The essence of the relationship is now expressive, except in a few rather special cases—as when the couple have a business they can manage together or when the husband is a man of much more than average accomplishments (in which case his wife can be his helpmate without any misgivings). The "first-lady image" of the President's wife provides the prototype for this tradition, and there are many corporation presidents' wives (and vice-presidents' wives, too) who take on this role. John Gruen (1968) tells how Charlie Chaplin's wife kept a constant vigil over her famous but aging husband, protecting him from overwork and rude intrusions and jogging his memory with bits of information as he told charming stories to friends. This, of course, is an elegant version of the wifely role; it has followed a much different course in rural and small town America. The helpmate tradition comes under unusual strain in the cities as more and more women work away from home. The husband must be a man of truly unusual achievement for his wife to see herself as his protector, nurse, and dutiful companion in middle and old age.

In most cases the essence of the middle-aged marriage is equalitarian companionship. (One of the spouses may still make most of the decisions, but it can be either husband or wife; sex dominance as such will not explain it.) This relationship is sustained by the couple's ability to give comfort to one another by just being together and by their ability to keep up the basic marriage work—mutual ego support. Ideally, the years of friendship between boys and girls in childhood, the lessons of dating in middle adolescence, and the homogamous tendencies in courtship pay off in middle age, and the couple are able to find mature heterosexual companionship.

But these years will probably bring both convergence and divergence; the couple will move closer to one another in some respects, further apart in others. One of the main reasons middle age is so hard to study, in fact, is because people in this stage do such a wide variety of things. Mothers are a little easier to investigate than fathers because they are easier to catch at home or to reach through the school system, and they are a relatively unified group. But even mothers change as they move through the adult years—in a process sociologists call "socialization after childhood"—and the general trend for both sexes is *differentiation*. For women the drift is simply less pronounced than for men.

Differentiation in adulthood is crucial for marriage as well as for personal adjustment. Probably the most important reason it occurs is the gradual wearing away of the power of the peer group, which seems to reach its greatest influence in adolescence. This is the time when the teen-ager is breaking away from parental controls and, for a relatively brief period, his liberation from one set of controls leads him directly into another—which can be even more imperious than home. But as people leave their teens, they are gradually freed from the hegemony of the peer group. We are never completely free, and middle-aged persons at public affairs may conform to group pressures even more than teen-agers, but the fact remains that as we grow older we tend to get a better perspective on what gives us pleasure. We are less easily swayed by the fads that are so powerfully built into the teen-age culture. One reason the peer group is so strong in adolescence is that teen-agers have not had a chance to work through all the activities available to them, not long enough to know the differences between what is truly enjoyable for them as individuals and what is simply fashionable. Some may never graduate from this need for group support, but many do in fact find their own personal freedom.

The ability of middle-aged couples to work out a satisfying expressive life together will depend to a considerable extent on whether they bring similar interests and tastes to their leisure affairs. An ability to do this is what brought them togther in the first place, but now fifteen or more years have intervened. Both have changed according to the differentiation process, and they may or may not find the kind of *couple resonance* they knew when they were younger.

Peter Pineo (1961) reports four progressive changes between the early and middle years of marriage:

1. A general decline in both marital satisfaction and marital adjustment, which Pineo calls *disenchantment*.
2. Such things as confiding, kissing, and the friendly settlement of arguments become less frequent. People report increasing loneliness. Pineo regards this as part of the more general process of disenchantment.
3. There is also a drop in the frequency of sexual intercourse and the sharing of various social activities. This, however, can be independent of disenchantment.
4. Although marriage disenchantment seems to be fairly universal, it is not necessarily accompanied by any comparable change in *personal* adjustment. Apparently people (Americans, at least) keep a sense of individuality separate from their sense of marriedness. Marriage can go sour without the personal life of each spouse taking the same turn, although obviously these two qualities are related.

But why does a generalized deterioration in marriage occur? Pineo argues that it strikes in two stages: early, in a rapid sequence of events, and again later, in a much slower fashion. At first it occurs because couples enter marriage with unreasonably high hopes for marriage and unrealistic expectations for one another. The realities of marriage force them to unmask and reevaluate. As the protective masks of each partner are stripped away, their true character is revealed, and the impact is more

often negative than positive. But this reaction is very quick. Disenchantment in the later years is due to unforeseen changes in the couple (physical and mental health problems, for example) or changes in their environmental setting. The surroundings to which they have to adjust may
change beyond recognition, by comparison with the earlier years. Pineo
argues that there is a *progressive loss of fit* as the grounds upon which the
couple decided to marry change or deteriorate.

Whenever a person makes a major, long-term commitment with information that is less than perfect, some disappointment is to be expected. "Fit" is best at the time when the commitment is made, and it
usually takes a turn for the worse over time. Pineo uses the example of
religion. At the time of marriage, religious attitudes of husband and wife
are likely to be very similar (assuming that religion is considered important by the couple). Religious attitudes at best can be expected to
hold this similarity after marriage; they are not likely to become even
more similar. By chance alone the fit could improve, but the *probability*
is greater that it will not. And yet it is also true that couples do not
diverge from each other nearly as much as they would if they were not
married. If the husband is a strong Unitarian, for example, the wife is
almost certain to have more interest in that group than she otherwise
would, and probably more sympathy for it, too. Perhaps the husband was
the loyal church member at the outset of marriage; by middle age he may
be the backslider and she the loyal one.

Some New Developments

Marriage in the middle years of life is no longer what it was on the
farm. Population changes also accompany people to the city, with further
implications for both marriage and middle age. The underlying fact is
that we live longer, but this is coupled with three other new developments which, in their combined impact, dramatically alter middle age.

One new development is that although formal education lasts longer
than ever before, people do not postpone marriage until later. Half a
century ago it seemed obvious that marriage would be postponed as people went to school longer, but a crucial factor was overlooked—affluence.
Either affluence itself, or the expectation that the bills will somehow be
paid, makes early marriage possible. In fact, the average age at first marriage seems to have declined in the twentieth century (until recently—it
has turned up slightly in the last few years). Difficulties in calculating the
average age at marriage are numerous, however, so we have to be cautious
in making generalizations.

The second fact is that couples have fewer children even though they
live longer. This is no accident. An inverse relationship between average

life expectancy and the birth rate seems to be inevitable. As the death rate goes down, we simply have to have fewer children or face an unmanageable growth in population. (As it is, we are only barely able to manage this problem in the United States, and it is not being managed at all in some countries.)

The third development is that children in any particular family are now born in a relatively short period of time after the couple marries. Paul Glick and Robert Parke, Jr. (1965) have outlined the pattern with careful precision. Their figures show that women who were born between 1920 and 1929 could look forward to about twelve years of joint survival with their husbands after their last child married, while women born forty years earlier could look forward to virtually no joint survival at all.*

Thus, contemporary women marry earlier and live longer, but they complete their child-rearing work sooner than women used to—at a median age of about thirty-one according to Glick's data. (It is also of interest that, when women marry, their husbands are not as much older than themselves as was once the case.)

In response to these new developments the postparental period has lengthened, and couples have more years to live together after the children are gone. But no significant upsurge in divorce hits couples at this time of life. In fact, the divorce rate slides steadily downward after the third or fourth year of marriage. Alfred Messer (1969) claims that there has been a sharp rise in divorce among older couples, which he calls the "twenty-year fracture." But he offers no convincing evidence to support this claim.

It seems that couples who may have planned to separate after their children leave home—remaining married just "for the sake of the kids" —find new reasons to hang on, despite marriage problems. One consideration, for example, is the promise of grandparenthood, which many middle-aged couples look forward to with eagerness and which is more likely to be fulfilled in the newly lengthened postparental phase. Of course grandparenthood is essentially an expressive role now; the modern grandparent has very little to do other than "relate" to grandchildren, which can help to compensate for any lack of expressive satisfaction in marriage. Expressive satisfaction can probably be derived from the very survival of the family. Couples find a variety of pleasures in this which are not directly related to the quality of husband-wife relations. The marriage makes them

---

* It should be apparent that this comparison refers to statistical tendencies. It is not a misleading comparison if we keep in mind that the joint survival of *some* couples in the earlier period was greater than for *some* in the more recent period. The figures were obtained by subtracting the median ages of women at the time of the first marriage of their last child from their median ages at the death of one or the other of the spouses.

possible nonetheless, and they are directly identified with the married couple.

The husband, for example, may lose the sparkling affection he had for his wife in their early years together, but he may find many conveniences associated with remaining married. After all, the couple has accumulated a useful set of "tools for living"—in the form of the house itself, the furniture and equipment in it, a car or two, an insurance policy, and so on. This domestic capital does not exist as a physical reality alone. The couple have worked out ways of using it to solve most of their daily problems. There is a certain satisfaction in knowing that the marriage has come a long way, that the couple have met a great many problems together, and that most of them have been handled reasonably well. These fundamental facts are a source of continuing pride even after the couple may have tired of one another.

The man may also find that many of his emotional needs are met at work, with his cronies, in clubs, or somewhere else away from home, and his wife may have made similar arrangements. Certainly one reason women turn to outside employment in mid-life is for companionship—not just for the money. As long as expressive needs are met in some way, and the marriage stands as no threat to them, it may be eminently worth keeping. The evidence leaves little room for doubt on this point.

Middle-Aged Sex

Since sex—or body caressing in general—was particularly important in forging the first bond between the couple, its place in middle age is of more than passing importance. All studies show that the frequency of sex relations will be sharply reduced at this time by comparison with the first years of marriage. The original level of *satisfaction* may hold up very well, however, depending on the quality of the total relationship between the spouses.

According to Kinsey's (1948) figures, males reach their highest total sex outlet between the ages of sixteen and twenty, with a slow but steady decline occurring from that time on, so that by age forty the average number of sex experiences is only about two-fifths of what it was twenty years earlier. In the case of women, the peak sex frequency occurs in the late twenties, after which there is only a slight decline until the age of fifty.

Since males have been found to have a much stronger sex drive than females at the beginning of the average marriage (without in any way implying that this difference springs from basic biological necessity), it is quite likely that the couple's sex drives will be most similar during middle age. This is especially true for couples whose relations are good out of bed as well as in, and particularly when they did well in the early stages of marriage (Clark and Wallin 1965). Some couples will have abandoned sex altogether by mid-life and may hardly miss it (although its *total* avoidance will probably point to something much deeper than a mere surface annoyance. Sex is a highly symbolic act; couples do not ignore it through oversight).

Occasional sex relations may be particularly important for keeping a reasonably satisfactory body image. Needless to say, such an image is harder to maintain as we grow older, heavier, more wrinkled, and more bowed and awkward. But the man likes to think he can still portray the image of a man, and his wife may be even more troubled by her body image than he is—personal appearance was probably more important for her marriageability in the first place, and women are bombarded with advice on how to look young, feminine, and sexy. In the absence of carefully collected data on this point we have to be very careful, but it seems likely that occasional sex activity in middle age functions as much more than sex release. It becomes symbolic not only of the couple's mutual respect for one another at the psychological level, but of mutual respect (or magnanimity) at the physical level as well.

The most feared aspect of aging in the United States seems to be the change associated with bodily appearance and performance. (This may not be quite so true in other societies.) Sex activity in middle age can aggravate this fear, or it can help to keep it under control. Recall (from the discussion of adultery in the previous chapter) that American men of higher social status participate more frequently in extramarital sex in the middle years of life than do men of lower social status. This reflects the fact that they have better opportunities for a broad variety of things at this time than do lower-class men. For such men, opportunities to reestablish a sense of *physical* masculinity can be terribly attractive, and even the chance to take a risk or two may hold some kind of fascination. (Women are not immune to this temptation either.)

PARENTS AND THEIR MATURE OFFSPRING

Troubles that aggravate parent-child relations as children approach the time to leave home have been mentioned in passing. It is to be expected that young people will become increasingly anxious to have complete personal freedom as the day of liberation nears, particularly from the advice and direction of parents—but not necessarily from their financial support. Almost all evidence suggests that contemporary youth are more worldly and sophisticated than in the past, but their dependence on parents (or parent surrogates) has actually been stretched out over a longer period of time. Attendance at college, for example, lengthens the stage of dependence because it requires either parental support or state subsidy, and yet modern college students are notoriously hostile to controls that parents and college administrators attempt to package with the support they give.

Let us move forward in the family cycle to the time when the children marry. The generation gap now begins to narrow and continues to constrict until late middle-age or the early stages of retirement. Parents almost always remain more emotionally attached to their adult offspring than the latter are in return (Streib 1965). Some continuing tension between the generations can hardly be avoided, given the contemporary theme of emancipation on the one hand and the traditional theme of filial respect on the other. It rests on the twin wishes to have close kinship ties and separate conjugal families, both at the same time (Glasser and Glasser 1962).

The literature on this point has been sharpened in the last thirty years by the clash of two opposed points of view. One, taking shape for over a century, holds that the modern family has drifted toward an isolated, nuclear arrangement with only two essential functions: (1) the rearing of children, and (2) ego stability for its members (Parsons and Bales 1955). But another point of view, largely in reaction to this, has also emerged. It argues that the larger kinship group retains many important functions inherited from the past and that it has even developed some new ones that can be very useful in the modern city (Sussman and Burchinal 1962). Everybody seems to agree that both the material and the ideological bases for the traditional large family have been cut back. The argument is over the extent to which the kinship network still exists and can be useful. The new arrangement has been called a "modified extended family system" (Litwak 1960a) or a "nonisolated nuclear family system" (Winch 1968).

Talcott Parsons, whose name is linked to the *isolation theory* more than anyone else's, stresses two characteristics of the nuclear family. One is residential. It rests on the premise that the family of the modern young couple normally has its own household, not shared with members of the parent generation and often far away from both parents and other kinsmen. Proof for this proposition is overwhelming, although some writers have objected on the grounds that three-generation households (consisting of grandparents, parents, and children) are still fairly numerous in the United States. According to census data, however, 97.2 percent of all married couples had their own households in 1959,* and in 1960 only one in ten husband-wife households had relatives other than children living in.†

---

* U.S. Bureau of the Census, *Current Population Reports—Population Characteristics,* Series P–20, No. 100 (April 13, 1960).

† U.S. Bureau of the Census, *United States Census of Population: 1960,* Final Report PC(2)–4A (Washington, D.C.: Government Printing Office, 1963).

Paul Reiss (1962) found that parents and mature offspring often want to live closer together than they actually do, but still not too close. The ideal of an independent household is neither weak nor precarious. And it is not simply an American pattern. In one country after another older people want to maintain family intimacy, but at a distance (Rosenmayr 1968). Whereas a sizable minority of older couples prefer to live alone, away from their relatives (Beyer 1962), an effort is usually made to avoid total or prolonged isolation. Widowed grandmothers in particular often live with their children, but not necessarily because they prefer to. Inadequate housing along with low income are the most common reasons (Sheldon 1958).

As a rule, common residence is strongly disapproved of by both generations, and Alvin Schorr (1962) says that this negative reaction tends to be exaggerated beyond good judgment. The younger generation objects to joint living arrangements, and it is only with great reluctance that most older people will give up their freedom and become members of their children's households (Gleason 1956). Thus, the three-generation family must be considered a special case; it is neither typical nor ideal any longer. Perhaps the fact that such shared arrangements do not necessarily cause problems for anyone, which Bert Adams (1968b) has shown in a North Carolina study, is beside the point.

The second characteristic of family isolation stressed by Parsons is that the households of most young couples are *economically* independent of all other households, including both the husbands' and wives' parents. Much greater controversy has been churned up by this point than by Parson's first one. Certainly parents help their children after they leave home if they can, offering financial aid and emergency assistance, making tactful gifts, giving constructive advice and encouragement, and providing a wide range of services—babysitting in particular (Sussman 1953; Moss and MacNab 1961).

Hope Leichter and William Mitchell (1967) found a surprisingly high level of *extended* familism among their nonaffluent Jewish sample in New York, involving parental assistance in the form of financial aid, information, and advice. And yet most of these people actually preferred nonfamily assistance in all three areas. Parents and other relatives are "resources" that can be useful when other sources either cannot provide help or charge too much.

Marvin Sussman and Lee Burchinal (1962) argue that financial aid from parents is available to an increasing number of families because people now have more *discretionary* income (money not needed for basic essentials). They contend that help from parents to married offspring has weakened the financial separateness of the young couple, though it has not replaced the ideal of separation. Moreover, Bert Adams (1964) notes that financial aid from parents is usually indirect in order to avoid any appearance of taking over the young father's role as provider. He found that financial aid in the middle classes begins immediately after marriage and soon diminishes. Services, too, reach a peak during the preschool years of the grandchildren. In a later study (1968) of a large group of young married couples, most of them said that their parents were the people they could rely on above all others.

But parents very seldom make specific decisions for their mature offspring. Their new role is indeed a postparental role, and it is supportive rather than coercive. The immunity of the young couple to parental controls is now guaranteed by strong and virtually unchallengeable social conventions. Only wealthy parents or parents whose offspring were never given a chance to be on their own in the first place have real leverage with their children. The help that parents give supplements rather than displaces the basic activities of the new family. The primary economic tie between the generations—occasional parental aid to the young marrieds—is itself based on neither a legal nor a cultural ideal, but rather upon ad hoc feelings and sentiments binding parents to their children (Sussman and Burchinal 1962).

After reviewing the above facts, only one conclusion can hold up: The relationship between parents and their mature offspring depends on the kinds of *expressive* relations that they have built up over the years. If the parents have been highly *managerial* toward their children, that is, if they have been busily running their lives as much as possible (most likely by urging them to be successful and trying to keep close supervision at all times), then the process of leaving home will probably be a stormy and unpleasant one as the parents persist in "helping out."

If the relationship has been based relatively more on friendly relations, the postparental period can be an agreeable one in most cases. Perhaps the ideal, especially in light of the current parent-to-child aid pattern, is for parental responsibility to be phased out slowly (but phased out nonetheless) and followed by a more congenial, equalitarian relationship. This is indeed what seems to happen, as suggested by the work of Bert Adams, Wayne Thompson, and Gordon Streib. Both financial aid and parental services reach a high point shortly after marriage, extending through the preschool years of the grandchildren, but by middle age—at least by later middle age—relations between the generations will be marked by simple friendliness, freed to a considerable extent from the old hang-ups.

After this, however, the relationship takes a decided turn toward renewed managerial or *instrumental* forms. As the parents enter old age and start having chronic health problems—about the age of seventy-five, but often earlier—the role of the mature offspring becomes problematic. Their job in the twentieth century is not so much to look after their parents in a direct way, but to see to it that their needs are met by people or agencies that can in fact do the job. Since we are as yet so inept in handling problems of the aged, the offspring are often just as bewildered as their parents. More and more attention will undoubtedly be focused on how middle-aged people can help the aged in years to come. Hopefully, our general understanding of what can be done and what the alternatives are will be greatly improved.

As families move from farms to cities, mothers tend to replace fathers as the key figures in kinship relations, and this trend becomes all the more important in middle age (Dore 1963). Dorrian Apple Sweetser (1966) points out that where fathers and sons work together, and the son is expected to replace his father both at work and as head of the family property when he grows up, men are very important in kinship affairs. When the succession from father to son serves as the basis for strong ties among male kinsmen, it is virtually essential that the family be an economic unit of production, and that kinsmen live close together. Such an arrangement is called a *corporate* or *stem family*. The life work of the son is a direct consequence of his family position rather than the operation of a labor market or educational achievement.

Where there is no father-to-son career pattern, relations are closer on the wife's side of the family. In that situation not only do sons choose careers that are unlike their fathers', but the father can only rarely give advice or direct capital assistance. Perhaps he can send his son to college, which is capital assistance of a sort, but the young man is thereby guided into a world that his father probably cannot enter, since it involves training and skills beyond his understanding. The son has to make most of the big decisions on his own or with the help of a faculty adviser.

Relatives are no longer of much use to men in their daily business, but they can be of considerable use to women—in child care, household decisions, and for purposes of companionship (wives seem to be closer to their parents, especially to their mothers, than husbands are to theirs). Closer relations between the wife and her family show up in a variety of ways: Parents of the wife are more likely to live with the couple than are the husband's parents; they are also more likely to live near her home; the intergenerational bond that carries the most *affect* is usually between mothers and daughters; the wife's relatives are more likely to visit unannounced (and even to have a key to the household); letters are more frequently written to the wife's parents than to the husband's (the wife often writes to both her own and her husband's parents); large family gatherings occur more frequently with the wife's relatives than with husband's; and assistance to the older generation involving money, care, and housework comes more often from the daughter than from the son. Although these patterns change during the family cycle, if anything the wife becomes progressively more involved than her husband, certainly not less.

The fact that relations are closer with the wife's family than with her husband's is not hard to explain, especially since the wife becomes the key to kin relations. She will usually have stormier relations with her mother-in-law than with her own mother, for example. Conflict between the husband and his mother-in-law can also be stormy, but it rarely approaches the antagonism of exchanges between wife and mother-in-law. For one thing, hostility is usually greater between persons of the same sex than between opposites (except in husband-wife relations). But even more important is the fact that the husband's work will probably take him away from home much of the time. When his mother comes to visit, the man's wife may have to spend more time with her than can possibly be filled with easygoing pleasantries. He will not be burdened by his mother-in-law nearly as much as the wife is burdened by hers. And the wife has probably already worked out ways of dealing with her own mother; her husband's mother poses a new challenge that may take years to resolve. Consequently the mother-daughter link is usually stronger than that between mother and daughter-in-law. (But it should be added that *all* in-law relations become a little more difficult when the stress is on expressive, leisure affairs rather than on working together. The old days of a kitchen full of women fixing dinner seem to be gone forever. The modern mother-in-law is usually urged to stay out of the kitchen.)

GRANDPARENTHOOD

Perhaps the greatest joys of later middle age are found in grandparenthood. (Many people still think of this as part of *old* age. But most new grandparents do not yet consider themselves senior citizens.) This role is without doubt the prime survivor of the extended family system. Grandparents remain closer to members of the nuclear family unit than any other relatives, followed at a considerable distance by aunts and uncles, then cousins (Robins and Tomanec 1962). Great-aunts and great-uncles are only rarely included among the relatives with whom core family members now have close relations.

A strong argument can be made for the proposition that the grandparent role has actually become a more important one in modern society than it was in the past, despite the general decrease in familism. Since people live longer, their chances of becoming grandparents are better than ever. The odds on their surviving as grandparents for an extended period of time have improved, too. Grandparents seem to play a relatively larger role in the lives of their grandchildren, especially since uncles and aunts are so much less important.

The fact of longer life expectancy adds to the general scope of grandparenthood in still another way, since the lengthened period of life corresponds to the retirement stage, a time of greater freedom to enjoy the family. This is especially true in the ages between sixty-five and seventy-five when health problems are not so bad—problematical maybe, but not immobilizing. Because families do not have as many children now, grandparents can concentrate their energies more narrowly on three or four.

But when all the pertinent facts are gathered together, they do not always point to a larger or more important role for the modern grandparent, particularly since the role faces special hardships in the modern city. As a case in point, Sydney Croog and Peter New (1965) found that many Americans have little or no knowledge of their grandfathers' occupations. Even the father's job tends to be invisible in the city compared to the work of farm fathers, and the careers of older men are almost totally unknown. Data collected by Croog and New suggest that people in the upper classes know most about their grandfathers; only men who have had impressive careers can be remembered for more than one generation by kinsmen in contemporary society.

Although grandparents typically make regular visits to their children's families, they neither have nor want responsibilities for the care of grandchildren (Albrecht 1954), and they take vicarious pride in the accomplishments of these children to a markedly lesser extent than the children's parents (Neugarten and Weinstein 1964). Indeed, grandparents apparently *avoid* an active and regular part in raising or providing for grandchildren unless there are special circumstances. Max Kaplan (1960) compares the contemporary grandparent to the second-generation immigrant of forty or fifty years ago; both are "marginal men." The immigrant received his basic cultural training in the old world but moved to a new one, and was marginal to both. Grandparents are caught between their knowledge of how to be useful in the old family setting and their children's independence from them in the new one.

Only where economic power and prestige rest with the aged, backed by strong family traditions, are grandparents and grandchildren likely to interact in terms of authority and deference. Where the grandparents are denied family authority, they take an equalitarian or even indulgent attitude toward their grandchildren (Apple 1956). Certainly grandparents are no longer authorities, not on family life in general nor even on their grandchildren in particular. Dr. Benjamin Spock, author of one of the most widely read books on child care ever written, once called himself a "substitute for grandmother."

Meanwhile, the modern grandfather often assumes the role of "fun seeker" with his grandchildren. He, too, exercises very little power. The most typical attitude of grandchildren toward him is one of "privileged disrespect," whereby grandchildren show greater respect for the authority of their parents than for that of grandparents, and parents are expected to maintain authority in a way not expected of the grandparents (Townsend 1957). Ruth Cavan (1962) says that the modern grandfather has to operate within a maternal, companionship setting in place of the patriarchal arrangement. He becomes a slightly masculinized grandmother. But Cavan also adds that most grandfathers do not seem to object, nor is their pride hurt. (Patriarchy has been dead for several generations now, so most of them have never learned to expect patriarchal deference.) Bernice Neugarten and Karol Weinstein (1964) contend that grandfathers, even more than grandmothers, attempt to do things for their grandchildren that they could never do for their own children, in large part because they were so absorbed by their careers when they were younger.

DISENGAGEMENT

Before leaving middle age behind it seems appropriate to call attention to the *disengagement theory* of aging (to be discussed in more detail in the following chapter). Some people argue that this general process starts in middle age. Elaine Cumming and William Henry (1961), for example, contend that normal aging is a process of *mutual disengagement* between the aging person and others around him. It begins with a reasonably stable level of social activity in middle age and leads to a much lower level in old age. The theory does not say that this begins with any kind of self-conscious effort by the middle-aged person to become a withdrawn senior citizen. It does suggest, however, that it happens because certain social and personal conditions appear for the first time in middle age, and, in what has become one of the most controversial parts of the theory, both the individual and society *implicitly* agree that aging people should disengage.

For example, Cumming (1963) contends that fundamental changes in our perception of things occur in middle age. One of the most important changes, she argues, is an urgent new awareness of the inevitability of death, a vivid apprehension of mortality in which the end of life seems closer than its beginning. This in turn radiates outward from the very core of the person's image of himself.

Whether such a realization is a truly important event in the lives of most middle-aged people remains unresolved, but it seems safe to allow that some heightened sense of mortality is part of a larger change in feelings and thoughts about life itself. The fact that the middle-aged couple's children are now marrying and settling into separate routines may actually be a more troubling realization than thoughts about death. In either case, the basic meaning of life begins to shift into a new focus.

Another psychological nudge toward disengagement occurs when the middle-aged person (who may have managed to avoid inner questioning before this time) reaches the point in life where losses begin to outrun his ability to replace them: a friend dies, a business closes, the children move away. Earlier in life losses could be replaced, if not in actuality, then in a spirit of hope for the future. Now with each loss the person must surrender a certain sense of his own life potential, replacing it with the symbolic echoes of memory. In a sense, this substitution of symbol for action amounts to a change in the *quality* of self.

Perhaps this is what is more popularly known as the *over-the-hill reaction*, which *can* occur in middle age, but which for many people does not occur until later in life, perhaps in the period of preretirement (from roughly fifty-five to sixty-five years of age). Nevertheless, Wayne Thompson and Gordon Streib (1961) suggest that such a reaction is associated with the self-conceptions of many middle-aged people. It stands at the end of one's "personal future," the point at which "onward and upward" is replaced by perseverance, tenacity, and an occasional fling "for old time's sake." To the extent that the perception of meaningful or even feasible activity is getting narrower rather than broader, the person has embarked upon a radically new phase in life.

A NOTE ON THE STUDY OF MIDDLE AGE

The first section in this chapter was entitled "Optimism and Emptiness," and there was no conscious intention to stress emptiness over self-confidence and high spirits. The disengagement theory with its pessimistic point of view has been subjected to a constant barrage of criticism as we shall see in the following chapter. For many people, middle age is the best time of life. The literature in sociology and psychology for this period is by no means rich and encouraging, however. Mainly it is just skimpy, and for several reasons. Childhood, adolescence, and old age receive much more attention (each by a ratio of at least four or five to one), and one of these three—old age—has itself only recently been discovered (by researchers, that is).

The pattern of discovery was not accidental. In the earliest development of social and behavioral science, attention tended to focus on social issues and philosophies of a very broad nature. As individuals were slowly isolated for study, the psychological problems of adults seem to have been noted first, leading fairly quickly to a concern for the cause of their troubles. This led inevitably to studies of childhood and to the rise of such provocative theories as those of Freud and his followers.

But even as the scientific study of childhood became respectable (especially with the work of such remarkable observers as Jean Piaget), a troublesome area of study associated with another age group was appearing—juvenile delinquency—and adolescence emerged as an isolable stage in life. After the study of both childhood and adolescence had gained momentum, attention turned toward old age, especially when it was recognized that the elderly were increasing in numbers out of all proportion to other age groups in the population. But the elderly did not emerge as a subject for extensive research until *after* the problems of adolescence had been recognized.

Perhaps the reader can see where all this is leading: Only after childhood, adolescence, and old age had been opened up to research was it possible to focus attention on the middle-aged population as a problem. Once the aged became subjects for scientific investigation, it was just a matter of time before we turned to middle age, because it was inevitable that the developmental approach upon which all behavioral theories are based would show that problems of old age have their roots in middle age. The logic may seem strained, but the sequence was perfectly rational. Research into adult abnormality led to the study of childhood, which happened to occur at the very time that adolescence was being recognized as a special stage in life causing distinctive personal and social problems.

The fact that children and adolescents were so convenient for study also helped to popularize research in this area. In fact, if there is any flaw in the present reasoning, it is that middle age has been slow to emerge as an object for study simply because its members are not as accessible as other groups. They are dispersed in a much wider variety of activities, and therefore they present an incredibly diversified range of life styles—and a moving target to researchers. The middle-aged also tend to be people of relatively high social status who follow established routines and who do not cause much trouble, at least not the kind that is newsworthy. Their very status gives them a measure of immunity from probing social researchers; people of lower social status, including the middle-aged who fall in this category, are studied most often.

Unfortunately, as this chapter is being written the study of middle age is still in its infancy. The field does not yet have a clear-cut identity, nor even a scientific-sounding name. The medical profession has been adept at giving impressive, if not intimidating, names to its fields of study, but so far only the age-graded specialties of *pediatrics* and *geriatrics* have emerged.

As the study of middle age gains momentum, we should expect research on problem behavior—especially reactions to emptiness or a sense of emptiness—to take precedence over studies of benign adjustment. Behavioral scientists have always tried to explain deviancy before attempting to explain what seems to need no explanation—problem-free behavior.

SUMMARY

The middle years of marriage can be years of fulfillment, but there is the possibility of emptiness, too. For many couples it is a time of family optimism, or at least of hopeful expectancy. The children are now coming of age; they will be starting careers and getting married, and in a quickly changing society such as ours their opportunities usually seem even more exciting than for the previous generation.

But the middle-aged couple usually worry as their children pass through the later teen years, which is justifiably called the launching stage. The offspring have now turned some of their best energies to the youth culture, not exclusively of course, but with unprecedented freedom from the family. They leave home psychologically before they go physically, and the parents can only watch, hoping that they have done everything parents should do. It is not clear just what they *ought* to do to guide and control their children as the process unfolds. Many young people say the answer is simple: as little as possible—but parents find that hard to accept. In any case, the full separation of youth from the family is a truly new thing when viewed in historical perspective.

The father usually takes stock of himself at this time, most often in terms of his success as a provider, while the woman reflects on her efforts as a mother. As authority figures, neither parent is very impressive, but the father's power has faded most notably. Ideally, parents are objects of affection for their children rather than figures of authority, and it is no accident that this new approach turned up at the very time in history when we started worrying about the generation gap. The tie between the generations now tends to be expressive in nature, based more on friendship (in the ideal case) than supervision. Obviously the switch from the old to the new is neither painless nor complete.

One possibility is that the middle-aged couple will move closer to one another as their children leave home. Another is that tendencies toward separation (which may have existed all along, but were muffled by the parents' mutual interest in the children) will become even more obvious. The couple find themselves in a period of redefinition of both their separate lives as individuals and their family life together. Certainly sex is not likely to be a strong binding force at this stage in life. It will occur less often and lack the old spark. And yet many psychic and social reasons exist for clinging to the marriage; the divorce rate does not go up in middle age. In fact, one reason for conflict during the child-rearing years was the daily tension over how to manage the children. Now this source of friction is gone.

The mother (if she has not been employed) will probably seek a new sense of usefulness and self-worth, which can mean employment, volunteer work, or club affairs. By contrast, the husband is more likely to be reaching the top of his career and may become even busier than before. Meanwhile, the adult offspring are settling in homes of their own, and the parents will give whatever help they can, especially financial.

Grandparenthood begins in the later stages of middle age, and it may very well offer a new enchantment. But the grandparent role, like parenthood, is like nothing before in history. Although it lasts much longer now (on the average), and there are fewer grandchildren, the grandparents will probably have no role in disciplining their grandchildren nor any very important function in advising the young parents. Furthermore, the activities of grandmother and grandfather overlap to a much greater extent.

Although disengagement from both the family and the larger community may begin at this time, opportunities for continued—even increased—social activity are plentiful in modern cities. Unfortunately, however, this is mainly true for couples with money enough to meet more than the bare essentials of life.

SELECTED READINGS

AXELSON, LELAND. "Personal Adjustment in the Postparental Period," *Marriage and Family Living*, Vol. 22 (February 1960), pp. 66–70.

CHILMAN, CATHERINE S. "Families in Development at Mid-Stage of the Family Life Cycle," *The Family Coordinator*, Vol. 17 (October 1968), pp. 297–312.

DEUTSCHER, IRWIN. "The Quality of Postparental Life: Definitions of the Situation," *Journal of Marriage and the Family*, Vol. 26 (February 1964), pp. 52–59.

GLICK, PAUL C., AND ROBERT PARKE, JR. "New Approaches in Studying the Life Cycle of the Family," *Demography*, Vol. 2 (1965), pp. 187–202.

NEUGARTEN, BERNICE L., AND KAROL K. WEINSTEIN. "The Changing American Grandparent," *Marriage and Family Living*, Vol. 26 (May 1964), pp. 199–204.

SUSSMAN, MARVIN B., AND LEE G. BURCHINAL. "Kin Family Network: Unheralded Structure in Current Conceptualizations of Family Functioning," *Marriage and Family Living*, Vol. 24 (August 1962), pp. 231–240.

SWEETSER, DORRIAN APPLE. "The Effect of Industrialization on Intergenerational Solidarity," *Rural Sociology*, Vol. 31 (June 1966), pp. 156–170.

THOMPSON, WAYNE E., AND GORDON F. STREIB. "Meaningful Activity in a Family Context," in Robert W. Kleemeier (ed.), *Aging and Leisure: A Research Perspective into the Meaningful Use of Time*. New York: Oxford University Press, 1961, pp. 177–211.

CHAPTER 12

The Family and Old Age

The total impact of longer life expectancy is beyond calculation. It leads to family changes in every stage of the life cycle. Its most obvious effects occur in the older age brackets, where both the absolute and the relative number of people have been increasing rapidly for several generations. About 9 percent of the American population is now over sixty-five years of age, and in absolute numbers the figure is near 20 million.

This *demographic revolution* is very recent and has needed no rebels or agitators to bring it about. It simply occurred as an inevitable consequence of the technical development of modern culture. The very fact that it was unplanned and as yet remains unplannable means that its effect upon the aged is not of man's own choosing. We may have "chosen" to cut the death rate (by our commitment to medical progress), but no deliberative body has ever placed its stamp of approval on the general condition of the aged in modern society. A visit to an average home for older citizens provides evidence that care for the aged is one area in which Americans do not seem to excel.

Nevertheless, the geriatric upheaval goes on. It is by no means slowing down, and new breakthroughs in life expectancy are still being made. The most revolutionary medical inventions so far have had their strongest effect upon infancy and childhood. We are still awaiting the most significant discoveries for cutting death rates among the elderly. Although it seems unlikely that medicine will provide any startling extension of maximum life in the immediate future, more and more people will live to a

239

ripe old age (Milne and Milne 1968). But the inequality in life expectancy for men and women—whereby women survive in larger numbers than men in every age category—remains a mystery, and the imbalance grows greater every decade. So one of the problems of old age in all industrial nations is a superabundance of women.

Study of the aged has progressed rapidly in the past quarter of a century, and the possibilities for sophisticated research in this area are now impressive. Yet society has not done very well by its older people—certainly not because the necessary wealth and resources are lacking. In fact, the conditions that permit longer life for the majority of people also seem to assure that the wealth needed to care for them (in a collective sense) will be available.

Thus, our failure to cope with the social and psychological problems of aging is a national embarrassment. We are much more successful in extending life than in improving its quality in the later years. American ingenuity in so many other areas simply fails to apply here. Irving Rosow (1965) suggests that our aged are an embarrassment to us because they are a mute reproach to our social conscience, somewhat comparable to our reaction to poverty. The elderly suffer primarily from lack of *function* and *status*; although the decline in their status seems to be a long-term trend over which we have no immediate control, their lack of function is another matter.

Industrial man has decades of experience in meeting the needs of children, but he is just learning how to provide for masses of older people. For example, the most challenging need of modern children is education, and this challenge has been met with considerable success through public efforts. With all its faults, the American school system ranks favorably with all contenders in the world, and there is virtually no popular opposition to the principle of free public education. The most pressing comparable needs among the aged are health care and housing. Not only do we not have decades of experience in meeting these needs through public efforts (whereby health and housing facilities would be provided for all as a matter of right), but strong opposition to the *idea* of such public facilities continues to exist. Housing for the aged—with all the facilities needed to meet their special needs—is still part of the private profit economy in America, and it is not working well at all.

THE PROBLEM

The problem, however, extends far beyond the difficulties involved in changing our health and housing systems to meet the most basic material problems of older people. In some respects we are just learning what old age is, since for many years it was thought to begin at age sixty-five. That may be a good time for retirement, but a more critical dividing line occurs at the age of seventy-five, when many chronic health problems first begin to show up. It is at this time that the person's sensory abilities—taste, smell, sight, hearing, and probably touch—decline most noticeably. And certainly the two key *family* problems of old age become almost universal at this time: (1) widowhood and (2) loss of the ability to maintain an independent household. These two problems appear at an accelerating pace between the ages of sixty-five and seventy-five, but at seventy-five the person who does not face at least one of them is a rarity, and the great majority will have to deal with both.

The changing population structure creates wholly new family problems, ones that have never been met in history before. For example, Peter Townsend (1968) points out that great-grandparenthood and the four-generation family are increasing at a brisk pace in industrial societies. They have never appeared on a substantial scale before. Most women reach great-grandmotherhood in the early seventies, whereas men more often become great-grandfathers in the middle seventies. Since men have shorter life expectancies than women and reach great-grandparenthood at a later age, they are notably underrepresented in this category. Nevertheless, Townsend found that over 40 percent of his sample of Americans sixty-five and over were great-grandparents. (The percentages were somewhat lower in European samples. Townsend believes that the higher rate in the United States is due largely to our higher American marriage rate and to our lower average age at marriage.)

Townsend shows that the increase in the four-generation family is not due to longer life expectancy alone. It results also from the fact that marriages of people now reaching sixty-five were entered at an earlier age than for people of an earlier time. Couples in the more recent era have also been having fewer children and within a shorter span of time after marriage. This means that they are not so old when the last child is born. In turn, they are younger when the last child marries and starts having children, increasing the likelihood that they will become great-grandparents.

The greatest significance of this shows up in new relationships within the family. Interchanges between the two older generations in the four-generation family probably become more intense and more frequent, as Townsend argues, and a situation emerges where the sixty-year-old grandmother may find her time divided between caring for her aged mother and doting on her grandchildren. The standard conception of the extended family usually covers only three generations, where the couple in the middle looks after both the older and the younger generations. Now two generations stand in the middle, and the range of possible relationships becomes much more complicated. The possibilities for familism would certainly seem to grow in this process, not dwindle.

But not all of the problems of the aged in modern society are family problems. Robert Butler (1963) says that a universal inner experience among older people is the continual, almost obsessive review of their lives. Although much of this concentrates on family matters, it is rather surprising how much is self-centered rather than familistic. Perhaps in highly familistic societies, where individualism is not so strong, things are different. Still, old age is the retrospective period when memories of a full family life can compensate for many physical infirmities.

And yet certain assumptions about the way people should spend their time almost inevitably create problems. For example, family activities are considered good and desirable by most of us, but family performance is almost always impaired as we grow older. As the number of elderly people increases, the scope of the problem grows, and the number of people in the younger age categories who feel embarrassed or threatened by it grows, too.

The problem can be divided into three parts: (1) As people grow older they are unable to do many things with and for the family that could be done before, but their commitment to familism and to the people in their own family circle does not decline—if anything, it grows stronger; (2) the older married couple must learn to adjust together in new ways as their involvement with the larger family declines; (3) younger members of the family (almost always the couple's children in contemporary society) must face the fact that the elders need their help.

Clearly, the family problems of old age are not limited to the elderly. Offspring in the middle years are drawn in, so that aging is not merely a future problem; it poses dilemmas of more than routine concern even before we grow old. At this stage in our knowledge of gerontology we do not know exactly what its impact on children and young adults is, but it no doubt hits them in a variety of ways, too.

AGING AND FAMILISM

One family challenge for the aged is their need to keep up family contacts while maintaining personal independence. In their younger years they were much more involved in trying to control the family's future—preparing for it and urging the children to become as successful as possible. Now their need is to conserve whatever sense of familism they have achieved as the family circle scatters. The problem is a formidable one because *family conservation* tends to be ill-fated in an urban environment. Not only are family members dispersed physically, but social and psychological differences can separate them even if they do not stray geographically.

This is particularly true for people at higher educational levels. The formal school system, especially at the higher levels, is probably the most revolutionary force for social and psychological diversity in modern society. It replaces the family (and the church) as the place to go for intellectual excitement (although the role of books, magazines, and the mass media should not be overlooked in this connection). To whatever extent this kind of excitement wins a person over, he will often—though not necessarily—turn away from his childhood home and relatives. He may resort instead to literature, drama, magazines, and like-minded people for mental stimulation. The elderly can still have a symbolic or sentimental importance for the younger generation, but their ability to fascinate is weak indeed—unless they are unusually spry for their age.

Not only do youth find relations with people their own age more satisfying, the sense of deference to age seems to crumble in the city. In agricultural societies, older people usually own the land. They have power because offspring are dependent on this basic form of wealth. In industrial societies, the aged do not control property as a rule; they may own stocks and bonds, but that kind of ownership rarely carries power over the day-to-day interests of youth. In fact, the ownership of land seems to be more widely distributed in agricultural societies than ownership of stocks and bonds in modern industrial ones, but reliable figures to prove this statement are not available. In any case, capital ownership is usually separated from business management, and hence the actual control of most companies is not in the hands of people over sixty-five. Even if we could assume that some of the old men who sit on boards of directors actually run things, we would have to admit that a very small percentage of all older men are employed in this way. (The same general principle applies to government power, despite the fact that the chairmen of crucial senate and congressional committees average over sixty-five years of age.)

In agricultural societies the elderly often have knowledge, or at least traditional lore, which younger people almost always respect. There are simply fewer areas where this can occur in rapidly moving societies. Knowledge now doubles every ten years or so, and past experience counts for less and less. Perhaps even in industrial nations the older people may possess useful "wisdom" for making decisions of a very broad nature, but again the number of men who are used in that way—as senators, supreme court justices, and so on—is small compared to the total old-age population.

A premium is placed on new ideas, and the elderly can only rarely compete. It is true that creativity differs considerably from one field to the next. Wayne Dennis (1966) studied 739 creative people, all of whom lived to be at least seventy-nine years old. He found the highest rate of output for nearly all groups occurred in their forties; after that there was not much decline until age sixty, when creative work dropped sharply. But the typical man (who is not particularly creative and was not included in Dennis' sample) probably stops toying with new ideas to any great extent in his late twenties or early thirties. Simply hanging on to a conventional point of view may have been useful in the past, but it guarantees obsolescence now, even before the age of sixty-five in many cases.

It is not easy for men over forty to start challenging careers unless they were specifically prepared for them earlier, and for men over sixty-five the problem of keeping up is often insurmountable. The best use of older workers occurs when jobs are tailored to their personal qualities, which is exactly the opposite of current bureaucratic practice (where the man is expected to adjust to his job). Bureaucracy inevitably rebels at personalized treatment for workers except at the very top of the hierarchy—among vice-presidents and above—but men at this level have had unusual opportunities to be resourceful in old age anyway.

The proportion of people employed over the age of sixty-five has dropped steadily in the past half century. Of those who are working, almost half are self-employed, but self-employment itself is a disappearing part of the total job structure. The best chance for the aged is found in a tight labor market, which has turned up only during wartime in the twentieth century. The bitter fact is that when we are at war the employability of older people goes up, but the war itself takes such a toll from the national economy that efforts to provide first-rate care for them is almost always postponed.

The main purpose of this discussion is to show why the ability of older men to influence, let alone control, younger members of their family declines sharply with industrial development. Older people are best off if they have middle-aged offspring who, for personal reasons, feel obligated to keep close contacts. Since this kind of obligation no longer gets strong social support, it is most likely produced by the style of the family itself. When adult couples plan the future of their families, that is, when they buy such things as life insurance policies and annuities, they might give some thought to the state of familism in their household. Unfortunately, such advice is much like that now given in the area of sex education. Since the traditional controls over sex have withered to a fraction of their old power, the key becomes education, but we are still not sure how to teach sex control in a society that stimulates impulse release at every turn. Similarly, how does a parent prepare children to be dutiful when the main thrust of our culture pushes them away from home?

The plight of the aged is dramatized by the fact that they have passed the stage in life for personal achievement, while a basic premise of modern culture holds that accomplishment is the measure of the man. The fact that achievement fades with age cannot be denied, and Talcott Parsons (1960) was certainly correct when he argued that "achievement needs a future." Our concern for the aged is not that they do not produce enough, although old people themselves sometimes worry about this very thing. They are simply not asked to be productive or creative, and they are much more concerned about their ability to keep up human contacts than to conquer new worlds. The concern for achievement shifts to concern for expressive relations.

But this shift—in an achievement-oriented society—may very well be a personal crisis. Such a reaction is most dramatically expressed in "youthful aging," as in the case of athletes. The thirty-five-year-old baseball pro faces a critical stage in life even if he is still a pretty good player. He knows his career is tailing off and that the main basis for his reputation will soon be exhausted. Aging for most people is a much slower process. For men it forces a realization that they have had their chance for a successful career. The results are now virtually in. For women, it means that they can no longer be a major influence on their children. The results of their mothering have now showed up (although the mother's influence on children is too often exaggerated).

Actually, most people in modern society are not achievers, despite our obsession with that possibility. Most of us reach a level of affluence made possible—in a sense, guaranteed—by the general state of the economy. During the middle years of life we acquire domestic capital, slowly paying off the mortgages on our homes and buying household furnishings that can be added to and improved over the years. Each household can compare reasonably well with others of approximately its own level—its *reference group*—which provide the most appropriate means of gauging one's own success.

But an inevitable problem is the fact that almost any success achieved by one generation will be surpassed by the next. The general level of achievement (reckoned in terms of domestic capital) keeps going up, very much like the inflationary spiral. Older couples had to work for a lifetime to accumulate what their children—certainly their grandchildren—can have fairly early in marriage. In fact, the new generation wants to start out where the old one left off and many succeed.

Reuben Hill (1968) studied households drawn from three generations of the same family line, comparing the grandparent generation, the parent generation, and the married grandchildren. His conclusions were devastating. The oldest family members proved to be severely underprivileged by comparison with the younger generations. For example, the grandfathers averaged considerably less educational achievement than the fathers, who themselves averaged much less than the grandsons. Occupationally, the grandfathers ranked lowest of the three generations, and they had made less upward progress in the course of their lives. In each succeeding generation a larger percentage of women had worked during the first several years of marriage and had returned to work after their children grew up. (This is not necessarily a sign of progress, but younger women are increasingly seeing it in that light.) Families in the youngest generation had already exceeded the grandparent generation in the percentage owning homes; they were at a level that took their parents twenty years of marriage to reach. The youngest generation had also caught up with the grandparent generation in the collection of durable goods; it had taken the parent generation thirty-five years of marriage to accumulate as much. A higher percentage of the young married group had firm financial plans for retirement, achieving the level reached by the parent generation only after thirty years of marriage. The grandparent generation occupied homes or apartments with the lowest rental values, and they more often lived in the poorest neighborhoods.

The only possible conclusion is that people in the older generation have not only reached a stage in life when they can no longer be concerned with personal achievement; the past achievements of most of them cannot be the basis for great esteem or respect in the eyes of the younger generation (although unequal levels of achievement apparently do not create bad relations between the generations [Adams 1968a]). Talcott Parsons (1963) has suggested that old age is the consummatory phase of life, a period of harvest when the hard work of the mature years is over. But for most older people it will not be a bountiful harvest. Any society that stresses creative achievement is a tough one to grow old in. This is true not only because achievement for the aged lies in the past, but because typical standards of achievement change from one generation to the next. Rarely does this kind of social progress give any advantage to the aged.

The older person's ego is not the only thing that suffers in the achievement-oriented society. The family itself is handicapped, since the stress on creativity does not favor familism. Anything that can release creative energies takes priority in an industrial society. If old age is not the time for achievement, almost by definition it will probably welcome an upsurge in familism. Both the need and the preference for family bonds take a step forward at this time, but the vital forces of society are busy undermining them in the younger age brackets.

There is at least one partial solution, however. People too old to be in the competitive scramble can identify with younger competitors, especially kinsmen. They can look to their middle-aged offspring or to their grandchildren (and increasingly to their great-grandchildren). Although achievement-striving in the middle years often draws people away from direct involvement in family affairs, identification with the deeds of younger relatives is more than ever a favorite family sport among the aged.

REVERSAL OF THE AID PATTERN

Although the trend is toward a more isolated, nuclear family, most households in the United States retain ties with at least some of their kinsmen. Relatives are usually spread out over the state or nation (despite some striking exceptions where relatives may cluster together in local neighborhoods, even in such places as New York City [Leichter and Mitchell 1967]), but contacts of various sorts are usually kept up—visits, telephone calls, letter writing, aid in the form of money and services, and the exchange of information and advice. Each kind of contact has been studied in recent years.

The evidence clearly shows that patterns change as the couple grow older. In particular, the flow of assistance changes pace over the years. Visiting, phoning, and letter writing may stabilize in the middle years, continuing more or less unchanged into old age, but financial assistance from parents to their offspring declines, and advice is certainly given more cautiously. Parents will usually make sacrifices for their small children and offer various kinds of help after they grow up, but as the parents grow old aid begins to travel in the opposite direction. Grandparents get substantially more help from younger family members than they give in return, except in the area of child care. Reuben Hill (1968) found this to be especially true with regard to help in time of sickness, help in managing the household, and help in the area of emotionial support.

In fact, Hill concludes that grandparents perceive themselves to be rather useless, especially in their ability to help younger members of the family. They are very conscious of the fact that they are receivers and readily admit being dependent (which is not to say they like it). By contrast, the middle-aged offspring are in a patronlike position—helpers of both the older and the younger members of the family, but they get relatively little help from either direction. The youngest generation (of married offspring in the three-generation family) has a status of greater interdependence with the older family members, since they both offer and take help. It is this generation that strikes the most even balance between giving and receiving emotional gratification, help in child care and household management, and aid in times of illness.

The tendency in a rapidly changing society is for the older generation to lose touch with the *technology of assistance*. Visiting never goes out of style, and the telephone can be used by the aged until almost total incapacity sets in, but the older generation becomes outdated on the subject of new information and techniques. One of the most useful services offspring can render is to try to keep them informed about the latest available facilities for the aged, public or private. This assumes that the younger generation will in fact be on the lookout for such things, an assumption that is not always met. Unfortunately, almost everybody seems to be sluggish in finding new ways to cope with the problems of old age; professional training for people who run homes for the aged is itself a relatively recent development.

The most critical need of the elderly seems to be help in making decisions about health care and living arrangements (Donahue 1954; Friedsam and Dick 1964). Younger members of the family can be extremely useful in helping the older ones decide where to live—in their own home, in an apartment, in a home for the aged, or where? The task of the younger generation is not to make the decision themselves, although perhaps at times they must, but to find out what the alternatives are and to *help* make the decision. They can also see to it that the various people who are paid to provide services for the elderly actually do what they are supposed to do and do it right. This need cannot possibly be underestimated. In the very nature of our mass, anonymous society each of us has to be on guard against swindlers and people who do not perform the services or supply the goods they promise. People without much education or who have to use highly specialized services are often easy marks under these circumstances, but almost all older people are vulnerable. In this respect they are a little like dependent children. They tried to protect their own children when they were small, and now they need their children's help. The roles are reversed.

What happens if older people have no close relatives to look out for them? Perhaps a friend will fill the need, and to some extent legal machinery has been set up to help. But, by and large, the person who has no kinsmen for protection goes unprotected. Or he is left to the good will of business and professional interests. Perhaps the good will is there, but it is probably unwise to abandon one's loved ones to that safeguard alone.

Ethel Shanas (1967) contends that the most important factors influencing help patterns in old age are the family's *size, structure,* and *living arrangements.* Between one-fifth and one-fourth of all old people have no surviving children, particularly the aged with white-collar backgrounds. She also found that those who did not have surviving children were more likely to receive help from brothers or sisters than from any other source.

The elderly get more help from their daughters than from sons in all social classes, but this seems to be especially true in the lower social levels (Young and Wilmott 1957; Shanas 1962). Maybe the explanation is simply that older people with white-collar backgrounds are less likely to have surviving daughters (Shanas 1967). But, generally speaking, when the aged parents do not have a daughter, the son will come to the rescue. Daughters give more help in the lower classes in part because they are more often available to give it, and it is at least possible that when old people decide to live near an adult child, they choose the daughter's area more often than the son's.

In fact, most older people live reasonably close to at least one of their adult children. Although white-collar parents often live at some distance from their nearest child, even they usually live close enough to get quick help when needed. Sharing a home physically with adult children is not too common, however, and it is most characteristic of older people in the working classes (Shanas 1967). An interesting commentary on modern life is the fact that as new technology pulls families farther apart, it also gives them the means to get together quickly in an emergency. (Telephones and jet planes are used most often for business purposes, of course, but family matters also occupy them day and night.)

THE ELDERLY COUPLE AND WIDOWHOOD

Elaine Cumming (1963) suggests that some people, because of their basic life style, may be better suited to old age than others. She refers in particular to the *impingers* and the *selectors*, who are presumed to differ in terms of their temperamental qualities.

Impingers are lively and brash; selectors are reserved and self-sufficient. Cumming argues that the former face greater anxiety as they grow old because they slowly lose their effectiveness in groups. This is shattering for them because they need group ties to preserve their sense of personal meaning. Selectors, on the other hand, are not threatened by this—their problem in old age is more likely to be apathy. In an achievement-oriented society, impingers are more suited to middle age; childhood and old age are more agreeable to selectors.

But Cumming's emphasis on temperamental (largely biological) qualities seems limited, if not misleading. Generally speaking, people react to crises late in life very much as they have reacted earlier. If they have had success, they will probably continue to be successful. Social differences among people may be even more relevant than temperament in this regard. And it is possible that some couples are better suited to the senior years because of the way they relate to each other. In fact, the style of the pair relationship may be more important than characteristics of either of the individuals considered separately. Emphasis has been placed on the degree to which couples give mutual ego support; there is no reason to believe that this ability should be any less useful in old age than at other stages in life.

If we take into account the fact that joint survival for the couple has been lengthened, then ego support may actually become more important. At the start of marriage the ego reinforcement pattern is crucial in determining whether the couple will stay together, and it influences the whole course that their psychological relationship will take. In old age the pattern is set; if mutual ego support is there, life will be much easier. There is every reason to believe that losses associated with aging are greatly softened if the aged have a close personal relationship to fall back on (Lowenthal and Haven 1968). Andras Angyal (1965) argues that keeping an intimate affinity with one other person is the ideal center of existence for most people up to the very end of life.

The fact remains that a gradual change in the aging person's self-concept can hardly be avoided, particularly as personal losses become harder to replace—when cronies of long standing die, for example. Among other things, the person needs new proofs of his own worth. Rewards for achievement may be replaced by expressive activity of one sort or another, but the former are more highly valued, and their distinguishing marks are clearer. With achievement a person knows where he stands; that is not as true with social-emotional relationships, especially among people who are not old friends.

Marriage work does not become less taxing in old age. Only if the pattern developed earlier in life is very effective—or the spouses have become completely resigned to their inability to help each other—can they coast through the later years (although older couples may typically slack off). But solidarity for them is based almost entirely on shared values and interests. Since homogamy was a key factor in their original attraction to one another, and they may have lived together forty, fifty, or even more years, shared values and interests in old age can be a profound reality. Although the couples may often *seem* miserable together, almost every body movement and every voice inflection has a meaning for them that is completely lost on outsiders.

But this need to be close with one other person makes widowhood all the more difficult, and the probabilities for joint survival drop at a disheartening rate after age sixty-five. Less than half of the population over that age still live with a spouse; one-fourth of the men and almost half of the women are widowed, and the rates go up steadily with each succeeding year.

The level of adjustment to loss of a spouse will depend on many things. Inviting controversy, Irving Rosow (1965) says that widowhood hits women particularly hard. His point is based primarily on the fact that many more women are widowed than men and that, contrary to the popular stereotype (of affluent widows who inherit their husbands' money), most of them are poorer than men of the same age. In 1960, for example, one-fourth of the widowed women had no income at all, three-fourths received less than $1,000 per year, and fewer than one out of ten received over $2,000 annually. By now inflation has raised these figures somewhat, but the essential fact has not changed: Old women are typically poor.

But a number of other factors have to be taken into account. Old men, though fewer than old women in both absolute and relative numbers, also have ample problems. Women, for one thing, are generally healthier. And they take care of themselves better—alone or with others. Men may have more money, but at no age are those who suffer economic distress as able as women to survive the social pressures of a household. Bear in mind that homelessness is not just a predicament for young and middle-aged men. It applies also to the older ones, and there is no comparable problem at any stage in the life cycle for women. Financial distress is simply not as dispiriting for them as it is for men.

Women without husbands are able to adjust to both the households of others and to a hospital or nursing home environment more smoothly than men without wives. Furthermore, between the ages of sixty-five and seventy-five the rate of suicide among American women drops rather steadily; among men it follows an upward trend (although this pattern does not necessarily hold true in other countries).

The fact that there are more women than men in the older age brackets seems to work to the women's advantage. Generally speaking, both men and women have had their most intimate relationships with members of their own sex (with the exception of the marriage bond itself). So women have considerably more opportunities to move into new relations with their own kind. In fact, there is greater continuity among female cronies in part because of the style that binds them together. Elaine Cumming (1963) claims, for example, that women usually specialize in social-emotional or *integrative* skills throughout life. These are the tools of human interaction everywhere. They are central to the traditional maternal and social roles of women, and it just so happens that they come in very handy in old age. It may even be that women, because of the style of life they most often take up in childhood, have a more favorable or perhaps more compassionate *attitude* toward old age than men (Stinnet and Montgomery 1968).

As breadwinners during their mature years, men specialize in adaptive or *instrumental* skills. These are most useful in specific work activities and, because of this, are not easily transferred to new situations. In many cases they are of no use in old age at all. Although career skills lose their relevance, the man may—without even thinking about it—maintain the instrumental approach he cultivated all his life. But the fate of this approach is like that of achievement; the social and psychological supports for it are absent in old age.

Even the basis for male bonding established in mid-life is hit by new and sometimes devastating pressures in old age. In most cases the common work interests of men are what hold them together in the middle years. They tend to associate with others doing the same kinds of things they do or with people working toward similar goals. Retirement has the effect of dissolving the cornerstone of masculine solidarity. When work stops, bonds between the man and his familiar work pals must be reforged if they are to survive. As Cumming argues, the *diffusely bonded* ties that are composed of a variety of interests tend to survive in old age, the *specifically bonded* ties based on narrow interests such as a job specialty wither. All in all, men simply find it harder than women to make new friends or to join new groups that can compensate for the old work routines.

Marjorie Lowenthal and Clayton Haven (1968) report that nearly half again as many women as men in their study of older people had an intimate companion. The confidant for either sex is most likely to be a spouse, child, or friend. For men, it will probably be the man's wife; women, on the other hand, are much more likely to have a child or friend as a close companion, which is not simply because more of them are widowed. Limiting the comparison to married men and women, women are still more likely to mention an offspring or a friend as an intimate companion. Lowenthal and Haven claim that older women have greater powers of personal responsiveness than men and that they are more versatile in choosing people to respond to. Lower-class men are especially handicapped, since they often cling to a concept of virility that undermines almost any kind of intimacy—except the purely sexual type. Irving Rosow (1967) found that, generally speaking, older people in the middle classes have more friends than those in the working classes. Thus, with the decline of sex or the loss of a partner, men in the lower social levels are left with fewer devoted friends than either women or middle- and upper-class men, but they are cut off from close, friendly relations with women in particular.

Complicating this general problem for men is the fact that retirement, unlike widowhood, has a tinge of failure to it. It involves a greater loss of *status anchorage*. Widowhood, by contrast, is a blameless end to a valued role. For almost all men, work was an important source of purpose and self-respect before retirement (Friedman and Havighurst 1962), and so retirement gives more emptiness to the man than widowhood gives to the woman. It also means freedom, but often without power or purpose. Actually, the man's authority at home tends to dip even before retirement. Robert Blood and Donald Wolfe (1960) have shown that the husband's power usually rises in the early stage of marriage, before children arrive and while the couple are young, and then it slowly sags in the various later stages, dropping sharply in retirement.

Ruth Cavan (1962) suggests three main ways in which a man can fill this vacuum: (1) by turning to recreation and hobbies; (2) by throwing himself into volunteer work; or (3) by spending time working around the home. She says that at least part of the man's efforts will probably go to housework, but this in turn may very well stir up conflict with his wife. The household was her own unchallenged domain while he was working, and it also served as an important basis for her self-image; how she managed it was an extension of her ego. It does seem likely that the retired man will move into some of his wife's territory. By comparison, widowhood can actually increase the woman's chances to do new things even as she keeps up many of her old activities.

John Ballweg (1967) found that retired husbands do turn to household work more than employed husbands of the same age, and that their wives do relatively less (though the wives still do more than their husbands). However, the work that retired men do is not necessarily shared with their wives. They usually take full responsibility for certain things—masculine or neutral in connotation—in areas that women are willing to let them have control. In this way the couple's sex identities are not threatened. Ballweg challenges Cavan's suggestion that retired husbands tend to invade their wives' tight little world. Ballweg's major point is that retirement for the husband in most cases does not cause trouble for the wife, and it does not challenge her self-image. The problem of retirement is pretty much the man's own personal problem.

SEX IN OLD AGE

There is no really good body of knowledge about the sex affairs of people in the later years of life. Studies of the older woman's sex life, for example, have been limited mainly to the impact of menopause or to the years immediately afterward. Still, there is little doubt that sex responsiveness for both men and women weakens even more quickly in old age than in the middle years.

Sexual inadequacy among men, for example, takes a sharp upturn after fifty years of age, according to Masters and Johnson (1966). They give several reasons, two of which are most basic: One is monotony, which Masters and Johnson say is the most predictable factor in the aging man's married sex life. But monotony may occur before age fifty, so some other explanation must account for the emphatic shift at this time. The answer seems to be fear of failure, which sharpens the withdrawal process. Masters and Johnson consider this of unquestioned importance. Whenever signs of impotence or sexual ineffectiveness begin to appear—and the signs show up ever more often as we grow old—many men simply avoid sex rather than face the ego-deflating impact of an unsuccessful effort. Failures increase only moderately as men grow older, but withdrawal due to *fear* of failure is much more exaggerated. This magnifies the effect of an occasional failure, but efforts at ego protection lead to exaggerated behavior in almost all spheres of life. Sex is hardly an exception.

Fear of failure seems to be of virtually no importance for women, however, although their interest in sex does decline in old age. The woman who has been plagued by lack of regular, enjoyable sex during her reproductive years will probably have a further drop in the sex drive during her post-menopausal years. The thought of *any* form of sex may become increasingly repugnant to her. Masters and Johnson suggest that women who take this approach are most likely to hold the Victorian notion that sex is a distasteful, if not immoral, indulgence for any woman beyond middle age.

Yet Masters and Johnson also claim that many women show a renewed interest in sex during their early fifties, for several reasons. One is because they no longer fear pregnancy. (This kind of worry will probably decline as women learn to use contraceptives regularly in their younger years.) They also often take greater interest in sex after the physical and mental demands of brood protection are finished.

On the other hand, a special difficulty for aging women is male attrition, a striking phenomenon in the over-seventy age group. Many of the surviving husbands, three or four years older than their wives on the average, suffer from severe physical disabilities which make sex relations with them either unattractive or impossible.

In general, the sex habits of people in the older years are directly related to the habits they worked out in the procreative stage of life (Kinsey *et al.* 1953). Women who have had a stimulating marriage may go through the years of later middle age and the early stages of old age with hardly any change. Men who have had high levels of sexual activity in the early years of marriage and are not plagued by some kind of physical incapability can have active sex lives into the seventy- and even eighty-year-old age categories. There seems to be no physiological reason—none that is an inevitable consequence of aging—why the sex frequency that seemed right during the younger years should not last into old age.

What we do not know is the potential effect on sex in old age of the more permissive attitudes that are now so common among people in the younger age brackets. The greatest attitude change occurred among women coming of age in the 1920s, and they are now in their sixties and seventies. This is the first generation of women in America to grow old who, collectively, had a permissive point of view when they were young.

Perhaps we shall soon discover that sex in old age is influenced in important ways by teen-age attitudes. This viewpoint is, in fact, implicit in the observations of Kinsey, Masters, and Johnson. One observer suggests that sex activity among the aged may show a definite increase in years to come if their health continues to improve and inhibitions are wiped out (Busse 1969). Still, there is reason to think that changes associated with aging are almost inevitably going to take much of the excitement out of sex. The image of sexiness pushed by movies and television just does not take old age into account.

DISENGAGEMENT IN THE LATER YEARS

Family problems for the elderly are part of a whole series of unhappy changes connected with aging—reduced activity, loss of function, and disengagement. This last aspect of growing old has been subjected to more controversy than almost any other issue in gerontology (Streib 1969). Since it is so closely related to problems of the family, we have no choice but to look into it. The *theory of disengagement* was first developed by a group of writers (Elaine Cumming, William Henry, Lois Dean, Isabel McCaffrey, and David Newell 1960; 1961) and has since been elaborated by Elaine Cumming (1963) in particular, but many others have contributed as well.

The theory holds that aging leads to a mutual withdrawal of the older person from younger and more active people in the community. This retreat is presumed to be a normal process, one that will ordinarily occur even if the person is in good health and has enough money to be financially independent. Gordon Streib (1969), citing data from a variety of nonliterate societies and from three literate ones as well, contends that it is a widespread, possibly universal, phenomenon. It is initiated both by the aging person and others in his circle. Once started it tends to be self-perpetuating.

Beginning at some relatively high level of activity in middle age—a mature equilibrium—disengagement proceeds until some fairly stable level is reached—a new equilibrium appropriate for old age. This is characterized by greater social distance all around, amounting to a new and different basis for personal relations. According to the theory, the entire process is consistent with our leading social customs and is, in a sense, agreed on by all concerned. Thus, the aging spend progressively less time with others and play progressively fewer social roles. The overall pattern is one of *reduction* and *simplification*, so the few roles that are retained become that much more important. They tend to be the person's fundamental concerns, the ones that are based on longstanding values.

This means that his individuality is centered ever more completely on viewpoints learned earlier in life when his most distinctive life style was formed. He will find it rather difficult to make new friends, especially with younger people whose approach to life reflects a very different point of view. Irving Rosow (1965) claims that it is almost impossible for the elderly to have close relations or relaxed affability with youth, at least in part because of their preoccupation with the past.

Elaine Cumming (1963) suggests that a good index of the depth and breadth of a man's social activity is the amount of disruption that would be caused by his sudden death. When an energetic person dies, he leaves many loose ends and unfinished obligations behind (although organizations often try to set up safeguards against this possibility). As people

grow old they cut down on their activities; the normal disengagement process thus "frees the old to die" without upsetting vital affairs. In fact, disengagement can be viewed as both a social and personal preparation for
death if, as the disengagement theorists contend, it is a *mutual* process,
tacitly agreed upon by everybody, including the person growing old.

But disengagement also gives the aging person new opportunities for freedom. He is liberated from social controls of both a positive and negative nature. He can be eccentric and get away with it as never before. Margaret Clark
and Barbara Anderson (1967) call it simply a process of relaxation—release
from social pressures, from the compulsion to compete, to produce, to succeed, and to hurry. The aged are given considerable license to be just plain
self-centered. Freedom from obligation replaces the confinement of being
needed. In some respects the ability to enjoy old age becomes the ability
to put the freedom it affords to good, uninhibited use. (But I wonder how
many of us have older relatives who, more than anything else, would prefer
to be needed.)

Wayne Thompson and Gordon Streib (1961) suggest that the processes
of aging can be divided into four stages: (1) late maturity, from about age
forty-five to fifty-four; (2) preretirement, from fifty-five to sixty-four; (3)
early retirement, from sixty-five to seventy-four; and (4) late retirement,
from seventy-five on up. Although they do not specifically accept the disengagement theory, lurking in their approach is the implication that a
certain amount of withdrawal occurs as the person moves from one stage
to the next. He may assume new commitments to be sure, but losses
usually outweigh gains.

Insofar as freedom is concerned, it would certainly seem that the golden
era occurs during the period of early retirement, providing the transition to
this stage is not too traumatic. It may be a rough time for the person who
has been heavily engaged, especially if he has held power that he now has
to let go. In any case, it is during the period from about age sixty-five to
seventy-four that the person is most likely to have extensive freedom along
with the health to use it. After age seventy-five chronic medical troubles
change all that.

But people are active in middle age in a variety of ways, and each may
lead to its own unique kind of disengagement. Obviously people who have
never been very active are in a much different position from those who
have been going strong for several decades. Some people will fight disengagement as long and as hard as they can, especially since activism is so
highly prized in nations like the United States (Williams 1965). Some
people spread themselves very thin, having many and varied contacts, but
none very deep; some are not so widely engaged, but they become deeply
involved whenever they take an interest; some have both broad and intense
affairs while others retain only narrow and shallow ones.

It seems reasonable to assume (from the viewpoint of the disengagement theory) that people who have never been greatly involved feel less sense of urgency about growing old than those who are strenuously active. Furthermore, some people are involved in direct interpersonal relations while others are active in a more symbolic way—the case of editors for example, or public figures such as lecturers and writers. Since the medium they deal with is relatively slow to change, they can keep contact longer in old age. Professional men who trade in concepts that change very slowly—lawyers, for example—can retain high professional status with greater ease than men who work in rapidly changing areas—physicists and chemists, for example. Nevertheless, the normal tendency according to the disengagement theory is for *all* kinds of activity to succumb to the general withdrawal pattern. Some of these simply move faster and more completely than others.

This entire theory has been subject to sharp, sometimes bitter, criticism. It is a predominantly pessimistic point of view, since most people prefer to be active, not inert, and the theory promises us—all of us—only a steady drift to the sidelines. Perhaps for those who like the sidelines anyway, growing old makes avoidance of center stage that much easier. But keeping busy is generally preferred. It seems likely that many people will not withdraw as willingly as the theory suggests, so the idea that it is a mutually desirable process is highly questionable. Every organization has a few old-timers who are not about to give up their piece of the action as rapidly as their younger associates would like, and perhaps most families do, too. Certainly Congress does. In fact, disengagement for the aged seems to be pushed by youth and the middle-aged much more than by older people themselves.

Furthermore, the persistence of older people does not necessarily create social problems. E. Grant Youmans (1969), for example, reviews most of the recent research on disengagement and concludes that empirical data refute the theory more often than not. Ethel Shanas and her associates (1968) have collected substantial evidence concerning the activities of persons sixty-five years of age and over in Denmark, Britain, and the United States; they conclude that these people are active and useful in industrial society—considerably more engaged than one might expect. The Shanas data suggest that, contrary to theory, the greatest reason for disengagement is physical infirmity. (Still, the aged sometimes face discrimination simply because they are old.)

Arnold Rose (1964) has offered several specific criticisms of the disengagement theory. He cites evidence that nonengagement in the later years is simply a continuation of patterns developed in the theoretically most active years of life. Thus, for example, one study concludes that people who have been highly engaged in the early and middle years remain highly engaged as they grow older, whereas people who have been minimally involved keep up their minimal involvements (Videbeck and Knox 1965). Even sex follows this "engagement breeds engagement" and "nonengagement breeds nonengagement" principle. Masters and Johnson (1966) say that men who are sexually active during the formative years of marriage and hold this pace during the thirty-one to forty age range will probably keep with it in both the middle and later years. Men who have high levels of sex expression in old age usually report that same pattern all along the way.

Rose also questions whether disengagement is as desirable as the theory leads us to believe. Generally speaking, active older people seem to have higher levels of life satisfaction than the less engaged (Havighurst, Neugarten, and Tobin 1968), and it is probable that their engagement works to the community's advantage. Many of our conceptions of old age are questionable in the light of new facilities for the aged or ones that an affluent society should be able to afford. Advances in preventive medicine and the control of communicable diseases permit an ever larger number of old people to be remarkably energetic.

Disengagement as preparation for death in these circumstances can become an extremely agonizing, even tragic, process when encouraged too soon, and perhaps it should not be encouraged at all. Hiram Friedsam (1969) raises this question: Why is it any more desirable (or functional) for the aged to prepare for death than to fight it with all their might, as in the mood expressed by Dylan Thomas (1958): "Do Not Go Gentle into that Good Night"? Thomas' advice was to "rage against the dying of the light." In *The Immortalist*, Alan Harrington (1969) states that man's every thought, action, and belief is conditioned by his desire to *avoid* death—and, we can add, by his desire to avoid total disengagement.

In his strongest objection to the disengagement theory, Rose contends that withdrawal among older people occurs only in certain kinds of cultures, especially ones like the United States that give unusually low status to the elderly. A study of the Israeli kibbutzim by Yonina Talmon (1961) suggests that disengagement is not the rule there and is not even encouraged. A shift toward relatively greater importance for the aged and perhaps even greater social engagement sometimes occurs. (Gordon Streib [1969], however, has cited this study in support of disengagement, not as a refutation of it, and hence its conclusions are open to conflicting interpretations.)

The notion that an equilibrium level of disengagement is reached in old age is also open to argument. The process seems to be progressive in nature, and its proponents argue that it feeds on itself in self-perpetuating fashion. The idea that some stable level of engagement is achieved in middle age followed by a slow slide to a new level in old age does not hold up. It implies that people get involved in a *socialization* process during the first half of life, becoming ever more involved in social affairs; the last half is spent in *desocialization*, assuring the community that they will not disrupt affairs too much when they die. In actual fact, an impressive variety of new involvements *can* occur in old age. For example, a trend in American society that helps to counteract disengagement is the new penchant among older people to form a subculture (Youmans 1969). The growth of retirement communities, homes for the aged, nursing homes, housing projects, specialized recreational facilities, and meeting places for the elderly (sponsored by churches, fraternal associations, and various private and public organizations) give opportunities for engagement in a wide variety of meaningful activities.

In a sense, the aging person finds himself caught in a three-way tug concerning the family: He is tempted to try to forge new family ties, to strengthen old ones, and perhaps to disengage. Although disengagement may be a common path for some (recognizing that attempts to breathe new life into old family bonds become increasingly difficult), in many communities of older people chances for new family commitments do exist—remarriage, for example. This is especially true for men, who are in relatively short supply. The possibilities of pairing-off without marriage are also reasonably frequent, not necessarily as permanent arrangements, but for short stretches of time, even "dates." Furthermore, opportunities exist for new group loyalties that are quasi-familistic in nature. A cluster of older people may regard themselves as a "family" even though they met for the first time only six months ago and are all over seventy. Communal arrangements in the youth culture follow a similar pattern. The ethos or mystique of familism runs so deep in our culture that almost any group of people who spend much time together, especially in daily household routines, come to think of one another as family.

Furthermore, a number of new trends serve to counteract, perhaps even reverse, the recent pattern of disengagement (Rose 1964). Social Security along with private pension plans and annuities can give better economic security to the retired and allow them to engage in a broader variety of activities. Older people in the United States are often involved in efforts to raise their own status, and this in itself provides a new kind of political engagement (and sometimes triggers a reaction on the part of younger people, who assist in the "movement").

Disengagement from the occupational role for men and the mother role for women—that is, from the chief traditional roles of both sexes—undoubtedly occurs at earlier ages now. This trend, along with better health and greater economic security, creates a strong pressure to *reengage*. The opportunities for this may very well be increasing, too, especially in the area of voluntary activities and hobbies (and jobs for women). Furthermore, the male role has been expanded to include things that were once ruled out as too effeminate—knitting, weaving, and painting, for example. Leisure-time activities in general are being redefined, giving them a more favorable rating relative to paid employment. Disengagement, with its pessimistic overtones, is thus certainly not the only choice in a progressive society.

SUMMARY

The number of older people has increased steadily in the last half century, but it is now agreed by almost everybody that longer life expectancy can be a mixed blessing. It would also appear that most problems of aging involve the family in one way or another. The main problem stems from a basic dilemma: The ability of people to meet family obligations declines as they grow older (especially after age seventy-five, an age now reached by many, women in particular), but their commitment to familism is usually as strong as ever.

The most appropriate way to cope with this dilemma is rarely self-evident. Older people find that the problem-solving skills they relied on in the mature years may not work in old age, and they need assistance from others. As the number of older people grows, the scope of their troubles grows too, and younger relatives (especially daughters) are drawn in to help.

In some respects aging is more difficult in a rapidly changing, achievement-oriented society. The elderly no longer have effective ways of controlling or even influencing younger members of the family (except as their personal problems exert an inescapable influence), and their achievements are dwarfed by the accomplishments of their children and grandchildren. The affluence of modern society is *not* fully shared by the older generation. All evidence suggests that the fruits of rapid economic growth are snapped up first by children and young adults. Middle-aged and older people do well by historical standards, but younger people do *exceptionally* well, expecting comforts and rewards much earlier in life than was possible or even conceivable in the previous generation.

Studies of the aging married couple are scarce, but mutual ego support seems to be just as important in old age as it was before. Since the couple's joint survival has been lengthened due to their closer age similarity at the time of marriage, along with longer life expectancy, ego support may actually become more important. Expressiveness makes up a larger part of the couple's life together, and effectiveness in this kind of relationship calls for male-female equality. It helps if the pattern can be traced all the way back to habits started in childhood and adolescence.

But if the couple have done well in their marriage work, widowhood is just that much more difficult, and the chances for joint survival drop at a gloomy rate after age sixty-five. Women are more likely to be widowed, and they are in fact more suited to this role than men, due to the life style usually cultivated when they were younger. That does not mean that women are constitutionally endowed for widowhood; the life styles they learn are products of cultural training (although these might possibly be influenced by the fact that they are, of necessity, the childbearers).

According to the disengagement theory, older people inevitably face a period of deactivation as their health and mobility wear away. Some theorists claim that older people have to drop out anyway—even if they keep their health. That is questionable. In fact, disengagement is by no means as inevitable as the disengagement theory suggests. A truly humane society is one where social participation is fully encouraged and where support for it stops only when physical and mental infirmities *force* a halt.

SELECTED READINGS

ADAMS, BERT N. *Kinship in an Urban Setting*. Chicago: Markham Publishing Company, 1968.

CUMMING, ELAINE. "Further Thoughts on the Theory of Disengagement," *UNESCO International Social Science Bulletin*, Vol. 15 (1963), pp. 377–393.

CUMMING, ELAINE, AND WILLIAM E. HENRY. *Growing Old: The Process of Disengagement*. New York: Basic Books, 1961.

ROSE, ARNOLD M. "A Current Theoretical Issue in Social Gerontology," *The Gerontologist*, Vol. 4 (March 1964), pp. 46–50.

ROSOW, IRVING. *Social Integration of the Aged*. New York: The Free Press, 1967.

SHANAS, ETHEL, et al. *Old People in Three Industrial Societies*. New York: Atherton Press, 1968.

THOMPSON, WAYNE E., AND GORDON F. STREIB. "Meaningful Activity in a Family Context," in Robert W. Kleemeier (ed.), *Aging and Leisure: A Research Perspective into the Meaningful Use of Time*. New York: Oxford University Press, 1961, pp. 177–211.

TOWNSEND, PETER. "The Emergence of the Four-Generation Family in Industrial Society," in Bernice L. Neugarten (ed.), *Middle Age and Aging*. Chicago: University of Chicago Press, 1968.

PART FOUR

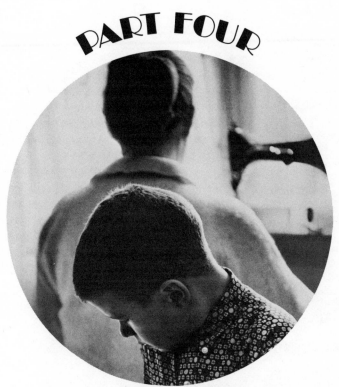

Breakup

CHAPTER 13

Domestic Deterioration

For some couples marriage brings increasing pleasure as the years go by. They never consider divorce nor have even the faintest thought that their marriage is a mistake. But many couples are not so lucky. For the majority, marriage slumps at least a little over the years. Peter Pineo (1961) claims that this is the most common pattern and that it usually includes a combination of three things: *alienation, disenchantment,* and *disengagement.*

Alienation is the opposite of idealization; it involves some degree of anger or resentment toward the spouse. Disenchantment is a sense of disappointment with the marriage, especially upon realizing that the high hopes of courtship have not been fulfilled. It centers on the person's current marriage rather than on marriage in general, although people frequently do become a little cynical about wedded life. Disengagement is the loss of intimacy that marked the couple's relationship in courtship and the early stage of marriage—a decline in confiding, kissing, sex relations, doing things together, the sympathetic settlement of disagreements, and so on.

Pineo claims that deterioration is a *generalized* process; almost all facets of the marriage decline together. A change in any area leads to changes in others, and losses and disappointment by one spouse usually force losses and disappointment by the other, too. This does not mean that everything is tied together in a perfect one-to-one relationship, nor does it mean that the deterioration is great enough to cause strong feelings of unhappiness or misery. But the typical *trend* in marriage is toward a general loss of adjustment and satisfaction with the passage of time (although time itself does not cause the deterioration). Robert O. Blood, Jr. (1967), studied marital satisfaction in marriages in Tokyo and Detroit and concluded that the degree of satisfaction in all measures decreased over time. This was true despite the fact that patterns of mate selection in the two cities were strikingly different. (Satisfaction curves did differ according to the way mate selection was handled, but the long-run trend was always toward less satisfaction rather than more.)

The purpose of this and the following chapter is to review the ways that couples perceive a turn for the worse in marriage and how they respond to their discoveries. We are not talking about mild or even moderate dissatisfaction—that kind of trouble was discussed in Chapters 9, 10, and 11—but to what is, from the point of view of the people involved, a truly chilling realization: Their marriage is an almost unbearable tragedy. In virtually all cases, the idealization that had led to love is reversed. It becomes alienation. And mutualization, which had made the couple so close, becomes disengagement.

Five different kinds of reactions can occur: (1) The couple may choose to "live with it"; (2) they may seek a legal separation; (3) they may live apart without making any change in their legal status as man and wife; (4) one spouse, almost always the male, may desert the household; or (5) the couple may end the marriage through divorce. In states where grounds for divorce are extremely limited, annulment can serve essentially the same purpose as divorce. (Without being altogether facetious there is one other possibility—murder. That recourse is suggested daily on television, and American audiences seem to be completely reconciled to it, at least in fantasy, if not in reality. Of course murder is infinitely more common on television than in real life. Still, it is a family affair more often than not.)

LIVING WITH IT

There are many reasons why people may be willing to put up with a marriage that gives them little pleasure and much heartache: religious or ethical scruples, a variety of inhibitions, or even a calculated review of the alternative possibilities. Surprisingly, hardly any research information is available on the subject.

Religious Scruples

It is often noted that the rising divorce rate in the twentieth century is correlated with the falling power of traditional religion. American church attendance has held up (at least until very recent years), but most observers add that the basis for attendance is now more often *secular* than *sacred*; it does not stem from deep religious piety, but from more practical, social considerations. Perhaps the fear of divine retribution for sinful behavior has always been exaggerated, but it certainly seems to have no great influence now.

Not only has the power of traditional religion declined, making it less effective in convincing people that they will be rewarded someday for submitting to their sorrows, but the weakening of religion is accompanied by a trend away from the ideal of family duty and personal sacrifice.

Nevertheless, there are certain facts relating family stability to religious affiliation that cannot be overlooked. Divorce rates are generally lower among Jews than Christians, for example. They are also lower among Catholics than Protestants. Is this because Jews learn to put up with more marriage trouble before seeking divorce than Christians? Are Catholics more willing to tolerate misfortune than Protestants? Perhaps, but it is also possible that forces other than inner religious controls are at work. In the case of Jews, it is possible that patterns of homogamy are stronger than among either Catholics or Protestants (Lenski 1961), and hence Jewish couples may actually face less marriage trouble than members of these other groups. As individuals, they may not be more resigned to their problems; they simply have fewer of them.

Another possibility is that there are greater pressures working to keep the Jewish couple together. There is plenty of evidence that the Jewish population is highly concentrated in certain urban areas and that the married pair is likely to have relatives living close by. When calamity hits, the preponderance of social pressures may help them cope and give them reinforcement at the points of greatest vulnerability. It is even possible that ethnic cohesion in the Jewish group, supported by nonreligious pressures as well as by religion, will help the couple weather the storm. By contrast, many Protestant couples have no close circles of strong ethnic supports that can help out.

To the extent that fear of actions by the Church, or by an angry Deity, will follow divorce, Catholics may be more likely than Protestants to resign themselves to their troubles. The Church has long taken a strong stand against divorce and threatened not only ecclesiastic but spiritual reprisals. We have to admit, however, that current knowledge about the ability of religious commitment to help couples stand up to their marriage problems is limited.

Ethical Scruples

The difference between religious and ethical scruples is this: Those of a religious nature imply commitment to the principles or rules of a religious body or to the wishes of a supernatural power; ethical scruples refer to commitment to principles falling outside this category. Thus, a person may have a strong objection to divorce on some other grounds than religion and may be willing to resign himself to an unhappy marriage as a result. In making this distinction there is no intention to suggest that religious scruples are not ethical. It simply means that there can be other sources for self-restraint or self-denial than religion.

In a sense, we no longer have a philosophy of resignation to unhappiness in marriage. If marriage becomes unbearable, it has become much more acceptable to look for something better. But that does not mean that people are less able to tolerate marital grief now than before. It is simply no longer considered a *virtue* to take that course.

No truly popular or effective argument in favor of enduring an unhappy marriage has appeared in recent centuries outside of religion. Perhaps a secular case *can* be made, such as the idea that social stability and child welfare require family stability and that every effort should be made to keep the divorce rate down because divorce contributes to social disorganization. In fact, such an argument can be found in contemporary textbooks on marriage and the family. But it would be foolish to think that these texts offer the *individual* any good reason why he personally should suffer in marriage for the good of society as a whole. The books are more likely to suggest that through marriage counseling or intelligent efforts by the couple, they may be able to solve their problems. If these remedies do not work, the author may suggest (not directly perhaps, but by the general tenor of his discussion) that separation or divorce may be the best solution.

One recent text suggests that Americans are becoming permanently available for new marriage arrangements, when these hold more promise than their current ones. Bernard Farber (1964) claims that this is a *desirable* approach, given the general nature of modern society. The argument offers virtually the opposite of a philosophy of resignation, because it suggests that everyone will be better off if each person keeps looking around. In this view a dynamic, fluid approach to mating replaces the traditional standard of lifelong monogamy.

The point of the present discussion is not to suggest that no good reasons exist to try to make the most of a difficult marriage. But in the past such reasons had strong religious support or sprang from a popular ethic stressing personal and family duty. No new arguments have gained broad appeal, and the trend is almost uniformly away from the old approach.

Inhibitions

Yet some couples suffer in marriage without making any effort to break away. The most obvious restraint is fear, especially fear that the children will be hurt (assuming that the couple have children). Surprisingly, evidence showing that couples will submit to unhappiness in marriage for the sake of their children is not impressive. Although couples who seek divorce are more often childless than those who remain married, when the length of marriage is held constant (so that divorced couples are compared only with still-marrieds who have been married the same length of time) it does not appear that having children is a deterrent to divorce (Monahan 1955). Furthermore, studies in the past ten or fifteen years clearly show that couples who remain married for the sake of their children—despite severe marriage problems—may be doing their children as well as themselves a disservice (Nye 1957; Landis 1962; Burchinal 1964).

Still, some couples do find it impossible to seek divorce because they fear it will have a crushing effect on their children. Or they may simply not want to give up the children, since at least one of the parents will probably be seriously cut off in case of divorce. The father will most likely be chosen for this role. In the past, American fathers were presumed to be more distant as parents than mothers and not too greatly upset by loss of daily contact with children. More recent studies show this image of father to be mistaken. Perhaps fathers are still moré willing than mothers to give up the child (as a rule) or to settle for occasional visiting privileges, but it is also possible that many men are now reluctant to take any action that threatens their ties with the children. Statistical data on this point are not available, but general trends suggest that modern men find greater expressive satisfaction as fathers—more than before the rise of the suburban style of life (Benson 1968).

If we can assume that some couples do stay married solely out of concern for their offspring, it would seem to follow that when the children leave home there would no longer be any good reason for the marriage. They can call it off at last, separating with a sigh of relief. This does happen sometimes, although the statistics on divorce show no sudden upsurge of divorces for couples between the ages of forty and forty-five, or between forty-five and fifty, when children usually leave home. The specter of a stampede to the divorce courts in middle age turns out to be an illusion. How can we account for this fact?

It seems that when children leave home a new set of conditions frequently comes into play, which works in favor of marriage. As a matter of fact, the very absence of children may turn out to be an advantage for the couple. A fact that has received relatively little attention is that one major source of trouble between spouses during the child-rearing years is conflict over child rearing itself. Although women often have feelings of emptiness and depression when the children move away, many get a new sense of freedom, their sex life often improves, and there is no longer any need to quarrel with husbands over how to handle the children. The possibility for a rebirth of spirit—personal and marital—suddenly appears.

As noted earlier, there is very little opportunity in courtship for young couples to find out much about each other as parents, especially on matters of discipline and control. Parents are almost never in complete agreement as to how to deal with the constant requests of contemporary children. Children have put pressure on their parents from the beginning of time, but only in recent decades has the authoritarian response collapsed. Furthermore, modern parents have much more money to spend on their children. The reply that "we can't afford it" is a casualty in the affluent society. All too often the parents *can* afford it, and they are forced to give less substantial reasons for denying requests or to take the easy way out—not deny them.

Another reason couples may stay together (despite serious misgivings) could be career interests of the husband. Some men are in lines of work where divorce could hurt their chances for promotion or even their ability to keep the job, so that they think twice before risking a possible scandal. This would be the case for men who feel that they must have an impeccable reputation. Politicians often feel this way, although it is not uncommon now for them to work divorce in without crippling their chances for election—Governor Rockefeller's success in New York politics after his divorce is a case in point. But there are others who do not want to risk it. Some men are simply afraid of the *possible* reactions of their employers. Wives may be less concerned than their husbands, although a man whose position is high enough that it matters is probably one who earns a handsome income; the wife will probably think twice before she gives up whatever status goes with his position. This is especially true if she can carry on most of her personal affairs without interference from her husband. She can have his rank and a life of her own, too—the best of two worlds.

There are still other reasons for hanging on. Divorce would require explanations to friends and relatives which could prove to be embarrassing, or (and this is even more likely) the divorced person may have to face people who act as if nothing has happened. He knows that his friends and colleagues are anxious to learn more about the affair and are probably talking about it behind his back. After all, an element of failure is still implied in divorce in the United States, and this part of it can be especially difficult to handle. It is not that these people are cruel. Even when they try to be helpful, they can do or say the wrong thing. By comparison, strangers pose hardly any problem.

One final reason for enduring an unhappy marriage is the *undernourished hopes syndrome*. Many people never fully understand just how bad their marriage is, and hence they hold no hope for a better life. It may never occur to a woman that her talents are being systematically underrated or sabotaged by a suspicious and insecure husband. Maybe her parents had always treated her very much the same way. This may be less likely to happen in contemporary society than in the past, partly because more stress is placed on sheer happiness in marriage now, but also because we are bombarded with questionnaires in the mass media urging us to find out whether we are really happy or whether our marriages are as good as they are supposed to be (or as good as the people who write on the subject say they should be).

The Awareness of Alternatives

The person's perception of his current state in life must be balanced against his awareness of alternative possibilities. Thus, John Thibaut and Harold Kelley (1959) suggest that as long as a couple find satisfaction in their relationship above the *comparison level for alternatives*, that is, above the level they consider possible in some other arrangement, the marriage is safe. Only when they can conceive of something better and perceive it to be within reach are they moved to action.

Thus, some people never fully grasp their own misfortune. Since it is taken for granted, they submit to it. One explanation is lack of mobility, either physical or psychological. The person who never travels far from home can be almost completely isolated from alternative possibilities, just as the person who reads very little may have very little insight into what might be. These are the people who are victimized by undernourished hopes. Expecting very little out of life, they do not even realize how little they get.

This may also help to explain why the divorce rate is so much higher in the United States than in most other industrialized countries where mobility rates are lower. It also supplies a clue as to why the divorce rate took such a leap at the end of World War II. Couples had been separated under circumstances in which alternative possibilities were highly visible and unusually numerous. In effect, almost anything that raises the level of marriage hopes and the visibility of alternatives lowers the contentment of people in their current marriages.

Even so, couples may put up with their problems if they are convinced that the alternatives are not really any brighter. We have no idea how common this is, but it may be more widespread than we might think. Such resignation depends in part on how marriageable the person considers himself to be. If we may assume that adults ordinarily prefer marriage to staying single, then a person who starts thinking about divorce will also try to figure his chances for remarriage. If he concludes that the odds are against him, he will probably take a more tolerant view of his present state.

It is also possible that people tend to underestimate their chances for remarriage. Although opportunities are actually very numerous (divorced women, for example, are much more likely to marry than women of the same age who have never married), a great many people do not know this.

It seems that one strong pressure toward divorce for many people is the fact that they already have a good prospect for remarriage in mind. In the absence of any immediate alternative, they let their marriage drift along. When a clear-cut replacement is spotted, the final divorce decision can come very easily. Thus, at least two factors disposing to divorce can be identified: marked unhappiness in marriage and the appearance of a promising new partner.

SEPARATION: LEGAL AND INFORMAL

Broadly speaking, legal separation can take two forms. One is separation by written agreement between the spouses. If properly executed, the courts of several states will uphold such a document (which may or may not include provision for support payments by the husband). The other form is separation by court order, governed strictly by court instructions. It is commonly known as "limited divorce." The limitation is that the couple's marriage is not dissolved in any absolute sense, and neither party is legally free to remarrry.

Separation in either form is particularly meaningful in light of the attitude of the Catholic Church toward divorce, which holds that a valid and sexually consummated marriage between two baptized Catholics can be terminated only by death and that even if separation occurs no true Catholic can be remarried during the life of his original spouse. But what does a member of the Church do if his spouse acts in illegal, provocative, or terribly disturbing ways? Separation offers a solution, imperfect though it is, since at least the aggrieved spouse can live apart.

Desertion and cruelty are the most common grounds for judicial separation (in those states where such separations are recognized). Strangely, adultery is sometimes not included as a basis for these actions (Ploscowe 1955). Thus, it may be possible to get a divorce in some states on grounds that are not admitted for legal separation. Still other states make no provision for legalizing separation, presumably on the belief that an unworkable marriage should not be given any encouragement at all by the law.

Defenders of legalized separation say it provides a useful period of time in which reconciliation may occur. It also gives relief to Catholics and Episcopalians, without violating Church rules, and to people in states where grounds for divorce are very limited. (This last point is becoming less and less important as divorce laws open up; legal separations are in fact very rare and apparently are becoming ever rarer.)

Much more frequent are informal separations where the couple simply live apart without bothering with legal agreements. This arrangement may last for a very short time or become permanent. The key to the difference between *informal separation* and *desertion*, as these terms are used here, is that the whereabouts of the deserting spouse are usually unknown, in addition to which desertion involves no mutual agreement. Informal separation implies that each of the parties knows where the other is living and that they acquiesce to the separation, either out of expediency or choice. (In actual fact, however, it is not always easy to distinguish between separation and desertion.)

If the couple separate out of expediency, the arrangement may be temporary and in no way imply marital discord or failure. Although this happens frequently enough—as in the case of husbands in the armed forces—it does not belong in a discussion of marriage deterioration. Our concern is with *symptomatic separation*, where the fact that the spouses live apart means that they prefer not to live together.

All kinds of considerations may be involved, such as how long the couple are separated, what sort of relationship they have during the separation, or what plans they have for the future. Short, trial separations usually lead to longer ones, although reliable statistics on this point are nonexistent. We would certainly like to know more about cases where one spouse moves out for a short period, later for a longer period, and sooner or later leaves altogether. Is there some typical sequence of events in this pattern? Generally speaking, it leads to divorce, so informal separation is actually only one stage in the overall divorce process.

The pattern of present concern, assuming that many informal separations are in reality part of the divorce process (to be discussed in the following chapter), is the one where spouses separate for an extended period without planning for divorce—when, indeed, they prefer to remain married but choose to live apart. Each knows where the other can be reached and agrees to the separation, so, at least technically, desertion is not involved. It is, of course, just one step removed from the case of the unhappy couple who continue living together. To whatever extent the "empty shell" marriage involves only a common residence, the couple have decided that living together is either a more practical arrangement or a more appropriate one for their particular needs. The fact that the marriage has no substance may not be apparent to friends, which may be exactly what the couple want. If they were to separate, the failure of their marriage would be known to all.

In a wartime study of separations, William F. Ogburn (1944) concluded that they occur most often among nonwhites, lower-income groups, city dwellers, residents of rapidly growing areas, childless couples, and young or old couples rather than those of middle age. Unfortunately, his analysis did not clearly distinguish between separation and desertion. In a somewhat later study Kingsley Davis (1950) concluded that separations and desertions tend to decline as the general level of education and affluence rises; couples increasingly turn to divorce to clear away insufferable marriages as their wealth improves.

It is probably in the middle and upper classes that informal separations follow a relatively stable pattern, however—that is, where the spouses agree to live apart but can still cooperate in certain ways (as when the husband gives regular financial support to his wife's household) and where they tacitly agree not to bother each other. But it is also at this level that divorce is usually a much better arrangement and is no doubt more frequently used. In the lower social classes, separations are more often unstable and nonamicable. Indeed, here is where the line between desertion and separation is most difficult to draw but where the formalities of divorce are most frequently ignored.

In sociological terms, patterns of separation are *anomic*, leaving a great deal of confusion and uncertainty. That is why the middle and upper classes prefer divorce; it provides standard procedures for dissolving the marriage and settling all legal claims. Then they can marry again, which they usually do.

DESERTION

By definition, desertion is not institutionalized. It is neither encouraged nor condoned, and each deserter (as well as the family he abandons) has to work out ways of handling the situation on his own. The community will help out in only the most minimal fashion. Public aid to dependent children, for example, is virtually never sufficient to cover even basic food, clothing, and shelter needs. It will have to be supplemented from other sources or else the children will suffer.

While desertion by the husband is often used as grounds for divorce, we are concerned here with cases that do not lead to divorce, at least not immediately. Customarily it is the father who leaves, but the fact that he does is rarely the *cause* of the trouble. Desertion reaches its highest frequency precisely where families are least likely to have any established order. In some respects, the deserter leaves a situation he cannot tolerate *because* of its lack of order, although the man probably contributed more than his share to household chaos in the first place. It would certainly be misleading to suggest that deserters are sensitive men who flee their families to find tranquillity. In most cases they have never known much personal organization, and desertion is just one more step in the same troubled direction that their lives have already taken.

Unfortunately, much more is known about divorce than desertion. Divorce exists to clarify obligations when marriage fails; desertion precludes all that. Only cases that reach the courts are recorded; whether they include all kinds of desertion is not known, but they probably do not. Furthermore, we have no way of knowing if cases that reach the courts represent a reasonably constant percentage of all desertions. And if they do, we still do not know what the percentage is.

Not only is the deserter reluctant to publicize his status, his wife may not want to spread the word either. Thus, when the census taker comes to her door and asks if she lives with her husband she may say yes, then add that he is temporarily out of town. For purposes of getting aid for families with dependent children, on the other hand, she may be all too willing to label him a deserter. Much will depend on her desire to be, or seem to be, conventional. The more of a conformist she is, the more likely she is to feel shamed by her husband's desertion and therefore make greater efforts to cover for him.

Oddly enough, the minimal satistics available on this subject confirm the speculation that accurate information is hard to find. For example, census surveys typically report more women separated from their husbands than husbands separated from wives. Obviously not all the men are being counted. Many deserting men simply disappear and even escape the diligent efforts of census takers to find them (as was suggested earlier in the discussion of masculine life patterns in the lower classes). And many of the men who manage to stay out of the "underworld of lost people" will not admit that they are married. (There are probably more bigamists in our society than anybody cares to admit.)

Perhaps because desertion is relatively easy to conceal, making the collection of reliable statistics on it difficult, it is publicized much less than divorce. In popular discussions of family breakup, for example, the center of interest is usually divorce, which has become the most typical index of family deterioration. Rates of desertion are probably about as high as divorce, but the very ambiguity of the practice seems to arouse less public alarm.

Ray Baber (1953), in a very conservative estimate, once suggested that there is roughly one desertion for every four cases of divorce. William Kephart (1955) made a much higher estimate, one that is more often cited, although his conclusions were based on Philadelphia statistics alone. Kephart argued that the ratio of desertion to divorce is more like one-to-one than one-to-four. Certainly it is no rare event. If his estimate is accurate, or even close, then the study of desertion is badly neglected.

Desertion takes two basic forms: *temporary* and *permanent*, although the first usually leads to the second. Thus, the man who deserts rarely does so all of a sudden. His final departure comes only after a string of "vacations" of varying—usually increasing—length. In fact, desertion is often just that in the mind of the deserter: a vacation from domesticity. The man wants a breather. It may even be good for marriage in some cases;

when the man returns he feels guilty and makes an extra effort to please. Both husband and wife are more aware of the need to try harder. This feeling may not last, but temporary desertion can still serve as an alternative to divorce.

The first departure may occur in the early weeks or months of marriage and may be nothing more than an unexplained absence for a day or perhaps overnight. In fact, this kind of respite may have occurred once or twice even during the courtship, before the couple married. Kephart's figures suggest that perhaps as many as three cases out of ten involve drinking problems, but he points out that still other family difficulties may lie behind trouble with alcohol. Drinking is usually only symptomatic of other probems—it can explain very little by itself.

Ray Baber (1953) found the median age for men at the time of their first desertion to be about thirty-three, and two-thirds of the desertions occurred within the first ten years of marriage. A pattern of occasional absences becomes established, with the man leaving for longer periods and perhaps ever more frequently, until he simply takes off for good. In the lower social classes the idea that men should have time off every once in a while is fairly well established. Wives are annoyed by it, but they often become resigned and may not even think of it as desertion, in the middle-class sense of the term. The middle-class woman is apparently quicker to consider her husband's absence a full-fledged abandonment. The "men need a breather" philosophy has never had strong support here, except perhaps in the sense that they ought to get a free evening with the boys now and then.

Sometimes the man will suddenly and unexpectedly disappear, but this kind of desertion is a rarity. Even then he will usually give at least some kind of forewarning. Certainly he will have grumbled about his marriage or shown dissatisfaction of some sort, unless he could communicate virtually nothing of his inner feelings.

Occasionally it is the woman who deserts, leaving no trace and abandoning children as well as husband. Her action is almost certain to lead to divorce. If she takes the children along, her ability to hide is greatly reduced, although a few women have been known to disappear with their children in tow. In fact, the nature of female desertion is basically different from that of men, just as their legal status is different. In many states, for example, the wife is expected to go with her husband when legitimate job pressures force him to move. But the man does not have to follow his wife. In a sense, the man's career and its requirements are conditions to which the wife has a legal obligation to adjust.

Class, Race, and Religion

Almost all available evidence points to the fact that desertion rates are highest in the lower-income brackets, among men whose occupational roots do not run deep. The more entrenched the man is (in terms of job status, ownership of financial assets of one kind or another, and having friends and relatives in the community), the less likely he is to abandon his family. In fact, it will be both more difficult and more troublesome for him to leave. In the middle and upper classes men usually turn to divorce when their marriages fail, to clarify money matters, protect the children, and allow remarriage. Both divorced and widowed mothers more often have formal support arrangements for themselves and their children than mothers hit by desertion.

Furthermore, it is much easier to trace middle- or upper-class men, because their web of relationships creates many more ways for them to get caught. If the deserting father has any status in the community he will be more visible (and there will be good reason to chase him down), unless he flees leaving all social ties and credentials behind. White-collar deserters probably move farther from home because they have to try harder to cover their tracks. The fact that the man of moderate to high status would be able to fulfill his obligations to wife and children if caught is crucial, since the court's concern is usually not so much with the stability of the family as with the fulfillment of the father's economic responsibilities. If he meets them, the law is not too concerned with where he lives while he does it.

The lower-class man often has little to lose through desertion—except his family, which may be the one social bond in his life, but an unpleasant one nonetheless. Agencies will attempt to catch him if his desertion is reported, and their chances for success are reasonably good. The man can no longer find asylum on the frontier or total anonymity in the metropolis. (It has been argued that at least one reason why desertion rates have been going up in recent years is that agencies like the Family Location Service do a better job in finding deserters; hence, the statistics are better.) Many states now have mutual working agreements for returning deserters.

Still, the man whose status is low and anonymous and whose apprehension is difficult may very well be one whose wife and family are not terribly anxious to have back. Social workers and civil authorities are reluctant to insist that such men support their wives and children. They *cannot* give support in many cases, and the most obvious alternative, imprisonment, seems pointless (Monahan 1958a).

At least one very reputable observer feels that emphasis on the class factor in desertion has been exaggerated. William Kephart (1955) admits that lower-class rates of desertion are high, but he says that they are not as much higher than middle-class rates as most people think. Racial factors, associated with prejudice and discrimination, are stressed by Kephart, and these complicate class comparisons. He found that nonwhite married men made up 17 percent of the total married male population in his sample, but they accounted for 40 percent of the desertions. Racial characteristics as such cannot explain this decrepancy, he notes, but job and social pressures associated with discrimination can. These make it difficult for black males to be stable breadwinners and offer neither them nor their wives much encouragement to observe the legalities of divorce. (Surprisingly, 44 percent of the white desertions in his study involved men from the upper half of the occupational ladder.)

Religious affiliation also seems to have some bearing on desertion rates. Catholics have somewhat higher rates than members of other religious groups, primarily because of the rigid attitude of the Church toward divorce and also because the Catholic population in some areas has a strong ethnic strain leading to job discrimination and low income. Kephart found that Catholics were overrepresented by nearly 40 percent in the desertion and nonsupport cases appearing in the Philadelphia courts he studied (with due consideration to their relative numbers in the Philadelphia population). However, the idea that Catholics have high rates of desertion independent of income or minority group status is by no means easy to prove using statistics from recent years.

On the other hand, desertion rates among Jews have always proved to be extremely low. (Not only is desertion rare, but divorce rates are too; this is taken up in the following chapter.) Jews in America have a minority group status, and they have not been immune to prejudice and discrimination, but such pressures by themselves have not led to high rates of desertion. So ethnic or minority status as such does not necessarily lead to family trouble, even if accompanied by prejudice and discrimination. The low rate of desertion among Jewish men can only be explained by the religious and ethnic values they hold toward the family combined with their relatively high economic status. Although these cannot guarantee 100 percent family success, they assure that most Jewish men will have a strong sense of domestic obligation and that they will also acquire the means to meet it. Under these circumstances desertion rates are bound to be low.

And yet desertion is undoubtedly frequent in the black population in the United States, where discrimination has had a much different impact. The explanation here must be found in the unique race history of the United States, where prejudice has had a crippling effect on many black husbands and fathers, both economically and psychologically. The key is not history or heritage per se, at least not in any abstract sense. It is the basic fact that job opportunities for black men have been systematically restricted. As has already been seen, the main basis for desertion in any group is family disorganization, and this is not so much the *result* of desertion as the *cause* of it. The basis for family disorder among blacks is the system in which many black males start at a disadvantage in the struggle to become stable breadwinners.

It is a curious fact that as the general status of blacks has improved, their divorce rate has risen—not the typical pattern when comparing divorce rates among whites of different social classes. Many blacks have lived in the ghetto culture where marriage and divorce follow a unique pattern. As their status improves, troubles in marriage increasingly lead to conventional divorce rather than desertion. They move into a status range where legal procedures for family affairs (and other matters) are available and are routinely followed. This is an important part of becoming first-class citizens, despite our misgivings about divorce itself.

The Children of Desertion

One of the tragedies of desertion, independent of race or ethnic status, is that it is likely to involve minor children to an even greater extent than divorce. In a study reported by Kephart and Monahan (1952), about three out of five divorces (58 percent) were granted to childless couples, but only about 25 percent of the desertion cases were childless. Marriages affected by desertion are not only likely to involve children, they involve more children in any particular household, and the impact is probably greater per child. This is because the family's average income is lower, so the mother is left with fewer resources to care for her children.

There are several reasons why there are more children, one of which is merely technical. Mothers with dependent children are more often put on the record books as having a deserting husband. If a woman has children she is more apt to seek financial help than a childless woman, so we are less likely to have statistics on deserted wives who do not have offspring. Also, since the deserting husband returns occasionally (as we have seen), the couple may keep having children even after the desertion pattern has been established. This rarely happens in divorce. For this same reason, the overall length of marriage is shorter in the case of divorce than desertion, thereby increasing the number of children the deserted family is likely to have. And lower-class couples, whose desertion rates are higher, have more children. Furthermore, it is quite likely that children are responsible (in part at least) for some desertion cases, in which the father cannot cope with his children or their annoying ways. Data collected in New Delhi by Prabha Malhotra and Lilian Khan (1962) suggest as much, and there are many supporting impressions in American case records. Children may indirectly cause couples to seek divorce, too, but their role in desertion is even greater.

The point at issue here is central to *fathering* in lower-income groups. Becoming a parent is a bigger crisis for men the less they earn (Hobbs 1965), and desertion rates are relatively higher. These men are likely to feel that children are the mother's responsibility. They have seen that attitude in their own homes as children, and so it seems normal. And yet the deserting father may regret the loss of his children even more than the loss of his wife (Hill and Becker 1942) and the loss of his role as parent more than that of husband. Although a desire to escape from the children can be an important factor, disgust for his wife (or her inability to compensate for his own problems) is usually more important. Jacob Zukerman (1950) has suggested that extramarital sex and drinking are the two leading reasons men desert, but both of these are at least partly due to the man's relations with his wife.

Desertion creates uncertainty for all concerned. The man cannot be sure how he should act (in giving credentials to prospective employers, for example), especially if he is trying to hide from his wife. He lives in a kind of social limbo, though he may have felt that way even before leaving his family. When children are involved, the image they have of their father (and of fatherhood itself) will no doubt take a beating, although the fact that the man is a scoundrel may never be stated out loud. Very little is known about what mothers actually say or do to describe runaway husbands in the presence of their children. An occasional unkind reference or a noticeable rigidity when the man's name comes up may be the only clues. But the children will probably pick them up, no matter how subtle they are.

The mere absence of the father can be a problem, of course, but it may be no more harmful than in the case of divorce. In fact, at the lowest income levels where desertion rates are high the children sometimes suffer from *too many* men in the household rather than too few. The mother may be visited by a series of men, and the children may not even be sure who is who. Above all, males in this setting do not have high esteem in the eyes of women, and masculinity is constantly humiliated. Boys reared here stand a good chance of becoming deserters themselves, so the pattern feeds on itself.

Despite the demeaning attitude these women hold toward men, they have extremely difficult child-rearing problems without them. They may receive "aid to families with dependent children," which is absolutely minimal despite popular middle-class beliefs to the contrary (McKeany 1960), but they are not likely to get support from their husbands. A large proportion of public aid to minor children is due to desertion, and its prevalence is increasing, not going down. The mothers have to work if they possibly can, and they will not ordinarily be able to get the best jobs.

Chances for remarriage are not good either because of the uncertainty of their marital status, but after a while they may settle this by getting a divorce.

Unfortunately, no quick solution to this general problem exists, certainly not in the sense that it can be suddenly eliminated; the chances are not even good that it will be greatly reduced in the next ten, or even twenty-five, years. The best hope lies in better opportunities for poor children, especially boys. If the school system could be made more attractive and meaningful to them—prime American talent has rarely been put to work on this problem—then it may be assumed that they could learn to make a steady living and develop habits of family dependability, too. Probably the key to family stability in any society is its ability to rear boys to be skilled and reliable workers. The overwhelming majority of men who are steady in this regard are also "family men." This even holds true when their marriages fail; they can be counted on to go through conventional divorce procedures and make regular child support payments. In fact, if they are steady workers, they will sometimes be given custody of the children. Desertion flourishes where males, beginning in childhood, are only weakly bound to the family and where their chances for getting jobs of dignity and esteem are all but lost by the time they reach their teens.

SUMMARY

A couple can respond to marital deterioration in several ways. Some may never even know they have marriage troubles because they have so many other problems as well. Those who recognize their troubles may still choose to keep the marriage, perhaps because of religious or ethical scruples against divorce. They may also fear the divorce process with all its legal mysteries or the embarrassment often associated with it. They may even calculate all the alternatives and conclude that they would be wise to remain married.

Research on why people endure unhappy marriages is surprisingly meager. One thing seems certain: No new philosophy of resignation to domestic unhappiness has become popular in the past century. Only attacks on earlier philosophies have come along. Apparently there are pragmatic reasons why people suffer marital misery even in a society that stresses personal happiness. Many couples do in fact persevere.

Among those who do not, some turn to legal separation—presumably the ones who have strong objections to divorce. Informal separations occur in an unknown number of cases (but the number is probably high). These usually lead sooner or later to divorce. But some of them represent practical means by which couples can part company and still cling to useful family ties. Because the pattern is not recognized in formal ways—it is not institutionalized—it is charged with uncertainty, and it precludes remarriage.

Desertion has much in common with informal separation, but it involves the additional element of "hiding out." As in the case of informal separation, it often ends in divorce, but in lower-income groups (where it is most common) it is least likely to be legally resolved. Hence, it becomes part of a general pattern of personal and family disorganization.

The disorder in lower-class family life begins even before marriage, radiating in all directions in the early stages, but not preventing a high birth rate. Desertion aggravates this already troubled situation, especially where sons have limited social and economic opportunities and grow up to have high rates of desertion themselves. Although abandonment of the family occurs in the middle classes more often than we like to think, it is the lower-class pattern that is part of a recurring social process. Any reform effort that can improve the job outlook for lower-class boys is likely to have a reassuring impact on rates of desertion—and an uplifting effect on American family life in general.

SELECTED READINGS

BLOOD, ROBERT O., JR. *Love Match and Arranged Marriage: A Tokyo-Detroit Comparison*. New York: The Free Press, 1967.

BURCHINAL, LEE G. "Characteristics of Adolescents from Unbroken, Broken, and Reconstituted Families," *Marriage and Family Living*, Vol. 26 (February 1964), pp. 44–51.

KEPHART, WILLIAM M. "Occupational Level and Marital Disruption," *American Sociological Review*, Vol. 20 (August 1955), pp. 456–465.

MONAHAN, THOMAS P. "Family Fugitives," *Marriage and Family Living*, Vol. 20 (May 1958), pp. 146–151.

PINEO, PETER C. "Disenchantment in the Later Years of Marriage," *Marriage and Family Living*, Vol. 23 (February 1961), pp. 3–11.

CHAPTER 14

Divorce and Remarriage

Divorce and remarriage are now entrenched in the American social landscape. They supply formal procedures for putting an end to marriage, clarifying family responsibilities, and starting fresh marriage ventures. Both occur so frequently in every city of any size that they can properly be called normal. They constitute no social problem in themselves; that is, no sense of emergency hangs over them. The community's crisis agencies deal with other matters. The police, for example, are hardly ever involved (although they are occasionally called in to restrain a belligerent spouse).

Divorce is like a funeral in some respects, since the death of a marriage usually calls for mourning, though it may also bring relief and freedom. Grief can be very intense, but the professional people who handle such matters—lawyers, judges, clerks—show little or no emotion, just as funeral directors and embalmers manage their disagreeable chores with perfect aplomb (though their clients are in agony). In fact, one might argue that the standard procedures for divorce are altogether too nonchalant and obliging. Perhaps there is something to be said for having someone in the community *care* deeply about what happens when a marriage dies (besides the couple involved). In fact, more fitting deaths for marriage probably could be arranged. Even before the "last rites" have been held, better arrangements for *community marriage care* could be worked out—to move in quickly when therapy or remedial action is called for. Otto Pollak (1967), for example, has called for a professional specialty in marital health.

But for the time being our task is to understand divorce in America just as it is and to see how the system works. We shall explore the pattern, the causes, and the trends in divorce, with a constant eye for the social significance of changing divorce rates.

SCOREKEEPING FOR DIVORCE

Divorce rates can be recorded in many ways, but they are usually stated in one of three forms: the number of divorces per year per thousand people in the population (which is the simplest and most commonly used measure in statistical reports): the ratio of divorces granted in a given year to the number of marriages entered into during that year (which can be very misleading, as we shall see); or the number of divorces in a given year for every thousand married women fifteen years of age and older. No matter how you figure it, the rate in the United States is extremely high by European standards—and the overall trend has been pushing steadily upward. In fact, the rise in divorce rates began in the nineteenth century, about one hundred years ago. The long-term climb has now covered a century, with 1975 as the centennial year for the birth of the modern era of rising divorce rates.

There have been short periods of falling divorce rates, as in the period from 1929 to 1933 when the rate dropped from about eight to six per thousand females over fifteen, and there was a great surge upward beginning in 1940, reaching the American historical peak in 1946 (see Figure 1). Between 1940 and 1946 the rate jumped from about nine to eighteen per thousand. Then, between 1946 and 1950, the rate plummeted just as sharply, back to about ten per thousand and continued to decline slowly in the 1950s. Even so, between 1946 and 1960 more than 6 million divorces were granted in the United States. In 1960 the rate was only slightly higher than it had been in 1940, but it inched upward again in the 1960s and early 1970s. If we look at divorce in terms of its cumulative impact, the statistics are impressive indeed. Considerably more than 10 million living Americans have been divorced at one time or another (and most of them have also remarried, some to divorce again).

If we view the American divorce statistics for the twentieth century in broad perspective, we see a steady rise through the first forty years, then the furious rise and fall of the 1940s associated with all the upheavals of World War II, a slow decline in the relatively serene 1950s during which the rate never fell as low as it had been before the war, followed by a return to the long-term climb in the 1960s. The 1940s stand out as years in which the basic century-spanning trend was grotesquely disturbed by the special events of that decade. Now it seems as if we are following the

FIGURE 1. Divorces Per Thousand Persons in Population

Computed from data from the United States Department of Health, Education, and Welfare; Vital Statistics of the United States

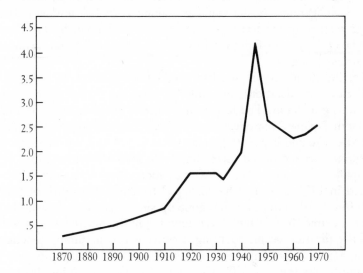

same trend that had been set before the volatile movements of the war years.

The divorce rate has also been rising in all the European countries, although the United States leads by a convincing margin. Among the Western nations, Denmark has approached the American divorce rate more closely than any other country, but even its high level in 1960 was slightly less than two-thirds of the American rate, and the rate for England and Wales was less than one-third of ours (Goode 1963).

In the Western experience, divorce rates have consistently accelerated with industrial development and the movement of people to the cities. But it would be misleading to say that industrialization always causes divorce rates to go up. In some parts of the world they have actually declined when the new technology was introduced. This was the general reaction in Japan and among the Arabic Islams (Goode 1963). Whether the divorce rate rises or falls depends largely on the rate of divorce and the dynamic forces associated with it at the outset of industrial growth.

Thus, divorce was no rarity in Japan before the factory system was initiated, but the basis for it was altogether different from that found in America. In neither Japan nor China had marriage been considered a sacramental affair. It was not even regarded as a concern of the state until the advent of industrialism, although divorce seems to have been very infrequent in China for centuries. This was not so for Japan. Japanese brides traditionally were expected to adjust, Madame Butterfly fashion, to a set of stern demands when they moved into their grooms' homes. Pleasing the man's mother and other in-laws was a large part of the young woman's obligations. If she could get along with her mother-in-law the chances were very good that her marriage would flourish. The husband would be no problem—failure to love him or even to like him was no cause for marriage breakup.

With industrialization, marriage and family adjustment is keyed to a wholly new consideration: husband-wife relations. In-law or kinship considerations grow faint. The fact is that conflict between husband and wife in modern Japanese marriages has not been as great so far as conflict between the wife and her mother-in-law used to be. And, for the time being, divorce rates have dropped. According to William Goode's (1963) figures, the Japanese divorce rate in 1890 was more than three times the level reported in 1950. In fact, it had dropped to about one-fourth of the 1890 rate before Pearl Harbor but has gone up since that time. It will not soon reach the extraordinarily high levels reported in the nineteenth century.

Industrialization seems to bring a convergence in family practices toward a standard contemporary pattern, but the starting points vary from one country to the next (Goode 1968). So the index for divorce may move up in some nations and down in others even as the end result tends to be about the same. In fact, the trend in Japan is now in an upward swing, having dropped to a level consistent with, or supported by, its current stage of industrial development. Further industrialization may now exert a disorganizing influence on the family or at least lead to the more frequent use of divorce as a safety valve in husband-wife relations.

One in Four

It is often said that about one marriage in four now ends in divorce in the United States, compared to a rate closer to one in eight at the turn of the century. But we must remember that divorces granted in any given year represent the end of marriages entered over the previous *two* decades (approximately). The rate usually given is the number of divorces per year per hundred marriages averaged over the previous ten years, which makes the assumption that the ten-year period is the one during which *most* of the marriages for the divorced group were started (Bogue 1959).

This does not mean that *your own* chances for divorce are one in four. It depends on what risk group you belong to. Speaking very generally, *your* chances are probably better than average—maybe much better— primarily because of certain status and educational factors working in your favor. Anyone who reads this page is probably at least a sophomore in college, and that alone makes him a better risk. The reader is also very likely middle class in background and cultural outlook. Class, race, education, rural-urban status, religion, even regional factors enter into the calculations; probabilities for divorce vary for different groups within every one of these categories. Furthermore, the divorce rate for remarriages is much higher than for first marriages, and the one-in-four cliché does not exclude two-time losers. When you marry for the first time, you are automatically in a relatively low risk group.

The one-in-four prediction is usually stated in such a way as to make it seem dangerously high, as if our marriage system and the whole modern family ethos must be near collapse. But if one out of four marriages is doomed, three out of four are not, which is a 75 percent success rate (assuming for the moment that nondivorce represents success, just as we usually assume that divorce means failure).

George P. Murdock (1950), for example, compared marriage breakup rates in a large number of societies, both nonliterate and literate, and concluded that contemporary divorce rates are well within the tolerable limits of a stable society. He made certain assumptions that can be challenged, such as the idea that divorce frequencies in nonliterate societies are truly comparable to those in advanced nations, but the thrust of his argument remains highly plausible. Americans have many reasons to worry about their nation and its future, but marriage seems to be one of its most stable institutions. Even the people who seek divorce usually remarry according to standard legal procedures, and quickly. Marriage is not just popular, it is *very* popular, and when people marry they still hope that it is for the rest of their lives. They know that it might not work out that way, but few regard marriage as just a temporary arrangement.

Religion

As for religious affiliation, both Jews and Catholics score low on divorce, while the frequency for Protestants is relatively high. Nonchurch members outdo all others (Monahan and Kephart 1954). Gerhard Lenski (1961) found the Protestants in his sample, both white and black, much more likely to have been divorced than either Catholics or Jews. (The sample consisted of 656 persons living in Detroit in 1958.) But the differences were not large among people currently divorced (and not remarried), because divorced Catholics were much less likely to remarry than Protestants. Only 8 percent of the Catholics had been divorced, compared to 16 percent of the white Protestants, and 22 percent of the black Protestants.

Jewish families had the lowest rate of all. Only 4 percent of those who had ever married reported a divorce. And yet of the three religious groups, Jews were the least critical of divorce, while Catholics were most strongly opposed to it. Only 11 percent of the Jews felt that divorce was always or usually wrong, compared with 66 percent of the Catholics—an almost staggering difference. Even Catholics judged to be low in Church ties were much more likely to be opposed; 40 percent of them considered divorce either always or usually wrong.

So religious convictions per se can hardly account for differences in divorce rates. They result from social patterns and interpersonal pressures that differ from one religious (or nonreligious) group to another (although religious doctrine is, of course, a part of these different social contexts). Despite their liberal attitude toward divorce, Jews are usually part of a network of social relations that can assure a high level of family stability. Furthermore, they marry at somewhat older ages than non-Jews, have completed more formal education on the average (Goldscheider and Goldstein 1967), and enjoy relatively high economic status. They use contraceptives in marriage earlier, more frequently, and more efficiently than either Protestants or Catholics. Jewish couples discuss the subject of family planning in marriage rather freely and more often agree on such matters (Westoff, Potter, Sagi, and Mishler 1966). This suggests a pattern of intelligent familism, and it is reflected in lower divorce rates.

Race

Blacks have had somewhat higher rates than whites throughout most of the twentieth century, according to figures compiled by William Goode (1956). Evidence from a variety of sources, much of it impressionistic, supports his figures. Richard Udry (1966; 1967a) analyzed 1960 census data and concluded that divorce rates among nonwhites were higher at all educational, income, and occupational levels and that these rates are probably a function of the blacks' inferior social position. A special report of the National Vital Statistics Division in 1957 estimated that about 20 percent of the nonwhite males in the United States had been divorced, compared to 14 percent of the white males. The corresponding figures for women were 20 and 17 respectively (NOVS *Special Reports* 1957). The greater discrepancy between black and white males than between black and white females is undoubtedly related to the special difficulties facing black men in America (discussed in Chapter 3).

National divorce statistics involving racial comparisons cannot be computed with precision, however. Much of the data collected by the National Vital Statistics Division do not identify people by race. As noted in the discussion of desertion, rates of divorce among blacks may actually rise as they gain first-class citizenship status, thereby sharing full partnership in the legal affairs of the community. Black lawyers have been admitted to the bar at an increasing rate for over a quarter of a century now. They stress legal divorce (Kephart and Monahan 1952), and more blacks can now afford to go that route. Desertion can be expected to decline (at least compared to rates for whites) as divorce becomes more available.

Socioeconomic Status

Social class, when measured by the occupation of the husband, seems to be inversely correlated with divorce, as William Goode (1951) and William Kephart (1955) have demonstrated. August Hollingshead had suggested such a relationship in 1950, but he did not supply convincing documentary support. Prior to this time even the experts assumed that the rich and powerful had higher divorce rates than the rest of us. They get the publicity, but publicity can be very misleading. For comparative purposes, Goode's proneness-to-divorce figures for occupational categories are as follows:

Professional and Proprietary	62.6
Clerical, Sales, Service	63.3
Skilled, Foremen	89.9
Semi-skilled, operatives	142.4
Unskilled	166.7

(These numbers express the relationship between the proportion of men who are classified as neither single nor married in each occupational category to the proportion who are married and living with their wives.)

The inverse correlation between occupational status and divorce helps to explain the higher rates among blacks. But no theory covering these data can also explain the rates for religious affiliation, although it would be helpful to explain both sets of data with just one theory. Economic hardship by itself is probably not at the heart of the matter, since both divorce and marriage rates usually increase during periods of prosperity and drop again when jobs and money are scarce (Goode 1966). A number of years ago—before the negative relationship between social class and divorce had been fully realized—Julius Roth and Robert Peck (1951) noted that couples who lose social status in the course of marriage face particularly severe domestic strain. They also claimed that the best prognosis for couples, independent of high or low status or high or low mobility, was class homogamy—roughly equal class status for husband and wife at the time of their marriage. But this is especially true at the middle- and upper-income levels.

Rural-Urban Differences

Rural divorce rates are generally lower than in the cities. A problem comes up, however, because the statistics are usually based on current residence and do not always reflect the person's whereabouts at the time of divorce or during the period when the marriage was deteriorating. Thus, census data clearly show that divorced women are most numerous in urban areas and are underrepresented on farms and in small towns (U.S. Bureau of Census 1960). But it is also known that women who divorce in rural areas do not always stay there; they move to the cities if they get a chance. Still, Thomas Monahan (1955a) found that farmers in Iowa contributed considerably less than their share to the total number of divorces in that state.

Region

Generally, divorce rates are higher the farther west you go on the American continent. They are low in New England, the Middle Atlantic states, and the Southeastern part of the country. In the Midwest they climb a little higher, while the peak levels are reached in the Southwest, Mountain states, and along the Pacific coast. The explanation is partly religious and ethnic. But it also reflects historical conditions, especially those that influenced customs in western areas at the time of their early settlement. Generally, these led to liberal attitudes toward marriage and divorce compared to the Old World flavor of the eastern states, where encrusted legal restrictions have tended to persist. As we have already seen, the American divorce rate has always been high compared to European rates, probably because of liberal influences along the expanding frontier, where women have had relatively high status. In a sense, the emancipating pressures (insofar as family life is concerned) extended westward with the growth of the nation. Wherever women have greater leverage in dealing with men, divorce rates nudge upward.

Age at Marriage

All studies on the relation between age at marriage and divorce rates come to essentially the same conclusion: The younger one or both parties are at the time of marriage, the more likely will their marriage end in divorce. Paul Glick (1957) once estimated that three times as many divorces occur among women who marry before age eighteen than among those marrying between the ages of twenty-two and twenty-four. Early marriage is associated with lower social status and also with expediency as the basis for marriage—early pregnancy in particular. Neither of these is conducive to marital stability.

Length of Marriage Before Divorce

The familiar one-in-four divorce prediction is almost completely meaningless if calculated in terms of length of marriage. Other things being equal, chances for divorce are much higher in the first five years of marriage and much lower after ten years of matrimony. The greatest number of divorces are granted in the second and third years after the ceremony. The rate goes up sharply until this peak is reached, after which it declines rather steadily, becoming a tiny fraction of 1 percent in the twenty-fifth year of marriage. (The only period of increase after the first peak that could possibly be considered significant was reached between the thirteenth and fourteenth year, but even that was negligible. This estimate was based on figures for separations collected in Philadelphia between 1937 and 1950 by William Kephart [1954].) The great majority of couples who seek divorce do it very soon after the wedding, and, strange as it may seem, some couples marry and divorce without ever even living together (Monahan 1962).

There is some evidence that the upsurge in divorce in the twentieth century has been due in part to an especially large increase in divorces during the first five years of marriage, but this was most evident in the sharp upswing of the 1940s (Jacobson 1950). It has been less true of the 1960s and 1970s, when the rate has gone up in all length of marriage categories.

DIVORCE AS A SOCIAL PATTERN

The laws governing divorce differ from one state to the next, but the underlying pattern does not vary to any great extent—except in a few unusual places. Reno, for example, is a strange town because divorce is so much more crucial to its day-to-day economic affairs. No doubt a selective force is also at work, since the people who go there are not really typical divorce hunters. They have more money as a rule, and they combine divorce with relatively expensive vacations. From the point of view of the Reno Chamber of Commerce, divorce seekers from other states are tourists. But *migratory divorce*—where the divorce is granted outside the couple's true state of residence—constitutes but a tiny fraction of all divorces granted in the United States.

In the typical home-state case, the first step toward divorce (after marriage has deteriorated to the point of insufferability) is taken when one of the partners consults a friend or relative. This is not an essential part of the legal process, of course. Increasingly, women who seek divorce have friends who have already groped their way through the process and can offer seasoned advice on how to proceed. In fact, one contributing factor to the high divorce rate is the existence in our cities of a large number of women who have been divorced and who stand as living proof that it can be done. This is the *reassurance factor*. People are easily intimidated by legal procedures, but they are a little less anxious if the process can be personalized. Perhaps some of the divorced women even advise married friends to follow their lead, especially when divorce has given them genuine relief from an intolerable marriage. They become, in a sense, testimonials, at least in part in reaction to the traditional stigma against the divorcee.

The next step toward divorce is to consult a lawyer. Most lawyers have virtually nothing to do with divorce work, and hence the divorce seeker in metropolitan areas will usually be referred to a lawyer who specializes in this kind of practice. According to one estimate, approximately 8 percent of the lawyers handle 80 percent of the divorce business in some cities, and the truly high-grade lawyers spend their time on other matters (Ehrlich 1959). Before referral, an attorney may try to halt or stall the action or possibly send the client to a marriage counselor, but he is certainly not obliged to.

Once the client reaches a lawyer who regularly handles divorce actions the case will probably be processed in a rather impersonal, technical way. As Stanton Ehrlich (1959) has observed, the lawyer receives his fee as a retainer, and his work load will be eased if he can arrange a reconciliation; he gets his fee in any case, so he does not, as is commonly believed, have a vested interest in the couple's breakup. Nevertheless, efforts at reconciliation by the lawyer at this stage are not very likely to work out. The lawyer's principal task is to manage the divorce in the most efficient manner possible, which means adjusting the facts of the case to the state's legal grounds for divorce and filing the necessary papers.

American divorce procedures have usually operated according to the *adversary system* (now under attack in many states)—one spouse acting as plaintiff, the other as defendant. The plaintiff is presumed to be guiltless; the defendant supposedly has done something that constitutes grounds for divorce. Ordinarily the couple agree, implicitly or explicitly, on who will play which role. In about three cases out of four the plaintiff is the wife, although it would be a gross error to assume that she is innocent and the husband, through guilty behavior, is responsible for all the trouble.

The adversary system is, in fact, a *legal fiction* insofar as divorce proceedings are concerned, since the lawyer knowingly adjusts the facts of the case to the state's legal requirements, and evidence that might call this set of facts into question is ignored. Less than one divorce out of ten is contested, and most of them take considerably less than half an hour of actual courtroom time. The defendant is only occasionally in attendance, although it is likely that he will be represented when property and child custody arrangements are made.

Generally, social pressures in the United States favor a nonadversary divorce system, and states are beginning to adopt *no-fault* procedures with incompatibility or irreconcilable differences as the grounds. California law, for example, no longer refers to divorce, but rather to dissolution of marriage. The petitioner whose action is not contested can get a decree (after filing his petition) by answering four questions put by the judge:

1. Do you now want to dissolve your marriage?
2. Are there irreconcilable differences between you and your spouse?
3. Have these caused an irremediable breakdown in your marriage?
4. Do you believe that marriage counseling or the assistance of a conciliation court or a waiting period before proceeding further could restore your marriage?

If the petitioner seeks *spousal support* (no longer called alimony in California law), several other questions are raised: Are you working now? Have you worked in the past? Is there any reason why you cannot work either part or full time? Making the final decision depends on the needs of the petitioner and the ability of the other person to pay, based on the size of their community property, their income pattern, the couple's standard of living, and related income information.

If the action is contested, testimony as to why the marriage has failed is heard and witnesses may be called. But the judge is obliged to listen only so long as he feels the need for further information. (Perhaps it should be added that people from out of state must establish residence in California at least six months before filing for dissolution of marriage, and the decree does not become final for six months after it is granted.)

Texas' divorce laws have also been changed, allowing dissolution on the basis of irreconcilable differences. The pressures to move in this direction come from both popular and professional sources. Marriage counselors and students of family life, for example, almost always speak against the adversary system. It dehumanizes the process, forces each case into a narrow legalistic mold, and makes official divorce records useless. Certainly these records are of little help in explaining the dynamics of marriage failure or the real causes of divorce (although the California system does not guarantee valid information either).

Thus, legal procedures in the United States are slowly changing and becoming somewhat more uniform from state to state. Trends in the grounds for divorce show this, especially with the use of incompatibility as the basis for legal action. Cruelty, too, has been used more frequently—currently in more than 60 percent of the divorce actions—and it is usually mental rather than physical. Legal standards for cruelty are ad hoc, meaning that its presence has to be judged by the special conditions of each case. There are virtually no standing criteria for cruelty in an absolute sense, so almost anything can qualify. This is what led to the current acceptance of incompatibility, since in its essential nature it boils down to mental cruelty. But when incompatibility is the issue, who is guilty and who innocent? *Neither* partner is at fault; the relationship itself is the culprit.

Legal codes, however, do not change as rapidly as their interpretations. Meanings of legal phrases change along with community standards, and therefore the *attitudes* of lawyers and judges are crucial—even more crucial than the laws and precedents themselves. This is not peculiar to laws for domestic relations. It has long been obvious in decisions of the United States Supreme Court. Thus, Supreme Court justices reflect the spirit of the times, much to the consternation of those who say that society runs by the rule of law rather than the rule of men.

Of critical importance for the main theme of this book—tension between familism and individualism—is the fact that legal interpretations now tend to favor the rights of individuals. The fate of the old idea that divorce should be granted only for grave and serious reasons illustrates this point. People should be served, not the institution of marriage. But laws themselves have changed little until quite recently. In the minds of the officials who run the judicial system and the public which uses it, a profound change occurred long before legal reforms were made.

The person who considers his marriage intolerable may find that he can take all the steps in the divorce process without ever being charged with violating the spirit of familism. He may be asked to reconsider on the grounds that he is acting too hastily or that there will be some stigma attached to his action, but the chances are excellent that he will never be accused of letting society down. If he feels guilt or shame, it is probably because he has *failed* in marriage—a personal failure—not because he has broken an intense social taboo. In this light, it is now taken for granted that the current crop of young couples entering marriage will produce a large number of divorces, but the ones who break up will not be considered traitors to a social norm. They are rather to be consoled, pitied, or rehabilitated because of their personal misfortune. This is not meant to suggest that the moral fiber of the nation has collapsed, but rather that society's concern has shifted from marriage per se to concern for the individuals who happen to be involved. The laws still tend to speak the conventional language protecting the institution of marriage, but the people who are closest to the divorce process are more likely to identify with the people whose lives are directly affected.

There is one legal procedure that has been widely used in the United States, however, that represents more than a token concern for the *institution* of marriage—that is the *interlocutory decree*. This kind of action is part of the divorce process in more than one-third of the states and serves, in a sense, as a preliminary divorce settlement. Only after a certain period of time has elapsed following the decree (from a month to a year, depending on the state) does the divorce become final. And only when it becomes final can the persons involved remarry. Since its ostensible purpose is to discourage impulsive divorce and to allow for reconciliation, it can be regarded as a kind of protection for the institution of marriage. The very fact that it hampers remarriage, which occurs as soon as possible after divorce in many cases, suggests that it is not intended to cater to anybody's personal wishes.

Before leaving this discussion, we should note that the general social pattern for divorce is greatly modified in certain groups. Many Catholics, for example, follow a unique course because the Catholic Church has its own procedures based on canon law. Thus, Church members approach divorce or annulment by first seeing their parish priest. According to Kenneth Salter (1969), this usually involves a couple (who may have married either within or outside the Church) who want to end their marriage *with* the Church's blessing so that they can remarry within it. This is a formidable undertaking, because the Church has set up elaborate rules to follow and obstacles to surmount. Salter's study shows that, although the priest's role in this is considered perfunctory by the Church and by many of the priests themselves, it will probably determine the success or failure of the couple's effort. The priest has great discretion over whether to take the case in the first place, and he in effect decides what the issues are. He guides the gathering of evidence, records, and forms necessary to bring the matter to trial in chancery court. In fact, according to Salter the priest's own feeling about canon law often determines whether the personal interests of the couple will take precedence over a strict interpretation of Church regulations. So this, too, is a social process influenced by local conditions—they can change whether the formal rules do or not.

MARRIAGE COUNSELING AND DIVORCE

Professional counselors have no necessary role to play in divorce in America, although a counselor may be consulted if the parties happen to know about one and choose to discuss their case with him. (And, as we have seen, the question of the possible use of counseling comes up under the marriage dissolution codes in California.) Most couples give at best only fleeting thought to that possibility. Even if they think about it or know of a person or agency not too far away, they probably have only a vague notion about what counseling can do—and they are not necessarily optimistic about it.

In fact, it seems likely that the first reaction of most people to counseling is fear. This can stem from many sources, but the main reason is that any badly corroded marriage is an extremely threatening and uncomfortable part of the person's life. Whoever has the job of probing around in this tormented area is automatically dangerous. He is at least as frightening as a dentist and probably a good deal more so. The very nature of counseling also poses a problem. Marriage partners at war usually blame each other for their troubles, and there is evidence that the more they do, the less likely will they seek professional aid—and the less likely will a counselor be able to help them (Gurin, Veroff, and Feld 1960).

It is not surprising, then, that professional counseling has never become a basic part of the divorce process in this country. And yet a few other countries have managed to work it in. Certainly most people are willing to see a dentist when their teeth give them unbearable pain. The question is this: Why have Americans been so reluctant to put counseling into the legal framework for divorce, especially by contrast with other industrial nations that have found more use for it?

The Effect of Pluralism

Unfortunately, we do not have any really good answer. Although many people argue that we ought to do better, few have tried to explain why we do not. Several factors are involved, and they overlap and reinforce one another. One is the *pluralism* of our social system. Americans cope with almost all personal and social problems in a remarkably diversified way, and it is rare for any group to gain a monopoly over the handling of any particular problem. Churches vie with each other in meeting the religious needs of people; business firms compete with each other in their sphere; colleges and universities abound in variety to meet all tastes; even medical doctors compete with osteopaths, assorted patent medicines, and a multitude of cure-all schemes in the treatment of America's health problems. Certainly pluralism characterizes the governmental health programs available to American families (Roemer 1967).

In fact, it is curious under these circumstances that the legal profession has gained as much control over the divorce process as it has, although we have seen that various extralegal solutions to marriage troubles are available and that some divorce seekers go to states where the divorce laws suit them better than those at home.

Given the general nature of American pluralism, it may seem unreasonable to expect all couples seeking divorce to look into the possibility of marriage counseling. But it should be noted that few people argue that counseling ought to be *required*. Most proponents feel that couples should have to make a *conscious decision* not to use it if that is what they want. At present, the decision is customarily made by default, without fully realizing what the alternatives are, or under the impression that counseling would be very inconvenient and possibly expensive.

The Professional Status of Marriage Counseling

Secondly, marriage counseling in America is a very young profession. It got its start in the 1920s and has only slowly acquired the bearings of a legitimate profession. Not until 1946 was the American Association of Marriage and Family Counselors founded, and twenty years later its membership had reached only about 500. The association still has a varied membership, including people with graduate degrees in theology, psychology, medicine, law, and sociology. (Although the following discussion deals largely with the AAMFC, it is not the only accrediting agency. Many psychologists have independent professional credentials for working with marital and family problems.) Admission to membership in the AAMFC calls for a graduate or professional degree (Ph.D., M.S.W., M.D., and so on) plus training in several specified areas, such as genetics, physiology, sociology of marriage and the family, and legal aspects of domestic relations. These specific requirements usually lead to considerable work beyond the counselor's professional degree, because they are not included in his basic degree requirements. Three years of professional experience are also required for membership, along with evidence of professional integrity, competence in accepted clinical standards, and emotional maturity.

The AAMFC has consistently stressed high membership standards. But the *licensing* of marriage counselors remains behind certification procedures for many other lines of work that have considerably less social importance. In most states, for example, almost anyone can call himself a marriage counselor or perhaps adopt an impressive synonym for that term, but relatively few marriage counselors earn a living through counseling alone. Furthermore, any respectable practice involves referrals to other professionals—medical doctors, psychiatrists, clinical psychologists, social workers, and perhaps lawyers or clergymen. A majority of the members of the AAMFC handle their practice on a part-time basis; they teach, preach, practice law, do research, or engage in some other professional or occupational work to supplement their income. The full-time practitioners are likely to work in agencies, many of which rely on subsidies from community chests of one sort or another or from public tax revenues.

The crux of the matter is that no prescribed training curriculum for marriage counselors exists as yet. Graduate schools that specialize in the training of professional counselors are slowly emerging, but most of the current practitioners have not been through a standardized training regimen specifically designed for the counseling of married couples. A large part of their training is at the postdoctoral level. The establishment of formal graduate programs will, among other things, lead to a more systematic re-cruitment of people into the profession. Then they will be able to prepare for careers during their undergraduate years with a clear conception of where they are going and what they will have to do (Leslie 1964). This is the way it is in law, medicine, physics, and other well-established profes-sions.

Reference to the heterogeneous training of counselors suggests another difficulty: Specific kinds of marital problems with well-defined syndromes —"textbook cases"—have not yet been isolated. This means that the whole issue of diagnosis is still controversial. How a particular case will be han-dled depends on the background of the counselor—theological, psychologi-cal, or sociological—and within each area there are several different schools of thought.

The counseling session itself can be organized in a variety of ways, al-though Gerald Leslie (1964) says that most counselors prefer to work with all parties to the affair—*joint counseling*—rather than parceling them out among different counselors or specialists. Group counseling, where several married couples meet with the therapist, also gets strong support. John Mayer (1967) points out that this approach helps couples to grasp the full scope and variety of marriage—most of us have extraordinarily limited im-aginations in this regard. No matter what we do, there are other ways to do it, and the chances are that one or two of them would be an improvement over our present methods.

Despite everything that has been said, many people advocate marriage counseling as a normal part of divorce procedure (even before it becomes a profession of high integrity in the public eye), especially to clarify the reasons for the marriage crisis, the rights and needs of all members of the family, the alternatives available, and the chances for reconciliation. This has been attempted in other countries with results that have earned popu-lar approval. The point of immediate importance is that the United States is a very special case. It may be that marriage counseling will have to earn much greater professional respect than has been necessary elsewhere for it to take a firm hold here. Other nations have not experienced the unique American drive to diversity and independence in problem solving.

Marriage Counseling for the Masses

Remember, too, that there are many persons, agencies, foundations, and so forth in the United States competing to meet almost every personal and social need associated with marriage and family problems. Almost every newspaper in the country has an advice to the lovelorn column; books are published to advise this same audience; cults and sects are formed with the express purpose of reaching it. Each may claim to have a particularly effective plan for dealing with domestic problems, but none has been successful enough to make any big impact on family patterns in general. In terms of classical economic theory, this is an almost perfectly competitive market—none of the suppliers (advice givers) has the power to materially affect the overall market for its particular service.

And yet never was there a market in which the consumer was so bewildered by the alternative possibilities and so in need of some kind of consumer's guide to help him cope. Perhaps there are some obvious frauds who can and should be exposed, but most of the advice givers cannot easily be censored, since in most cases what they have to say is not without some redeeming social merit.

There are questionable offenders, however—even the columnists who give advice so freely in the daily press. The formula is very simple. In most cases the columnist-counselor gets letters from troubled readers, and certain ones are picked out and printed. Then advice is given in writing—for a mass audience. The statements of the letter writer are taken at face value as a rule, and hence the symptoms as reported by the client are used to diagnose the case.

The columnist's next step is usually to supply reassurance, which is often built into the columnist's basic style and seems to say that most problems can be solved.

The advice is brief and usually seems to be practical, since it is given in response to a human problem expressed in a letter by one troubled person. How effective it is remains unknown; there seems to be no way to determine how such advice is used.

There is an interesting contrast between journalistic advice to the lovelorn and advice given on medical matters. In the latter, the columnist is always a member in good standing of the American Medical Association. He will occasionally give suggestions on the basis of very meager information supplied in the reader's letter, but inevitably he tells the reader to see his own physician. This is the crux of the matter. The medical columnist provides a very useful service—as an information giver who can help people decide when to consult a doctor. It is assumed that the reader will see a physician if an actual medical diagnosis is called for, and therefore professional practitioners are not by-passed. Newspapers, in fact, *reaffirm* the importance of the medical doctor's role. By contrast, journalistic counseling on family matters often turns out to be a *substitute* for professional counseling. But, again, this merely underscores the tenuous status of professional marriage counseling in the United States.

The overall impact of this discussion may seem negative, but that is certainly not its intention. Members of the AAMFC are a thoroughly dedicated group, and they can be extremely helpful—in premarital counseling and for both mild and severe marital troubles. They work in a referral setting so that problems can be handled by the most appropriate professional specialty for each case. Although strategies of help are diverse, they are almost always ones that have proved useful in terms of the style and clientele of the particular counselor involved. There is every reason to believe that the profession will take a giant stride forward in the decade ahead. This is the best hope available for couples in trouble.

THEORIES OF DIVORCE

Theoretical explanations for the divorce rate are both cheap and dear—they are cheap in the sense that there are scores of them and almost anyone can make one up, but they are dear in the sense that a theory that can explain most of the known facts is extremely hard to come by, and devising one that can be put to a truly critical test is most difficult of all. The purpose of this section is to review the ones that have gained wide attention among professional students of the family and to call attention to both their strengths and weaknesses.

Kinship Theory

Anthropologists study family relations in all kinds of societies. The key to their approach is the search for a general theory that can account for the great variety of divorce rates in the world or at least organize the facts in a useful way. Information about divorce in scores of societies is available in the Human Relations Area Files (a collection of data about many cultures that has been carefully cross-referenced to enable comparisons for different topics) including groups in almost every stage of cultural and technological development. Is there any general explanation that can bring order out of this mass of divorce data?

One interesting approach was developed by Max Gluckman (1950; Fallers 1957; Mitchell 1961). After studying the Zulu and Lozi of Africa, he concluded that divorce patterns are an integral part of the kinship system itself. He found *descent* customs to be particularly important, that is, the way kinship duties are determined and, even more crucial, the way authority is wielded over the woman's procreative power. For example, in *patrilineal* societies—where kinship is traced through the male side of the family—divorce is rare according to Gluckman. In effect, the woman in such societies has children for her husband. That is her duty, and that is likely to be her goal in life. Consequently, the legitimacy of children becomes an obsessive concern, and illegitimacy, a serious problem. In such *father-right* societies marriage is supposed to last a lifetime; divorce is a humiliation.

In *matrilineal* societies, on the other hand, kinship is traced through the female side of the family. Hence the woman produces her own lineage, and divorce under these circumstances is not rare. In effect, the woman has children for herself and her relatives rather than for her husband and his kinsmen. In this arrangement barrenness on her part will probably not be considered a breach of the basic reason for marriage (which, in patrilineal societies, is to have children for her husband). By the same token, no particular husband is of special importance to the woman, at least not for kinship purposes. Since the husband has no strong claim to his wife, and the wife has no great need for any particular husband, the divorce rate is high.

In *bilateral* societies, such as ours—where people trace their kinship through both the male and the female sides of the family—divorce may also be frequent, although not necessarily. Bernard Farber (1966) has suggested that bilateral kinship is appropriate in modern society precisely because it neither stresses kinship nor entirely ignores it, and it has no built-in need for sharp restrictions on divorce.

Gluckman's basic premise seems to be rather limited for two major reasons. The most critical objection is that facts from some parts of the world do not fall into line with the theory. Studying a sample of societies drawn from the Human Relations Area Files, Charles Ackerman (1963) concluded that bilateral societies do not generally have high divorce rates. In fact, Ackerman was forced to conclude that the descent part of the kinship system was not very useful in accounting for differences in divorce rates in his sample.

The second criticism of Gluckman's approach is almost as crucial, and it may help to explain why there is no good correlation between kinship patterns and the divorce rate. Rates of divorce have been known to change within a single society, often quite radically, without any basic change in the way kinship is traced. This has happened in the United States, for example. It seems obvious that the kinship system itself cannot be used to explain change when it remains constant. Furthermore, even if a fluctuation in kinship happens to be associated with changes in the divorce rate, it does not follow that kinship necessarily *causes* it. Much deeper forces might very well be at work. For one thing, industrial growth could force changes in both kinship and the divorce rate at the same time. The underlying cause could turn out to be technological change.

Industrial and Urban Growth

Most of the sociological theories of the past seventy-five years—the period during which our divorce rate has risen—have been based on technical progress and the growth of cities. In fact, the earliest attempts to study the family in terms of industrial development predicted closer and stronger husband-wife bonds, not their breakdown.

Frederick Engels (1902), for example (the coauthor with Karl Marx of *The Communist Manifesto*) argued that monogamous marriage had been founded for the purpose of subjugating women and that women's miserable status was but one part of a larger pattern of exploitation found in all presocialist societies. Engels further claimed that power and property relationships between the sexes are determined by the kinds of work men and women do—that is, they are caused by the "forms and relations of production"—and that only when women's work is socially as important as men's can there be any hope for equality between the sexes. (Current proponents of women's liberation often express similar views.)

Thus, he regarded the economic emancipation of women as absolutely essential for their liberation at home. Their full freedom becomes possible only when they take part in production away from home on a large scale. And this becomes possible only when modern industry demands it—when household work is reduced along with the massive growth of service industries, and women are needed as industrial workers just as much as men.

Engels forecast the time when the family would no longer be the basic economic unit in society. This would follow the rise of mass production and social ownership of all key parts of the economy—factories, utilities, and so on. Then the care and education of children would become a community rather than a household responsibility, relieving wives of their degrading household burdens and leading to a higher level of intimacy in marriage. The anxieties associated with bequesting and inheriting would be eliminated. With sex equality, genuine romantic love would become possible, and freedom to choose a mate would exist for the first time in history.

Although family strife might accompany this process, Engels considered the general trend completely desirable. Through socialist planning, the economic foundations for a higher form of family life could be formed. He foresaw a marriage of equals—a marriage that would be stable, not because of religious sanctions or laws making divorce difficult, but because it would be based on mutual love. Such a marriage would be devoid of coercion and the traditional male condescension.

Engels took little note of divorce as such, but he clearly felt that rules against it were, above all, devices to keep women down. Conflicts within the capitalist system would become ever fiercer as industry grew, he thought, and there would be efforts to change the laws governing marriage. Still, the thrust of his argument seemed to suggest that marriage would become more stable, not less, as the economic system moved ahead.

A long discussion of this approach is probably unnecessary. There is very little evidence that the higher form of marriage that Engels predicted has appeared only in Marxist nations. If anything, marriage in Russia, for example, has moved toward a bourgeois pattern in the past thirty years, much like that in capitalist America (although there was a brief period shortly after the Bolshevik Revolution when both marriage and divorce rules were radically relaxed). The point of most interest in Engels' work is that he linked marriage patterns to the processes of industrial development at an early date. His era was the one when such theories began to monopolize social thought.

Another writer of even greater sociological interest also related marriage and family patterns to industrial growth at about this time. In a lecture on the family delivered in 1892 (eight years after the first publication of Engels' work), Emile Durkheim (1965) argued that the main theme in the whole history of family life had been a decline in the number of members in each family along with closer personal ties binding the remaining members together. The family becomes smaller as the industrial environment gets larger, and *individuation*—the freeing of the individual from rigid, traditional controls—goes right along with this drift. He called this new family the *conjugal family*. It becomes a "little social world" where special rules of morality apply. The nonfamily sphere of life is a less friendly place where people must conform to much more formal, bureaucratic standards.

Family solidarity becomes almost completely *personal* in this process. People cling to the family only because they are attracted to the personal qualities of their fathers, mothers, wives, or children. Ties had previously been based on things rather than interpersonal relations. The whole organization of the family was designed mainly to control goods and property and to keep them within the family. Personal considerations had to be suppressed. Durkheim believed that the day would come when the individual would not be allowed to bequeath property to his children even by means of a will, since keeping property in the family line is but the last and most basic form of hereditary privilege. This kind of link between the generations becomes an affront to the public conscience in a society that believes in merit and efficiency.

Durkheim argued that only one kind of social bond is powerful enough to hold men together in an industrial society: their occupational or professional groups. At the same time, these are broad enough to allow for a wide social perspective. They are the only social units able to perform the economic and moral functions that the family used to take care of. And yet Durkheim felt that marriage grows stronger both implicitly and explicitly as it is held together by personal ties of affection, replacing the economic and moral pressures of society and the larger kinship group.

Although Durkheim's ideas are different in several ways from Engels', he was reacting to the same set of social facts. He dropped the constant reference to class struggle and exploitation and gave scant attention to emancipation for women. Still, he saw a drop in traditional controls over the family, a trend toward greater individual freedom, and a drift toward companionship relations at home as basic economic affairs are taken over by outside agencies. But, like Engels, Durkheim did not specifically consider the question of divorce. Neither of them could tell at the time they wrote what the trend would be, since reliable data were simply not available.

In the twentieth century a succession of writers have offered theories about marriage that either elaborate the basic ideas of Engels and Durkheim, or modify them somewhat. It became ever more apparent that the divorce rate was going up, so attention tended to concentrate on this fact. Blame for this trend was repeatedly laid on industrialization and the growth of cities. One important landmark for this approach was an influential textbook on the family published in 1945 by Ernest Burgess and Harvey Locke. These two men were not terribly original, but they did state a theory of family change covering many of the same points put forward by Engels and Durkheim, with this new twist: They saw in industrial progress the basis for both higher divorce rates and a higher form of family life. In a sense, this was the Americanization of what had become the standard view of industrialism's impact on the family.

The key to their approach was one central idea: With American industrial development there had been a rapid change from the rural, *institutional* family (essentially a preindustrial arrangement) to the *companionship* family of the city (the industrial pattern). The earlier family was based on permanence and duty as the highest obligations of family members. By contrast, the companionship family has personal happiness as its main goal and relies on divorce to straighten out mistakes in mate selection. Because the switch from the traditional to the modern family has happened so quickly, it brings disorganization, but, as always happens in the course of social change, it also carries the seeds for its own reorganization.

Family members in the old order were bound together not only by their common possession of material things (to use Durkheim's expression), but by the need to cooperate in order to get the necessary work done. The rural family was a work unit, and the land was its capital. Even the youngest children could see the need to help. This family was also held together by pressures from outside, especially the community stigma on divorce. Marriage breakup inevitably led to gossip and enough shame to make most people avoid it.

By contrast, the city family is not held together by a need for joint work efforts or by pressures from outside. It is a consumers' unit and, if anything, city life tends to pull family members apart. It certainly offers a dizzying variety of ways to spend leisure time. It is also a place of exaggerated anonymity, where the person is free in part simply because nobody knows him, so nobody cares what he does. This is most true in precisely those parts of the city that offer the most action. The family is united only by its ability to give companionship and ego support. If it cannot do that, then divorce is a tempting way out, and facilities for obtaining one are readily available.

Burgess and Locke noted the increasing likelihood that spouses would have different religious, ethnic, and class backgrounds in the cities, since this is where diversity is greatest. In fact, if there is any one reason for the rise in divorce with the quick shift of people from farms to cities, it is the much greater chance for mixed marriage—mixed not just in terms of race and religion, but in almost every conceivable way. That is not the only source of trouble, however; couples also have to adjust to new and changing problems.

The Burgess-Locke theory thus says that a rapid change from one kind of family system to another has occurred, and for the brief period of transition high levels of family trouble can be expected. This theory combines short-term pessimism with long-term optimism, since it holds that the time will come (after we adjust to city life) when we can take its challenges in stride. But in the short run we falter, largely because we bring too much folklore from the past into our new setting, most of which simply does not apply. But Burgess and Locke predict that eventually the outmoded ways will be discarded and new ways to cope will be discovered. The day will come when the prophecies of Engels and Durkheim can come true, bringing a higher form of marriage and family life, freed from the stereotypes and narrow vision of the old way.

In fact, eight years after the Burgess-Locke thesis was published, E. Gartley Jaco and Ivan Belknap (1953) argued that a *new* transition was already upon us, superseding the one outlined by Burgess and Locke. The latter had talked mainly about the exodus of people from small towns and rural areas to the congested, central parts of big cities. In particular, they stressed the trend from single-family to multifamily housing then found in the inner areas of the cities. But even as they were writing their thesis, a new switch to the suburbs had started. This involved several new trends, according to Jaco and Belknap, such as the return to a slightly higher birth rate (higher than what had turned up among the first wave of American city dwellers) and higher rates of employment for both single and married women.

Now that a few years have passed since the flight to the suburbs, the Jaco-Belknap thesis has been almost forgotten. Most people seem to assume that the farm-to-city migration was always essentially a move to the suburbs. But if suburbanism was in fact a second phase in city growth—

a second period of transition—maybe another one is about to begin. Maybe *no* stable family system can ever emerge in the cities. The modern city seems to be in constant flux; whether a new equilibrium—one with standing traditions passed on from one generation to the next—can ever be formed under these circumstances is questionable to say the least. It is possible that unless a moratorium on new inventions is called, the human community will be in rapid change for decades to come, even centuries. So the family will be in constant transition. Society will never again stand still long enough for people to perfect a family style suited to their current needs.

Before leaving this discussion, we should recall industrial growth does not *always* cause the divorce rate to go up (as demonstrated by William Goode [1966]). Generally speaking, it has led to higher divorce rates, but several countries had very high rates long before modern times. The industrial pattern has actually had the effect of lowering divorce in these places.

Friendship and Divorce

One intriguing approach with implications for modern city life attempts to pinpoint the people who are most susceptible to divorce. Almost all observers agree that social controls over the small family are relaxed in the urban setting. But few people become *completely* anonymous. It is doubtful that any human society could last in a city that aloof. Nevertheless, some people are caught up in more active and sympathetic social circles than others, and some couples share friends more than others. Charles Ackerman (1963) suggests that the key to family stability is the degree to which the couple have *shared* as distinguished from *separate* friendships.

He contends that the key to the sociological study of divorce rates has usually centered on mate selection. Homogamy (where couples have similar social backgrounds) is associated with marriage stability; heterogamy (where their backgrounds are different) is linked to instability. Burgess and Locke had called attention to the greater chances for mixed marriages in the cities, but they did not put this at the heart of their theory. Ackerman goes beyond similarities between husband and wife to include similarities between their friends and relatives. He suggests that the *network of affiliations* surrounding the marriage determines, more than anything else, the probability of divorce. If they are *conjunctive*—that is, if the friends and associates of the wife are the same or nearly the same as her husband's— divorce is unlikely. If they are *disjunctive*, each spouse having separate friends and group memberships, divorce is more likely. With conjunctive affiliations, both husband and wife will have similar values and will react to similar social pressures which, in most cases, will help bind them together. But if they have separate friends, they will respond to different social pressures, more often than not pulling them apart.

It does seem likely that the modern city breeds separate friendships for spouses, especially when contrasted with the small town or rural area. Not only are young people with different social and personal traits more likely to meet and marry, but couples who have similar backgrounds at the time of courtship may drift apart in marriage simply because they are more likely to meet people of divergent views.

Nevertheless, whatever leads to joint friendships fosters marriage stability. The low divorce rate of Jews, noted earlier, is undoubtedly aided by this kind of influence. Various writers have shown that couples in the lower social classes, where divorce rates are high, tend to be pulled apart by divided *kinship* loyalties. By contrast, middle-class couples have greater independence from kinsmen and more often enjoy a shared circle of friends, resulting in lower divorce rates (Bott 1957; Rainwater and Handel 1964; Scanzoni 1965).

It is even possible that the custom of having separate social circles is part of a subculture, passed on from one generation to the next and linked to the class system. Judson Landis (1956) studied three generations within single family lines and found that divorce rates in all three were correlated; if the grandparents had high rates, both the second and third generations were likely to have high rates, too. In fact Landis suggested that youth from divorce-prone families tend to go steady with, become engaged to, and marry persons from other divorce-prone families.

How this applies to preindustrial societies remains a mystery. If Max Gluckman (1950) was right, a key to differences in divorce rates in such societies is their kinship practices (although other factors are also undoubtedly involved). If the divorce rate is low when industrial trends are introduced, the chances are good that it will start going up. Many forces will be at work, but of special importance will be (1) greater diversity in mate selection, (2) the fact that marriage relies so heavily on the couple's ability to give mutual companionship, and (3) the fact that outside pressures more often lead to disjunctive than to conjunctive friendships.

Resources-Demands Theory

In the most general sense, almost any approach to divorce must recognize two basic factors: the *resources* that couples have to work with and the *demands* or problems that they have to face. If the balance is favorable, the couple's resources will pull them through. If it is unfavorable, they will not. Couples with limited resources may not have serious trouble, however—provided that they do not have to contend with unusual difficulties. And the well-endowed couple may still fail if they are pushed into extraordinary challenges. It is the *balance* of resources and demands that counts. If the divorce rate starts to rise in a society, we have to assume that something has upset the previous balance between resources and demands.*

The couple's "resources" refer to any personal qualities they may have or any social or material facilities that can help them cope with their problems. The personality of the wife, for example, or contraceptive information shared by the couple, or readily accessible counseling help, or financial assistance from parents may come in handy. "Demands," on the other hand, refer to anything that taxes the couple's ability to make their life together a happy one. These could include the husband's special weakness for alcohol, the wife's dependence on her mother, community pressures pulling the couple apart, or a job that eats away at the husband's self-respect.

Obviously, both resources and demands can take an almost infinite variety of forms. It may not even be possible to classify them all, let alone name them. And a resource for one couple may prove to be a demand for another. Wealth, for example, would seem to be a plus factor for most families, but it can be a serious problem for others. The theory is not as specific as we would like, yet it remains the essential basis for all explanations of divorce. In the case of Charles Ackerman's model, for example, conjunctive affiliations are resources for the couple while disjunctive affiliations are demands. But even the couple surrounded by mutual friends may be overwhelmed by demands of one sort or another and fail to make their marriage work. And neither will the husband and wife with separate friends necessarily break up.

No divorce theory can pinpoint with precision the balance of pluses and minuses for all couples. But looking at the resources-demands approach in broad perspective, we can ask: What are the trends? How is the balance shifting? Below are listed eight trends usually linked to industrial growth:

1. More education for more people
2. Greater wealth per capita
3. Greater personal and social diversity
4. Fewer traditional controls over people (such as kinship and religious restraints)
5. Better health care and longer life expectancy
6. Higher rates of geographical mobility
7. Fewer restrictions on women and generally higher status for them compared to men

* George Levinger (1965) stated an approach to marriage rather similar to this, based on two forces: (1) attractions or repulsions in the relationship and (2) barriers to its breakup. These are the driving and restraining pressures in any social group. Marriage cohesion is just a special case of the more general condition, group cohesion.

8. Better knowledge of psychology, sociology, and the dynamics of inter-personal relations (This point is not always included among industrial trends. Still, it is part of the general change occurring, and it is important for the present discussion.)

Recognizing that no complete consensus exists, it is still possible to ask whether, in general, each of these trends has the effect of helping couples meet their marriage problems or of putting new demands on them.

New Resources. At least three of them are clearly desirable: more education, better health, and greater wealth. Nobody can deny that education usually comes in handy in marriage, and research linking marriage adjustment to educational achievement bears this out. The same is generally true for wealth. In the nineteenth century most people were convinced that universal education and prosperity would solve all problems, in and out of marriage. They were far too hopeful, but we still push for more of the same—the alternative is certainly not the answer.

The relation between health and marriage may be somewhat more questionable, especially since we have no proof that it has anything to do with marriage success or failure. It does seem, however, that a healthy couple has an advantage; poor health can hardly help. (This would obviously be true for mental health as well, but whether people are mentally healthier today than they were in the past is anybody's guess. We can only be sure of an improvement in physical health.)

New Demands. While three of the factors add to the resources of couples, three of them also pose new problems: social diversity, the decline of traditional controls, and increased geographic mobility. Almost all available evidence suggests that heterogeneity in the city leads to higher rates of heterogamy in mate selection, and that pushes the rate of marriage failure up. The collapse of traditional controls gives individuals more freedom, as Engels and Durkheim noted, but this includes more ways to escape from an unhappy marriage. It also makes escape more morally defensible than it used to be. Mobility can be a resource for the couple, especially since it gives them a way to find better job opportunities elsewhere. But at the same time it gives them many more chances to find new and different marriage partners. People who are immobile are more likely to resign themselves to their marriage, happy or not.

The Imponderables. This leaves two of the eight trends unaccounted for: the rising status of women and increased knowledge about interpersonal relations. Their impact is debatable. Although the fact that modern women have greater freedom and relatively higher status *may* make them more companionable in marriage, this is also one of the key factors in our higher divorce rate. The rise in divorce in the United States has been correlated historically with the rising status of women (although this has not been the case everywhere—not in Japan, for example). Engels felt that freedom for women would lead to closer relations between the sexes. And it probably has, all things considered, but it also means that dissatisfied wives no longer have to resign themselves to their fate. If freedom is escape from fate, than that is what the sex revolution is all about. This is one of the truly new pressures on the urban family, and it is essentially a pressure on husbands. Breadwinning is not enough; the man is expected to be a companion, too, and sometimes a helpmate. The feminine connotation of "helpmate" is being stripped away, so it is no longer the wife's obligation alone (although many men have not yet made the transition).

What can we say about modern psychology and sociology—the new knowledge of interpersonal relations? Does the fact that people now know more make them better husbands and wives—or worse? One would think better, at least at first. Ideally, when people learn about the dynamics of human relations they become better cooperators, and they have greater control of themselves—but not always. In fact, the spread of revolutionary ideas throughout the world has accompanied greater knowledge about social relations—is there some relationship between the two? And certainly the spread of modern psychology has led to greater sensitivity to neurotic behavior. Modern parents are awed by the dangerous possibilities lurking in almost anything they may do to their children, whether disciplinary or permissive. Certainly Freudian psychology has the general effect of crushing parental self-confidence.

What, then, can be said about the spreading impact of psychological and sociological knowledge on married life? It can be interpreted either way—as a resource or as a demand. The modern husband, for example, may have greater insight into himself and his motives and perhaps be a little easier to live with as a result. But, he may also have greater insight into his wife's behavior. He may even remind her occasionally of the possible hidden meanings of her actions, and she may not be grateful for his diagnosis. When couples start analyzing one another with the concepts of modern psychology, they sometimes unleash forces beyond their control. Perhaps it would be best to regard the popularization of social psychology as a questionable factor insofar as divorce is concerned. It may help in some cases; in others it may only make it easier to find your spouse's most secret, sensitive nerve.

Let us summarize:
    New resources associated with industrial growth are:
        educational advancement,

    health improvement, and
    general affluence.
New demands associated with industrial growth are:
    heterogeneity in the cities, the
    decline of traditional controls, and
    mobility.
Question marks are: the
    rising status of women, and
    popularization of psychology and sociology.

One final observation is in order. A new factor—standing between resources and demands—has arisen in the past century: the greater accessibility of divorce. Although we might consider this as merely one aspect of the decline of tradition, it can be considered as an independent factor, since limited access to divorce is not always traditional in the cultures of the world. If it is given an independent place, then the resources-demands theory becomes the resources-accessibility-demands theory.

Although the balance between resources and demands is certainly important, the availability of divorce becomes a critical factor, too. If the laws and mores in this regard are strict, then no matter how hopeless a couple's marriage may be, they are stuck with it. Only as divorce becomes a fairly accessible alternative can it serve as an index of the changing nature of marriage problems. This seems to be what is happening.

RATES OF REMARRIAGE

After divorce most Americans try again. The remarriage rate is extremely high, and yet in the 1920s, 1930s, and early 1940s it was commonly believed that most divorced people were through with marriage forever (Monahan 1958b). Dissenting opinions were strictly in the minority. Now our error has been exposed, and the figures are impressive indeed. In 1948 a nationwide sample of twenty-five thousand households conducted by the Bureau of the Census revealed that about three-fourths of the people divorced in the preceding five years had remarried (Glick 1949). Approximately two-thirds of the women and three-fourths of the men eventually make a second effort (Glick 1957). Samuel Johnson called this the triumph of hope over experience, but never was hope so well documented. At the present time about one marriage in three involves remarriage for at least one of the partners, and in more than one out of eight cases both partners are entering marriage a second time. We now know that high remarriage rates are found in virtually all nations having high divorce rates (Goode 1956).

In 1950 Paul Landis called attention to the fact that a larger number of people in America run through two or more marriages than in some so-cieties classified as polygamous. He called the American system *sequential marriage*. The term *serial polygamy* has also been used in recent years. As might be expected, the younger people are when they divorce, the more likely they are to marry again. At the same time, the older they are at the time of the wedding, the greater the chances are that it will be a remar-riage. Only about half of the brides between the ages of thirty and thirty-four marry for the first time, and less than one-fifth of those between forty-five and forty-nine are first-timers (Schlesinger 1968).

Whereas widowhood once accounted for nearly all remarriages, most re-marriages now follow divorce, since the divorce rate has greatly increased. The overwhelming majority of persons who remarry in the United States have been divorced, and they are more likely to marry fellow divorced people than widows, widowers, or never-before-marrieds (Monahan 1958b). A divorcee of any given age is more likely to remarry than a widow of the same age, and she is much more likely to marry than a single woman of that age.

Not only is the remarriage rate high for divorced people, they seem to remarry in a certain haste. According to one study, the medium number of years elapsed prior to remarriage for the divorced population was 2.7; for the widowed it was 3.5 (Glick 1957). One-third of the divorced women remarry within a year, half within two years, and two-thirds within five (Jacobson 1959). Apparently women marry sooner after divorce than men (on the average), although a smaller percentage of them ever remarry.

William Goode (1956), however, found that when men take the first step toward divorce, they are likely to get back into married life sooner than women who are initiators of divorce. It is at least possible that the man who makes the first move has a replacement for his wife already in mind. The woman who makes the first move is somewhat more likely to seek divorce simply because she finds her husband intolerable. This is not inconsistent with a point made in Chapter 10—that women have his-torically had greater adjustment tasks in marriage. This traditional role has been relaxed, especially because divorce is now more accessible. Women have more personal security and greater immunity from criticism when they divorce their husbands. But they still have fewer chances than men to find new partners. We should expect this to become less true as women work more often in jobs that bring them near eligible men. August Hol-lingshead (1952), for example, found that people marrying for a second time were much more likely to meet their partners on the job than those entering a first marriage.

However, there is no strong moral code in America insisting that people remarry. William Goode (1966) argues that remarriage rates are high mainly because it is difficult to live alone, especially for people who have already tried marriage. Even a bad experience does not kill marriage's generally favorable image—at least for most people. This being so, the remarriage rate may be a sensitive index of the relative attractions of familism on the one hand and individualism on the other. For example, we might expect the appeal of single life to be somewhat greater if there are no children to care for (from the broken marriage). And yet divorced men, who only rarely take custody of the children, actually have higher remarriage rates than divorced women.

This does not mean that divorced women who have children are necessarily handicapped in finding a second husband. They have virtually no disadvantage vis-à-vis other women of the same age and social status. This suggests that lack of opportunity is what keeps women's remarriage rates down, not any strong desire to remain single. Some writers, however, say that men actually *need* marriage more than women, especially by comparison with women who are financially self-sufficient (Bernard 1956; Edwards 1967).

Age patterns certainly do not favor remarriage for women. In 1959 the median ages at the time of marriage for Americans were:

Single men	22.8
Single women	20.3
Men marrying for the second time	38.3
Women marrying for the second time	34.0
Men marrying for the third time	46.9
Women marrying for the third time	41.4

These figures show that differences in ages for men and women become greater in second and third marriages (Schlesinger 1968). Stated another way, as the age of men at the time of marriage goes up, their brides become increasingly younger than themselves. Apparently the male holds onto an image of the youthful bride as he grows older. He may not be able to marry a girl in her early twenties—perhaps he would not even want to— but he does seem to prefer a woman considerably younger than himself. Obviously this decreases the chances for remarriage for women as they grow older. The pattern takes on added weight when we recall that male death rates are higher than women's, creating a shortage of men in middle age and beyond.

But there is still another factor to consider. The rate of remarriage is higher for the poorly educated than for high-school and college graduates (Glick and Carter 1958). It seems that the more education people have, the less they rely on marriage. This is consistent with almost everything that has been said so far about women, but not about men. The more educated women are, the less likely they are to marry a first, second, or third time. Though statistics are not available, it is possible that the more educated men are actually more likely to remarry, which is known to be the case for men in first marriages. Certainly they are highly marriageable, and they have a wide range of women to choose from—their own age as well as some considerably younger and women of their own status as well as attractive women from the lower classes. The well-educated, higher status woman has a smaller circle of eligibles to pick from.

Thus, the relationship between family attitudes and remarriage rates becomes rather complex, with much still to be learned. And it is even further complicated by religious practices. According to Gerhard Lenski's (1961) Detroit data, for example, Catholics have much lower remarriage rates after divorce than Protestants, and yet his data also suggest that Catholics usually have stronger commitments to familism. As Lenski points out, if Catholics find any rewards at all in family life, they are under greater pressure than Protestants to make their first marriages work. This is especially true for those who are better educated and highly committed to the faith.

ADJUSTMENT TO REMARRIAGE

A point of continuing interest is the success rate for remarriage. The most common measure is in fact an index of failure: the rate of divorce in first marriages compared to the rate in second or later ventures. William Goode (1956) once argued that second marriages are usually happier than first ones and that failure in second marriages occurs less often than in first ones. Evidence gathered since his observation casts doubt on this viewpoint, however. Even before Goode stated his case, Thomas Monahan (1952) had collected data showing that divorced people are, on the average, substantially poorer marital risks than singles, widows, or widowers. Later (1958b) he studied the divorce rate in Iowa (where extensive data were available) and concluded that the rate for couples where both husband and wife had been divorced was about twice as high as for couples where neither had been divorced. If both spouses had been divorced two or more times, the rate shot up to more than four times the level for first-time couples. Not only do remarriages have higher divorce rates, they do not last as long as first marriages before the lawyers are called in (Monahan 1959).

By contrast, widows who remarry have very low divorce rates. But Monahan points out that widows tend to remarry at relatively older ages, so their low rates are due in part to the shorter time they have together before one or the other dies. Of course personality and social factors are no doubt also involved.

But what if some measure other than lack of divorce is used as a criterion for success in remarriage? Then a whole new set of conclusions may be called for. William Goode (1956), for example, has suggested that the happiness scores of remarried women are no lower than those in first marriages. Furthermore, he claimed that nine out of ten divorced women in his sample—almost all of them—had a happier second marriage than their first. If accurate, this is a surprising statistic, since there are many reasons why women in second marriages could be expected to have particularly difficult problems. Jessie Bernard (1956) once argued that about one-third of the people in the divorced population are neurotic to begin with, that is, they suffer *role disturbance* and are not adept in handling emotional problems. Although critics have attacked Professor Bernard for this accusation, she did not state her case glibly; it is explained with great care and caution. The special problems of adjusting to stepparenthood may have to be faced, too, not to mention alimony payments (which can be problematical to both the divorced husband and his ex-wife—to the husband because of the financial burden and to the divorced woman because payments tend to dwindle over time).

It is likely that at least some remarriages are entered into without ordinary prudence. There may be a greater urgency to marry among divorced persons than for those who are younger and have never married. The *expediency factor* (discussed in Chapter 7) can exert a powerful pressure. As yet, however, no careful study comparing the compulsive need to be married among divorced and never-married people has been made. Sex differences may occur in this regard due to the relatively greater pressures to marry for single women. All of us probably know an eighteen-, nineteen-, or twenty-year-old girl, never before married, whose eagerness for marriage is stronger than any suicidal death wish we have any personal knowledge about.

Goode says it may be misleading, however, if not unfair, even to attempt to compare remarriages with first marriages. Marital adjustment not only follows a different pattern in the two categories, it may not even mean the same thing. Sex, for example, poses a unique set of problems in remarriage. Furthermore, if remarriages are compared only with the first marriages of people who eventually divorce, then they cannot help but appear more successful. *All* of the first marriages are failures by the divorce criterion; certainly not *all* remarriages are failures by that standard. As a matter of fact, most of them are not. If we judge remarriage solely from this point of view, recognizing that virtually all the people in the remarried population have had more than their share of domestic trouble, then remarriage offers a merciful second chance. And in this sense it is, more often than not, a successful venture.

Maybe most second marriages are entered into with just this comparison in mind. They mark a special determination to succeed, and they offer the chastening experience of a bad marriage to reflect on. Under these circumstances we might expect people to grasp a little more clearly the *relative* nature of personal happiness. Almost any marriage can be more satisfying than a dismal failure, even if the later one also fails.

SUMMARY

Divorce and remarriage go together in the great majority of cases in the United States, as they do in virtually all societies where divorce rates are high. Together the two represent formal, well-established means to dissolve marriage, to clarify family commitments, and to set up new living arrangements.

The divorce rate has climbed in the United States for almost a century, the most volatile period occurring in connection with the social upheavals of World War II. Since that time the general drift seems to have returned to its long-term upward climb.

Legal codes for divorce change much more slowly than the social realities of marriage breakup, since divorce is not solely a legal matter. The social and psychological implications go much deeper than laws can take into account. Divorce seekers consult lawyers who adapt the facts of each case to the divorce codes of the state, then proceed to file the appropriate papers. Professional marriage counseling has no essential place in this process, neither in the court proceedings nor in the crucial preliminary maneuvers. It seems likely, however, that it will slowly assume a larger role as the years go by.

Theories attempting to explain the divorce rate stress kinship factors and industrial growth. Of the two, the latter gets the most support. It stresses the progressive emancipation of people (women in particular) from marriage and family obligations in the modern city. Many couples are stripped of the strong, conjunctive relations that forged powerful family bonds in the past. Without these, divorce is no remote possibility. In the last analysis, however, any theory of divorce must try to explain the balance between the *resources* that couples bring to marriage and the *demands* that their marriages face. (But if there are immovable obstacles to divorce —as in Spain, for example, largely due to the strict position of the Catholic Church—then couples have to deal with domestic problems in other ways.)

The relation between divorce and remarriage rates was only recently discovered. Changing widowhood rates have undoubtedly clouded the picture. As the rate of widowhood has dropped in the past century (due to falling death rates in the middle years), the divorce rate has gone up. And it is in this context that the divorce-remarriage pattern shows up. Although rates for widowhood are inevitably linked to remarriage to some extent, this link is not as pronounced as the one with divorce.

Success rates for remarriage are not as good as for first efforts. Still, the phenomenal appeal of second efforts speaks well for the institution of marriage, and it highlights the problems of living alone. In fact, for all its potential trouble, remarriage offers people stricken by marriage trauma a heartening chance to try again. Many second attempts are enviably successful.

SELECTED READINGS

ACKERMAN, CHARLES. "Affiliations: Structural Determinants of Differential Divorce Rates," *American Journal of Sociology*, Vol. 69 (July 1963), pp. 13–20.

BERNARD, JESSIE. *Remarriage: A Study of Marriage*, New York: Dryden, 1956.

GLUCKMAN, MAX. "Kinship and Marriage Among the Lozi of Northern Rhodesia and the Zulu of Natal," in A. R. Radcliffe-Brown and Daryll Forde (eds.), *African Systems of Kinship and Marriage*. London: Oxford University Press, 1950, pp. 166–206.

GOODE, WILLIAM J. *After Divorce*. New York: The Free Press, 1956.

GOODE, WILLIAM J. *World Revolution and Family Patterns*. New York: The Free Press, 1963.

LESLIE, GERALD R. "The Field of Marriage Counseling," in Harold T. Christensen (ed.), *Handbook of Marriage and the Family*. Chicago: Rand McNally, 1964, pp. 912–943.

LEVINGER, GEORGE. "Marital Cohesiveness and Dissolution: An Integrative Review," *Journal of Marriage and the Family*, Vol. 27 (February 1965), pp. 19–28.

MONAHAN, THOMAS P. "The Changing Nature and Instability of Remarriages," *Eugenics Quarterly*, Vol. 5 (June 1958), pp. 73–85.

MURDOCK, GEORGE PETER. "Family Stability in Non-European Societies," *Annals of the American Academy of Political and Social Science*, Vol. 272 (November 1950), pp. 195–201.

SCHLESINGER, BENJAMIN. "Remarriage—An Inventory of Findings," *The Family Coordinator*, Vol. 17 (October 1968), pp. 248–250.

PART FIVE

Past, Present, and Future

CHAPTER 15

Historical Roots, Evolutionary Pressures

Everyone seems to agree that family life in the United States is unique. This is a rich and powerful nation, and it has been enormously successful in mass production. In technical matters, Americans excel. Beyond that, we are in a position to take advantage of almost every progressive development achieved in the entire history of mankind. Because of this, American homes have many material comforts.

The American family has also been influenced by special historical forces beginning in the Middle East over three thousand years ago. Many of our family ideals can be traced all the way back to the Hebrews of the Old Testament, subject to change and elaboration by the ancient Greeks and Romans, the medieval Europeans, the Europeans of the Renaissance and Protestant uprisings, the political revolutions of the seventeenth and eighteenth centuries, and the migration of people from the Old World to the New. In fact, the family customs of the ancient Hebrews can be linked to still earlier customs associated with the rise of agriculture and written language in the Middle East.

By contrast, the American family has been influenced very little by the history of Asia, Africa, South America, Oceania, Polynesia, Melanesia, or Micronesia. A history of the American family is therefore by no means a history of family life in general.

The effect of history on our present culture may not be obvious. But if you wonder why you are expected to do certain things that may—in the cold light of reason—seem rather silly, history often holds the answer.

Family customs accumulate slowly, and they change just as slowly. You may wish you could feel free and easy about premarital sex, for example, but perhaps you still have doubts and guilt feelings. That is not so difficult to explain, however, especially in the case of a middle-class American girl reared in even a moderately devout Catholic, Protestant, or Jewish home in the twentieth century. The guilt is a product of centuries of sexual conditioning. It will take more than a rash of free swinging novels, movies, and plays to wipe out this influence.

But people are always fighting their cultural heritage, and nowhere is this more obvious than in family matters. Whether you want to fight it or uphold it, knowing what it is helps.

HISTORICAL PERSPECTIVE

Five influences from the past have had a special impact on the American family:

1. The ancient Hebrew family pattern has retained an important place in our thinking because of its familiarity in the Old Testament.
2. Family ideals expressed by the early Christians have maintained a position of influence.
3. In the medieval period the Catholic Church slowly climbed to its position of moral leadership in family matters.
4. The Protestant Reformation unleashed several alternatives to the Catholic position.
5. Urban, industrial society now molds family trends, but it is always subject to traditions and moral standards inherited from the past.

The Hebrew Family Pattern

Most Americans are familiar with the ancient Hebrew family because they were schooled in the lore of the Old Testament as children. Even those who never attended Sunday school are exposed to bits and pieces of the story of the ancient Hebrews, partly because teachers often refer to the Bible and also because many biblical references are made in the mass media.

It is not surprising, then, that certain early Hebrew practices are still regarded as ideal. The pioneers who moved westward on the American frontier often tried to live up to biblical codes of conduct, which had been developed three or four thousand years earlier under entirely different conditions. And yet these codes were not completely irrelevant to American frontier circumstances. They probably helped settlers to survive under extremely difficult conditions.

The Hebrew family system was held together by several key rules. Most of them were probably not invented by the Hebrews—they were common throughout the Middle East (Patai 1959) and are attributed to the Hebrews simply because we are familiar with their sacred literature. The stories, myths, and legends of other groups in the Middle East are unknown or ignored (in the West)—unless they happen to have been recorded in the Old Testament.

The Hebrew family was an extended family which put great emphasis on the large circle of kinsmen. By contrast, relatively little stress was given to the nuclear family (Cross 1927). Many references to nuclear families can be found in the Bible, and in places there is more concern for relationships between husband and wife than can be found in the classical Greek literature (Gouldner 1966). But clearly the individual person reckoned his social position by the place assigned to him in the larger, extended family.

One's position was traced through the father's side of the family, a practice that has been retained throughout the entire history of Western man. It is still nominally followed. (Anthropologists refer to the modern American family as a bilateral system, tracing lineage through both the mother's and the father's side of the family, although only names of the paternal line are usually retained.) Not only was the paternal lineage system followed, but authority within the family was highly patriarchal (Mace 1953). Paternal power is dramatically expressed in the biblical account of the contemplated sacrifice of Isaac by his father Abraham. Hebrew customs gave power to the older males, a pattern that has also dominated the Western tradition. Although this system has been greatly weakened within the family itself, it has been maintained without serious interruption in the world of politics, economics, and religion.

The Hebrew father was granted the right to choose his son's wife, and it was not uncommon for the wife to become a part of the household of the groom's family, a *patrilocal* residential arrangement. Wives were expected to be dutiful to their husbands, and unmarried women were obligated to their fathers or older brothers (Goodsell 1934). The groom also had greater rights in the area of divorce than his wife, although divorce was apparently rare. In the earliest stages of Hebrew history (the Hebrews passed through several stages during the time covered in the Old Testament), the father served a distinctly religious function by virtue of his position as head of the household.

One aspect of the patriarchal pattern that tends to be forgotten is the fact that, according to Mosaic law, the male could have more than one wife—hence it was a polygynous system. (Solomon apparently had seven hundred wives and three hundred concubines.) In this respect the Hebrews were not the least bit unusual among their contemporaries in the Middle East. Of greater interest than polygyny itself is the fact that it died out

early among people whose culture was based largely on the Hebrew beginnings. This was not true (until quite recent times) of most other
groups that can be traced back to the Middle East. The Greeks in particular influenced the Western tradition toward monogamy.

The practice of using *concubines* was also common among the Hebrews,
especially as a means of conceiving children for the man whose wife happened to be barren. The principal role of the concubine was to bear children; this function should not be confused with that of mistress or sex
companion. But concubines had much lower status than wives; they were
usually taken from among slaves and women captured in war. This practice
died out rather quickly in the Western world.

The patriarchal pattern was perhaps merely a reflection of the deeper
and more pervasive double sex standard that the ancient Hebrews shared
with all other groups in the Middle East. Males were judged by entirely
different moral standards from those for women. This double standard is
usually given a rather narrow sexual-erotic significance, by which males
are allowed greater freedom in sex play, but it actually extends to a broad
range of activities.

In fact, a better term to describe it is *triple sex standard,* since the pattern includes one set of moral principles for men, one for "good" women
(who prove they are good by being virgins until marriage and, in general,
by remaining naïve about sex and worldly matters), and a third set of codes
for "bad" women (who serve men in various ways, mainly sexual, and receive certain rewards; the price they must pay is loss of respectability). The
triple standard has been passed on from generation to generation; only in
modern times have trends appeared that foretell a genuinely revolutionary
change. Conceivably, the age-old pattern could be wiped out by the end
of this century in advanced parts of the world, but more will be said about
that later.

Patriarchal practices did not consist solely of special rights and privileges
for men. Males who were thoroughly trained in the traditional pattern
held themselves accountable in various ways; they took their obligations
seriously. A patriarchal system that works well is one that contributes to
the stability of the entire society, not just to the welfare of older men. One
of the reasons why dating has now become so common, along with the idea
that love and romance should perk up marriage, is to help compensate
modern men for the loss of power they once held in the family (see Chapters 4 and 6). If men are needed to make the human family system work,
but they are not as dependable as mothers, something must make them
want to meet their obligations. The authority they wield in patriarchal
societies is undoubtedly one powerful reason why men of even moderate
social status can be relied upon to perform family duties. In modern
societies middle-class men are bound to their families not so much by the

power they wield as by the affection and companionship they receive. For the ancient Hebrews, the situation was quite different.

Related to the patrilocal living arrangement was the *levirate*, which persisted to some extent in Jewish communities well into the Middle Ages. This was a practice whereby, in case of the death of a childless husband, one of his unmarried brothers was expected to marry the widow. The reason for this was to provide an heir for the deceased, since the Hebrews considered a man very unfortunate if he died without children. Although others in the family felt that an unmarried brother should marry the widow, he was not forced to, and some brothers for various reasons did not. If the brother was strongly committed to the traditions of the group, however, he would accept his duty. Upon taking the role of *levir*, he gained possession of his brother's land and wealth and took responsibility for managing them.

This makes sense in a patrilocal society where the bride lives among her husband's people. When the husband dies childless, his family is more or less obligated to supply a husband in his place. Although the circumstances are different in many ways, the psychosocial forces that once contributed to the levirate explain why it seemed so right in the 1960s for the remaining brothers of a slain American President to offer profound solace to his widow; when one of these brothers was also slain, it seemed altogether appropriate for the last and youngest brother to stand as the representative of the family as guardian of the widows.

In the Old Testament repeated references are made to adultery, which the Hebrews thoroughly condemned; the taboo against it stands as one of the Ten Commandments. Generally, they regarded sex as strictly a family affair. Adultery was condemned in part because it represented a form of sex relations that not only occurred outside the family but also constituted a threat to its very existence. The student may note a slight flaw in this logic, however, since adultery is a threat to the family system at least in part because it is a basis for divorce. Whenever it occurs and the offended spouse knows it, especially in the case of a husband, he is *supposed* to be humiliated and to contemplate divorce. The very attitudes that are taught about adultery make it a threat to the family system; if it were defined less harshly it would not be such a threat. But it remains true that adultery can lead to a new relationship of genuine affection, and thus cause divorce or desertion.

But there was still another reason for the attitude toward adultery: the need among Hebrews and others throughout the Middle East to establish with absolute certainty the paternity of their offspring. Men wanted to be fathers, and they wanted to be sure that their children were actually their own. Quite obviously adultery calls into question the paternity of the child.

Fornication, or sex relations between unmarried couples, was also regarded as a thoroughly reprehensible practice in the Old Testament, but it received far less attention than adultery. Since marriage usually occurred at an early age, premarital sex does not seem to have been a terribly serious problem. The main reason for opposition to it was that it constituted a threat to the family. It represented a deviation from the moral code which held that sex was appropriate for reproduction only and was proper only in marriage (or as an adjunct to marriage, as in cases where concubines were used to bear children for married men of high status).

Still another sex practice specifically condemned in the Old Testament was homosexuality; it is forbidden in Leviticus and punishable by death. The hostility toward it today may be traced at least as far back as biblical times. But homosexuality is considered a threat to the family and condemned in virtually *all* cultures in the world. The biblical strictures against it may contribute to our furious reactions, but they would probably be much the same if we had never heard of the Old Testament.

One other taboo held by the Israelites which influenced later generations was the taboo against incest, which is mentioned in several places in the Old Testament. In Leviticus the male is forbidden to marry his mother or stepmother, his sister, his half-sister, his paternal or maternal aunt, or his daughter-in-law. Comparable restrictions are listed for the female, but cousin marriage is not prohibited and seems to have been preferred. Once again, this was a social pattern shared with almost all groups in the Middle East, but biblical references to it have probably helped to dramatize its reprehensibility for succeeding generations of Jews and Christians.

By way of summary, the legacy of the ancient Hebrews has been transmitted to us through the Old Testament. It became sacred literature with the rise to power of the Christian Church and has had further impact because of the continuing influence of the Jewish community in Western history. Though a minority group, the Jews have always wielded more influence than their numbers alone could explain. Their legacy includes a positive regard for the extended kinship system, with strong patriarchal controls in the hands of fathers and older men; a double sex standard (strictly speaking, a triple standard) by which men are given greater freedom in sex exploration and other areas than women; a patrilocal household arrangement in which the wife lives with her husband's people (extended in our own day to the idea that the wife should go wherever her husband goes to further his career); and strong hostility toward adultery, fornication, and homosexuality. Thus, in spite of the fact that the modern American family is much different from that of the ancient Hebrews and must adapt to an altogether different social environment, it still takes moral and ethical cues from the earlier family system.

But not all that was acceptable to the Hebrews in the Old Testament is acceptable today; their tolerance of polygyny is a case in point. Very early in Western history, especially through the influence of the Greeks, it was weeded out in favor of monogamy, and hence the Hebrew practice in this regard has been almost totally ignored.

We should also remember that the Old Testament has become much less popular in modern society than it was in our earlier history. Even in the nineteenth century it was not uncommon for each family to possess a giant Bible (passed from one generation to the next) whose text was carefully explained and simplified in the margins. The Bible often served as the only reading material available to the family. Not only did it have little competition from other books and magazines, it was considered sacred and holy. All literature becomes less sacred as the total volume of written material increases and as people become more sophisticated in using it.

The Early Christian Influence

We will not attempt to trace in detail the rise of Christianity from its humble beginnings to the peak of religious power—that would take us far afield. Suffice it to say that Christianity took hold slowly, first as a tiny group of dedicated people (considered either curious cranks or dangerous fanatics by outsiders), gradually becoming a respectable group of much greater numbers and perhaps less total dedication to their original principles. By A.D. 312 the Church was recognized and sanctioned throughout the Roman Empire.

The Christians only gradually gained social and religious power, but their spokesmen had much to say about marriage and the family along the way. This is the one area in which the Church has remained most powerful even in modern society, but it is also the one in which it has had its greatest troubles. The fiercest controversies in the twentieth century, for example, have been in response to Church and papal actions in the area of divorce, celibacy, and birth control.

Two aspects of the Church's rise to power are especially relevant to our study of marriage and the family. One concerns the attitudes toward family life stated by the founding fathers; the other concerns a string of developments by which the Church set as its proper function the establishment of rituals, philosophical premises, and precise codes of conduct for marriage and family affairs.

Jesus never married, and he had little to say about the family as reported in the New Testament, although some of his remarks have been interpreted as authoritative on the subject of adultery, sex, and marriage. Paul was much more explicit. His statements are customarily believed to favor celibacy (the avoidance of marriage) for those who truly seek to serve Jesus and the Christian cause. In 1 Corinthians Paul says: "But I say to the unmarried and to widows, it is good for them if they abide even as I. But if they have not continency, let them marry; for it is better to marry than to burn" (1 Cor. 7:8, 9). Paul linked virginity with purity and godliness and spoke often of the need for Christians to be self-denying. Such denial clearly included restraint in sex relations as well as other "pleasures of the flesh." Although Jesus seemed to have a tolerant, even democratic, attitude toward women, Paul apparently preferred to keep them in their traditional place—the place they had occupied throughout the Middle East (and which they continued to have in Greece and Rome). He charged that women should accept subjugation to their husbands (Ephesians, 5:22, 23). Peter said that husbands should in turn give honor to their wives "as unto the weaker vessel" (1 Peter, 3:7). Tertullian went further, referring to women as the "devil's gateway." Of course Eve had played the role of temptress in the Old Testament story, urging Adam to eat the forbidden fruit.

Opposition to divorce is apparent in various statements of the founding fathers, as is opposition to abortion and infanticide. There is some evidence that the abandonment of infants and small children had become a fairly common practice by the time Christianity appeared, and the Church very early set up foundling institutions for homeless children. It has been argued that this helped to establish an extremely warm image of mother care, which the Church has never lost (Bossard and Boll 1966).

Actually, the attitude of the early Church fathers toward marriage and family life is open to stubborn differences of opinion among scholars. The record of what was said is awkwardly phrased and limited in scope; the interpretation of this scant evidence can only be considered debatable. That the early Christian leaders had attitudes concerning the family cannot be denied, and that the Church has consistently claimed a religious and moral obligation to make pronouncements in this area is also absolutely clear. John Randall, Jr. (1968–1969), argues that conventional Christian ethics have concentrated on erotic conduct ever since Augustine, who he claims transformed the notion of sin from something primarily social in nature to a quality that is essentially sexual.

Slowly the views of Church leaders on family matters took on the sanctity of revealed truth. Their views were codified and institutionalized in the rituals and offices of the Church itself (Howard 1904). One reason why the Church became so strong was that its powers were acquired gradually over many generations. For example, even after the early growth of Christianity, marriage remained for centuries an essentially secular affair in which the priest had virtually no role except to deliver a benediction after the bride was given to the groom. The payment of an appropriate bride price was a much more significant part of the proceedings. Beginning in about the fourth century A.D., it became increasingly common to stage a bride mass after the marriage, thereby giving the Church a stronger position at this important occasion. It was several centuries before another Church ritual became common, that of conducting the marriage at the door of the church—not inside, but at the church nonetheless, with the priest performing an important role in the ceremony. His role gradually grew in importance, until he replaced the person who acted as the bride's guardian and assumed the right to give the bride away.

By the thirteenth century the priest's role in the marriage ceremony had become essential. Without him the wedding was not legal in the eyes of the Church. (The Church kept a distinction between *legal* and *valid* marriages which we need not pursue here.) By the fifteenth century marriage had become one of the key sacraments, regarded in religious theology as a major crisis in life over which the Church is divinely ordained to preside. The sacramental theory of marriage was approved by the Council of Florence in 1439.

Somewhat later celibacy was established in no uncertain terms for members of the priesthood, and rigid rules against divorce were proclaimed. Both priestly celibacy and the *indissolubility of marriage* have remained cardinal features in the Church's philosophy of wedlock, although they are also sources of unending irritation for many laymen and some members of the clergy as well. (The number of priests who have left the priesthood in order to marry has been unusually high in recent years.) The rule of *religious endogamy* (marriage to a person of one's own faith) had also been firmly established by the seventeenth century, and all the marital possibilities (including marriage between two Catholics, a Catholic and a Protestant, a Catholic and a non-Christian, and marriage between Catholics outside the Church) had been thoroughly explored. The position of the Church with regard to each was stated in detail. Even opposition to birth control had begun to take shape, to be formalized by Pope Pius XI much later (not until 1930).

This brief survey of the rise of the Church should make it clear that its position was not won easily. It came as the result of painstaking efforts to define precisely what the Church's role ought to be in response to heated differences of opinion and continuing struggles for religious power. The full impact of the Church upon our marriage and family ideals is beyond calculation.

The Protestant Reformation

Reactions to the power of the Church were becoming intense in some quarters even as it approached the full extent of its authority. Although dissenters had no shortage of issues to debate, most of them dealt either directly or indirectly with Church doctrines concerning the family. Martin Luther, John Calvin, John Knox, and Ulrich Zwingli all raised objections.

Luther, for example, had many reservations about the Church's role in marriage and was inclined to favor relatively greater power for non-Church authorities. He attacked celibacy and argued for a more lenient attitude toward divorce. He was not particularly original, however; most of his complaints had been voiced in dissident religious circles for decades.

The long-run effect of the Reformation is what is most important. Protestant groups did manage to break away, to persevere, and to establish themselves. They set up new groups from schisms within their own ranks in ever-increasing numbers, a process that continues in the twentieth century. In one sense, Protestants simply introduced uncertainty into the entire question of Christian attitudes toward sex, marriage, and family life. Whereas the Catholic Church was attempting to move in the direction of greater uniformity and centralized control for the great mass of Christians, Protestant groups created a variety of new centers of religious power.

Another way to view the Protestant impact, however, is to say that it ushered in an era of greater variety and pluralism. Protestantism not only enabled Christianity to become more flexible in a critical period of social change, it may have enabled it to survive. Its influence spread Christianity to a much broader segment of the world's population than might otherwise have been possible. According to one popular theory, for example, it was no accident that Protestantism appeared at the very time that the spirit of industrial capitalism was showing signs of life (Weber 1930; Tawney 1938). Among other things, the Reformation supported capitalism by stressing aspects of the Christian heritage that the Catholic Church tended to play down. If William Goode, whose theory will be discussed later in this chapter, is correct, the very structure of the family system in Western Europe, particularly that associated with Protestantism, fostered a comparatively rapid development in the capitalistic, industrial sector of the economy. That is not to say that the Catholic family system was wholly unsuited to industrialism; it has adapted quite well. But Protestants stressed greater flexibility in family life and freed individuals (to some extent) not only from priestly controls but from the supremacy of the family itself.

The long-term influence of Protestantism has probably been felt less in the area of economic development than with regard to family values as such. Thus today, as never before in Western history, the person who happens to live in one of the major cities in the United States should have no trouble finding a Christian denomination or sect that will look tolerantly upon almost any idea of marriage he is likely to have. In part, these various churches mold people's thinking about family life, but they also stand ready to accept members whose beliefs are already formed. Almost anyone can conceive of himself as a Christian and find a church somewhere that will not condemn his preexisting notions too harshly.

We have discussed the influence of the ancient Hebrews, the Church fathers, the Catholic Church, and finally the Protestant Reformation. Although the United States is usually thought of as a Protestant nation, all of these influences have had a powerful effect, including the Catholic Church. The reason for this influence is that Protestantism could never rid itself of the idea that it was threatened by Catholicism, and therefore the Catholic Church was influential not only because of its initial effect, but also in the continual Church pressure felt by the Protestants.

The Early Industrial Impact

By the eighteenth century the industrial revolution was being felt in America with a force that it could not have in the Old World. North America, with its minimal commitment to the past and an almost total lack of feudal traditions, responded to industrialism in a direct and spontaneous way—not inhibited by any deeply entrenched customs. The family along with almost everything else was tailored to the industrial order. Children were freed from parental controls more quickly than in the Old World, women gained new freedoms from their fathers and husbands (and even brothers), and the household was capitalized in a new sense— from sheer material abundance.

Even as the American population moved westward, picking and choosing among new inventions that had been so slowly and painstakingly achieved by Western civilization, the country developed a remarkably effective industrial economy. Free movement had always characterized Americans, and the very people who came to the New World in the first place were in most cases persons who had no great stake in the past and no strong commitment to any particular family system.

The Americans were Europeans in many respects, but they were not fenced-in by their own history. It is true that a well-established family was useful in coping with the constant problems of a rapidly growing nation, but rarely did families stay permanently in any one place. There were many temptations for children, no matter how hard they may have worked to help their parents, to strike out on their own when they reached maturity—which they reached at a relatively young age. Certainly the revolutionary idea that children *should* grow up and leave home was pioneered in the United States. This was rarely possible in other parts of the world, and it has had an extraordinary influence on the American character. Perhaps it would have occurred even if the country had not made rapid industrial progress. It might have been simply the product of a frontier to be conquered, but certainly that could not have been tamed by technologically backward people. The most common justification for taking the Indians' land was that white men could make better use of it (unacceptable as that argument may seem today). They succeeded in taking it in an incredibly short period of time because their guns and organization were better than those of the natives. In the very nature of the changing frontier pattern young people had to establish homesteads of their own in the newly acquired territories. Thus, the early American society was one where young people had every opportunity to leave home, and there was a growing economic base to support their foot-loose ways.

While these conditions were breaking the hold of parents over children, these and other forces were also breaking the control of men over women. Women were relatively scarce among the immigrants to the New World, and in the westward movement the sex ratio favoring women was extraordinary. It is almost always characteristic of a frontier for women to be in short supply, and that certainly does not hurt their ability to upset the sexual status quo. Industrial growth also gave women better leverage in relations with men. The nineteenth century impact did not win new career opportunities for them; that came later. But it did succeed in setting the stage for all of the twentieth-century reforms. It created a much more receptive state of mind for the principle that women *should* have sex equality.

The industrial revolution brought about a rising standard of material comfort. New firms had products to sell, many of which could be used by women to lighten their work at home, releasing them for pursuits formerly closed to women. The new stress on mass production and mass consumption also had the effect of turning women into shoppers. They have played this role throughout history to some extent, but industrial development made shopping a way of life—both stimulating and liberating at the same time. This role has grown spectacularly in the United States, where women were first shoppers for their families, then shoppers for both their families and themselves. Indeed, as more and more married women get jobs away from home, they usually regard at least some if not all of the money they make as their personal treasury, further enhancing their freedom. This point should be qualified by adding that many women work mainly for money to spend on their children. In this way maternal employment is often considered an extension of the role of mother (Glenn 1959; Jephcott 1962). But the fact remains that many women also feel that the money they earn is their own, a point of view developed even before they marry. Today most single girls who are not in school are employed, and they relish the opportunity to use their earnings on occasional shopping sprees.

In summary, industrial development in the United States had a unique effect because of the special circumstances of the new American nation. This has been most obvious in the reactions of women and children. Above all, the American historical experience has been a liberating one. Nevertheless, the family system has not collapsed or in any sense withered in the process. If industrialism offers people opportunities to leave home and find pleasure in a variety of highly personal or nonfamily ways, it also provides the means for a very comfortable household, now most often found in the suburbs.

THE EVOLUTION OF THE FAMILY

The American family has its own unique history, but it is also influenced by general changes occurring in the world at large. In a broad sense, the human family has evolved through several stages, from its earliest position in nonliterate or "primitive" societies to its current place in highly complex, modern nations. Although scholars are not agreed on any particular pattern of evolutionary development, efforts to outline the main trends have often been made. Three of the more influential attempts will be discussed here. Two of them are quite recent and take an evolutionary approach; the other one rejects much current thinking about the place of the family in man's history. The two evolutionary approaches are William Goode's *convergence theory* and Robert Winch's *curvilinear theory* (which he developed in association with Rae Lesser Blumberg); the critical one is Carl Zimmerman's *cyclical theory*.

A word about the meaning of "social evolution" is in order. It refers to gross social changes over time, one change leading to another and all of them together having a cumulative effect. In the area of technical inventions, for example, each new development makes another one possible, and there is progressive advancement toward ever more complicated and powerful tools and machines. But each new step does not necessarily occur in the same society that developed the previous one. In terms of general social advancement, the Middle East was once the world's most progressive area. Greece took over for a while, as did England at a much later time. The United States has had its moment of glory; the next major development may very well occur somewhere else.

The human family, however, does not necessarily evolve in a progressive way. Man's tools—his productive machinery—become more effective all the time, according to standards of progress that everyone can agree on. But the family does not improve in this sense. We can only say that certain general trends have occurred in the past, and it seems likely that they will continue into the future.

The Convergence Theory

In its most concise form, William Goode's (1963; 1968) approach is this: Throughout the world the nuclear family unit (consisting of mother, father and children) has been dependent upon its larger circle of kinsmen for survival until the recent emergence of an urban-industrial way of life. With the growth of industrialism, the nuclear unit became the primary basis for family stability, no longer relying so heavily on the extended family. The trend is toward a relatively tiny family, set apart and operating on its own, although not completely isolated from kinsmen.

Goode identifies six facets of this trend, all spurred by industrialization:

1. Decline of the extended family as a close-knit social unit
2. Decline of marriage between kinsmen
3. Decline of traditional authority, including parents' authority over their children and the husband's authority over his wife
4. Growth of equality between the sexes and equality for all children in the family in the inheritance of wealth from parents
5. Decline of marriage involving either the dowry or the bride price
6. Rise of free choice in mate selection with love serving as the primary reason for marriage.

Goode argues that the pressures for modern industrial growth are closely tied to those that promote greater freedom from traditional family controls. Thus, the family customs that exist in a nation when it first faces industrial pressures will influence the speed and form of its industrial development. In particular, economic growth moves ahead more rapidly if the large kinship system is weak at the outset. When that is the case, people will be able to move more freely in response to industrial needs; they can advance in their careers without feeling obligated to kinsmen; industrial decisions can be made without waiting for approval by relatives; hiring and promotion can be based on merit rather than nepotism (favoring relatives); women can be used with fewer restrictions based on their traditional family roles; and the family itself becomes more adept at giving intimate emotional support, which can be very helpful in the midst of urban tensions.

But there are many possible variations in the relation between industrialism and familism. In Pakistan, for example, the longstanding bride price has evolved into a dowry system that serves as insurance for brides in case of marital trouble. It contributes to family stability in a rapidly developing society (Korson 1967). The trend in China seems to be in the direction of free marital choice, and yet there is still strong solidarity among related families, providing *cooperative family networks* in the midst of industrialization (Stoodley 1967).

Although the kind of family that exists in the early stages of national development may influence the rate of industrial growth (Goode argues that it was no accident that industrial capitalism developed rapidly in the Western world), the development of an industrial economy inevitably undermines the large family system. It is this point that makes Goode's theory an *evolutionary* one, because industrialism in his view is a social force that has a predictable effect upon a nation somewhat independent of its particular history. Although some nations have backgrounds that favor industrial progress, while others impede it, the convergence theory claims that trends in both cases will be toward an essentially similar family system—some variation on the nuclear family pattern.*

The Curvilinear Theory

Robert Winch (with Rae Blumberg 1968) concurs with almost everything Goode has to say, but he attempts to add another dimension to the argument. In particular, Winch traces the pattern of family life back to its earliest human beginnings, whereas Goode was primarily concerned with the world revolution brought about by industrialization.

According to Winch, the key to change in history is *societal complexity* brought about by an expanding division of labor. He argues that the nuclear family was the basic social group in man's earliest development; it was *not* closely tied to any large kinship system. This was the era in which man relied on hunting and gathering for his livelihood, and the division of labor was very simple. A basic fact about the life of hunters and gatherers is that they almost always live in small family clusters that are rather isolated from one another (Hart and Pilling 1960). Survival problems are so pressing that a large kinship system is of no use and cannot be supported. Work is assigned according to the person's sex and age rather than parceled out among a variety of men, each contributing highly specialized skills. Therefore the most effective means of coping with life is by direct, cooperative efforts within a small family.

With the growth of an agricultural economy the large family system not only became feasible, it became the basis for much greater social stability. This characterized the great middle period of man's history. It was accompanied by the appearance of a few great cities, but most people were still peasants, dependent upon simple, nonmechanized farming. More recently, as the industrial order took over, the nuclear family once again became the key unit for family stability (for reasons cited by Goode). This, then, is the curvilinear family pattern; *nuclear* in man's most primitive beginnings, *extended* during the long middle centuries of history, and returning to the *nuclear* system in the modern industrial era (see Figure 2 on page 336).

Winch claims that there are four underlying conditions that determine the degree of complexity in a society: (1) the reliability of the food supply,

---

* Sidney Greenfield (1961), on the other hand, contends that there is no necessary connection between industrial development and the nuclear family. His point of view does not seem to be popular, but he presents it forcefully, and it cannot be totally disregarded.

FIGURE 2. Curvilinear Theory

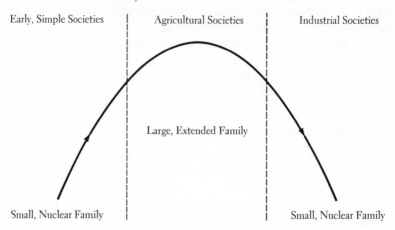

Early, Simple Societies   Agricultural Societies   Industrial Societies

Large, Extended Family

Small, Nuclear Family   Small, Nuclear Family

(2) the extent to which the family itself serves as the basis for work activities, (3) the extent to which family units are geographically mobile, and (4) the extent to which land is the primary wealth owned by the family.

The earliest hunting and gathering societies are similar to modern industrial ones in certain respects, especially in terms of points (3) and (4); in both, families are geographically mobile and the ownership of land is not the primary source of family wealth. Furthermore, hunting and gathering societies often have an unreliable food supply which, in combination with their mobility and limited ownership of land, helps to explain their stress on the nuclear family. High levels of mobility, an absence of landed wealth, and the fact that work is done away from home help to explain why the nuclear family is strong in modern industrial nations.

Agricultural societies, on the other hand, have problems that are different from those of both hunting-gathering and industrial societies; their work is family-centered, they are not very mobile, and wealth is rooted in the land. These conditions favor an extended kinship system.

Winch emphasizes societal complexity as the key to long-run changes in the family. An alternative is the concept of *culture base*, which refers to the accumulated knowledge, tools, and skills of a society. The more highly developed the culture base, the more proficient the people will be in meeting their material needs. And as the culture base develops, the family must also change. For example, as knowledge expands, it takes children longer to learn the nation's basic skills. A public school system is needed, and the development of formal education is probably the key to loss of functions of kinsmen. Children must attend school and learn from professionally trained teachers, replacing parents and relatives. Parents are still important

—more important than uncles and aunts and so on—but even they teach less. Parents are now important to their children mainly in providing motivation and emotional security.

In the earliest stages of human history the culture base was too poorly developed to support an extended family. People had to move in small family clusters. With agriculture the large family complex became very useful, and it remained so for several thousand years. Only with the explosion in knowledge brought about by modern science was the kin network undermined and the critical importance of the nuclear family revived. But, as we have seen, even this family arrangement is now challenged by the incredible progress in science.

The Cyclical Theory

A theory contrasting sharply with both Goode's and Winch's is one worked out by Carle C. Zimmerman (1947). In his key work Zimmerman argues that the family in each major civilization goes through three fairly distinct phases; he rejects the idea of an evolutionary sequence for mankind in general. ("Major civilizations" refer to cultures such as classical Rome and Greece, and modern Western civilization.) Zimmerman argues, furthermore, that the style of the family at any stage in a nation's history determines the basic quality of its national life, because the family supplies the fundamental form of social organization. Every other principle of organization is dependent upon it. In place of other forces that have been called the key to history—technology, class struggle, religion, ideology—Zimmerman offers the family.

Civilization, he claims, grows out of familism, but as it grows, it loses its original connection with this basic life force. Inner family decay is the main reason for the fall of the great civilizations. When the process of rotting away has progressed as far as it can go, the civilization exhausts its inventory of social and moral resources, which is followed by self-destructive reactions and almost total social collapse. The length of the "dark ages" that follow will depend upon how quickly people find their way back to the fundamental mother-source—familism.

According to Zimmerman, this approach to historical change does not ignore all other causes of change set forth by philosophers of history. It simply points out that the final outcome in great historical movements has always been decided by fundamental changes in the family. Hence, the family has a unique place in explaining historical trends, and family change is itself the final, decisive force.

Family patterns reflect the prevailing state of the culture, and in certain important ways Zimmerman believes that the family *determines* the state of society. Although his point of view is extremely hard to support against criticism from anyone not disposed to accept it, it is based on a very popular idea—that the family is the backbone of society and that any weakening of family virtues must lead to general catastrophe.

As noted in Chapter 1, Zimmerman argues that most of the scientific study of the family since the Renaissance has been a tragic blunder; scholars have almost always challenged traditional family values and have occasionally held them up to ridicule. Zimmerman says that this has happened many times before in history, especially when civilization is under unusual stress (during the decline of the Roman Empire, for example). In fact, he seems to say that intellectuals have been largely responsible for the decay of familism. When they turn against the family, it may be decades or centuries before the damage can be repaired.

Zimmerman claims that each of the high civilizations can be subdivided into three family stages. The first one he calls the *trustee stage*, in which members of the family who are living are considered trustees of its blood, rights, property, name, and position during their lifetimes. Children are brought up to respect all the tribal traditions, and they acquire a strong sense of duty to the family. Marriage and family bonds are as close to total organic unity as human beings can make them. This type of family has more power than any other human family system, amounting in extreme cases to the right of life or death over its members. Although living conditions are not easy, since this usually occurs in the early stages of economic development, the family is stable and its members are thoroughly disciplined. They are capable of improving their style of living. Society is hardly more than a collection of families and must count on each one to govern, protect, support, discipline, and take responsibility for its own.

The second period is the *domestic stage*, during which trustee ties are loosened. Forms of marriage begin to appear that are not as binding as before, although marriage is still regarded as a lifelong arrangement. Divorce becomes possible, though disreputable, and love loses some of its sacrificial meaning. The social rules by which a man and his wife and sometimes even his kinsmen are mutually responsible for a crime are relaxed. The culture grows large and gains power. Formal types of political control are set up, and the older men are no longer trustees for the tribe simply because they are heads of families. Political control is assigned to certain men who are designated community leaders. In this stage it is also common for organized religion to appear, with full-time priests, and so the family is surrounded by priests and officials who have critical powers independent of family membership.

But the family remains strong and stable, and children are still reared to fulfill duties to the family and to all the established institutions of society. The domestic family is the most common family system in the world according to Zimmerman. It satisfies to some extent the natural desire for freedom from family bonds and for individualism, yet it also preserves social order. The state can depend upon it for support. Cultures with domestic family patterns may achieve the rank of first-class civilizations because of the hard working, duty-oriented people they produce.

The third period is the *atomistic stage*. (There are periods of transition between stages, of course, but as each one develops, its distinguishing characteristics are clearly revealed.) In the atomistic stage the family begins to show signs of weakness, decay, and disintegration. The civilization itself, which reached its peak in the later stages of the domestic period, is now wealthy but undisciplined, and it begins to show signs of collapse. Disorganization within the family is the key. Whereas in trustee times the *family* was sacred, in the atomistic stage the *individual* becomes sacred. (Zimmerman says that this change can be measured by the rise of the idea that illegitimate children should have the same rights as other children.)

Children are now taught to look for happiness rather than to develop a sense of duty and obligation. Adults, too, seek sex pleasure above all, and married persons—even parents—file for divorce for trivial reasons. Common property, common names, and common theories of origin begin to break up. The strength of the marriage bond changes from mutual guardianship to a loose contractual arrangement; husband, wife, and children no longer "belong" to each other in any real sense. The family is held together mainly by the pleasure it can offer. Children often have no guiding principles and no self-sustaining discipline. All of the key signs of cultural vitality waver in the direction of deterioration and lack of purpose.

Zimmerman suggests that out of such chaos a new order will be formed, most likely around the nucleus of the trustee type of family. The atomistic period ultimately brings about a renewal of familism because of its self-defeating doctrines, making it impossible for civilization to expand in its present form. Therefore antifamilistic and antisocial atttudes keep feeding upon themselves until there is some vital reaction around which a new society can grow (see Figure 3 on page 340).

Zimmerman attempted to prove his point, that these three stages have indeed appeared in all the great civilizations. The classic Greek and Roman periods in particular lend themselves to his kind of historical analysis, each having progressed through a trustee period (or something rather like it), then the civilization-building stage dominated by the domestic family, and finally a stage of atomistic decline. In ancient Greece, according to Zimmerman, the trustee family lasted from the Homeric period to the end of the ninth century B.C.; the domestic family appeared in the eighth century and continued until the fifth century B.C., roughly from

FIGURE 3. Cyclical Theory

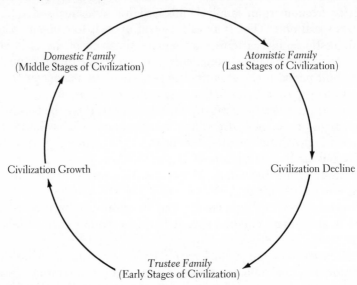

Hesiod to Pericles and the ascendancy of sophism, and lasted until the end of classical Greece (when it merged with the Roman atomistic family system).

The trustee family of Rome existed from the time of the earliest tribes to the period of the Twelve Tables Code, about 450 B.C.; the domestic family lasted from the decline of the trustee family until the reign of Augustus; the atomistic family prevailed from Augustus to the time of Justinian. In modern Western civilization the trustee family prevailed between the sixth and twelfth centuries A.D., from the rise and dominance of canon law over the "barbarians" until the decline of Thomist philosophy; the domestic family lasted from the thirteenth to the eighteenth centuries, by which time both capitalism and the Protestant Reformation were dominant; the atomistic family appeared along with eighteenth century rationalism. It has lasted until the present time, when it may be reaching its limits.

How should we evaluate such an ambitious view of history? That civilizations have waxed and waned cannot be denied, nor can it be argued that the growth cycle of any particular civilization involves changes in family life, somewhat along the lines Zimmerman has outlined. But whether there is any *causal* connection between family patterns and the rise and fall of civilizations remains questionable and unproved.

In fact, an explanation of why the family *must* go through these three stages never becomes clear. Certainly it is difficult to see a cyclical continuation of modern society along the lines Zimmerman suggests. We can forsee only a rush of new developments in the last part of the twentieth century—and an even more explosive twenty-first century. Zimmerman himself seems to be more confident when he searches for evidence from the past to support his theory than when he attempts to project it into a genuinely calculable or meaningful future. The theories of Goode and Winch, on the other hand, suggest reasonable projections into the future. These are the ones that we shall explore in greater depth when talking about the future of the family.

SUMMARY

The history of the family is not as controversial as its evolution, although historians have not written as much about family life as we would like. There can be no doubt that the views of the ancient Hebrews have had a continuing influence in the Western world, even on people living in the United States in the 1970s. Views of the early Church fathers have also been influential, along with the slow rise to power of the Catholic Church. The position of the Church was crystallized and solidified over a long period of time, making its influence all the more important. But the Protestant Reformation introduced a new pluralism into the realm of family beliefs, followed (or accompanied) by the liberating influence of industrialism itself. Thus, many of the family doctrines that had been accepted by the ancient Hebrews and those formulated by the Catholic Church during its rise to power have been under siege during the past several centuries.

One may choose to call the current era a period of atomism, but it is also correct to say that current trends have simply reduced family obligations, stripping the family of many of its kinship supports. Even parents and children in the nuclear family are granted new opportunities to go their separate ways. And yet familism persists; the marriage rate in the United States was never higher—it is now higher than in any other Western nation. In some respects, family life offers satisfactions today that it could never offer before.

William Goode argues that industrial growth causes family patterns all over the world to become more similar no matter how different they may have been at the outset. In particular, the nuclear, small family system is the one most adaptive to modern conditions. This point of view is not new; Goode's work is distinguished primarily by his effort to provide supporting evidence and to state the theory as carefully as possible.

Robert Winch carried Goode's approach backward through history to the earliest stages of human development, when the nuclear family was more effective than a large kinship system. His thesis turns on the degree of complexity in human culture. In the earliest stages, food getting is very primitive, and the small family pattern is adequate. In the long, middle stages of man's development society becomes more complex, and the large family system is needed for both social stability and personal security. But in modern society complexity and change are so pronounced that the kinship system is too sluggish, and the nuclear family becomes more effective. The concept of the culture base may also be used to explain this pattern, because a major reason for change in the family is man's accumulated knowledge. When the culture base is very limited, the large family system is not too effective, and when culture is highly advanced, the large family again poses difficult problems. It works best in the middle stages of cultural development.

Carle Zimmerman strongly opposes all evolutionary approaches to society. He argues that every great civilization has passed through three stages in the course of its history. The first is the trustee stage, where children are reared to serve the family. Although life is severe, people work hard and are capable of building toward a more comfortable future. In the second, domestic stage, family obligations are relaxed somewhat, but people still regard the family as the basis for social order and pledge their lives to its service. This is the kind of family system still found in most parts of the world according to Zimmerman. The third stage is the atomistic period, when the family loses its earlier sense of purpose. People live for personal happiness rather than for the good of the family. Zimmerman claims that an abandonment of family duties characterizes this era, leading to the disintegration of all major forms of cultural vitality. Society begins to decay along with the inner erosion of the family, and renewal can come only from a resurgence of familism.

The theories of Goode and Winch are most consistent with the main currents of contemporary thinking, and their views will be discussed again when we turn to possible developments in the future.

SELECTED READINGS

GOODE, WILLIAM J. *World Revolution and Family Patterns*. New York: The Free Press, 1963.

GOODSELL, WILLYSTINE. *A History of Marriage and the Family*. Rev. ed. New York: Macmillan, 1934.

GREENFIELD, SIDNEY M. "Industrialization and the Family in Sociological Theory," *American Journal of Sociology*, Vol. 67 (November 1961), pp. 312–322.

PATAI, RAPHAEL. *Sex and Family in the Bible and the Middle East.* Garden City, N.Y.: Dolphin Books, 1959.

WINCH, ROBERT F., AND RAE LESSER BLUMBERG. "Societal Complexity and Familial Organization," in Robert F. Winch and Louis Wolf Goodman (eds.), *Selected Studies in Marriage and the Family.* New York: Holt, Rinehart and Winston, 1968, pp. 70–92.

ZIMMERMAN, CARLE C. *Family and Civilization.* New York: Harper, 1947.

CHAPTER 16

Kinds of Families

It is well known that family life varies from one place to another. The important questions are: What causes the differences, what limits their variation, and what can we learn from studying them? If people were infinitely flexible, we might have any kind of family at all—or choose to do without it. Some people might prefer an arrangement with three husbands and five wives; sex relations might be encouraged between brothers and sisters or between parents and children, or include all members of the family; exclusive sex relations between a man and woman might be considered sinful; mothers might not be allowed to see their own children because they are considered too ego-involved; perhaps family life could be so highly bureaucratized that almost all acts would require official permission, with forms to be filled out and supervisors and inspectors to be reckoned with. A survey of the world's family customs will reveal some improbable arrangements—and some of them seem to have worked for a long time. But the fact remains that Homo sapiens is limited in the kind of families that can meet his needs, or at least those of the great majority of people.

Monogamy, for example, is by far the most common marriage practice, and for good reason. Polygyny (the marriage of one man to more than one woman) was fairly common until the rise of industrial nations, but polyandry (the marriage of one woman to more than one man) has always been extremely rare. Its drawbacks greatly outnumber its advantages. In fact, polyandry is self-limiting in its very nature, because one wife can have no more children with four husbands than she can have with one. Another conceivable alternative—group marriage—has never worked. Due to the fairly equal numbers of men and women in most societies, monogamy is the most efficient way to establish a small cooperative group for a long-term relationship (although there are places where a surplus of women could be used to argue for permitting polygyny). It reduces rivalries within the family, which always become more difficult to control as the group becomes larger. The one man–one woman arrangement is workable in a very pragmatic way. It is strengthened by mutual sex attraction, so it can perpetuate itself through childbirth. The most likely basis for a successful polygynous marriage, on the other hand, is the existence of a rich and powerful husband. Since all men cannot be rich and powerful, it is best for most men to remain monogamous or not to marry at all. It is an observable fact that, as the general affluence of a society improves, women gain greater equality with men, and then they inevitably rebel against polygyny.

In other words, family organization must not violate certain biological and social-psychological requirements for human survival. Although it can take many forms, there are limits beyond which it had better not go. Thus, certain family patterns recur over and over again throughout the world, repetitiously enough to suggest that the basic forms of family life are remarkably similar across national boundaries. It also seems likely that the subjective personal feelings of family members cannot differ as much from place to place as we might suppose. The sensations associated with sex relations are relatively constant, and the feelings associated with pregnancy, childbirth, infant nurturing, and early child care are probably quite similar among the women of the world. The feelings that infants and young children have toward parents and older people are probably also very limited in range.

It becomes a question of what we choose to look for: similarities or differences. The current chapter is concerned with differences, but it would be a mistake to lose sight of the underlying sameness of family life in human experience.

THE EXTENT OF DIVERSITY

Diversity occurs in both time and space. The history of man's behavior has long been studied, in part because we are curious about people who lived before our own time and also because studying the past can be useful for the present; not only can we learn something about ourselves, but we may even avoid the mistakes of the past. The study of history became popular long before the rise of modern social science, and it continues to be an important bridge between the humanities on the one hand and sociology and psychology on the other.

The most critical developments of contemporary social science, however, provide two entirely different ways of understanding human behavior. One is the careful collection of data to test a theory, thereby accepting it as valid or rejecting it as invalid (or simply unproved). This approach was borrowed from the physical sciences. A second is the cross-cultural approach, by which social patterns in different cultures are described and compared. This is the most striking new way to achieve broad social perspective, and it is the guiding influence for this chapter.

Adopting such an approach, George P. Murdock (1957) has identified four kinds of family patterns that have become typical in certain parts of the world:

Independent families are family groups that include no more than one nuclear family (consisting of parents and children).

Stem families usually consist of two nuclear families, one of the parent generation and the other of the offspring generation, which have close and continual interaction.

Lineal families consist of one nuclear family from the older generation and two or more from the offspring generation, again with close relations.

Extended families are large in size and normally include the families of at least two siblings or cousins in both the parent and the offspring generation.

The last three family types are often lumped together and simply called extended families; that term is used in this broad sense in this book. We should bear in mind, though, that the extended family actually takes several different forms, with different consequences for family attitudes and behavior (Chu 1969).

THE WAYS FAMILIES CAN DIFFER

There are five basic differences in human family patterns: (1) differences in *composition*, (2) differences in *spatial arrangement*, (3) differences in *division of labor*, (4) differences in the *placement pattern*, (5) differences in *family and kinship imagery*.

These differences can be outlined as follows:
Composition
    Size
    Presence or absence of key members
    Age make-up
    Genetic characteristics

Spatial arrangement
    Structure of the household
    Location of kinsmen
Division of labor
    Work roles of family members
    Authority pattern
Placement pattern
    Socioeconomic pattern
    Family reputation
    Special traditions or lore retained in the family
    Procedures for transmitting wealth and status from one generation
      to the next
Family and kinship emphasis
    Subjective: the importance people attach to family membership and
      familism
    Objective: the degree to which people are handicapped by not being
      part of a family

The important thing to keep in mind is that the patterns in all five areas
are joined together to make up the total family system. Changes in any
part will usually lead to changes in all the others.

Composition

Size. The composition of the family can vary greatly from one society
to another; the most basic difference is in size. In the United States, for
example, the average family will have between four and five members,
but in some countries the average may be closer to seven or eight. If all
kinsmen living under one roof and very close by are counted, the number
may be much higher. There is evidence that most people have some conception of an ideal family size and that it is related to the actual size of
their families; these attitudes are transmitted from one generation to the
next (Hendershot 1969).

Most people think of the modern American family as a small independent family system because the household of parents and children is somewhat isolated from relatives and also because the birth rate is so much
lower than it has been in the past. But the average number of people in
the household does not vary as much as changes in the birth rate might
suggest. In peasant countries, where the birth rate is high, the death rate
is usually also high, so the number of children in the family may be no
greater than in many contemporary suburban homes. Still, the modern
family tends to be smaller after eight or ten years of marriage than a
comparable family of a century or more ago. Although families with five
to ten children (and some with more) can be found even in modern

cities, their basic life style will be more like that of other contemporary families with two or three children than that of the large farm and peasant families of the past. Thus, we can speak of the *small family system* as a special kind, found most often in modern nations.

Presence or Absence of Key Members. More important than sheer size are the *roles* that are included in the ideal family. Thus, marriage is monogamous in the United States, and it is considered appropriate for the married couple to have children; the ideal household consists of mother, father, and offspring. If other persons are present, some explanation is usually called for. (Polygyny has been an ideal pattern in many parts of the world, but monogamy is always the most practical arrangement for the great majority of people.)

Although the nuclear family in industrial nations may be somewhat smaller than earlier families, its most distinguishing quality is the fact that it is more likely to be *intact*. None of the children have died as a rule, and both biological parents are likely to be living. Children apparently grow up with less sense of loss insofar as death in the family is concerned, and parents, too, are more likely to enjoy many years of family life without having to face widowhood or the loss of a child. Although the full significance of this is not yet known, it would seem to allow family members to rely on one another for both material and emotional support, especially the latter, with greater assurance than in the past.

It has often been noted that emotional relations in nonliterate and peasant families tend to be rather shallow. Relations between husbands and wives are usually distant, formal, and impersonal. The woman in tropical Africa, for example, often feels like an alien in her own marriage; her enduring emotional ties are with kinsmen (Paulme 1963). The major strains within the household in Zinacantan, Mexico, are between brothers or between mother-in-law and daughter-in-law (Cancian 1964), and it is not uncommon for a husband to beat his wife. The degree of personal disrespect tolerated in marriage is almost incomprehensible to citizens of the United States.

These patterns occur in part because the nuclear family is not stressed or romanticized. Only the larger kinship group can offer a strong basis for personal security; the nuclear family is too unstable. High death rates are part of the problem, too. People simply cannot rely too heavily for emotional security on one or very few other people. It is safer to count on the large family.

Age Make-up. The typical age make-up of the family also varies from one culture to another and among different groups within any particular society. Insofar as the nuclear family is concerned, there are differences between the ages of husband and wife, parents and children, and siblings. The range of possibilities is greater than we might imagine. A strong tendency existed among the Australian Tiwi, for example, for husbands to be either very much older than their wives (as a result of their practice of "infant bestowal," an agreement for the infant's future marriage) or very much younger (as a result of widow remarriage)—or some combination of both. Hence many Tiwi husbands had a few wives much older than themselves, including some already dead (but still counted). They also had some very much younger than themselves, including a few who were still babies or perhaps not even born yet, but bestowed (Hart and Pilling 1960).

Historically, husbands have been much older than wives in most societies, but the trend in the past seventy years or so, for which we have reasonably good data, is clearly toward fewer and smaller differences (Glick and Parke 1965). In the short run, differences in the ages of spouses may be due to special population problems, such as a shortage of men two or three years older than women in the marriageable ages. This occurred in the United States in the mid-1960s; it was caused by a sharp increase in the birth rate twenty years earlier (at the end of World War II). Girls born at that time outnumbered males who were born two or three years earlier. Therefore, many of these women were virtually forced to marry men closer to their own age. But in the long run, quirks like this cannot account for the continuing trend. A plausible explanation is that, broadly speaking, the difference in the ages of husbands and wives reflects the degree of inequality between men and women. As women gain greater equality, they marry men nearer themselves in age.

As discussed in Chapter 4, dating in the twentieth century seems to be closely associated with the decline of the double sex standard. As dating begins at earlier ages, young people become more accustomed to intimate social (as well as sexual) relations with members of the opposite sex of their own age, which in turn leads to closer ages at the time of marriage. Samuel Lowrie (1961) found that the age disparity of adolescent daters from families of lower social status and weak educational background was consistently greater than average. Similarity in the ages of couples was associated with high social status, extensive education, and smaller families. All of these last-mentioned qualities are correlated with greater equality between the sexes.

The pattern of age disparity between parents and children varies from culture to culture. No single theory can explain it. Among the Tiwi, age differences were extreme; it was even possible for the father's stepchildren to be older than himself. Early marriage for couples means that they will be closer to their children in age, but early marriage is found in countries that are not the least bit similar in other respects—it occurs in both rich and poor nations, for example. For several decades in the twentieth century the average age at marriage in the United States has gone down, apparently because of prosperity, but there have also been periods of prosperity when the average marriage age has risen.

Differences between the ages of parents and children are not, so far as we know, related to any particular pattern of child rearing. Thus, if the average mother in a society is about twenty-five years older than her children, she will not necessarily be a different kind of mother than women in another society who average only eighteen years older than their children. The full significance of the fact that black women in the United States have more children in their late thirties and early forties than whites (Rainwater 1965), and hence are often much older than their children, is not fully known. It certainly seems to be a product of the special status of blacks in American society. Any differences in mothering behavior between white and black women are more likely to be caused by the lower average social status of blacks than by the fact that more of them are so much older than their children. Nevertheless, the age discrepancy itself could be of some significance.

Age differences among siblings are products of marriage patterns, the birth rate, and spacing practices. Where women start having children in their early teens and continue to have them until they die, which has been a common pattern throughout history, the last child is often much younger than the oldest one. The only reason the children may not follow a one-a-year age pattern is because several of them are likely to die. What often occurs in nonliterate societies is that children are grouped together in terms of age and sex, rather than family membership, and hence little emphasis is given to particular brothers and sisters. The boy's "brothers" are all the other boys in the tribe who are about his own age. (The actual age of each will probably be unknown.)

By contrast, in contemporary society most women have their two or three children quite early in marriage (Glick and Parke 1965), as a result of which the offspring are fairly close together in age. They conceive of themselves as a sibling unit, and relatively few have brothers or sisters who are much older or much younger than themselves.

Current theories of sibling relations suggest that brothers and sisters who are close together in age tend to be highly competitive toward one another. When their ages are further apart, the older ones play a kind of parental role; they are more protective and disciplinary toward the younger children, and the latter are respectful in response. Contemporary sibling relations, involving high levels of competition and jealousy within a small family group, seem to be in harmony with the high levels of competitiveness and achievement demanded by modern industrial society.

Genetic Characteristics in the Family. Families are composed of people who have similar physical characteristics. Since they share genetic traits, or a tiny *gene pool* passed on from one generation to the next, children often resemble their grandparents or even greatgrandparents, and many families now have photographic records to prove it. We cannot yet manipulate genes and tailor-make our children's physical characteristics, although some geneticists forsee such a state of affairs in the not-too-distant future.

Right now that point of view must be considered science fiction, but there is one *current* trend, especially in the United States, that may prove to be very important. That is the tendency for young people to travel farther from home and therefore to meet and marry persons who have genes quite different from their own. It is well known that the constancy of genetic traits in any given locality is largely due to the practice of intermarriage among people in that area. Residential propinquity is still a major force governing marriages in most parts of the world, where people ordinarily do not move very far from home during the courtship stage of life. Hawaii is a special case, where racial intermixtures are common even without extensive travel; about two out of five Hawaiian marriages are interracial. But the trend in modern society is toward greater mobility, and hence toward greater diversity in mate selection almost everywhere. William Goode (1963) argues that geographic mobility has probably enlarged the area from which eligible partners are drawn in every Western country. The pattern has slowly expanded since the late sixteenth century, when a nationwide marriage market appeared for the first time in London.

This trend is very strong in the United States. Almost all teachers are reminded of it in the classroom, where the last names of students are remarkably diverse and where a casual glance at the students' facial features, complexions, hair colors and textures attest to genetic interbreeding. Anthropologists contend that this is becoming more characteristic of many populations. They also seem to agree that, from the standpoint of population vigor, it is a good thing (Dobzhansky 1967; Brace and Ashley Montagu 1965).

Spatial Arrangement

One of the unique qualities of Homo sapiens is the fact that he almost invariably has a "home base" from which to operate. *Nesting* is found in other species, but higher primates such as the chimpanzee and gorilla usually build a new nest each day rather than return to the one of the day before (Washburn and DeVore 1961). There are various ways of housing the human family—look at the homes in any single community, let alone the incredible variety in the world. The "houses" of the Australian Tiwi represent the bare minimum, often nothing more than a few piled-up tree branches used as shelter for several nights, then abandoned.

Structure of the Household. The study of household ecology concerns (1) the most common architectural designs for the home, (2) the uses to which it is put, (3) its influence on the family's daily affairs, and (4) its effect upon their general style of life. The households of the Swazi and of the people of Vasilika provide examples of how household structures can differ.

The homestead of the Swazi, a Bantu-speaking people of Swaziland in southern Africa, is usually built according to a plan that reflects the main interests of its polygynous occupants (Kuper 1963). In the center is a heavily fenced cattle pen to which men and boys have free access, but which women only enter on special occasions. Grouped around the western end of this pen are the living quarters. The main gateway to the compound is at the other end, facing the rising sun. Near the main enclosure is a "great hut" which is supervised by the mother of the male head of the family. It is often decorated with skulls of cattle sacrificed to the head-man's ancestors and is used as the family shrine. Menstruating women, people in mourning, and adults "hot" from sexual intercourse are never allowed to enter the great hut.

Separated from this enclosure are the quarters of the wives of the head-man. Among most southern Bantu groups the wives are usually segregated in order of rank. Each wife has her own sleeping, cooking, and storage huts, and within her enclosure she leads a rather private existence with her children. She is also allotted land, and, if possible, cattle. Thus, her quarters are a semi-independent social and economic unit. Young children sleep with their grandmothers; adolescent girls have their own huts behind their mothers', while adolescent boys build barracks at the entrance to the compound. A room of one's own is considered antisocial, and unattached individuals always live with people of their own age and sex.

These homesteads are so closely identified with the occupants that the idea of selling or renting them to strangers is repugnant. When a headman dies, the site is abandoned, and a new one is built in the vicinity of the main heir, whose duty it is to perpetuate the family. The key principle illustrated by the Swazi pattern is that the spatial arrangement of the household—in this case a *compound household*—reflects both the leading values and the daily concerns of its people.

The typical household of the people of Vasilika, a village in modern Greece, is entirely different. Ideally it is a two-story home having a terrace and a highly stylized arrangement of rooms (Friedl 1962). The ground floor usually consists of two chambers, one of which has a concrete floor and a fireplace. Families use this room for various purposes: as a kitchen, living room, and bedroom for all members of the family. The other ground level room has an earth floor used for storing supplies. If the family is poor, the lower floor may have only one room with a curtain separating the living section from the storage area.

The upper story usually has several rooms. In one of these a second fireplace is the focus of what the villagers call their winter quarters; this is a smaller version of the all-purpose room below. Women often hang their wash on the terrace, and the entire family may sleep there in the summer. The remaining second-floor room is the ceremonial sanctum and showplace of the house, comparable to the American front parlor, which the family presents to the outside world. Visitors are usually brought to it and expected to remain there. Most of the time it is not used but, because it is the family showroom, its furnishings are the best in the house, and the room is always kept neat and clean.

Every house in Vasilika, regardless of wealth, has a corner of one room set aside for religious objects. An icon of one of the saints of the Greek Orthodox Church is usually the central object. The house's deep symbolic importance is seen in the fact that a priest is requested to bless all new homes before families will move in. The blessing is presumed to place the home and its family under God's protection.

American households offer a striking contrast with those of both the Swazis and the Vasilikas. The ideal suburban home in modern America has a "ranch style" architecture, with a living room, kitchen, one or more indoor bathrooms, a place for modern labor-saving devices (washing machine, dryer, and so on), a bedroom for the married couple, and (ideally) a room for each of the children. The popularity of the dining room waned for a while but apparently has returned to fashion more recently. Having a den or recreation room has become popular, and each house (again ideally) has a front lawn and a backyard with trees and a patio area. The house itself is by no means considered sacred, nor is any part of it subject to religious or magical taboos. Many Americans, perhaps most, hope to move to a bigger and better place.

There is thus a common and ideal pattern in the United States, as elsewhere (Mercer 1967). Communities with special problems and special histories have somewhat different arrangements, as in Manhattan or San Francisco where multiple-dwelling units are more common and space is very expensive. It is obvious that the family budget usually determines the size of the home and the presence or absence of all the ideal features.*

---

* Slightly less than 3 percent of the 60 million households in the United States in 1969 had second homes reserved throughout the year for their use ("Current Housing Reports" 1969).

Trends in Housing. Generally, the birth rate of families tends to go down as their wealth increases, so living accommodations become more spacious. Thus, a trend associated with modern affluence in America is toward more space and privacy per member, although the trend is not as rapid as affluence alone might allow (Glazer 1967). While people have more personal space within the household, they actually have less outside as families crowd together in the city. This may have been reversed somewhat in the suburbs, but increasingly children play in public areas clearly designated for this purpose. We are beginning to question whether it is a good idea for each family to have a yard, play facilities, and a swimming pool of its own—or even to want to.

The privacy that modern parents have in their own bedrooms beyond the eyes of children seems to be correlated with the rise of love and romance in marriage. At the same time, the greater privacy afforded children is associated with generally higher status for them and the fact that childhood lasts longer.

Social scientists have not done much research in this area (Glazer 1967), but the most general conclusion to be drawn is that the spatial arrangement of family life is broadly correlated with changes in the entire range of family interests. As the status of children changes, as child-rearing practices change, as marriage interaction focuses upon different kinds of relations between the spouses, as the role of religion and magic in family life changes, the physical structure of the household changes, too.

Location of Kinsmen. One's relatives may be scattered all over the country, or they may live within a few blocks of home. In the past, most people in America lived in small towns and, except in the newly settled frontier communities, each nuclear family was surrounded by relatives. Thus, the child was influenced not only by his immediate family but also by relatives nearly everywhere he went. He was judged mainly by his position in the large kinship pattern. He was known as one man's nephew, another's cousin, and the brother of still another. In such a community the person's status was largely determined by his family connections. He could not escape the pattern, except by leaving town (which many Americans did).

In contemporary America the child is likely to be born in a large city with few kinsmen living nearby, in many cases none at all. He is still influenced by family members at home, but when he steps outside, he deals with people who are not his relatives. Most teachers, coaches, employers, and policemen, for example, are nonkinsmen. They judge the child by his performance, not by his family name. This is in complete harmony with the changing stress on *ascribed* and *achieved* status in industrial society. Ascribed status is determined by birth or conditions beyond our control.

Achieved status is earned. As achievement is stressed more, children grow up having less and less contact with people who will judge them on the basis of kinship.

The degree to which children are surrounded by kinsmen varies from group to group. A study of Jewish welfare recipients in New York, for example, showed that they lived in the midst of kinsmen to a surprising extent (Leichter and Mitchell 1967). For Catholics the pattern was less common, and for Protestants it was rare indeed (Winch 1968). The rise of an educational system where children (and people in general) can be judged by their performance rather than by family position is a key part of the changing physical structure of the family.

The spatial arrangement of the kin group has been given much attention by sociologists, especially since Talcott Parsons (1943) asserted that the modern family tends to be an isolated, nuclear unit. The contemporary family is not totally isolated from its kinsmen by any means, but the facts clearly show a trend in that direction. While modern technology lets people move about more freely, separating family members, it also gives them the means to keep in touch—telephones, jet planes, and so on. We are not physically embedded in a neighborhood full of kinsmen any longer, but we are not isolated either.

Division of Labor

Work Roles of Family Members. The duties and chores assigned to family members differ in predictable ways from one society to the next.

For example, in Rusembilan, a Malay fishing village in southern Thailand, the husband is the main provider for his household, engaging in such occupations as fishing or rice cultivation (Fraser 1966). He is head of the family—of which there is no doubt—although authority may be delegated to his wife or to an elder child when he is absent from the house. The husband also represents the family in most religious and political activities of the communty. Women may be observers in religious matters, but they are allowed to play no role whatsoever in political decision making.

However, the wife *is* manager of the household. Assisted by her elder daughters, she takes care of virtually all domestic chores. Children are expected to obey both their parents and their elder siblings, and as they grow older they assume an increasing share of the daily work. A six-year-old girl, for example, may be seen playing on the beach in complete charge of her infant siblings. As a girl approaches puberty, she spends more time with her mother and other mature women, from whom she learns female skills, but as she enters the childbearing years, she must remain in virtual seclusion until marriage. Very early in life, boys are given the responsibility of tending cattle; later they begin to accompany their fathers and other men on fishing trips in order to learn the lore and skills of manhood.

In some respects, the American pattern is not so different from this. The father's duty is to leave home each day to attend to his job, for which he is paid in wages or a salary; his earnings serve as the basic wealth of the family, and each family's budget is determined largely by the father's value on the labor market. Mother's work is to fix meals, care for the household, see to the needs of her children—the traditional housekeeping and child care duties. (She, too, often works for wages now, but more will be said about that later.) In the modern household, children have few chores to do; their work is primarily the daily task of attending school in preparation for the future.

In terms of the broad sweep of history, the role of children as full-time students is a new one of revolutionary proportions. But the most disruptive recent development in family life is the movement of women away from home to work for wages. The woman's work role is the most inadequately structured position in the modern family, since women—especially the ones who receive the most education—are not sure exactly how they should use their talents. If they choose to have full-time careers away from home, they will usually find that the opportunities open to them are considerably less appealing than those available to men. If, on the other hand, they turn to housework and child rearing, their work usually becomes less rewarding as they gain more experience in it. This is just the opposite of the career pattern of husbands in the middle classes; men usually reach a career peak only after the children have grown up and left home.

The confusion in the work role of women is reflected in a somewhat comparable confusion in the work role of girls. They compete with boys in school in the early years (and can surpass them more than half the time), but on reaching adolescence they pull back—and sometimes live to regret it. This reflects the career doubts of their mothers and of women in general. As a result, they do not choose the majors in college that could prepare them for the most rewarding adult careers.

The division of labor in the family traditionally separates work for men and women and creates sex tension in the process. The pattern still exists, but the most agonizing development in recent times is the marked confusion over what women should do. We are only slowly reforming the wife and mother role; to many observers, a high price is still paid by everybody —men, women, and children—in keeping women down (Bird 1968).

Authority Pattern. The most common authority arrangement is patriarchy, where the fathers (and older men in general) have the right to make the most important decisions (those affecting the overall operation of the family and the community at large). Fathers cannot always play the role that society says they should, however, and women have always proved adept at getting their own way in a "man's world." Nevertheless, the *ideal* in culture after culture has been for men to be wise and masterful, and they are expected to cultivate a personal style that reflects these qualities. The pattern is linked to their size and strength and to the fact that they are not encumbered by pregnancy and the burdens of infant care.

The size and strength advantages of men are neutralized somewhat by modern technology, however, and pregnancy no longer occupies such an enormous part of the lives of women, as we have seen. Therefore the patriarchal ideal persists primarily in hunting, fishing, and agricultural societies; it fades rapidly with industrialization. It is strongest in peasant societies: The Mexican family is a good example (Penalosa 1968).

Authority in the modern family is characterized by its sheer absence more than anything else. Nobody has any clear-cut right or mandate to be boss. Even the age advantage that parents inevitably hold over their children loses its significance when parents try to create a warm atmosphere at home and when they worry about inhibiting their children. They are bombarded with advice on child rearing, but even the experts disagree. The stress on democracy in politics is carried over into all aspects of life, and it is not surprising that the family itself (ideally) is democratic, nonauthoritarian, and permissive.

Since it is not considered wholly legitimate, authority in the contemporary family is wielded by whoever can get away with it. The strong person (and there is likely to be one, despite the fact that none is supposed to exist) may be father, mother, or even one of the children. But those who have authority wield it with more guilt now, because they do not receive strong social support. And those who must be submissive are likely to be resentful for the same reason. Being submissive and obedient are never virtues where democracy and equality are held up as ideals.

The decline of authority takes a particularly critical turn at the time of marriage for young couples. Where authority is based on age and kinship, children are either given little freedom in choosing mates, or they have few eligibles to choose from, or both (Freeman 1968). The authority of the family declines along with the power of age and kinship, and consequently new forms of dating, courtship, and romance are developed in industrial societies.

Placement Pattern

In virtually all societies the family confers a social position or status on its children, which is important both for society in general and for the particular child.

Socioeconomic Status. Which family the child is born into determines whether he is upper, middle, or lower class and, more specifically, what material goods he will have and what services will be made available to him. Wealthy families teach their children the culture of wealth just as poor families inure their children to poverty. Such differences are found in all societies, although the amount of difference is greater in some than others, and the relative number of people who are rich or poor will vary (Barber 1957).

Modern society differs from the past, in that it is no longer tolerable to be poor. In the past the great majority of people were poor; only in recent memory has poverty as such been considered a problem, that is, a form of community sickness. Growing up poor is now a much greater handicap because it disqualifies the child for success in the school system, making jobs much harder to find and keep later in life. Poor families often create a burden for the community at large, taking from the economic system more than they can give in return and contributing much less than they might if they could help their children to do well at school.

Family Reputation. The child takes the name of his parents and is judged, to some extent, by his family membership, especially in small communities. This pattern tends to break down as cities grow and as talent becomes more important than family status. Of course some families, especially those holding great wealth, still confer a reputation on their children. But the very emergence of a celebrity-conscious society, where masses of people constitute a market for the person who can perform some unusual feat, reduces the traditional reputation-conferring function of the family; celebrities often come from families of no previous distinction.

Special Traditions or Lore. Families continue to serve a *screening function* for their children by directing their attention toward some things and censoring or simply ignoring others. The Catholic family encourages its children to learn about Catholicism and systematically (although perhaps largely unconsciously) keeps them from learning other religious views. If parents enjoy classical music, their children will certainly have an opportunity to learn about it.

Probably the most significant differences among families in this regard are not caused by the family as much as by changes in the community itself, especially the growth of public school programs and mass communications. As the scope of formal education and the mass media grows, the family's ability to control what children learn or hear about is greatly reduced. Parents do attempt to influence the school curriculum, and they can try to control what their children read or see on television, but their efforts are not usually very effective.

This trend, like others that have been discussed, seems to be part of a more general pattern: Parents and kinsmen have less control over children than they once had. The business of transmitting culture from one generation to the next tends to become professionalized, and new procedures are introduced to determine how to train the incoming generation. In fact, a reaction to the basic trend has already set in (Kitsuse and Cicourel 1962); the objection is not that new patterns ignore the family (which Robert Morison [1967] and others suggest they should), but rather that these procedures are not always as effective, or as wise, or as scientific as they are intended to be. Nevertheless, the trend away from family controls is firmly established.

Family and Kinship Emphasis

It is very hard to measure people's subjective feelings about the family, hence our systematic knowledge in this area remains limited. One way of suggesting the range of possibilities is to ask this question: How does the person gain (or lose) esteem in his community by being (or not being) a member of a family? For example, it is common all over the world for the person who does not marry to forfeit some social status as a result, although he can usually compensate for this loss by accomplishments in other areas. People without families are not necessarily stigmatized, but they have to suffer through songs, movies, and casual remarks that constantly extol the pleasures of family life. There are pressures to marry, to remarry after divorce (remarriage seems to be a partial atonement for the "sin" of divorce), to have children, to be heterosexual rather than homosexual, and so forth.

Societies differ in the extent to which people without families can find aid and comfort in the community and also in whether they are allowed to compete with others for jobs and social rewards on an equal basis. Modern industrialism certainly rejects family standing per se as a qualification for important careers, although a family scandal can still ruin a man's chances in some kinds of work. This is most apparent in careers where a public image of morality and propriety is needed (as in politics, the ministry, banking and brokerage institutions, and so on).

Perhaps the most important question does not concern the degree of familism found in a culture, which would be very hard to measure in any case, but the extent to which familism is consistent with other leading social themes. For example, the family receives as much attention in the United States as any other institution, and it does not ordinarily create conflicts with leading religious values. Despite the fact that family values do not conflict with private enterprise, they are deeply at odds with certain trends toward the welfare state and equal opportunities for children. Some of our most progressive social goals can only be achieved by relaxing traditional family values, such as those that urge each family to guard its wealth in jealous competition with all other families and therefore to become blind to the general good. We still operate largely in terms of Adam Smith's theories about the virtues of competitive striving: If each family will look after its own members and actively seek what is to their advantage, the "invisible hand" of competition will assure that all families will be better off. But this idea is in conflict with almost every attempt to solve urban problems through community efforts (whether governmental, philanthropic, or profit-seeking) above the family level.

THE IRREDUCIBLES OF FAMILY LIFE

The essential conditions of a human family system have already been mentioned in our discussion of composition, spatial arrangement, division of labor, placement pattern, and kinship emphasis.

But what are the conditions that make these irreducible features possible? Could an intelligent creature on some other planet have a family system essentially like our own? How would we identify it?

Symbolic Language

The first requirement would seem to be the existence of a species capable of using symbols—one that can create meaning and project its creative imagination onto its surroundings (White 1959). This is something no other earthbound species besides man has been able to do as far as we know, and hence none has a family system that is truly human in form. We often project human values and motives onto other animals, especially dogs; and we like to act as if they can think in terms of human language, but the fact remains that they cannot enter the realm of semantics and ideas.

Any species capable of symbolic behavior would have the ability to create a human kind of language; its vocabulary could be infinitely expanded. Words (symbols) could be mixed in any imaginable combination, and hence anything members of the species could think of—real or unreal, true or false—could be communicated to others.

Language as such does not make family life inevitable, but only with it can kinship in the social sense be created. It becomes possible to invent words for mother, father, uncle, brother, or nephew without which the human family is not possible. Other species cannot know their uncles, or even their fathers in most cases (although the mother may be identified by an imprinting process, which remains somewhat mysterious to this day). Man can know his kinsmen because he creates symbols to identify and stereotype them. Nobody knows what the first human words may have been—distinguished from the *calls* of primates such as the chimpanzee and gibbon—but it seems likely that *kinship terms* appeared very early in human evolution. These would certainly be among the first words dealing specifically with the man-made social order, and only after such an order was created could human survival be assured.

It is quite possible that a word for father may have been even more crucial than that for mother, despite the fact that mother-child bonds are stronger than father-child bonds among all mammals, including man. That is why the invention of the *social* father and a word to designate him was so crucial; fatherhood in the human sense of the term had to be a social creation. The role of father, after pregnancy, is in no way dictated by instincts, hormonal pressures, or physiological imperatives. Among primates, other than humans, most adult males have virtually no role in the care of children except when they guard the troop against predators. They share food with neither the females nor the infants and juveniles. Only human males work cooperatively with women to ensure the feeding of children, and it is plausible that the *idea* of a social father—a father who will help mother take care of infants and children—had to be created early in the evolution of a human type of species. If it had not been, Homo sapiens could never have evolved and thrived. The basis for the creation of such a role was the evolutionary development of a species capable of symbolic language.

Incest Taboos

One other feature of the human family is so universal and so essential to man's survival that it would seem to qualify as one of the irreducibles. This is the *incest taboo*. Without such a taboo, it is difficult to imagine a human family system at all. In all human cultures rules against sex and marriage between members of the immediate family (other than between mother and father) are sharply enforced.

The one taboo that is most carefully guarded is the prohibition against mating between mother and son; nowhere is that permitted (and hence tales of incest between mothers and sons are almost always the most obscene tales that can be told). Men must be willing to assume responsibilities toward their families, of course, and the mother-son taboo helps immeasurably in solidifying the social obligations of the father. Father-daughter mating is usually forbidden, although it is condoned under certain rare circumstances. This is also true for brother-sister mating (Middleton 1962). These exceptions usually occur in upper-class or elite segments of the population. There seems to be some truth to John Updike's (1969) observation that incest is the sexual sin of the aristocracy; adultery is for the middle classes, and rape is for the mob. Extensions of the incest taboos to kinsmen outside the immediate family are found in all cultures, but they are not guarded so closely.

The mystery surrounding these taboos has never been fully unraveled, but there is a satisfactory general explanation—and it is not based on physiological or instinctive grounds alone. The basic explanation for incest taboos runs along this line: Father is the weak link in the human family system; he is needed in the vast majority of families if they are to work well, but there are many reasons why men might wish to defect. One appeal, certainly not the only one, holding father to his obligations is sex attraction to his wife. This particular lure becomes much more powerful if there are strong taboos within the family limiting the woman's sex interest to her husband. Quite obviously taboos against adultery serve a similar purpose, but sex rivalry within the family would be even more disruptive than rivalries from outside (which may help to explain why societies virtually never use sex attraction for daughters as an added means of holding fathers to their families).

We should not get the idea that early man was wise enough to recognize the social importance of incest taboos or that women promise fidelity simply to keep their husbands. The necessity of the taboo for family survival was by no means apparent to nonliterate tribes, and its function is debatable to this very day. But any group that did not hit upon it would simply fail to meet the minimum level of social cooperation needed for group survival (Mead 1953; Sahlins 1959).

In fact, its function in holding father within the family is only one part of the taboo's social importance. By also forbidding father-daughter and brother-sister mating, it helps to eliminate *all* sex rivalry within the family. Some writers, however, claim that incest becomes difficult mainly *because* family members learn to cooperate with one another. Allan Coult (1963) suggests that most people avoid incestuous mating because they fear the role strain it would cause. It is simply too difficult to adjust in marriage to a person with whom you have already learned to adjust in a distinctly nonmarital way. After learning to interact with a person in an intense relationship such as that found in the family, it is almost impossible to establish a radically different relationship with that same person (Catton 1969).

But the incest taboos have still other uses. Since siblings and parents are ruled out as sex partners, children must seek mates from other families. The need to marry outside one's household creates strong ties among families, thus enlarging the scope of the family network and expanding the range of kinship cooperation. Over time, the incest taboos create a great circle of kinsmen who become more willing to join together for the common good. Thus, the taboos serve as an *associative mechanism* cementing relatively small groups together within larger communities, as Yonina Talmon (1964) has shown in a study of mate selection in Israel.

One final use for these taboos is worth noting, although it has been the subject of much controversy: their genetic, or eugenic, function. Incestuous inbreeding would magnify any biological weakness existing in the breeding group, which could be fatal—especially in a small, slow-breeding, late-maturing population such as Homo sapiens (Aberle *et al.* 1964). Undoubtedly early man had no knowledge or understanding of this fact, nor could he have understood the other uses that have been attributed to incest taboos. Nevertheless, since he could use symbols in a creative way, it was quite possible that the idea of restricting incest occurred quite frequently. It is certainly an ancient idea (by no means an invention of the classic civilizations of the Middle East, for example). Some early hunting and gathering bands may not have enforced incest taboos, but, as already indicated, these groups did not last very long and we have no record of them. The incest taboos are placed among the irreducibles for one crucial reason: Without them it is very doubtful that man could have survived.

Three basic elements in the human family have been defined: (1) the existence of a symbol-using species, (2) the development of a language for family membership and obligation (especially obligating the father; mother could be counted on to a much greater extent because of her mammalian female physiology), and (3) the creation of incest taboos that restrict sex rivalry within the family, extend the family circle, and reduce the potential ill effects of genetic inbreeding.

DUET OR TRIO?

The role of the father in the human family seems to be a crucial one, but an intriguing—and conflicting—point of view has been expressed by Richard Adams (1960). He argues that the nuclear family consists of three pair relationships or *dyads:* the mother-father or *conjugal* dyad, the mother-child or *maternal* dyad, and the father-child or *paternal* dyad. Adams claims that the real core of any family system is the maternal dyad, linking mother and child. The mother-father pair sometimes amounts to little more than occasional sex relations, and the father-child relationship does not even exist to any appreciable extent in many families. He cites communities in Central America, for example, where women head almost 40 percent of the households and where adult males often have a secondary role in the family or none at all except for sex relations. He contends that the prevalence of female-headed households in Central America is not a confused and random pattern. It is a standard part of the *Ladino* culture, mixing Spanish and Indian traditions, and it is concentrated in certain regions. He concludes that the nuclear family, with a stable father figure in addition to mother and child, is neither universal nor absolutely necessary for the stability and survival of human society.

Although one may question whether the adult males in these Central American communities are as free from family obligations as Adams claims they are, they certainly do not live in the family household as fathers are ordinarily expected to do. Nevertheless, it is worth noting that even in the most mother-centered of these communities more than half of the households are headed by fathers, and they are the men who have gained high status.

Adams, referring to research done by Raymond T. Smith (1957), observes that woman-headed households are most likely to be found in places where large numbers of men are poor. This, of course, is a condition known in the black ghettoes of American cities, where black men face economic discrimination, and the household is often headed by a woman. It is no random pattern; this arrangement is a practical adjustment to the ghetto culture. It is not regarded as an ideal situation, however, and it is questionable whether the term "social stability" applies to the family that results. Many people contend that the absence of a father creates serious problems for both the mother and the child and indeed for the entire black community (Rainwater 1965).

But an even stronger criticism can be leveled against Adams' argument. How can we explain the fact that in no society are women-headed households in the majority? Or, carrying this question a step further: Why is it that in no society are almost *all* households headed by women? This would be somewhat like the pattern found among other mammalian species where the male role is simply to supply sperm during the reproductive process. Then he fends for himself, serving only to ward off predators (if he has any troop duties at all). There is no evidence of the existence of such a society among human beings. The fact is that although not every household in a stable, flourishing community has to have an active male member, the majority do seem to need such a father figure. Households that are organized around a father-mother combination supply an essential basis for social order. Families headed by women can then function reasonably well, but only because they are part of a larger community in which fathers perform absolutely essential services.

Adams stresses the mother-child dyad as the basic unit in society rather than the nuclear family. But if he is wrong, and the nuclear family is the core social unit, then the key arrangement is a trio—consisting of mother, father, and child—not a dyad. In fact, it is difficult to accept the idea that the family needs to be subdivided into pairs as the best way to explain its elementary relations. The social unity of mother-father-child is actually a three-sided affair, and relations between mother and child are not isolated from mother-father and father-child interaction. When a mother deals with her children, she takes the father's interests and wishes into account. It seems likely, for example, that mothers who have pleasant relations with their husbands can be more relaxed and confident in relations with their children. Not only are they and the children better off, society is, too.

SUMMARY

Man has a complex biological, psychological, and sociological nature which enables him to survive in a great variety of ways. But he always uses symbols to identify members of his family and to define their obligations. And he always establishes incest taboos to control sexual rivalry within the family, to extend his circle of cooperating kinsmen, and to control the possible ill effects of inbreeding. Above all, the human family takes a giant step beyond the "family" life of nonhuman primates by creating a *social* father (as distinguished from the *biological* father). A range of duties are designated for the father to perform, thus creating the nuclear trio of mother, father, and child.

There are five basic features of the human family. In terms of composition, it varies in size, in the designation of key members, in its age make-up, and in its gene pool. The American family, for example, tends to be small, monogamous, intact insofar as key members are concerned, and relatively undispersed in the ages of its members. It is slowly moving toward greater genetic variety. Each of these traits can be contrasted with comparable ones in other countries. But the American pattern is no random collection of characteristics. Each is molded through interaction with the others and by the major social pressures in American life.

Trends in the spatial arrangement of the family parallel trends in its composition. Although there is now less space between American homes than in the past, each family member tends to have more room inside the home, affording greater privacy for both children and the married couple. Kinsmen, on the other hand, are now widely scattered. This is different from arrangements in most other parts of the world, but it is consistent with general trends in American family and social life.

The most unique features of the American family's division of labor is the work assigned to children—virtually all of them go to school for ten to fifteen years—and the most troublesome new development is the confused work role of women. Family authority is also in a state of confusion, since no member of the American household has a clear-cut right to be boss. Ambiguity at home is reflected in general uncertainty about authority in the culture at large. Such a pattern seems to be workable only in a small family system which places little emphasis on kinship obligations but gets its work done through large organizations.

The placement function of the family is also linked to characteristics of society at large. The family continues to pass its social status on to children, a perilous arrangement for low-income families. But urban families tend to be anonymous, so only rarely do children have any family reputation in the community.

Parents still have opportunities to teach various things to their children and to screen certain ideas out. But even here the family has to compete with many new sources of information that reach children whether their parents approve or not.

Patterns of family belief and ideology are deeply imbedded in the cultural practices of every community. But people who flout conventional family customs are much less likely to be censured today than was true in nonliterate, peasant, or small-town agricultural communities.

SELECTED READINGS

ADAMS, RICHARD N. "An Inquiry into the Nature of the Family," in Gertrude Dole and Robert L. Carneiro (eds.), *Essays in the Science of Culture: In Honor of Leslie A. White*. New York: Thomas Y. Crowell, 1960, pp. 30–49.

FREEMAN, LINTON C. "Marriage Without Love: Mate-Selection in Non-Western Societies," in Robert F. Winch and Louis Wolf Goodman (eds.), *Selected Studies in Marriage and the Family*. New York: Holt, Rinehart and Winston, 1968, pp. 456–468.

GLICK, PAUL C., AND ROBERT PARKE, JR. "New Approaches in Studying the Life Cycle of the Family," *Demography*, Vol. 2 (1965), pp. 187–202.

MURDOCK, GEORGE PETER. "World Ethnographic Sample," *American Anthropologist*, Vol. 59 (August 1957), pp. 664–687.

PARSONS, TALCOTT. "The Kinship System of the Contemporary United States," *American Anthropologist*, Vol. 45 (January–March 1943), pp. 22–38.

SPIRO, MELFORD E. "Is the Family Universal?" *American Anthropologist*, Vol. 56 (October 1954), pp. 839–846.

CHAPTER 17

The Future of the Family

The twentieth century is three-fourths gone, and it has been a hectic era for the family. What about the next twenty-five years? Or the century to follow? Wars, technological revolutions, political upheavals will undoubtedly occur in response to issues and discoveries beyond the scope of our contemporary imagination and certainly beyond the reach of our current headlines. The future is so murky in a rapidly changing society that practical readers may feel it deserves no comment at all. Some people say we already suffer from *future shock*—a dizzying disorientation caused by social changes occurring so fast that the human mind cannot adjust (Toffler 1970).

But for many people family life provides a stable sanctuary in the midst of all the turbulence. Even the future of the family is debatable, however, primarily because it is subject to relatively little direct control or manipulation. We may anticipate increasing efforts to harness it, if for no other reason than to bring it into line with other areas that have been organized and tamed. Nathan Cohen and Maurice Connery (1967), after reviewing the role of government in this regard, argue for a much larger and more conscientious government role in planning family change, and they give good reasons for it.

But the family is not easy to govern. It is subject to no established techniques of legislative or administrative planning. Although its enormous value to society is recognized by everybody, the countless new laws passed each year rarely apply directly to it. Legislators attend to more pressing matters, influencing family life by their actions, but in indirect and largely unanticipated ways. Laws that may have a rather direct bearing on the family are usually introduced to right a wrong or to correct a clear-cut abuse, not to chart a whole new course in domestic life. In fact, the courts are usually more concerned with family needs than lawmakers are, but they are in no position to initiate new family customs. Thus, values and opinions that affect family life change for reasons that are very poorly understood, and they do not ordinarily change very much from one generation to the next. Not even a dictator in the most authoritarian society is powerful or wise enough at the present time to change family habits to satisfy his own wishes.

Therefore, projections for the future can only be based on (1) trends already established, (2) general developments in culture that seem very likely to affect the family (study of which is becoming more disciplined than it was in the past, led by "futurologists" like Daniel Bell [1968] and Herman Kahn [1967]), and (3) proposals for change or reform that have been expressed often and loud enough to actually be influential.

Just how fast the family is changing is open to question. Ivan Nye (1967) claims that science is now making more of an impact on domestic life than ever before. He says that a speed-up in family change is inevitable as rapid changes hit other parts of society. In 1950, Kingsley Davis argued that marriage, divorce, and reproduction were already quick to respond to new conditions; he claimed that a *major* revolution had occurred in the first half of the twentieth century. But it does not seem that a similar revolution has yet materialized in the second half of this century. It is possible that we exaggerate change, seeing "revolutions" where there are really only ripples and trends. We get so accustomed to speaking about rapid change that we underestimate how stable society really is. At the same time, we look for reasons for change rather than for the forces underlying constancy.

FAMILY PLANNING

One trend is not exaggerated, however. Increased family planning is a fact, and its most fully documented consequence is a decline in the birth rate. But this may not prove to be its most significant effect in the decades to come. We can look forward to a nation where family life is much more rational, where family planning is completely accepted, and where children can be absolutely assured of the right to be wanted.

Population Control

There is continuing concern about the birth rate when we talk about world population trends. Broadly speaking, two contradictory ideas have gained popularity, both of which have been seized by science fiction writers (Kenkel 1969). The premise of one group is that the human race may never be able to solve its population problems. Death rates will continue to decline more quickly than birth rates, and people will multipy beyond our powers of sensible regulation. Billions of people will inhabit the globe, suffering horrendous consequences. A related assumption is that, although the long-term trend is toward smaller families, it still lags behind the ever increasing *need* for small families, so that population problems will become more and more disastrous.

The alternative assumption is that mankind can harness the birth rate to its better interests. The authorities are not this optimistic, but it is difficult to generate popular national concern about the world's birth rate. Certainly adequate family planning must inevitably mean more than the use of birth control by affluent middle-class parents. It must include planning by virtually all married couples, with active social agencies on hand to help, not just when asked, but in an aggressive, almost belligerent way. Young people should be expected to learn the philosophy and strategies of family planning—*responsible parenthood*—as a matter of course. All this should take place in school even before they enter courtship (as we expect teen-agers to learn to drive before they get a driver's license). We should expect *explicit* information to be spread through the mass media— especially television and the newspapers—and much more open, hard-sell appeals by advertisers of contraceptives.

Unfortunately, the concept of responsible parenthood is just developing. William Kenkel (1969) has reviewed its course so far. At first, he claims, it had a strong economic emphasis. The argument was that couples should have no more children than they could feed, house, and support. Later the idea was enlarged to include their ability to meet the emotional needs of children and to provide a good social environment. Only recently, and still only rarely, has it been enlarged still further to include responsibility to the larger community. Rarer still is concern for the optimum size of the population instead of the maximum size. Kenkel claims that there is a need for the broadest possible concept of family planning and for efforts to introduce it into the thinking of *all* citizens. In fact, we can expect the growth of social agencies for just this purpose.

The Right To Have Children

Kenkel did not put *genetic* planning into his concept of responsible parenthood, but we should expect greater interest in this area and maybe stronger controls over the right to have children. In Chapter 8 it was suggested that the day may soon come when marriage licenses will require more than the blood tests found in most states. Biologists have already called attention to various problems in store for the offspring of genetically mismatched marriages.

We hear more and more people plugging for two stages in family formation—one in which couples marry and show evidence of their ability to live together in harmony, the second where they bear children, but only after proving their compatibility (Mead 1966). When concern turns to the question of qualifications for parenthood, *marriage* is not so much at issue as the *family* it will create. It would certainly be possible to distinguish between the legal right of couples to live together in marriage and their right to have children.

When that time comes, the social and psychological considerations involved in family planning may prove to be even more important than genetic matters. Although genetic counseling has made great progress in recent years and is now available in all the major metropolitan centers, marriage counseling at the social and psychological levels has an even longer and more fundamental record of service.

It is not likely, however, that a legal distinction between the right to marry and the right to have children will be made in the very near future. Despite the ease of making such a distinction, it represents one of the most radical departures from traditional family customs imaginable. Politically, it has no chance at the moment.

Furthermore, in the Western nations where the most progressive attitudes toward family relations have been pioneered, as in the Scandinavian countries, mutual living arrangements by young couples have become very informal. In Sweden, for example, there has been a marked tendency for young couples to live together without any formal wedding ceremony. In a high proportion of cases, marriage occurs only after the woman becomes pregnant. Neither premarital sex nor premarital pregnancy carry the stigma they once did, so there is no public outcry. The new attitude seems to be that people have a right to pair off and live together as they choose, without legal controls. This is the right of free, mutual association. Only with childbirth and the need to protect the rights of immature infants do legal controls become inescapable.

This means that relatively little attention is given to family planning before the birth of the first child. Planning can assume an important role later, but the first baby comes very soon after the partners start living together, sometimes when they are still quite young. Neither genetic nor premarital counseling is likely to be part of this pattern, so at least some of the advantages of family planning are by-passed. (Nevertheless, it was calculated that only one birth occurred for every 1,100 sex episodes during a month's study period in Sweden in 1967, because contraceptives were so frequently used [Moskin 1969].) We can assume that the trend toward more liberal abortion laws will continue and that "compulsory pregnancy" (as Garrett Hardin [1968] calls it) will be virtually abolished.

Consequences of Family Planning

No matter how the preparenthood phase of married life is managed, family planning becomes routine in most middle-class homes after one or two babies are born, and it takes the form of deciding whether or not to have a third or fourth child. The decision *not* to have a fourth (or more) is very common, and even the third child is vetoed by more and more couples. The evidence is not yet overwhelming, but everything available suggests that for couples who plan, the higher their social status, the more children they have. Historically, poor people have had the most children. But when they plan, they break the longstanding pattern.

This has staggering social implications. If it really takes hold, we can expect big changes. In the first place, it would mean that parents in the lower classes would have fewer children to care for than in the middle classes—they have traditionally had more—so their resources would more nearly cover their obligations. In effect, lower-class children would have a better chance to compete with those in the middle classes. In fact, planned children have relatively equal opportunities because of the social and psychological qualities that go with planning as a way of life.

The possibility of success in interclass competition was rarely even considered in the past. This was but one part of the larger pattern; parents had children "when the gods decreed" and their destiny was presumed to be part of this inscrutable plan. Human choice had very little to do with it (except in a negative way, since it was sometimes argued that they had yielded to temptation and therefore had to suffer the consequences of sin and indolence).

We can predict that as planning takes over, fewer children will be put up for adoption. Most adopted children at the present time are originally unwanted and unplanned. Indeed, we can see the day when hardly any children will be available for adoption proceedings. Perhaps this will lead to even greater research in the area of nonfertility and underfertility, since many couples now turn to adoption without exploring all the possible ways of correcting their own fertility problems.

Actually, a drop in the number of children up for adoption may have no important effect on child rearing, since adopted children are certainly wanted by the parents who take them in modern society. The care these parents give is at least as diligent and loving as the kind that natural parents give, so these children have a better chance to compete with other children than stepchildren used to have.

Another reason why stepparenthood is not what it used to be is that there are so few ways to exploit children in modern society. The major continuing problem is that in the lowest classes, where children are least likely to be planned, they are also least likely to be put up for adoption (Jeffery 1962). Where incomes are higher—precisely where planning is most likely to occur—there are strong pressures to place children for adoption when planning breaks down. Thus, the middle-class single girl who becomes pregnant is more likely than the poor girl to give her baby up for adoption. The child of the poor girl will probably be reared by her mother or relatives with sporadic help from the girl herself. The middle-class girl's child will be adopted by a couple meeting middle-class standards, so the child will not be handicapped. In fact, adoption has the effect of erasing the stigma of illegitimacy. So once again the greatest gain to be made by better family planning is in the lower social classes.

Community welfare services would also profit from family planning. Many of them are now designed to meet the needs of families that cannot care for their children adequately. If these families had only as many children as they could reasonably support, the burdens of the welfare agencies could be eased. This does not mean that such agencies would be phased out of existence, but that they could turn their efforts to other matters. Rather than dealing with problems of sheer survival, which is what they usually do now, they could turn their attention to lifting the general level of family life above the basic survival point.

Generally, family planning holds extraordinary promise for the future, assuming that trends move ahead in their current course. It is tempting to think that universal planning, where every child is wanted, would be the magic solution to all our problems. That, of course, is not so; family planning cannot possibly be overestimated, but it is still no cure-all.

One questionable side effect, for example, has to be watched. If almost all children were planned, hence endowed with more equal opportunity, we should expect greater competition among them than has ever existed before. One reason why children of upper-middle-class status usually do so well at school is that they have an initial advantage. Their life at home is well suited to the demands made upon them at school. Because they do well at school, they get the best jobs when they graduate. But as children from lower social levels learn to compete (which is also fostered by efforts to make the school system more effective in reaching them), we should expect youth from the middle classes to try even harder. And their parents will probably put a little extra pressure on them. Meanwhile, both parents and children in the lower classes, sensing that they have a chance, will probably make a real effort, too.

As family planning becomes truly universal, we can expect the birth rate to fluctuate in a sensitive way from year to year, more so than in the past.

It already shows signs of unprecedented shiftiness. The American birth rate rose slightly while the last three chapters of this book were being written. It may turn down again before the final printing. Throughout most of man's history the fertility index has been consistently high; when it starts dropping in response to industrial growth, in most countries it falls about as low as it can go. Then it begins to fluctuate from year to year. Decisions are made by each new generation, based on many considerations, especially the typical age of couples at marriage and their attitudes toward having third and fourth children.

If for some reason having a third child becomes more popular, for example, the birth rate swings up. If there are reservations about having third children, it turns down. As yet we cannot be sure what determines the nation's "parental mood," but undoubtedly perceptions about the cost of rearing children and sensibilities to national and even international affairs are involved. It seems likely that the birth rate will become more and more sensitive to conceptions of the *quality* of family life among young adults. Any new note of pessimism will divert the birth rate to a lower course—temporarily. Then grounds for optimism will probably show up—but again only temporarily.

Some remarkable biological innovations could introduce entirely new considerations. Thus, if couples could pick the sex of their offspring—and they soon may be able to do just that—problems we never had before will have to be faced. There might be an imbalance in the ratio of the sexes at birth, followed by hasty, no doubt clumsy, bureaucratic efforts to regulate the process. Edward Pohlman (1967) figures that the ability to control the child's sex would lead to a reduced birth rate, because if the couple preferred to have children of both sexes, which is very often the case, they could reach their goal in exactly two pregnancies. Now it often takes three or more tries to get that result. But what if most couples want boys, or if some couples want certain combinations of boys and girls, or several children of one sex for special reasons? Would there be fads and fashions in birth planning? Problems of managing the sex ratio in a society with highly effective contraception plus the ability to choose the sex of each child stuns the imagination.

MERITOCRACY

A society generating strong competition among children across class lines for the rewards of an affluent society is a meritocracy—a society where people actually reach the level of achievement they deserve (Young 1959). It may prove to be an anxiety-ridden place for both parents and children. We already face a reaction to pressures inherent in this kind of society, especially among bright but alienated college students. They often come from middle- or upper-middle-class backgrounds where they grew up under relentless pressures to succeed. To many, the rewards do not seem to be worth the effort. No similar reaction from the lower classes has yet appeared on a broad scale. They are still striving for the right to compete on an equal basis. Only when that right has been fully guaranteed and competition is heated-up still more will we see the mass reaction.

But for the great range of middle-class children the school system is a competitive arena where those who do best are doubly rewarded: They are honored while they attend school, and they continue to receive larger pay checks and bigger expense accounts throughout life. The school system selects and channels. Any child who meets its requirements with distinction is paid off with thirty or forty years of high and rising income. In a lifetime he can earn anywhere from $100,000 to $500,000 more than the slow or merely average student. A boy who wants to be a medical doctor, for example, has to get into medical school, and without high marks in college he can forget it. But in order to do well in college he has to lay a solid foundation in the secondary schools, and he will do better there if he has pleased his teachers at the elementary level. With help from home his initial advantage improves with each passing year.

But now more than ever we stress equal opportunity, which calls for an end to all family-linked advantages. Charles Hobart (1963), among many others, has called the decline of the family's power to determine its children's status—that is, to transmit high or low status from one generation to the next—one of the most powerful forces in the world today. In particular, it goes with the growth of corporations and federal civil service as distinguished from small business enterprise, especially for technical jobs and in the middle levels of management. Not only do big organizations have to base their salary and promotion standards on a merit system to a greater extent than in smaller firms, but the life styles they encourage implicitly tend to stress merit. For instance, people who work in them seem to be more likely to hold *themselves* accountable for their level of achievement than do people employed in smaller businesses. The latter, according to a study of Joel Nelson (1968), shift the blame; they are prone to explain lack of personal success by forces outside themselves.

It is not surprising that contemporary parents see the report card as a projective index of their children's future. Everything is recorded—failures as well as successes—and it becomes harder and harder to rationalize failure except on the basis of incompetence or poor health. Many parents are forced to search for some kind of failure in themselves if their children fall behind at school. Certainly the ones whose children succeed feel a sense of personal pride and accomplishment.

But what does all this "drivenness" do to the quality of family life? What happens to family cohesion? Or the mutual ego support function of the family? As yet we cannot be sure, but the one assumption that *seems* safe is that competitiveness within the school system will become more intense, not less, and that a larger percentage of all children will be thrown into competition on an even footing. It is possible, of course, that even this assumption may prove wrong. At the time of this writing some black parents want the schools to produce not just equal opportunity, but *equal attainment*. This is a denial of meritocratic assumptions, but the demand is understandable in the light of current pressures to make up for lost time in the area of racial equality.

One possible reaction to increased competition is to drop out entirely. A variety of observers have claimed that more and more young people are doing just that (Keniston 1969). They claim that worldly success is meaningless in an imperfect world and become wanderers or protesters, in some cases turning to voluntary poverty. The ones who legitimately fall into this category are those who have shown that they can succeed in the school system if they want to. Some dropouts cannot, but many in fact can.

There is not much to suggest that parents of the legitimate dropouts are enthusiastic about their course of action, although they may be more sympathetic than one would think. Charles Hobart (1963) claims that the family serves as a basic humanizing influence in the midst of current trends. If this is true, parents might be expected to offer shelter to youth who rebel against the system. Still, we might wonder whether modern parents are any more protective in such matters than parents have been in the past.

Let us assume for the moment that the long-term trend is toward greater competitiveness among children and that most of them do not hold out against the system. They gripe about it, but they still persevere in the main task assigned to modern youth—going to school and striving to rank as high in their class as their talents will allow. We should expect parents with gifted children to want them to move rapidly ahead and to be rewarded for their efforts. Parents with average children will push, too, but gradually accept the fact that their children are not really exceptional. How parents in a competitive society will act when their children are inept is not so easy to predict, but in most cases they, too, can be expected to resign themselves to reality. Bear in mind that even children who do rather poorly at school can still do reasonably well in an affluent society, if they do not get totally discouraged and quit.

Maybe in the next decade or so we can work out better ways of spotting each child's potential, so that parents can have a more realistic idea of what to expect. Mental ability tests have taken root already and help to set parental and teacher expectations for particular children. Perhaps parents who have some kind of scientific basis for thinking that their children are gifted can be counted on to demand more of them, and those that have reason to expect only mediocre performance may learn to make the best of it. The possibilities for misuse of such information are obvious, too. In fact, the use of such devices by the family is an extremely hit-or-miss matter right now. Teachers often know things that parents do not know, and many prefer to keep this information to themselves.

We can hope that better ways will be devised to help parents cope with their children's aptitudes. Having invented ways to measure such things, we would like to know how to react in the most useful and humane ways. Most of the energy has been spent making new and better tests, with no corresponding concern for how to put them to use by the family.

In an interesting switch, Otto Pollak (1967) sees a new function for the family—defense of its own integrity against experts in the field of education, health care, and public welfare. He argues that the most regrettable loss experienced by the family in recent years is the loss of the ability to set its own standards. The idea that mother and father know as much (or maybe more) than the experts is an interesting point of view, though not really new. It has long been voiced by parents and by some of the experts themselves. Pollak enters a plea for coordination, or "orchestration," of the family with all these outside agencies that are now so active.

The point of this discussion of meritocracy is to suggest two things: (1) that meritocracy does have implications for the family, and (2) that these implications have tended to go unnoticed. As the pressures of competition among children and youth are tightened, it is helpful for parents to explore the available alternatives with their offspring. Guidance in such matters may be handled increasingly by school counselors and the peer group itself, but it does seem that a vital family system would attempt to play a major role in the process.

SELF-KNOWLEDGE

Family planning and meritocracy are tied up with a third trend: increased self-knowledge. We are said to live in an age of psychology, so modern couples bring more knowledge about personality into marriage than ever before. They also know more about interpersonal, group, and family dynamics. As our understanding expands, it seems safe to presume that we become more self-conscious about our family performance.

Being a good parent, for example, is no longer viewed as an innate expression or property of sex, as when it was assumed that women would be good mothers simply because they were women (so long as they did not willfully defy their instincts) and that men would be good fathers (maybe just a little undependable) simply because they were men. Now we see parenthood as a challenge to be mastered only by learning how, and even then we have to keep working at it. Some people deplore this trend, yearning for the good old days when men and women simply did what came naturally. One of the attractions of Dr. Spock's book (1954) for parents is that it is not terribly demanding. Be that as it may, the trend is toward a more self-conscious kind of parenthood, with an effort to find new, workable solutions to very real problems.

But this can only mean that some people may not be qualified for parenthood or may simply have the wrong background for it. If we carry this only a little further, we face the issue of setting minimum requirements for the rights to rear children. As already noted, the popular reaction to this is strong and visceral indeed. And yet we seem to be pushing toward it on a voluntary basis anyway. In an age of unprecedented ego sensitivity, more than a few people voluntarily admit that they are unsuited for parenthood. The only thing unusual about this is that it developed so slowly. It emerges as a new kind of personal disqualification, rarely met in history before.

It seems that people are more self-conscious about themselves as husbands and wives than before. The mass media is filled with advice on how to do better, and it repeatedly implies that most of us have a lot to learn. The idea that many couples fail in the area of communications keeps popping up, and there is no shortage of advice on how to correct this fault. In actual fact we are still in the embryonic stage when it comes to domestic self-improvement. That couples ought to try harder is commonly acknowledged, but the kind of advice they get is still nonscientific for the most part. We accept the idea that drugs and medicines must be rigorously tested for direct effectiveness and the absence of side effects before they can be put on the market, but behavioral advice can be—and is—given freely by anyone, and there is virtually no such thing as malpractice in its use.

As a somewhat retarded development in the age of psychology, people seem to have become more concerned about their family performance and more aware of the cultural and social alternatives available to them. The process continues, and its most intensive growth undoubtedly lies in the future, as bright young men and women turn to careers in the family service fields. A number of years ago Nelson Foote and Leonard Cottrell, Jr. (1955), talked about *interpersonal competence*, claiming that better skills in this area require knowledge, training, and constant application. This point of view stands as a basic premise among students of the family, and it is now being popularized. In the next quarter of a century we may expect better training for close personal relationships—as distinguished from training for jobs, which schools now stress. Bureaucratic competence may still be a backward area, too, but the marshaling of resources to improve it is enormous compared to what we have yet done for interpersonal competence.

THE RECONSTRUCTION OF SEX ROLES

We have talked about *masculinization* and *feminization*: one set of learning experiences for boys, another for girls. We used to think that these were dictated by instinct, and so little attention was paid them by researchers and philosophers. Now we know that they vary from place to place and respond with remarkable sensitivity to changing social conditions.

A great tangle of forces has conspired to make growing up male and growing up female much more similar than they used to be. If anything, we now exaggerate their similarities, losing sight of the deep, persistent differences that still exist. Of course the processes do overlap to a greater extent, since boys and girls now have many identical experiences and social pressures as they grow up. This was discussed in Chapter 3, but three areas of similarity were not stressed at that time: (1) new forms of personal identity for children, (2) new ways of preparing for adult sex roles, and (3) sharper competition between the sexes.

Identification

Historically, girls have identified with older girls and women, looking to them as models to be respected and emulated. Little girls have always admired men, but they have rarely been expected to identify with them or to think of them as models for their own behavior. In fact, the overwhelming majority of girls have always been satisfied to stay close to their mothers in day-to-day behavior, becoming very much like them in the process. Boys identify strongly with their mothers in the early years of life, too, due to close physical contact and extreme personal dependence, but they gradually shift attention to fathers, older boys, and men in general.

These traditional patterns are now changing, especially among girls. They still identify with older females for the most part, but men are coming into view in a new way, and the female models are themselves doing remarkable things. The masculine models are usually teachers and counselors in high school and college or perhaps television figures. Elizabeth Almquist and Shirley Angrist (1970b) found that college women with strong career aspirations were considerably more likely to have been influenced by college professors than the non-career women in their sample, and many of these professors were undoubtedly male.

And yet there is no reason to believe that contemporary boys in the preadolescent or adolescent stages of life are strongly attracted to women as personal models. It is possible that they stay under the thumb of women longer now than in the past, especially in the period from about age ten to fourteen or fifteen—a period during which boys used to begin working closely with grown men. Now they stay in school, and women still predominate as teachers at this time. Men take over in the middle and later stages of adolescence, at the very time when the academic achievements of boys usually begin to equal or exceed those for girls and when boys typically begin to identify with their favorite male instructors.

Preparation for Adult Sex Roles

In preparation for adult sex roles, masculinization and feminization have converged in the most striking, even revolutionary, ways. Historically, girls have prepared almost solely for the standard roles of wife and mother. Boys have had a little more choice, but mainly their work has taken them out of the immediate household. Girls were under pressure to meet a set of stereotypes based on housework and child care. But all current signs point away from home. Most elementary-school girls now say that they want careers—positions away from home comparable to those available to boys (though they are still unimpressed by most blue-collar occupations).

We can only speculate about the social-psychological forces churning away in this changing pattern, but it is obvious that girls are finding a taste for careers that were once closed to them. Whom do they identify with when they say that they want to be doctors or lawyers, for example? What specific individuals catch their eye—and their imagination? In most cases, girls still identify with women, and they choose traditional female career patterns for which there are many female models. This is most common because it is still the easiest solution to a girl's career dilemma. Many male occupations are virtually invisible to girls precisely because they tend to see what other *women* are doing rather than what the men are up to.

But since girls now show a desire for careers in areas once closed to them, they must certainly learn about them and become interested in them in new ways. Does the modern girl who wants to be a lawyer identify with a male model, somehow transposing the man's role into a female pattern in her own imagination? Or is she more likely to know or have seen a woman attorney whose life style captured her imagination?

Apparently modern girls are increasingly attracted to the relatively few women who go into areas dominated by men. At the same time, the average woman is less likely to be in a traditional female role; she is more likely to be *both* a mother and a career woman. The first requirement is not likely to be dropped in the near future, but the woman who "makes it" in a male stronghold is clearly the prototype for the brightest and most highly motivated teen-age girls today, and the trend is toward more of the same.

Competition Between the Sexes

As a result of changing sex roles, boys and girls now compete with each other to a much greater extent as they grow up. This happens mainly in the classroom, but it is just this academic competition that has set the trend for other aspects of child behavior. It is here that preparation for an exciting future can occur. Girls vie with boys for grades, and it seems almost certain that the more the sexes compete, the more alike they become.

Similarity shows up most clearly in standards of ideal behavior. To whatever extent both boys and girls strive to make high grades in class, they have no choice but to adopt similar ideas about what is good. In acquiring certain kinds of knowledge, for example, they not only learn the same things, but they also develop identical conceptions of what is worth learning. Similarity also shows up in the fact that girls and boys who compete in class must take each other seriously—explicitly as competitors and implicitly as individuals who are part of the same *reference group*. They begin to compare themselves with one another in terms of achievement and personal tastes. Quite obviously comparisons do not occur in all areas; boys and girls cannot compete on an equal basis in athletics, for example, at least not after the age of eight or nine. But they now compete in more areas than ever before, and that is no trivial innovation.

The most striking kind of competition affecting family life is the one that cuts into job opportunities. Elina Haavio-Mannila (1969) claims that the rising educational level of women and their greater participation in economic affairs have at least two important consequences: (1) The sexes are brought closer together outside the family; and (2) women begin to compete for the prize achieved statuses, instead of settling for the dependent status of wife to a prominent man. (On this last point, Arlie Hochschild's [1969] study of the role of the ambassador's wife is most interesting. By contrast, hardly anything has been written about the role of husband to a prominent woman.)

F. Ivan Nye (1967) predicts that we can expect six latent consequences of the trend toward equal economic opportunity for men and women:

1. The principal or only provider in an increasing number of families will be the wife, with the husband in some instances becoming housekeeper. (It is now well established that the more either partner takes part in affairs outside the family, the more power that person will have at home, other things being equal [Lupri 1969].)
2. As the wife's occupation makes more demands upon her time and underscores her financial independence, the divorce rate will continue to rise.
3. As the number of full-time homemakers drops, nurseries and day-care centers will be set up in ever greater numbers to care for their children.

4. Women will probably turn to sex patterns more nearly like those of men.
5. As exciting, or at least interesting, alternatives to child rearing come into view, the birth rate will fall until it reaches some rock-bottom level.
6. The age of women at marriage will probably increase as finishing college becomes more important to them.

John Edwards (1967) adds still another forecast—that further economic progress will have a repressive effect on the marriage rate. As women discover economic independence, marriage will lose some of its appeal. Their attraction to marriage has always been primarily economic, he claims, not domestic, nor even maternal in nature. He sees no alternative but that women will begin to regard economic dependence on husbands as a cowardly vice rather than a comfortable virtue and that more and more of them will say no to marriage. The need to say yes was a burden from which they could never really feel free before.

A few reservations with regard to these forecasts are in order. For one thing, economic equality between the sexes is easily exaggerated. Even in Finland, where the proportion of women at universities and colleges is one of the highest in the world and where women are more active away from home than in almost any other Western country, the income of working women is (on the average) only 59 percent that of men. They have jobs of generally lower prestige than men, and their number in leading positions is discouraging (Haavio-Mannila 1969).

Furthermore, the rate of marriage was never higher. This fact does not square with Edwards' prediction concerning the decline of marriage. It seems that an increasing percentage of wives work by choice rather than out of necessity; it is working out of necessity that has a depressive effect on marriage. In fact, Susan Orden and Norman Bradburn (1969) argue that an increase in the number of wives working in good jobs will have the effect of strengthening marriage for both sexes. It is even possible that the divorce rate will fall along with continued economic progress (Parke and Glick 1967), thus bringing into question one of Nye's predictions.

Feminization is still different from masculinization in key ways. Boys and girls still have distinctive personal identities, and they do not compete in *all* areas of human interest. The breadwinner ethic, with father as a main provider for his family, remains enormously powerful. Most girls are still taught to like it, despite its implications for economic dependence upon men (Benson 1968).

Implications for Mothering and Fathering

All these trends, of course, are tied in with the growth of an industrial-urban society. Industrial development has the effect of freeing women from housework and child care, upgrading their lives in one sense, but downgrading the role of mother in no uncertain terms. For the first time in history motherhood is on the defense. In *Brave New World* Aldous Huxley made "mom" a dirty word. A sentimental image of mother love persists —and nobody can truthfully say that any society can get along without it— but the trends cannot please people who cherish the traditional image of motherhood.

Almost every new trend linked to feminization draws the girl's attention away from mothering. And almost every other kind of female opportunity is getting more attention. Certainly the new sex freedom is not good news for the traditional mother. It is no surprise that most opponents of sex education in the public schools are also strong advocates of the traditional mother role; the new outlook on sex not only puts a greater stress on the rights of women and challenges the double sex standard, it is part of the family planning and birth control movement which itself is strongly committed to the proposition that women have been having too many children. (Perhaps you could say that family planning lets women become *better* mothers by having fewer children, so it is not a part of the anti-mother uprising. But the fact remains that it stresses birth control, freeing women for all sorts of things in addition to or in place of motherhood.)

There is a remarkable historical paradox here. At the very time that mother faces new criticism, industrial trends have upgraded both the work and family roles of father (Mogey 1957; Benson 1968). His skills are more advanced, his pay is higher, he has more leisure, he is more interested in his children (in a personal rather than an exploitative way), he is more expressive in relations with both his wife and his children, and so on.

People have two basic sets of roles to play: one within the family and one outside. Modern industrial development undermines the woman's family roles, at least in their older forms, leading to a disenchantment with kitchen and nursery work and with the whole idea of devoting her best years to housekeeping. At the same time it has enlarged women's opportunities outside the home. By contrast, men find new possibilities both inside and outside the family. Critics of modern society can say it is rotten, and we have mentioned the highly competitive nature of both school and work, but the fact remains that by past standards more men have more chances to do more things than ever before. They have all this and time for their families, too, if they want to spend it that way, and many do.

In fact, more than ever it seems that the key to real quality in family life is father, not mother. Mother's energies are drawn away from home as never before, and the trend will continue. Working women can still be counted on to devote time to their children, and they probably go to extra lengths in this regard to compensate—they know that working mothers are accused of neglecting their children (Nye and Hoffman 1963). Fathers remain less dependable, and that is why they represent the key to maximum family well-being and our hope for the future. Since mother has to be away more—the modern economy has settled that—there is a greater urgency for father to take up the slack. Absolute proof that fathers will, or even can, meet this challenge is not yet available, but the signs are favorable. (But it is a striking fact that people who write about the family of the "postindustrial" future often suggest that the male role in reproduction may become obsolete, or almost so, because of the enormous potential for storing male sperm. One man's sperm could impregnate all the women in the world.)

Implications for the Couple

The drift toward companionship in marriage, based on greater equality between the sexes, has been documented throughout this book. Couples are now bound together by affection, and affection alone, more than before. Although there are many reasons why they may live together after the first excitement of romance has died, they no longer have to. Maybe we will see a more candid acceptance of the fact that mutual endearment does not always prevail but that there are good reasons to stay married anyway.

John Edwards (1967) predicts that we can expect a more practical emphasis in marriage as our economy expands. He argues that a highly materialistic outlook dominates contemporary society—a "technological drivenness" (he cites Jules Henry 1963) which seeps into all aspects of life, even marriage. Therefore, he forsees matter-of-factness in marriage in direct response to economic abundance. Partners become interested mainly in what they can get from the relationship, and what they want is not so much psychic or emotional as it is material—economic security. If Edwards is right, the more completely our material needs are met, the more materialistic we get, and the less we rely on marriage for emotional security. This approach is intriguing but erroneous, I think, because it runs counter to almost all current thinking about the modern family's stress on affection and ego support.

Some people argue that the divorce rate will continue to go up as incompatibility becomes legally and morally acceptable as a basis for divorce and that we may expect the ideal of permanent availability to take over. Such a pattern may be inevitable when there are no children, but the wish for children (that is, two or three of them) seems to run as strong as ever. Even parents may find marital breakup a manageable, if disagreeable, experience as long as trends toward greater affluence and rapid remarriage continue. The remarriage rate climbs with the divorce rate, and most middle-class families are not broken for any extended period of time. Lower-class patterns, however, involve considerably more personal and family disruption. In an optimistic note, Robert Parke, Jr., and Paul Glick (1967) contend that a decline in the relative frequency of divorce and separation should result if we can cut poverty down and raise the general socioeconomic level, because divorce rates are lower among affluent people than among the poor.

But what are the chances for entirely new conceptions of marriage? Strangely, there is not much speculation in this area. William Kenkel (1969), for example, reviewed a collection of science fiction stories and found remarkably few references to either marriage or the family. This might mean that marriage as we know it is about as solid as man can devise; maybe tampering is futile. Or it could mean that domestic affairs just are not important enough to get the attention of imaginative writers. It could even mean that science fiction writers are themselves culture-bound, that a society like ours, where technological change is so immensely popular, forces people to limit their dreaming to technical matters. Science fiction that has anything to do with the family is usually concerned with birth control or with the extension of life through medical developments and transplants. As George Steiner (1968) has noted, very few of us can visualize the "not yet," the truly unprecedented, but this is especially true of family organization.

However, unusual marriage arrangements for the future are imaginable. Kenkel talked about one plan where people would have three marriages, each meeting the special needs of a certain period in the life cycle. In the late teens and early twenties men would marry to satisfy their strong sex needs. The man's second marriage would be for reproduction and would be based on a different set of assumptions about his needs. His third marriage would be for mature companionship. This sequence is altered for women, whose first marriage would be for reproduction, the second for sex enjoyment (since sexuality builds up later in women than men), and the third for companionship.

But no such scheme as this represents the wave of the future. No major change in marriage patterns in the next quarter of a century seems likely—unless other social conditions are drastically altered. The majority of married couples do in fact live together until one of them dies. They may not find complete happiness, but it is questionable that searching for new partners at various stages along the way would make personal and social tensions any easier to manage. Staffan Linder (1969) puts it another way; it simply takes too much time to establish new contacts in middle age, especially compared to the possibilities for relaxation at home. Most of us are too lazy to scurry around trying to find new partners who *might* be more appropriate for the stage of life we are in.

Actually, the trend toward greater sex equality seems to be a good thing for the principle of monogamy. Maybe the sexes are getting to be more alike at all stages in the life cycle. Do women have to reach their stride in sex relations later than men just because they have in the past? Are men and women of the same age only compatible in middle age? In fact, current trends contradict any assumptions about the *need* to change partners at different life stages. The monogamous, "pairing-off-in-youth" system has proved both stable and flexible, and the most striking developments of recent years make it seem only more desirable.

For one thing, young people in the United States are now more likely to marry than ever before. A first marriage has almost become *de rigueur* for the girl of about twenty to twenty-three and for the man of about twenty-two to twenty-five. The marriage rate among *very* young women reached a peak in the mid-1950s and is now in decline. Extremely young age at marriage has never been very widespread among men, but it has become a little more characteristic of them in recent years. Result: They are not as much older than their brides when they marry. Still another development is the fact that couples are marrying at about the same age to a greater extent than before; those who marry for the first time, both male and female, tend to be clustered closer together in age. As noted in the chapters on dating, love, and courtship, most of the recent trends seem to have the effect of bringing the sexes closer together in terms of age grading. Couples are therefore probably capable of closer personal relationships (not merely sexual ones) than ever before.

Robert Parke, Jr., and Paul Glick (1967) argue that the compression of age differences between husbands and wives along with decreasing mortality rates will cause a big jump in the chances for joint survival of the married couple into retirement age and should reduce both the average length as well as the frequency of widowhood. Furthermore, the ability to enjoy close marriage relations in middle age may be at least partly due to close relations in late adolescence and early maturity. Changing partners in mid-life (on the assumption that one's first partner now has interests and tastes different from one's own) would certainly not seem to apply to the majority of couples.

And yet the possibility of longer life and longer joint survival for married couples does raise some questions. Even the reasons for marriage, or our conceptions of them, may change. Edward Suchman (1968), for example, contends that people are becoming the agents of their own diseases more than ever before, since health is often determined more by what we do to ourselves than by what some germ or infection from outside does to us. A new function for the family is suggested: Family members, especially spouses, can help each other stay healthy. More emphasis may be placed on this, Suchman says, leading to new ways of thinking about the control of health and illness. We already know that dental and medical habits are molded by the life style in each family (Lambert, Freeman, *et al.* 1967), but with very little conscious concern.

Although many signs suggest that monogamy is firmly entrenched, it is possible that the practice of couples moving into homes of their own, separated physically from one another by yard and fence and economically by independent budgets, may be changed. The suburban pattern of sharply separated households has been popular for at least two generations, and its roots can be traced back to an agricultural pattern of farmhouses separated from one another by even greater distances. In this arrangement, each household handles its problems more or less on its own; cooperation among neighbors does occur, but the tendency is for each family to work independently—in making purchases, preparing meals, planning for the future, taking care of the children, and so forth.

Rumblings among young people suggest a desire for less exclusiveness in family life. We see a reaction against the standard suburban life style, with a trend toward greater density in living arrangements. Without in any way suggesting group marriage, this pattern could include much closer cooperation and intimacy among clusters of married couples, not only in social relations, but in the more practical matters of feeding, clothing, and housing their families, and caring for their children (Stoller, 1970). The need for cooperative family efforts to adjust in the modern city gives this trend an urgency that has not yet gained widespread public awareness.

THE GLOBAL VILLAGE

Family affairs have always been notoriously parochial. In some respects, this is the essence of family life. It gives us a manageable little niche, something we can comprehend and be enveloped by. The powers of kinship are stripped away as the secular state expands, so the nuclear family actually becomes more isolated at the very time that almost everything else is turning more cosmopolitan.

And yet the kind of society we are moving toward gives greater opportunities for people to travel far from home, both physically and psychologically, than ever before. When Marshall McLuhan (1964) argued that modern mass media bring the world's population closer together into what he calls a *global village*, he spotted a truly important trend. McLuhan has been known to exaggerate, but on this point he is completely justified. The world's people *are* becoming entangled in a world-wide political and economic network (although in the short term this obviously does not make them get along with each other any better than before).

If we can assume that there are basic, irreversible trends toward greater international contacts at almost all levels, what happens to the family? How do trends affect domestic life, or how does the family influence these trends (if it has any effect at all)? Maybe we should put the question another way: How *should* family life change to meet the new facts of life?

Many observers have been heartened by the fact that people now travel more. They learn more about life styles in other lands, and they are more aware of family variety around the world (Hobart 1963; Rapoport and Rapoport 1965; Edwards 1967). We might expect this increased mobility to make people a little quicker to take up new family ideas. As noted in the chapter on courtship, greater mobility probably also leads to higher rates of heterogamy in mate selection, and this may very well have the effect of speeding up change in society (Wassink 1967).

Generally, however, the parochial nature of the family makes it a conservative influence. There is very little evidence that familism fosters sophistication in international affairs. It usually breeds narrow family commitments, not broad intercultural loyalties. As Yonina Talmon (1965) says with regard to the nuclear family in Israel, a strong interest in collective social goals seems to be fundamentally at odds with close family solidarity.

In fact, Claude Bowman (1963) has suggested that the constant international conflict of recent decades has caused people to turn inward upon the family for reassurance even more than before. The family becomes a sociopsychological shelter, an antidote to fear, but not one that helps to solve international problems.

Two basic characteristics of the family illustrate its conservatism: (1) its role in determining the social status of its members and (2) its role in indoctrinating children. An upper-middle-class family in the United States, for example, enjoys a very high standard of living by world standards. When members of this family travel abroad, their wealth (compared to that of the natives) will usually be high, and they will not be anxious to share their good fortune. The family is the primary spending unit in virtually all nations, and rarely do families with high status want to divide things up equally—not with people of lower status in their own countries, let alone with foreigners. The urge to pass wealth and advantages from one generation to the next through the family line is one of the most parochial, narrow-spirited forces operating in the world today.

But the family's role in indoctrinating children is almost as restrictive. Parents not only teach children their personal prejudices (in politics, religion, economics, and so on), they ordinarily consider it their duty to do so. The public school system, by contrast, is not quite as single-minded in its indoctrination, although the established American economic and political systems are reinforced. Of course teachers often push their prejudices, but they are not supposed to. And there are usually several of them with different points of view, so they may counteract each other. The school, in general, adopts progressive social innovations more quickly than the home (Shostak 1967).

And yet Nathan Cohen and Maurice Connery (1967) claim that similarities in family life throughout the world far exceed differences. They say that this common bond may yet give us the basis for a world community. The family does not always resist social improvement, nor for that matter do people avoid all innovations in family affairs (van den Ban 1967). An idea that seems fanciful indeed is one suggested by Otto Pollak (1967); he envisions a family system of the future in which family members are expected to act out their aggressive impulses toward one another, thus lessening the need for aggression at higher social levels. The family becomes a community of sufferers, an organization of regeneration for life in the cold, bureaucratic world.

What is the possibility of rearing children who can rise above their parents' narrow interests? The push will probably have to come from outside the family—where all modern reform movements have originated. Apparently new forces are in fact making their impact, since a significant number of contemporary youth already show signs of an international spirit.

Kenneth Keniston (1969), for example, contends that a *postconventional morality* is now emerging. "Youth," as he defines the term, includes people in the marginal stage between adolescence and adulthood; they are characterized by *disengagement* from many adult institutions, *confrontation* with new moral viewpoints, and traumatic *discovery* of the true extent of corruption in the world. This opens possibilities for both greater moral development and greater moral regression than ever before (which has also been suggested by Lewis Feuer [1969]).

Keniston identifies three stages in the moral growth of most youth: (1) Preconventional morality comes first, based on self-centered notions about right and wrong. Whatever leads to personal pleasure or can be done without getting caught is perfectly all right to small children. (2) Conventional morality develops next, in preadolescence and early adolescence, when good and evil are based on current community standards, and law and order are stressed. In this stage we feel the need to be "good boys" and "good girls." (3) Keniston argues that postconventional morality takes hold among an increasing number of youth in the later stages of adolescence and youthful maturity. It takes two forms. In one, right and wrong are believed to stem from some sort of social agreement, but they can and should be changed as social conditions change. People who see the need to make changes have to take a stand, and youth are in the best position to volunteer. In the second form, personal principles are believed to transcend both the conventional morality and the social contract; these can be very self-centered.

The first of these two forms is most relevant here. Moral principles ordinarily stressed by the family tend to be highly conventional. Keniston (and many others) argues that much of the unrest among modern youth is the bubbling over of reactions to moral premises strongly entrenched in their own families. They do not rebel against their parents in a highly personal way as a rule—there is a certain sympathy for parents, in fact, though not very visible to the parents themselves—but they do question the older generation's values. These seem much too provincial to be helpful in meeting the problems of modern society.

Certainly modern youth do go through an internationalizing experience in college, but what happens then? If they follow the path of previous generations, most of them will marry and settle down. The urge to reform a very imperfect world will slowly fade. By the age of thirty-five their sense of status and personal dignity will become rooted in the local community, reflected in the image of success and stability of "a home of their own."

But maybe the current generation of youth will prove to be different. Richard Flacks (1970) suggests that a social transformation of extraordinary proportions is now occurring, and its impact on youth as they "come of age" may not be temporary. Many have grown up in liberal, humanistic homes under circumstances of affluence, and they are more interested in careers with intrinsic appeals than ones that are primarily devoted to making money and gaining status. College attendance is much more widespread than before, so the scope of its impact is very extensive. What is more, there are careers in education itself and in social service that stress other values than those associated with personal success and the acquisition of power. These career opportunities are growing more rapidly than the traditional ones, and wholly new life styles become possible as the number of people involved increases. The gap between the generations may or may not widen, but our self-consciousness about it certainly boils over as the age-old parochialism of the family comes under attack.

And around the corner is a life-expectancy standard that may make the generation gap of the 1970s look like a petty squabble among chronological peers. With childbearing strictly controlled, old people may actually outnumber youth—by a big margin—and perhaps insist upon commensurate political rights. Since families would be small, relatively more children would be first born, and they tend to be more conservative than second, third, or later children (Kammeyer 1966; Tomeh 1969). Idealistic pressures will continue to come from youth, but in a crowded society with many well-educated older people, political forces may follow a strange, new pattern.

We are justified in thinking that the family will continue to be useful for generations to come, perhaps precisely because of its conservative nature. As F. Ivan Nye (1967) has argued, the family seems to be here to stay, not because of its intrinsic value (which is considerable), but because it is *instrumental* in maintaining life itself, in training and humanizing the infant, and in meeting basic needs of people in all stages of the life cycle. The family retains these functions beyond question; alternatives that work for masses of people exist only in science fiction.

Furthermore, the nuclear family unit gives a powerful impetus to striving among its members. It is the basic social source for *endeavoring behavior*. We know, for example, that parents play a crucial role in the school and job aspirations of their children, probably more than siblings, kinsmen, friends, teachers, or any other adults (Tomeh 1968). We would like the school system to provide built-in motivation for students, but it does not always do that.

In fact, the family may very well become even more important for meeting fundamental human aspirations in the future, as revolutionary social changes occur. It is the one social institution that man has relied upon for continuity and stability in every stage of his evolutionary existence. Only by imagining wholly new kinds of personal and social security (and let us hope that man proves to be ingenious in this regard) can we conceive of an end to the family. It provides an incomparable source of reassurance and endurance at the small group level; its one major drawback is that it often aggravates tensions at the larger national and international levels.

THE BIOLOGICAL TIME BOMB

Complacency is under attack from all directions, and we now face a biological revolution bearing directly on our most basic family assumptions. We are accustomed to thinking about the future in terms of breath-taking technological leaps, but our present exploits, in space for example, are absolutely trivial when viewed in the perspective of the biological future. If all that is technically feasible should come to pass, the present discussion may be woefully dated within a quarter of a century. Gordon Rattray Taylor (1968) argues that the surge of achievement happening right now in genetics, biochemistry, medicine, and molecular biology is so far-reaching in its social, economic, and familial implications as to represent the first total crisis in the history of the species. He has outlined the possibilities and has even attempted to supply a timetable for new developments, as follows:

Phase One, by 1975:
Extensive transplantation of limbs and organs

Test-tube fertilization of human eggs
Implantation of fertilized eggs in the woman's womb
Indefinite storage of female eggs and male spermatazoa
Choice of sex of offspring
Extensive power to postpone clinical death
Mind-modifying drugs: hence, regulation of personal urges
The ability to erase memory
Creation of artificial viruses
Creation of artificial placenta (but imperfect)

Phase Two, by 2000:

Extensive mind modification and personality reconstruction
Enhancement of intelligence in men and animals
Memory injection and memory editing
Perfected artificial placenta
Life copying: reconstructed organisms
Hibernation and prolonged coma
Prolongation of youthful vigor
First "cloned" animals (growth from cuttings)
Synthesis of unicellular organisms
Organ regeneration
Man-animal chimeras (combined tissues and organisms)

Phase Three, After 2000:

Greatly improved control of aging; extension of life span
Synthesis of complex organisms
Preservation of disembodied brains
Linkage between the brain and computers
Gene modification
Cloned human tissues
Linkages between brains
Man-machine chimeras
Indefinite postponement of death

Since social and economic considerations are involved, these are dates of technical achievement, not necessarily of widespread application.

Taylor was confronted by new developments during the year he wrote his book, so he may prove to be conservative as often as not. Predictions that he made while writing the first draft came true before he could finish the last one. He foresees a human animal of the not-so-distant future as

a strange biped that will combine the properties of self-reproduction without males, like the greenfly; of fertilizing his female at long distance like the nautiloid mollusc; of changing sex like the xiphophores; of growing from cuttings like the earthworm; of replacing its missing parts like the newt; of developing outside its mother's body like the kangaroo; and of hibernating like the hedgehog (p. 55).

Primarily, the biological revolution at hand will change patterns of reproduction and longevity. But these will in turn change patterns of parenthood, old age, social stratification, and relations between the generations. The range of sexual, medical, and psychic options open to man could be fantastically widened. In fact, if the potentialities for genetic rearrangement are as great as contemporary geneticists report, then the entire social structure might as well prepare for upheaval. In one of his more controversial forecasts, for example, Taylor contends that techniques for raising the level of intelligence must inevitably lead to an elite caste, ruling over lesser individuals assigned to work of only routine importance.

The textbook written ten years from today will explore this subject in depth, and there will be scores if not hundreds of research reports and professional treatises to document the discussion. These do not exist today, but the ideas for them are already in embryonic form. It is possible that a truly scientific study of the family can grow only in response to revolutionary biological developments. The entire history of the family revolves around conventional reproduction and child-rearing patterns. In a sense, the modern family is not terribly different from the one described in the Old Testament; its basic biological assumptions are the same. So here we are, for the first time in history, toying with the possibility of truly new assumptions.

SUMMARY

One reason why it is so hard to forecast future developments in the family is that it is subject to hardly any direct control or manipulation. Organized efforts to guide social change rarely try to change basic family arrangements. Family values have always changed only imperceptibly from one generation to the next; it will be a totally new era for man when we leave this historic pattern behind.

One trend is clear: a drift toward broader and more effective family planning. The day may soon arrive when family life will be much more rational than it has been, including a full guarantee of the right to be wanted for children, greater use of genetic knowledge, and perhaps stronger controls over marriage and the right to have children. Implications for the birth rate in the lower social classes, for premarital and early pregnancies, adoptions, welfare services, and short-term fluctuations in fertility are impressive when viewed one-by-one. They are staggering in their cumulative impact.

If almost all children were planned, we should expect competition among them to be even greater than it is today, since the supervision of each child may very well become intense. This is tied to the trend toward meritocracy, a society where people succeed on the basis of their abilities, not family background. But parents still have a strong urge to pass their status and possessions on to their children.

As people learn more about the nature of their personal and social existence, they become more self-conscious about family performance. Parenthood, for example, is no longer accepted naïvely, but is seen as a challenge to be mastered. The concept of responsible parenthood is now getting attention; it is a much more sophisticated idea than it was just a quarter of a century ago, and it will surely become even more so.

Industrial growth has led to the liberation of women from traditional social roles, upgrading the quality of their lives in a sense, but stripping the appeal from the role of mother. At the same time, it has upgraded both the work and family roles of father. Industrialization also changes patterns of personal identification for boys and girls, and it changes the way they prepare for adult roles (especially for girls). It has greatly expanded the range of competition between the sexes. Implications for mothering and fathering are far-reaching, but it remains questionable whether husband-wife relations will become different in any basic way from what they have been. Greater equality between the sexes should bring them closer together and open even greater possibilities for monogamous marriage.

A contrast exists between the parochial nature of family life and the growing need for cosmopolitanism. Can children be reared whose social loyalties rise above the provincialism that has historically restricted their parents? Already a vocal minority among youth are becoming international. After they form families of their own, however, they may become parochial in outlook again—that has always happened before. Adult couples root themselves in the local community; they gain status, which is reflected in their home and family life. In this way the family clings to its conservative function, and it supplies an elementary basis for social order. But such an order does serve as a stumbling block to creating higher forms of personal and social loyalty. It is possible that contemporary youth now have experiences so unlike those of previous generations, and develop career goals or life styles so devoid of the traditional stress on wealth-seeking and social status, that a profound social transformation is occurring.

The biological time bomb is a question mark. A revolution in the biological sciences is currently in progress, whereas spectacular advances in physics and chemistry have been around for some time. The full impact of the newest scientific revolution is extremely difficult to contemplate. In the next decade we should expect its implications for the family to become clearer, yielding a much better understanding of the basic family alternatives available to mankind.

SELECTED READINGS

COHEN, NATHAN E., AND MAURICE F. CONNERY. "Government Policy and the Family," *Journal of Marriage and the Family*, Vol. 29 (February 1967), pp. 6–17.

EDWARDS, JOHN N. "The Future of the Family Revisited," *Journal of Marriage and the Family*, Vol. 29 (August 1967), pp. 505–511.

——— (ed.). *The Family and Change*. New York: Knopf, 1969.

NYE, F. IVAN. "Values, Family, and a Changing Society," *Journal of Marriage and the Family*, Vol. 29 (May 1967), pp. 241–248.

OTTO, HERBERT A. (ed.). *The Family in Search of a Future: Alternative Models for Moderns*. New York: Appleton-Century-Crofts, 1970.

PARKE, ROBERT, JR., AND PAUL C. GLICK. "Prospective Changes in Marriage and the Family," *Journal of Marriage and the Family*, Vol. 29 (May 1967), pp. 249–256.

POHLMAN, EDWARD. "Some Effects of Being Able to Control Sex of Offspring," *Eugenics Quarterly*, Vol. 14 (December 1967), pp. 274–281.

POLLAK, OTTO. "The Outlook for the American Family," *Journal of Marriage and the Family*, Vol. 29 (February 1967), pp. 193–205 .

TAYLOR, GORDON RATTRAY. *The Biological Time-Bomb*. London: Thames and Hudson, 1968.

ABERLE, DAVID F., *et al.* "The Incest Taboo and the Mating Patterns of Animals," in William J. Goode (ed.), *Readings on the Family and Society.* Englewood Cliffs, N.J.: Prentice-Hall, 1964.

ACKERMAN, CHARLES. "Affiliations: Structural Determinants of Differential Divorce Rates," *American Journal of Sociology,* 69 (July 1963), 13–20.

ADAMS, BERT N. "Structural Factors Affecting Parental Aid to Married Children," *Journal of Marriage and the Family,* 26 (August 1964), 327–331.

———. *Kinship in an Urban Setting.* Chicago: Markham Publishing Company, 1968a.

———. "The Middle-Class Adult and His Widowed or Still-Married Mother," *Social Problems,* 16 (Summer 1968b), 50–59.

ADAMS, RICHARD N. "An Inquiry into the Nature of the Family," in Gertrude Dole and Robert L. Carneiro (eds.), *Essays in the Science of Culture: In Honor of Leslie A. White.* New York: Thomas Y. Crowell, 1960, pp. 30–49.

ALBRECHT, RUTH. "The Parental Responsibilities of Grandparents," *Marriage and Family Living,* 16 (August 1954), 201–204.

ALMQUIST, ELIZABETH M., AND SHIRLEY S. ANGRIST. "Career Salience and Atypicality of Occupational Choice Among College Women," *Journal of Marriage and the Family,* 32 (May 1970a), 242–249.

———. "Role Model Influences on College Women's Career Aspirations," paper read at meetings of the American Sociological Association, Washington, D.C., September 1970b.

AMERICAN COUNCIL ON EDUCATION. *Higher Education and National Affairs.* 17, December 23, 1968, 7–8.

AMERICAN SOCIOLOGICAL ASSOCIATION COMMITTEE ON MARRIAGE AND DIVORCE STATISTICS. "The Need for Nationwide Marriage and Divorce Statistics," *American Sociological Review,* 23 (June 1958), 306–312.

ANDREW, GWEN. "Determinants of Negro Family Decisions in Management of Retardation," *Journal of Marriage and the Family,* 30 (April 1968), 612–617.

ANGRIST, SHIRLEY S. "The Study of Sex Roles," *Journal of Social Issues,* 25 (January 1969), 215–232.

ANGYAL, ANDRAS. *Neurosis and Treatment: A Holistic Theory.* New York: Wiley, 1965.

APPLE, DORRIAN. "The Social Structure of Grandparenthood," *American Anthropologist,* 58 (August 1956), 656–663.

ARIES, PHILIPPE. *Centuries of Childhood.* New York: Vintage Books, 1965.

AXELSON, LELAND J. "Personal Adjustment in the Postparental Period," *Marriage and Family Living,* 22 (February 1960), 66–70.

BABER, RAY E. *Marriage and the Family.* New York: McGraw-Hill, 1953.

397

BACH, GEORGE R., AND PETER WYDEN. *The Intimate Enemy: How to Fight Fair in Love and Marriage.* New York: Morrow, 1969.

BALL, DONALD W. "Toward a Sociology of Toys: Inanimate Objects, Socialization, and the Demography of the Doll World," *The Sociological Quarterly*, 8 (Autumn 1967), 447–458.

BALLWEG, JOHN A. "Resolution of Conjugal Role Adjustment After Retirement," *Journal of Marriage and the Family*, 29 (May 1967), 277–281.

BARASH, MEYER, AND ALICE SCOURBY (eds.). *Marriage and the Family: A Contemporary Analysis of Contemporary Problems.* New York: Random House, 1970.

BARBER, BERNARD. *Social Stratification: A Comparative Analysis of Structure and Process.* New York: Harcourt, Brace and Company, 1957.

BATES, ALAN. "Parental Roles in Courtship," *Social Forces*, 20 (March 1942), 483–486.

BAYER, ALAN E. "Early Dating and Early Marriage," *Journal of Marriage and the Family*, 30 (November 1968), 628–632.

BECK, DOROTHY F. "The Changing Moslem Family of the Middle East," *Marriage and Family Living*, 19 (November 1957), 340–347.

BECKER, HOWARD. "Current Sacred-Secular Theory and Its Development," in Howard Becker and Alvin Boskoff (eds.), *Modern Sociological Theory in Continuity and Change.* New York: Holt, Rinehart and Winston, 1957.

BEIGEL, HUGO G. "Romantic Love," *American Sociological Review*, 16 (June 1951), 326–334.

BELCHER, JOHN C. "The One-Person Household: A Consequence of the Isolated Nuclear Family?" *Journal of Marriage and the Family*, 29 (August 1967), 534–540.

BELL, DANIEL (ed.). *Toward the Year 2000.* Boston: Houghton Mifflin, 1968.

BELL, ROBERT R. *Premarital Sex in a Changing Society.* Englewood Cliffs, N.J.: Prentice-Hall, 1966.

BENSON, LEONARD. *Fatherhood: A Sociological Perspective.* New York: Random House, 1968.

BERGER, BENNETT M. "Adolescence and Beyond," *Social Problems*, 10 (Spring 1963), 394–408.

BERNARD, JESSIE. *Remarriage: A Study of Marriage.* New York: Dryden, 1956.

BEYER, GLENN H. "Living Arrangements, Attitudes, and Preferences of Older People," in Clark Tibbitts and Wilma Donahue (eds.), *Social and Psychological Aspects of Aging.* New York: Columbia University Press, 1962.

BILLINGSLEY, ANDREW. *Black Families in White America.* Englewood Cliffs, N.J.: Prentice-Hall, 1968.

BIRD, CAROLINE. *Born Female: The High Cost of Keeping Women Down.* New York: David McKay, 1968.

BLOOD, ROBERT O., JR. "Uniformities and Diversities in Campus Dating Preferences," *Journal of Marriage and the Family*, 18 (February 1956), 37–45.

———. *Love Match and Arranged Marriage: A Tokyo-Detroit Comparison.* New York: Free Press, 1967.

———, AND DONALD M. WOLFE. *Husbands and Wives.* New York: Free Press, 1960.

BOGUE, DONALD J. *Population of the United States.* New York: Free Press, 1959.

BOLTON, CHARLES D. "Mate Selection as the Development of a Relationship," *Marriage and Family Living,* 23 (August 1961), 234–240.

BOSSARD, JAMES H. S., AND ELEANOR S. BOLL. "Marital Unhappiness in the Life Cycle," *Marriage and Family Living,* 17 (February 1955), 10–14.

———. *The Sociology of Child Development.* 4th ed. New York: Harper & Row, 1966.

BOTT, ELIZABETH. *Family and Social Network.* London: Tavistock Publications, 1957.

BOWERMAN, CHARLES E., AND JOHN W. KINCH. "Changes in Family and Peer Orientation of Children Between the Fourth and Tenth Grades," *Social Forces,* 37 (March 1959), 206–211.

BOWMAN, CLAUDE C. "The Family and the Nuclear Arms Race," *Social Problems,* 11 (Summer 1963), 29–34.

BRACE, C. L., AND M. F. ASHLEY MONTAGU. *Man's Evolution.* New York: Macmillan, 1965.

BRAV, STANLEY R. "Note on Honeymoons," *Marriage and Family Living,* 9 (Summer 1947), 60.

BREHM, H. P. "Sociology and Aging: Orientation and Research," *Gerontologist,* 8 (Spring 1968), 24–31.

BRODERICK, CARLFRED B. "Social Heterosexual Development Among Urban Negroes and Whites," *Journal of Marriage and the Family,* 27 (May 1965), 200–203.

———. "Socio-Sexual Development in a Suburban Community," *Journal of Sex Research,* 2 (April 1966), 1–24.

———, AND STANLEY E. FOWLER. "New Patterns of Relationships Between the Sexes Among Preadolescents," *Marriage and Family Living,* 23 (February 1961), 27–30.

———, AND GEORGE P. ROWE. "A Scale of Preadolescent Heterosexual Development," *Journal of Marriage and the Family,* 30 (February 1968), 97–101.

———, AND JEAN WEAVER. "The Perceptual Context of Boy-Girl Communication," *Journal of Marriage and the Family,* 30 (April 1968), 618–627.

BRONFENBRENNER, URIE. "The Psychological Costs of Quality and Equality in Education," *Child Development,* 38 (December 1967), 909–925.

BRYAN, JAMES H. "Occupational Ideologies and Individual Attitudes of Call Girls," *Social Problems,* 13 (Spring 1966), 441–450.

BURCHINAL, LEE G. "Research on Young Marriage: Implications for Family Life Education," *Family Life Coordinator,* 9 (September–December 1960), 6–24.

———. "Characteristics of Adolescents from Unbroken, Broken, and Reconstituted Families," *Marriage and Family Living,* 26 (February 1964), 44–51.

———. "The Premarital Dyad and Love Involvement," in Harold T. Christensen (ed.), *Handbook of Marriage and the Family.* Chicago: Rand McNally, 1964b, pp. 623–674.

BURGESS, ERNEST W. "The Family as a Unity of Interacting Personalities," *Family,* 7 (March 1926), 3–6.

————, AND LEONARD S. COTTRELL. "The Prediction of Adjustment in Marriage," *American Sociological Review*, 1 (August 1936), 737–751.

————, AND LEONARD S. COTTRELL. *Predicting Success or Failure in Marriage*, Englewood Cliffs, N.J.: Prentice-Hall, 1939.

————, AND HARVEY J. LOCKE. *The Family: From Institution to Companionship*. 2nd ed. New York: American Book, 1960.

————, AND PAUL WALLIN. "Predicting Adjustment in Marriage from Adjustment in Engagement," *American Journal of Sociology*, 49 (January 1944), 325–330.

————, AND PAUL WALLIN. *Engagement and Marriage*. Philadelphia: Lippincott, 1953.

BUSSE, EWALD W. "Physical Fitness and Aging." Report presented to the annual convention of the American Medical Association, New York, 1969.

BUTLER, ROBERT N. "The Life Review: An Interpretation of Reminiscence in the Aged," *Psychiatry*, 26 (February 1963), 65–76.

CALDERWOOD, DERYCK. "Differences in the Sex Questions of Adolescent Boys and Girls," *Marriage and Family Living*, 25 (November 1963), 492–495.

CANCIAN, FRANCESCA M. "Interaction Patterns in Zinacanteco Families," *American Sociological Review*, 29 (August 1964), 540–550.

CAREY, JAMES T. "Changing Courtship Patterns in the Popular Song," *American Journal of Sociology*, 74 (May 1969), 720–731.

CATTON, WILLIAM R., JR. "What's in a Name? A Study of Role Inertia," *Journal of Marriage and the Family*, 31 (February 1969), 15–18.

CAUDILL, WILLIAM, AND HELEN WEINSTEIN. "Babies East and West," report on paper presented at meetings of the American Anthropological Association, Denver, Colorado, 1965, in *Trans-action*, 3 (March–April 1966), 28–29.

CAVAN, RUTH SHONLE. "Self and Role in Adjustment During Old Age," in Arnold M. Rose (ed.), *Human Behavior and Social Processes*. Boston: Houghton Mifflin, 1962.

————. *The American Family*. 3rd ed. New York: Crowell, 1963.

CHEKKI, D. A. "Social Legislation and Kinship in India: A Socio-Legal Study," *Journal of Marriage and the Family*, 31 (February 1969), 165–172.

CHILMAN, CATHERINE S. "Families in Development at Mid-Stage of the Family Life Cycle," *The Family Coordinator*, 17 (October 1968), 297–312.

CHRISTENSEN, HAROLD T. "Cultural Relativism and Premarital Sex Norms," *American Sociological Review*, 25 (February 1960), 31–39.

————. "Pregnant Brides—Record Linkage Studies," in Evelyn M. Duvall and Sylvanus M. Duvall (eds.), *Sex Ways—In Fact and Faith*. New York: Association Press, 1961.

————. "Child Spacing Analysis via Record Linkage: New Data Plus a Summing Up from Earlier Reports," *Marriage and Family Living*, 25 (August 1963), 272–280.

————. "Children in the Family: Relationship of Number and Spacing to Marital Success," *Journal of Marriage and the Family*, 30 (May 1968), 283–289.

————, AND KENNETH E. BARBER. "Interfaith Versus Intrafaith Marriage in

Indiana," *Journal of Marriage and the Family,* 29 (August 1967), 461–469.

―――, AND HANNA H. MEISSNER. "Premarital Pregnancy as a Factor in Divorce," *American Sociological Review,* 18 (December 1953), 641–644.

―――, AND BETTE B. RUBENSTEIN. "Premarital Pregnancy and Divorce: A Follow-up Study by the Interview Method," *Marriage and Family Living,* 18 (May 1956), 114–123.

CHU, HSIEN-JEN. "A Note to Utilizing Murdock's Ethnographic Survey Materials for Cross-Cultural Family Research," *Journal of Marriage and the Family,* 31 (May 1969), 311–314.

CLARK, ALEXANDER L., AND PAUL WALLIN. "Women's Sexual Responsiveness and the Duration and Quality of Their Marriages," *American Journal of Sociology,* 71 (September 1965), 187–196.

CLARK, MARGARET, AND BARBARA G. ANDERSON. *Culture and Aging.* Springfield, Ill.: Charles C. Thomas, 1967.

CLARKE, HELEN I. *Social Legislation.* New York: Appleton-Century-Crofts, 1957.

COHEN, NATHAN E., AND MAURICE F. CONNERY. "Government Policy and the Family," *Journal of Marriage and the Family,* 29 (February 1967), 6–17.

COLEMAN, JAMES S. *The Adolescent Society.* New York: Free Press, 1962.

COOLEY, CHARLES HORTON. *Human Nature and the Social Order.* New York: Charles Scribner's Sons, 1902.

COOMBS, ROBERT H., AND WILLIAM F. KENKEL. "Sex Differences in Dating Aspirations and Satisfaction with Computer-Selected Partners," *Journal of Marriage and the Family,* 28 (February 1966), 62–66.

CORBIN, HAZEL. *Getting Ready To Be a Father.* New York: Macmillan, 1944.

CORY, DONALD WEBSTER. "Homosexuality," in *Encyclopedia of Sexual Behavior.* New York: Hawthorn, 1961.

COULT, ALLAN D. "Causality and Cross-Sex Prohibitions," *American Anthropologist,* 65 (April 1963), 274–275.

CRAWLEY, LAWRENCE Q., *et al. Reproduction, Sex, and Preparation for Marriage.* Englewood Cliffs, N.J.: Prentice-Hall, 1964.

CROOG, SYDNEY H., AND PETER KONG-MING NEW. "Knowledge of Grandfather's Occupation: Clues to American Kinship Structure," *Journal of Marriage and the Family,* 27 (February 1965), 69–77.

CROSS, EARL B. *The Hebrew Family.* Chicago: University of Chicago Press, 1927.

CUBER, JOHN F., AND PEGGY B. HARROFF. *The Significant Americans: A Study of Sexual Behavior Among the Affluent.* New York: Appleton-Century, 1965.

CUMMING, ELAINE. "Further Thoughts on the Theory of Disengagement," *UNESCO International Social Science Bulletin,* 15 (1963), 377–393.

―――, LOIS R. DEAN, DAVID S. NEWELL, AND ISABEL MCCAFFREY. "Disengagement: A Tentative Theory of Aging," *Sociometry,* 23 (March 1960), 23–25.

―――, AND WILLIAM E. HENRY. *Growing Old: The Process of Disengagement.* New York: Basic Books, 1961.

"Current Housing Reports," series H–121, No. 16, June 1969.

CUTLER, BEVERLY R., AND WILLIAM G. DYER. "Initial Adjustment Processes in Young Married Couples," *Social Forces*, 44 (December 1965), 195–201.

DAGER, EDWARD Z., GLENN A. HARPER, AND ROBERT N. WHITEHURST. "Family Life Education in Public High Schools: A Survey Report on Indiana," *Marriage and Family Living*, 24 (November 1962), 365–370.

DAVIS, ALAN J. "Sexual Assaults in the Philadelphia Prison System and Sheriff's Cans," *Trans-action*, 6 (December 1968), 8–16.

DAVIS, KATHARINE B. *Factors in the Sex Life of Twenty-two Hundred Women.* New York: Harper, 1929.

DAVIS, KINGSLEY. *Human Society.* New York: Macmillan, 1949.

———. "Statistical Perspective on Divorce," *Annals of the American Academy of Political and Social Sciences*, 272 (November 1950), 9–21.

———. "Sexual Behavior," in Robert K. Merton and Robert A. Nisbet (eds.), *Contemporary Social Problems.* New York: Harcourt, Brace & World, 1966.

DELORA, JACK R. "Social Systems of Dating on a College Campus," *Marriage and Family Living*, 25 (February 1963), pp. 81–84.

DEMOS, JOHN, AND VIRGINIA DEMOS. "Adolescence in Historical Perspective," *Journal of Marriage and the Family*, 31 (November 1969), 632–638.

DENNIS, WAYNE. "Creative Productivity Between the Ages of 20 and 80 Years," *Journal of Gerontology*, 21 (January 1966), 1–8.

DE TOCQUEVILLE, ALEXIS. *Democracy in America.* Phillips Bradley (ed.). New York: Vintage Books, 1956, Vols. I and II.

DEUTSCHER, IRWIN. "The Quality of Postparental Life: Definitions of the Situation," *Journal of Marriage and the Family*, 26 (February 1964), 52–59.

DICK, HARRY R., HIRAM J. FRIEDSAM, AND CORA ANN MARTIN. "Residential Patterns of Aged Persons Prior to Institutionalization," *Journal of Marriage and the Family*, 26 (February 1964), 96–98.

DOBZHANSKY, THEODOSIUS. "Changing Man," *Science*, 155 (January 1967), 409–415.

DONAHUE, WILMA. "Where and How Older People Wish to Live," in Wilma Donahue (ed.), *Housing the Aging.* Ann Arbor: University of Michigan Press, 1954.

DORE, RONALD P. *City Life in Japan.* Berkeley: University of California Press, 1963.

DOUGLAS, ROBERT R. "Dinnertime Dynamics," *The Family Coordinator*, 17 (July 1968), 181–184.

DOWNING, JOSEPH. "The Tribal Family and the Social Awakening," in Herbert A. Otto, (ed.) *The Family in Search of a Future: Alternative Models For Moderns* (New York: Appleton-Century-Crofts, 1970).

DURKHEIM, EMILE. *The Division of Labor in Society.* George Simpson (tr.). New York: Free Press, 1947, first published in 1893.

———. Lecture on the family given in 1892, recorded by Marcel Mauss, George Simpson (tr.), "A Durkheim Fragment," *American Journal of Sociology*, 70 (March 1965), 527–536.

DUVALL, EVELYN M. "Teenage Boys and Family Living," *Marriage and Family Living*, 23 (February 1961), 49.

DYER, EVERETT D. "Parenthood as Crisis: A Repeat Study," *Marriage and Family Living*, 25 (May 1963), 196–201.

EARLE, JOHN R. "Parent-Child Communication, Sentiment and Authority," *Sociological Inquiry*, 37 (Spring 1967), 275–282.

EDMONDS, VERNON H. "Marital Conventionalization: Definition and Measurement," *Journal of Marriage and the Family*, 29 (November 1967), 681–688.

EDWARDS, JOHN N. "The Future of the Family Revisited," *Journal of Marriage and the Family*, 29 (August 1967), 505–511.

——— (ed.). *The Family and Change*. New York: Knopf, 1969.

EGGERS, OSCAR. "The Future of the American Family," *The Bulletin of Family Development*, 1 (1960), 1–4.

EHRLICH, STANTON L. "What Is a Divorce Lawyer?," *Marriage and Family Living*, 21 (November 1959), 361–366.

EHRMANN, WINSTON W. *Premarital Dating Behavior*. New York: Holt, Rinehart and Winston, 1959.

ELKIN, FREDERICK, AND WILLIAM A. WESTLEY. "The Myth of Adolescent Culture," *American Sociological Review*, 29 (December 1955), 680–684.

ELLIS, ALBERT. "The Value of Marriage Prediction Tests," *American Sociological Review*, 13 (December 1948), 710–718.

ENGELS, FREDERICK. *The Origin of the Family, Private Property, and the State*. Ernest Untermann (tr.). Chicago: Charles H. Kerr & Co., 1902, first published in 1884.

ENGLAND, R. W., JR. "Images of Love and Courtship in Family-Magazine Fiction," *Marriage and Family Living*, 22 (May 1960), 162–165.

ENGLISH, O. SPURGEON, AND STUART M. FINCH. *Introduction to Psychiatry*. New York: Norton, 1954.

ERIKSON, ERIK. *Childhood and Society*. New York: Norton, 1963.

———. *Identity: Youth and Crisis*. New York: Norton, 1968.

FALLERS, LLOYD A. "Some Determinants of Marriage Stability in Busoga: A Reformulation of Gluckman's Hypotheses," *Africa*, 27 (January 1957), 106–121.

FARBER, BERNARD. *Family: Organization and Interaction*. San Francisco: Chandler, 1964.

———. *Kinship and Family Organization*. New York: Wiley, 1966.

FELDMAN, HAROLD. *Development of the Husband-Wife Relationship*. Ithaca, N.Y.: Cornell University Press, 1965.

FELIPE, NANCY JO, AND ROBERT SOMMER. "Invasions of Personal Space," *Social Problems*, 14 (Fall 1966), 206–214.

FEUER, LEWIS S. *The Conflict of Generations*. New York: Basic Books, 1969.

FLACKS, RICHARD. "Social and Cultural Meanings of Student Revolt: Some Informal Comparative Observations," *Social Problems*, 17 (Winter 1970), 340–357.

FOLSON, JOSEPH KIRK. *The Family and Democratic Society*. New York: Wiley, 1943.

FOOTE, NELSON N., AND LEONARD S. COTTRELL, JR. *Identity and Interpersonal Competence*. Chicago: The University of Chicago Press, 1955.

FOSTER, GEORGE M. *Traditional Cultures and the Impact of Technological Change.* New York: Harper, 1962.

FRANCIS, ROY G. "Family Strategy in Middle Class Suburbia," *Sociological Inquiry*, 33 (Spring 1963), 157–164.

FRASER, THOMAS M., JR. *Fisherman of South Thailand: The Malay Villagers.* New York: Holt, Rinehart and Winston, 1966.

FRAZIER, ALEXANDER, AND LORENZO K. LISONBEE. "Adolescent Concerns with Physique," in Jerome M. Seidman (ed.), *The Adolescent: A Book of Readings.* New York: Dryden, 1953.

FREEDMAN, DEBORAH S. AND RONALD, AND PASCAL K. WHELPTON. "Size of Family and Preference for Children of Each Sex," *American Journal of Sociology*, 46 (September 1960), 141–146.

FREEDMAN, RONALD, AND LOLAGENE COOMBS. "Childspacing and Family Economic Position," *American Sociological Review*, 31 (October 1966), 631–648.

FREEMAN, LINTON C. "Marriage Without Love: Mate-Selection in Non-Western Societies," in Robert F. Winch and Louis Wolf Goodman (eds.), *Selected Studies in Marriage and the Family.* New York: Holt, Rinehart and Winston, 1968.

FREUD, SIGMUND. "Some Psychological Consequences of the Anatomical Distinction Between the Sexes," in *Collected Papers.* London: The Hogarth Press, 1956, Vol. V.

FRIEDAN, BETTY. *The Feminine Mystique.* New York: Norton, 1963.

FRIEDL, ERNESTINE. *Vasilika: A Village in Modern Greece.* New York: Holt, Rinehart and Winston, 1962.

FRIEDMAN, E. A., AND ROBERT J. HAVIGHURST. "Work and Retirement," in Sigmund Nosow and William H. Form (eds.), *Man, Work, and Society.* New York: Basic Books, 1962.

FRIEDSAM, HIRAM J. "Theory, Practice, and Ideology: The Case of 'Applied Social Gerontology.' " Paper read at meetings of the Southern Sociological Association, New Orleans, April 12, 1969.

————, AND HARRY R. DICK. "An Exploratory Study of Resident and Relative Views of Involvement in Admissions to Two Homes for the Aged," *Journal of Health and Human Behavior*, 5 (Spring 1964), 45–50.

FROMM, ERICH. *The Art of Loving.* New York: Harper and Row, 1956.

FURSTENBERG, FRANK, JR., LEON GORDIS, AND MILTON MARKOWITZ. "Birth Control Knowledge and Attitudes Among Unmarried Pregnant Adolescents: A Preliminary Report," *Journal of Marriage and the Family*, 31 (February 1969), 34–42.

GASS, GERTRUDE ZEMON. "Counseling Implications of Woman's Changing Role," *Personnel and Guidance Journal*, 37 (March 1959), 482–487.

GENNÉ, WILLIAM H. *Husbands and Pregnancy.* New York: Association Press, 1956.

GENNEP, ARNOLD VAN. *Les Rites de Passage.* Paris: Emile Nourry, 1909.

GINOTT, HAIM G. *Between Parent and Child.* New York: Macmillan, 1965.

GLASSER, PAUL H. AND LOIS N. "Role Reversal and Conflict Between Aged Parents and Their Children," *Marriage and Family Living*, 24 (February 1962), 46–51.

GLASSER, PAUL H., AND LOIS N. GLASSER (eds.) *Families In Crisis*. New York: Harper & Row, 1970.

GLAZER, NATHAN. "Housing Policy and the Family," *Journal of Marriage and the Family*, 29 (February 1967), 140–163.

———, AND DANIEL P. MOYNIHAN. *Beyond the Melting Pot*. Cambridge: The M.I.T. Press, 1963.

GLEASON, GEORGE. *Horizons for Older People*. New York: Macmillan, 1956.

GLENN, HORTENSE M. "Attitudes of Women Regarding Gainful Employment of Married Women," *Journal of Home Economics*, 51 (April 1959), 247–252.

GLICK, PAUL C. "First Marriages and Remarriages," *American Sociological Review*, 14 (December 1949), 726–734.

———. *American Families*. New York: Wiley, 1957.

———, AND H. CARTER. "Marriage Patterns and Educational Level," *American Sociological Review*, 23 (June 1958), 294–300.

———, AND ROBERT PARKE, JR. "New Approaches in Studying the Life Cycle of the Family," *Demography*, 2 (1965), 187–202.

GLUCKMAN, MAX. "Kinship and Marriage Among the Lozi of Northern Rhodesia and the Zulu of Natal," in A. R. Radcliffe-Brown and Daryll Forde (eds.), *African Systems of Kinship and Marriage*. London: Oxford University Press, 1950, pp. 166–206.

———. *Custom and Conflict in Africa*. Oxford, England: Basil Blackwell, 1955.

——— (ed.). *Essays on the Ritual of Social Relations*. Manchester, England: Manchester University Press, 1963.

GOLDSCHEIDER, CALVIN, AND SIDNEY GOLDSTEIN. "Generational Changes in Jewish Family Structure," *Journal of Marriage and the Family*, 29 (May 1967), 267–276.

GOLDSTEIN, JOSEPH, AND JAY KATZ. *The Family and the Law*. New York: Free Press, 1965.

GOODE, WILLIAM J. "Economic Factors and Marital Stability," *American Sociological Review*, 16 (December 1951), 802–812.

———. *After Divorce*. New York: Free Press, 1956.

———. "The Theoretical Importance of Love," *American Sociological Review*, 24 (February 1959), 38–47.

———. *World Revolution and Family Patterns*. New York: Free Press, 1963.

———. *The Family*. Englewood Cliffs, N.J.: Prentice-Hall, 1964.

———. "Family Disorganization," in Robert K. Merton and Robert A. Nisbet (eds.), *Contemporary Social Problems*. New York: Harcourt, Brace & World, 1966, pp. 479–552.

———. "The Role of the Family in Industrialization," in Robert F. Winch and Louis Wolf Goodman (eds.), *Selected Studies in Marriage and the Family*. New York: Holt, Rinehart and Winston, 1968.

GOODMAN, NORMAN, AND RICHARD OFSHE. "Empathy, Communication Efficiency, and Marital Status," *Journal of Marriage and the Family*, 30 (November 1968), 597–603.

GOODSELL, WILLYSTINE. *A History of Marriage and the Family*. Rev. ed. New York: Macmillan, 1934.

GORER, GEOFFREY. *The American People*. New York: Norton, 1948.

GOULDNER, ALVIN K. *Enter Plato*. New York: Basic Books, 1966.

GOVER, DAVID A., AND DOROTHY G. JONES. "Requirement of Parental Consent: A Deterrent to Marriage?" *Journal of Marriage and the Family*, 26 (May 1964), 205–206.

GRAVATT, ARTHUR E. "Family Relations in Middle and Old Age: A Review," *Journal of Gerontology*, 8 (April 1953), 197–201.

GRAY, HORACE. "Marriage and Premarital Conception," *The Journal of Psychology*, 50 (October 1960), 383–397.

GREENFIELD, SIDNEY M. "Industrialization and the Family in Sociological Theory," *American Journal of Sociology*, 67 (November 1961), 312–322.

———. "Love and Marriage in Modern America: A Functional Analysis," *Sociological Quarterly*, 6 (Autumn 1965), 361–377.

GRIBOV, I. "Marriage Palaces in Moscow," *Marriage and Family Living*, 22 (August 1960), 274.

GROVES, W. EUGENE, PETER H. ROSSI, AND DAVID GRAFSTEIN. "Life Styles and Campus Communities," preliminary report, Campus Community Studies, Johns Hopkins University, December 1970.

GRUEN, JOHN. *The Private World of Leonard Bernstein*. New York: Viking, 1968.

GURIN, GERALD, JOSEPH VEROFF, AND SHEILA FELD. *Americans View Their Mental Health*. New York: Basic Books, 1960.

HAAVIO-MANNILA, ELINA. "Some Consequences of Women's Emancipation," *Journal of Marriage and the Family*, 31 (February 1969), 123–134.

HALVERSON, HENRY M. "Genital and Sphincter Behavior of the Male Infant," *Pedagogical Seminary and Journal of Genetic Psychology*, 56 (March 1940), 95–136.

HAMILTON, GILBERT V. *A Research in Marriage*. New York: Albert & Charles Boni, 1929.

HARDIN, GARRETT. "Abortion—or Compulsory Pregnancy?" *Journal of Marriage and the Family*, 30 (May 1968), 246–251.

HARLOW, HARRY F. "The Nature of Love," *The American Psychologist*, 13 (December 1958), 673–685.

HARRINGTON, ALAN. *The Immortalist*. New York: Random House, 1969.

HARRIS, DANIEL. "Age and Occupational Factors in the Residential Propinquity of Marriage Partners," *Journal of Social Psychology*, 6 (May 1935), 257–261.

HART, C. W. M., AND ARNOLD R. PILLING. *The Tiwi of North Australia*. New York: Holt, Rinehart and Winston, 1960.

HART, HORNELL, AND WILMER SHIELDS. "Happiness in Relation to Age at Marriage," *Journal of Social Hygiene*, 12 (June 1926), 403–407.

HARTLEY, RUTH E. "Some Implications of Current Changes in Sex-Role Patterns," *Merrill-Palmer Quarterly*, 6 (April 1960), 153–164.

HAVIGHURST, ROBERT J. *Developmental Tasks and Education*. New York: Longmans, 1950.

―――. *Human Development and Education*. New York: Longmans, 1953.

―――, BERNICE L. NEUGARTEN, AND SHELDON S. TOBIN. "Disengagement and Patterns of Aging," in Bernice L. Neugarten (ed.), *Middle Age and Aging*. Chicago: University of Chicago Press, 1968, pp. 161–172.

HAWKINS, JAMES L. "Associations Between Companionship, Hostility, and Marital Satisfaction," *Journal of Marriage and the Family*, 30 (November 1968), 647–650.

HEDRICH, A. W., AND CHARLOTTE SILVERMAN. "Should the Premarital Blood Test Be Compulsory?" *American Journal of Public Health*, 248 (February 1958), 125–132.

HEER, DAVID M. "Negro-White Marriage in the United States," *New Society*, 6 (August 1965), 7–9.

HENDERSHOT, GERRY E. "Familial Satisfaction, Birth Order, and Fertility Values," *Journal of Marriage and the Family*, 31 (February 1969), 27–33.

HENRY, JULES. *Culture Against Man*. New York: Random House, 1963.

HENTOFF, MARGOT. "The Curse," *New York Review of Books*, January 16, 1969, p. 3.

HILL, REUBEN. "Education for Marriage and Parenthood in the United States." Paper read at Social Scientists' Advisory Meeting, sponsored by the Social Security Administration, June 20–21, 1960.

―――. "Decision Making and the Family Life Cycle," in Bernice L. Neugarten (ed.), *Middle Age and Aging*. Chicago: University of Chicago Press, 1968, pp. 286–295.

―――, AND HOWARD BECKER. *Marriage and the Family*. Boston: D. C. Heath, 1942.

―――, J. M. STYCOS, AND KURT W. BACK. *The Family and Population Control*. Chapel Hill: University of North Carolina Press, 1959.

HILSDALE, PAUL. "Marriage as a Personal Existential Commitment," *Marriage and Family Living*, 24 (May 1962), 137–143.

HILTNER, SEWARD. *Sex Ethics and the Kinsey Reports*. New York: Association Press, 1953.

HOBART, CHARLES W. "Commitment, Value Conflict and the Future of the American Family," *Marriage and Family Living*, 25 (November 1963), 405–412.

HOBBS, DANIEL F., JR. "Parenthood as Crisis: A Third Study," *Journal of Marriage and the Family*, 27 (August 1965), 367–372.

HOCHSCHILD, ARLIE. "The Role of the Ambassador's Wife: An Exploratory Study," *Journal of Marriage and the Family*, 31 (February 1969), 73–87.

HOLLINGSHEAD, AUGUST B. "Class Differences and Family Stability," *Annals of the American Academy of Political and Social Science*, 272 (November 1950a), 39–46.

―――. "Cultural Factors in the Selection of Marriage Mates," *American Sociological Review*, 15 (October 1950b), 619–627.

―――. "Marital Status and Wedding Behavior," *Marriage and Family Living*, 14 (November 1952), 308–311.

HORNEY, KAREN. "The Denial of the Vagina," Harold Kelman (ed.), in Karen Horney, *Feminine Psychology*. New York: Norton, 1967, pp. 147–161.

HORTON, DONALD. "The Dialogue of Courtship in Popular Songs," *American Journal of Sociology*, 62 (May 1957), 569–578.

HOWARD, GEORGE S. *A History of Matrimonial Institutions*. 3 vols. Chicago: University of Chicago Press, 1904.

HURLEY, JOHN R., AND DONNA P. PALONEN. "Marital Satisfaction and Child Density Among University Student Parents," *Journal of Marriage and the Family*, 29 (August 1967), 483–484.

JACO, E. GARTLY, AND IVAN BELKNAP. "Is a New Family Form Emerging in the Urban Fringe?" *American Sociological Review*, 18 (October 1953), 551–557.

JACOBSON, PAUL H. "Differentials in Divorce by Duration of Marriage and Size of Family," *American Sociological Review*, 15 (April 1950), 235–244.

———. *American Marriage and Divorce*. New York: Holt, Rinehart and Winston, 1959.

JEFFERY, C. RAY. "Social Class and Adoption Petitioners," *Social Problems*, 9 (Spring, 1962), 354–358.

JENCKS, CHRISTOPHER. Review of Gael Greene's *Sex and the College Girl*, *New Republic*, April 4, 1964, 18–21.

JEPHCOTT, PEARL, with NANCY SEARS AND JOHN H. SMITH. *Married Women Working*. London: G. Allen, 1962.

JOHANNIS, THEODORE B., JR. "Participation by Fathers, Mothers, and Teenage Sons and Daughters in Selected Child Care and Control Activity," *The Coordinator*, 6 (December 1957), 31–32.

———. "Married College Students and Their Honeymoons," *Family Life Coordinator*, 7 (March 1959), 39–40.

———, AND JAMES M. ROLLINS. "Teenager Perceptions of Family Decision Making," *The Coordinator*, 7 (June 1959), 70–74.

KAHN, HERMAN, AND ANTHONY J. WIENER. *The Year 2000*. New York: Macmillan, 1967.

KAMMEYER, KENNETH. "The Feminine Role: An Analysis of Attitude Consistency," *Journal of Marriage and the Family*, 26 (August 1964), 295–305.

———. "Birth Order and the Feminine Sex Role Among College Women," *American Sociological Review*, 31 (August 1966), 508–515.

KANIN, EUGENE J., AND DAVID H. HOWARD. "Postmarital Consequences of Premarital Sex Adjustments," *American Sociological Review*, 23 (October 1958), 556–562.

KAPLAN, MAX. "The Uses of Leisure," in Clark Tibbitts (ed.), *Handbook of Social Gerontology*. Chicago: University of Chicago Press, 1960.

KARGMAN, MARIE W. "Legal Obligations of Remarriage: What Is and What Ought To Be," *The Family Coordinator*, 18 (April 1969), 174–177.

KATZ, ALVIN M., AND REUBEN HILL. "Residential Propinquity and Marital Selection: A Review of Theory, Method, and Fact," *Journal of Marriage and the Family*, 20 (February 1958), 27–35.

KELL, LEONE, AND JOAN ALDOUS. "Trends in Child Care over Three Generations," *Marriage and Family Living*, 22 (May 1960), 176–177.

KENISTON, KENNETH. "Youth as a Social Force." Paper read at meetings of the American Psychiatric Association, Miami Beach, 1969.

KENKEL, WILLIAM F. "Marriage and the Family in Modern Science Fiction," *Journal of Marriage and the Family*, 31 (February 1969), 6–14.

KENNEDY, RUBY JO REEVES. "Premarital Residential Propinquity and Ethnic Endogamy," *American Journal of Sociology*, 48 (March 1943), 580–584.

KEPHART, WILLIAM M. "The Duration of Marriage," *American Sociological Review*, 19 (June 1954), 287–295.

———. "Occupational Level and Marital Disruption," *American Sociological Review*, 20 (August 1955), 456–465.

———. *The Family, Society, and the Individual.* Boston: Houghton Mifflin, 1961.

———. *The Family, Society, and the Individual.* 2nd ed. Boston: Houghton Mifflin, 1966.

———. "Some Correlates of Romantic Love," *Journal of Marriage and the Family*, 29 (August 1967), 470–479.

———, AND THOMAS P. MONAHAN. "Desertion and Divorce in Philadelphia," *American Sociological Review*, 17 (December 1952), 719–727.

KERCKHOFF, RICHARD. "Teaching Ethical Values Through the Marriage Course: A Debate, Con," *Marriage and Family Living*, 19 (November 1957), 330–334.

KINSEY, ALFRED C., WARDELL B. POMEROY, AND CLYDE E. MARTIN. *Sexual Behavior in the Human Male.* Philadelphia: W. B. Saunders, 1948.

———, AND PAUL H. GEBHARD. *Sexual Behavior in the Human Female.* Philadelphia: W. B. Saunders, 1953.

KIRKENDALL, LESTER A. "Circumstances Associated with Teenage Boys' Use of Prostitution," *Journal of Marriage and the Family*, 22 (May 1960), 145–149.

KIRKPATRICK, CLIFFORD. *The Family as Process and Institution.* 2nd ed. New York: Ronald, 1963.

———, AND THEODORE CAPLOW. "Courtship in a Group of Minnesota Students," *American Journal of Sociology*, 51 (September 1945a), 114–125.

———, AND THEODORE CAPLOW. "Emotional Trends in the Courtship Experience of College Students as Expressed by Graphs, with Some Observations on Methodological Implications." *American Sociological Review*, 10 (October 1945b), 619–626.

———, AND CHARLES HOBART. "Disagreement, Disagreement Estimate, and Non-Empathic Imputation for Intimacy Groups Varying from Favorite Date to Married," *American Sociological Review*, 19 (February 1954), 10–19.

KITSUSE, JOHN I., AND AARON V. CICOUREL. "The High School's Role in Adolescent Status Transition," in B. J. Chandler, L. J. Stiles, and J. I. Kitsuse (eds.), *Education in Urban Society.* New York: Dodd, Mead, 1962.

KNOX, DAVID H., JR., AND MICHAEL J. SPORAKOWSKI. "Attitudes of College Students Toward Love," *Journal of Marriage and the Family*, 30 (November 1968), 638–642.

KOHN, MELVIN L., AND ELEANOR E. CARROLL. "Social Class and the Allocation of Parental Responsibilities," *Sociometry,* 23 (December 1960), 372–392.

KOLLER, MARVIN B. "Residential Propinquity of White Mates at Marriage in Relation to Age and Occupation of Males, Columbus, Ohio, 1938 and 1946," *American Sociological Review,* 13 (October 1948), 613–616.

KOMAROVSKY, MIRRA. *Blue-Collar Marriage.* New York: Random House, 1964.

KOOS, EARL L. "Class Differences in Family Reactions to Crisis," *Marriage and Family Living,* 12 (Winter, 1950), 77–78.

KORSON, J. HENRY. "Dower and Social Class in an Urban Muslim Community," *Journal of Marriage and the Family,* 29 (August 1967), 527–533.

KRONHAUSEN, PHYLLIS AND EBERHARD. *Sex Histories of American College Men.* New York: Ballantine Books, 1960.

KTSANES, THOMAS AND VIRGINIA. "The Theory of Complementary Needs in Mate-Selection," in Robert F. Winch and Louis Wolf Goodman (eds.), *Selected Studies in Marriage and the Family.* New York: Holt, Rinehart and Winston, 1968, pp. 517–529.

KUBIE, LAWRENCE S. "Psychiatric Implications of the Kinsey Report," in Jerome Himmelhoch and Sylvia Fava (eds.), *Sexual Behavior in American Society.* New York: Norton, 1955.

KUPER, HILDA. *The Swazi: A South African Kingdom.* New York: Holt, Rinehart and Winston, 1963.

KURTZ, RICHARD M. "Body Image—Male or Female," *Trans-action,* 6 (December 1968), 25–27.

LAMBERT, CAMILLE, HOWARD E. FREEMAN, *et al. The Clinic Habit.* New Haven, Conn.: College & University Press, 1967.

LANDIS, JUDSON T. "The Pattern of Divorce in Three Generations," *Social Forces,* 34 (March 1956), 213–216.

———. "A Comparison of Children from Divorced and Nondivorced Unhappy Marriages," *The Family Life Coordinator,* 11 (July 1962), 61–65.

LANDIS, PAUL H. "Sequential Marriage," *Journal of Home Economics,* 42 (September 1950), 625–628.

LEGMAN, GERSHON. *Rationale of the Dirty Joke.* New York: Grove Press, 1968.

LEICHTER, HOPE JENSEN, AND WILLIAM E. MITCHELL. *Kinship and Casework.* New York: Russell Sage Foundation, 1967.

LEMASTERS, E. E. "Parenthood as Crisis," *Marriage and Family Living,* 19 (November 1957), 352–355.

LEMASTERS, E. E. *Parents in Modern America.* Homewood, Ill.: Dorsey Press, 1970.

LENSKI, GERHARD. *The Religious Factor.* Garden City, N.Y.: Doubleday, 1961.

LERMAN, PAUL. "Argot, Symbolic Deviance and Subcultural Delinquency," *American Sociological Review,* 32 (April 1967), 209–224.

LESLIE, GERALD R. "The Field of Marriage Counseling," in Harold T. Christensen (ed.), *Handbook of Marriage and the Family.* Chicago: Rand McNally, 1964.

———. *The Family in Social Context.* London: Oxford University Press, 1967.

LEVINGER, GEORGE. "Marital Cohesiveness and Dissolution: An Integrative Review," *Journal of Marriage and the Family*, 27 (February 1965), 19–28.

LEWIS, OSCAR. *Life in a Mexican Village*. Urbana: University of Illinois Press, 1951.

LICHT, HANS. *Sexual Life in Ancient Greece*. London: Routledge and Kegan Paul, 1932.

LINDER, STAFFAN BURENSTAM. *The Harried Leisure Class*. New York: Columbia University Press, 1969.

LIPSET, SEYMOUR MARTIN. "The Activists: A Profile," *The Public Interest*, 13 (Fall 1968), 39–51.

LITWAK, EUGENE. "Three Ways in Which Law Acts as a Means of Social Control: Punishment, Therapy, and Education," *Social Forces*, 34 (March 1956), 217–223.

————. "Occupational Mobility and Extended Family Cohesion," *American Sociological Review*, 25 (February 1960a), 9–21.

————. "Geographic Mobility and Extended Family Cohesion," *American Sociological Review*, 25 (June 1960b), 385–394.

LIVELY, EDWIN L. "Toward Concept Clarification: The Case of Marital Interaction," *Journal of Marriage and the Family*, 31 (February 1969), 108–114.

LOCKE, HARVEY J. *Predicting Adjustment in Marriage*. New York: Henry Holt, 1951.

LOPATA, HELENA Z. "The Secondary Features of a Primary Relationship," *Human Organization*, 24 (Summer, 1965), 116–123.

LOWENTHAL, MARJORIE FISKE, AND CLAYTON HAVEN. "Interaction and Adaptation: Intimacy as a Critical Variable," *American Sociological Review*, 33 (February 1968), 20–30.

LOWRIE, SAMUEL H. "Dating Theories and Student Responses," *American Sociological Review*, 16 (June 1951), 334–340.

————. "Early and Late Dating: Some Conditions Associated with Them," *Marriage and Family Living*, 23 (August 1961), 284–291.

————. "Early Marriages: Premarital Pregnancy and Associated Factors," *Journal of Marriage and the Family*, 27 (February 1965), 48–56.

LUPRI, EUGEN. "Contemporary Authority Patterns in the West German Family: A Study in Cross-National Validation," *Journal of Marriage and the Family*, 31 (February 1969), 134–144.

MACE, DAVID R. *Hebrew Marriage*. New York: Philosophical Library, 1953.

MADDOX, G. L., JR. "Disengagement Theory: A Critical Evaluation," *Gerontologist*, 4 (June 1964), Part 1, 80–82.

MAGRABI, FRANCES M., AND WILLIAM H. MARSHALL. "Family Developmental Tasks: A Research Model," *Journal of Marriage and the Family*, 27 (November 1965), 454–458.

MAINE, HENRY SUMNER. *Ancient Law*. New York: Henry Holt, 1885.

MALHOTRA, PRABHA, AND LILIAN KHAN. "Factors Favoring Acceptance of Family Planning Among Women Attending Some New Delhi M.C.W. Centers," *Journal of Family Welfare*, 8 (1962), 1–18.

MALINOWSKI, BRONISLAW. "The Principle of Legitimacy," in Rose Laub Coser (ed.), *The Family: Its Structure and Functions*. New York: St. Martin's Press, 1964, pp. 3–19, first published in 1930.

——. *A Diary in the Strict Sense of the Term*. Norbert Guterman (tr.). New York: Harcourt, Brace, and World, 1967.

MARRIS, PETER. "Individual Achievement and Family Ties: Some International Comparisons," *Journal of Marriage and the Family*, 29 (November 1967), 763–771.

MASTERS, WILLIAM H., AND VIRGINIA E. JOHNSON. *Human Sexual Response*. Boston: Little, Brown, 1966.

——. *Human Sexual Inadequacy*. Boston: Little, Brown, 1970.

MAYER, JOHN E. "The Invisibility of Married Life," *New Society*, February 26, 1967.

MCCAGHY, CHARLES H., AND JAMES K. SKIPPER, JR. "Lesbian Behavior as an Adaptation to the Occupation of Stripping," *Social Problems*, 17 (Spring 1969), 262–270.

MCDANIEL, CLYDE O., JR. "Dating Roles and Reasons for Dating," *Journal of Marriage and the Family*, 31 (February 1969), 97–107.

MCINTOSH, MARY. "The Homosexual Role," *Social Problems*, 16 (Summer 1968), 182–192.

MCKEANY, MAURINE. *The Absent Father and Public Policy in the Program of Aid to Dependent Children*. Berkeley: University of California Press, 1960.

MCLUHAN, MARSHALL. *Understanding Media*. New York: McGraw-Hill, 1964.

MEAD, MARGARET. *Sex and Temperament*. New York: Morrow, 1935.

——. *Male and Female: A Study of the Sexes in a Changing World*. New York: Morrow, 1953.

——. "Marriage in Two Steps," *Redbook*, July 1966, pp. 48ff.

——. *Culture and Commitment*. New York: Doubleday, 1969.

MENCHER, SAMUEL. "Social Authority and the Family," *Journal of Marriage and the Family*, 29 (February 1967), 164–192.

MERCER, CHARLES V. "Interrelations Among Family Stability, Family Composition, Residence, and Race," *Journal of Marriage and the Family*, 29 (August 1967), 456–460.

MESSER, ALFRED A. "Dissolution of Long-Standing Marriages," *Mental Hygiene*, 53 (January 1969), 127–130.

METROPOLITAN LIFE INSURANCE. *Statistical Bulletin*. New York: May 1950.

MIDDLETON, RUSSELL. "A Deviant Case: Brother-Sister and Father-Daughter Marriage in Ancient Egypt," *American Sociological Review*, 27 (October 1962), 603–611.

MILNE, LORUS J. AND MARGERY. *The Ages of Life*. New York: Harcourt, Brace & World, 1968.

MIRANDE, ALFRED M. "Reference Group Theory and Adolescent Sexual Behavior," *Journal of Marriage and the Family*, 30 (November 1968), 572–577.

MITCHELL, J. C. "Social Change and the Stability of African Marriage in Northern Rhodesia," in Aidan Southall (ed.), *Social Change in Modern Africa*. London: Oxford University Press, 1961, pp. 316–329.

MOGEY, JOHN M. "A Century of Declining Paternal Authority," *Marriage and Family Living*, 19 (August 1957), 234–239.

――――. "Research on the Family: The Search for World Trends," *Journal of Marriage and the Family*, 31 (May 1969), 225–232.

MONAHAN, THOMAS P. "How Stable Are Remarriages?" *American Journal of Sociology*, 58 (November 1952), 280–288.

――――. "Divorce by Occupational Level," *Marriage and Family Living*, 17 (November 1955a), 322–324.

――――. "Is Childlessness Related to Family Stability?" *American Sociological Review*, 20 (August 1955b), 446–456.

――――. "Family Fugitives," *Marriage and Family Living*, 20 (May 1958a), 146–151.

――――. "The Changing Nature and Instability of Remarriages," *Eugenics Quarterly*, 5 (June 1958b), 73–85.

――――. "The Duration of Marriage to Divorce: Second Marriages and Migratory Types," *Marriage and Family Living*, 21 (May 1959), 134–138.

――――. "When Couples Part: Statistical Trends and Relationships in Divorce," *American Sociological Review*, 27 (October 1962), 625–633.

――――, AND WILLIAM M. KEPHART. "Divorce and Desertion by Religious and Mixed-Religious Groups," *American Journal of Sociology*, 59 (March 1954), 454–465.

MOORE, BERNICE M., AND WAYNE H. HOLTZMAN. *Tomorrow's Parents*. Austin: University of Texas Press, 1965.

MORISON, ROBERT S. "Where Is Biology Taking Us?" *Science*, 155 (January 1967), 429–433.

MOSKIN, J. ROBERT. "The New Contraceptive Society," a preview of *On Sexual Life in Sweden* by Hans L. Zetterberg, in *Look*, February 4, 1969, pp. 50–53.

MOSS, J. JOEL, AND MARIAN MYERS MACNAB. "Young Families," *Journal of Home Economics*, 53 (December 1961), 829–834.

MURDOCK, GEORGE PETER. *Social Structure*. New York: Macmillan, 1949.

――――. "Family Stability in Non-European Societies," *Annals of the American Academy of Political and Social Science*, 272 (November 1950), 195–201.

――――. "World Ethnographic Sample," *American Anthropologist*, 59 (August 1957), 664–687.

MURSTEIN, BERNARD I. "Empirical Tests of Role, Complementary Needs, and Homogamy Theories of Marital Choice," *Journal of Marriage and the Family*, 29 (November 1967), 689–696.

MURTAGH, JOHN M., AND SARA HARRIS. *Cast the First Stone*. New York: McGraw-Hill, 1957.

NELSON, JOEL I. "Anomie: Comparisons Between the Old and New Middle Class," *American Journal of Sociology*, 74 (September 1968), 184–192.

NEUGARTEN, BERNICE L., AND KAROL K. WEINSTEIN. "The Changing American Grandparent," *Marriage and Family Living*, 26 (May 1964), 199–204.

NIMKOFF, M. F. (ed.). *Comparative Family Systems*. Boston: Houghton Mifflin, 1965.

NOVS Special Reports, Vol. 45, No. 12 (1957).

NYE, F. IVAN. "Child Adjustment in Broken and in Unhappy Unbroken Homes," *Marriage and Family Living,* 19 (November 1957), 356–361.

————. "Values, Family, and a Changing Society," *Journal of Marriage and the Family,* 29 (May 1967), 241–248.

————, AND LOIS W. HOFFMAN (eds.). *The Employed Mother in America.* Chicago: Rand McNally, 1963.

OGBURN, WILLIAM F. "The Changing Family," *The Family,* 19 (July 1938), 139–143.

————. "Marital Separations," *American Journal of Sociology,* 49 (January 1944), 316–323.

ORDEN, SUSAN R., AND NORMAN M. BRADBURN. "Working Wives and Marriage Happiness," *American Journal of Sociology,* 74 (January 1969), 392–407.

OSBORNE, RUTH FARNHAM. "Boys and Family Life Education," *Marriage and Family Living,* 23 (February 1961), 50–52.

OTTO, HERBERT A. (ed.). *The Family in Search of a Future: Alternative Models for Moderns.* New York: Appleton-Century-Crofts, 1970.

PARKE, ROBERT, JR., AND PAUL C. GLICK. "Prospective Changes in Marriage and the Family," *Journal of Marriage and the Family,* 29 (May 1967), 249–256.

PARSONS, TALCOTT. "The Kinship System of the Contemporary United States," *American Anthropologist,* 45 (January–March 1943), 22–38.

————. "Toward a Healthy Maturity," *Journal of Health and Human Behavior,* 1 (Fall 1960), 163–173.

————. "Old Age as a Consummatory Phase," *Gerontologist,* 3 (June 1963), 53–54.

————, ROBERT F. BALES, et al. *Family, Socialization and Interaction Process.* New York: Free Press, 1955.

PATAI, RAPHAEL. *Sex and Family in the Bible and the Middle East.* Garden City, N.Y.: Dolphin Books, 1959.

PAULME, DENISE (ed.). *Women of Tropical Africa.* Berkeley: University of California Press, 1963.

PENALOSA, FERNANDO. "Mexican Family Roles," *Journal of Marriage and the Family,* 30 (November 1968), 680–689.

PETERSEN, DAVID M. "Husband-Wife Communication and Family Problems," *Sociology and Social Research,* 53 (April 1969), 375–384.

PETERSON, JOYCE, AND MARILYN MERCER. *Adultery for Adults.* New York: Coward-McCann, 1969.

PINEO, PETER C. "Disenchantment in the Later Years of Marriage," *Marriage and Family Living,* 23 (February 1961), 3–11.

PLOSCOWE, MORRIS. *The Truth About Divorce.* New York: Hawthorn Books, 1955.

POHLMAN, EDWARD. "Some Effects of Being Able to Control Sex of Offspring," *Eugenics Quarterly,* 14 (December 1967), 274–281.

POLLAK, OTTO. "The Outlook for the American Family," *Journal of Marriage and the Family,* 29 (February 1967), 193–205.

POMEROY, WARDELL B. *Boys and Sex.* New York: Delacorte Press, 1968.

POPE, HALLOWELL. "Unwed Mothers and Their Sex Partners," *Journal of Marriage and the Family,* 29 (August 1967), 555–567.

POTTER, ROBERT G., JR., PHILIP C. SAGI, AND CHARLES F. WESTOFF. "Improvement of Contraception During the Course of Marriage," *Population Studies,* 16 (November 1962), 160–174.

PUTNEY, SNELL, AND GAIL J. PUTNEY. *Normal Neurosis: The Adjusted American.* New York: Harper & Row, 1964.

QUEEN, STUART A., ROBERT W. HABENSTEIN, AND JOHN B. ADAMS (eds.). *The Family In Various Cultures.* New York: Lippincott, 1961.

RAINWATER, LEE. "Social Status Differences in the Family Relationships of German Men," *Marriage and Family Living,* 24 (February 1962), 12–17.

———. "Crucible of Identity: The Negro Lower-Class Family," *Daedalus,* 95 (Winter 1966), 172–216.

———, AND GERALD HANDEL. "Changing Family Roles in the Working Class," in Arthur B. Shostak and William Gomberg (eds.), *Blue-Collar World.* Englewood Cliffs, N.J.: Prentice-Hall, 1964.

———, AND KAROL KANE WEINSTEIN. "A Qualitative Exploration of Family Planning and Contraception in the Working Class," *Marriage and Family Living,* 22 (August 1960), 238–242.

RAMSEY, GLEN V. "The Sexual Development of Boys," *American Journal of Psychology,* 56 (April 1943), 217–234.

———. "The Sex Information of Younger Boys," in Jerome M. Seidman (ed.), *The Adolescent: A Book of Readings.* New York: Dryden, 1953.

RANDALL, JOHN HERMAN, JR. "The Manifold Experience of Augustine," *The American Scholar,* 38 (Winter 1968–1969), 127–134.

RAPOPORT, RHONA. "Normal Crises, Family Structure, and Mental Health," *Family Process,* 2 (1962), 68–80.

———, AND ROBERT N. "New Light on the Honeymoon," *Human Relations,* 17 (February 1964), 33–56.

———. "Work and Family in Contemporary Society," *American Sociological Review,* 30 (June 1965), 381–394.

REEVY, WILLIAM R. "Premarital Petting Behavior and Marital Happiness Prediction," *Marriage and Family Living,* 21 (November 1959), 349–355.

REISS, ALBERT J. "Sex Offenses: The Marginal Status of the Adolescent," *Law and Contemporary Problems,* 25 (Spring 1960), 309–333.

REISS, IRA L. *Premarital Sexual Standards in America.* New York: Free Press, 1960.

———. "Sexual Codes in Teen-Age Culture," *Annals of the American Academy of Political and Social Science,* 338 (November 1961), 53–62.

———. "Social Class and Campus Dating," *Social Problems,* 13 (Fall 1965), 193–205.

———. *The Social Context of Premarital Sexual Permissiveness.* New York: Holt, Rinehart and Winston, 1967.

———. "How and Why America's Sex Standards Are Changing," *Transaction,* 5 (March 1968), 26–32.

REISS, PAUL J. "The Extended Kinship System: Correlates of and Attitudes on Frequency of Interaction," *Marriage and Family Living*, 24 (November 1962), 333–339.

RHEINGOLD, JOSEPH C. *The Fear of Being a Woman*. New York: Grune and Stratton, 1964.

RICARDS, SHERMAN L., JR. "The Secret Marriage," *Marriage and Family Living*, 22 (August 1960), 243–247.

RICHTER, STEPHEN. "The Economics of Child Rearing," *Journal of Marriage and the Family*, 30 (August 1968), 462–466.

RIESMAN, DAVID. "Some Continuities and Discontinuities in the Education of Women," in David Riesman, *Abundance for What?*. Garden City, N.Y.: Doubleday, 1964, pp. 324–348.

RILEY, MATILDA AND JOHN, AND MARY MOORE. "Adolescent Values and the Riesman Typology," in Seymour Lipset and Leo Lowenthal (eds.), *Culture and Social Character*. New York: Free Press, 1961.

ROBINS, LEE N., AND MIRODA TOMANEC. "Closeness to Blood Relatives Outside the Immediate Family," *Marriage and Family Living*, 24 (November 1962), 340–346.

RODGERS, DAVID A., AND FREDERICK J. ZIEGLER. "Social Role Theory, the Marital Relationship, and Use of Ovulation Suppressors," *Journal of Marriage and the Family*, 30 (April 1968), 584–591.

RODGERS, ROY H. "Toward a Theory of Family Development," *Journal of Marriage and the Family*, 26 (August 1964), 262–270.

RODMAN, HYMAN. "Marital Relationships in a Trinidad Village," *Marriage and Family Living*, 23 (May 1961), 166–170.

RODMAN, HYMAN (ed.). *Marriage, Family, and Society*. New York: Random House, 1965.

ROEMER, MILTON I. "Governmental Health Programs Affecting the American Family," *Journal of Marriage and the Family*, 29 (February 1967), 40–63.

ROGLER, LLOYD H. "A Better Life: Notes from Puerto Rico," *Trans-action*, 2 (March–April 1965), 34–36.

ROSE, ARNOLD M. "The Adequacy of Women's Expectations for Adult Roles," *Social Forces*, 30 (October 1951), 69–77.

———. "A Current Theoretical Issue in Social Gerontology," *The Gerontologist*, 4 (March 1964), 46–50.

ROSENBERG, BERNARD, AND JOSEPH BENSMAN. "Sexual Patterns in Three Ethnic Subcultures of an American Underclass," *Annals of the American Academy of Political and Social Science*, 376 (March 1968), 61–75.

ROSENMAYR, LEOPOLD. "Family Relations of the Elderly," *Journal of Marriage and the Family*, 30 (April 1968), 672–680.

ROSENSTIEL, EDITH E., AND HAROLD E. SMITH. "The Growth of Family Life Education in Illinois," *Marriage and Family Living*, 25 (February 1963), 109–111.

ROSENWAIKE, IRA. "Parental Consent Ages as a Factor in State Variation in Bride's Age at Marriage," *Journal of Marriage and the Family*, 29 (August 1967), 452–455.

ROSOW, IRVING. "And Then We Were Old," *trans-action*, 2 (January–February 1965), 21–26.

———. *Social Integration of the Aged.* New York: Free Press, 1967.

ROSSI, ALICE S. "Transition to Parenthood," *Journal of Marriage and the Family*, 30 (February 1968), 26–39.

ROSSI, PETER. Preface to Norman M. Bradburn and David Caplovitz, *Reports on Happiness.* Chicago: Aldine Publishing Co., 1965.

ROTH, JULIUS, AND ROBERT F. PECK. "Social Class and Social Mobility Factors Related to Marital Adjustment," *American Sociological Review*, 16 (August 1951), 478–487.

RUBIN, ZICK. "Do American Women Marry Up?" *American Sociological Review*, 33 (October 1968), 750–760.

RUTLEDGE, AARON L. *Pre-marital Counseling.* Cambridge, Mass.: Schenkman, 1966.

RYDER, NORMAN B., AND CHARLES F. WESTOFF. "Use of Oral Contraception in the United States, 1965," *Science*, 153 (September 9, 1966), 1199–1205.

SAHLINS, MARSHALL D. "The Social Life of Monkeys, Apes and Primitive Men," in Morton H. Fried (ed.), *Readings in Anthropology.* New York: Crowell, 1959, Vol. II.

SALTER, KENNETH W. "Canon Law Divorce and Annulment of the Roman Catholic Church at the Parish Level," *Journal of Marriage and the Family*, 31 (February 1969), 51–60.

SAUBER, MIGNON. "The Role of the Unmarried Father," *Welfare in Review*, 4 (November 1966), 15–18.

SCANZONI, JOHN. "A Reinquiry into Marital Disorganization," *Journal of Marriage and the Family*, 27 (November 1965), 483–491.

SCHAEFER, GEORGE, AND MILTON ZISOWITZ. *The Expectant Father.* New York: Simon and Schuster, 1964.

SCHLESINGER, BENJAMIN. "Remarriage—An Inventory of Findings," *The Family Coordinator*, 17 (October 1968), 248–250.

SCHNEPP, GERALD J. "Survey of Going Steady and Other Dating Practices," *The American Catholic Sociological Review*, 21 (Fall 1960), 238–250.

SCHORR, ALVIN L. "Current Practices of Filial Responsibility," in Robert Winch, Robert McGinnis, and Herbert Barringer (eds.), *Selected Studies in Marriage and the Family.* New York: Holt, Rinehart and Winston, 1962.

SCHWARTZ, GARY, AND DON MERTEN. "The Language of Adolescence: An Anthropological Approach to the Youth Culture," *American Journal of Sociology*, 72 (March 1967), 453–468.

SCOTT, JOHN FINLEY. "The American College Sorority: Its Role in Class and Ethnic Endogamy," *American Sociological Review*, 30 (August 1965), 514–527.

SHANAS, ETHEL. *The Health of Older People: A Social Survey.* Cambridge, Mass.: Harvard University Press, 1962.

———. "Family Help Patterns and Social Class in Three Countries," *Journal of Marriage and the Family*, 29 (May 1967), 257–266.

———, et al. *Old People in Three Industrial Societies.* New York: Atherton Press, 1968.

SHELDON, HENRY D. *The Older Population of the United States.* New York: Wiley, 1958.

SHIPMAN, GORDON. "The Psychodynamics of Sex Education," *The Family Coordinator,* 17 (January 1968), 3–12.

———, AND H. YUAN TIEN. "Nonmarriage and the Waiting Period," *Journal of Marriage and the Family,* 27 (May 1965), 277–280.

SHOSTAK, ARTHUR B. "Education and the Family," *Journal of Marriage and the Family,* 29 (February 1967), 124–139.

SHUTTLEWORTH, FRANK K. "A Biosocial and Developmental Theory of Male and Female Sexuality," *Marriage and Family Living,* 21 (May 1959), 163–170.

SIMON, WILLIAM, AND JOHN H. GAGNON. "Femininity in the Lesbian Community," *Social Problems,* 15 (Fall 1967), 212–221.

———. "Homosexuality: The Formulation of a Sociological Perspective," *Journal of Health and Social Behavior,* 8 (September 1967b), 177–185.

———, AND DONALD CARNS. Selected research findings reported in *The New York Times* December 14, 1968, Section 1, p. 84.

SKIPPER, JAMES K., JR., AND GILBERT NASS. "Dating Behavior: A Framework for Analysis and an Illustration," *Journal of Marriage and the Family,* 28 (November 1966), 412–420.

SLATER, PHILIP E. "On Social Regression," *American Sociological Review,* 28 (June 1963), 339–364.

SLIEPCEVICH, ELENA M. Study described by Elizabeth Force in the *Journal of Marriage and the Family,* 27 (February 1965), 96.

SMITH, RAYMOND T. "Family Structure and Plantation Systems in the New World." Paper presented at the Seminar on Plantation Systems of the New World, San Juan, Puerto Rico, 1957.

SPIRO, MELFORD E. "Is the Family Universal?" *American Anthropologist,* 56 (October 1954), 839–846

———. *Kibbutz: Venture in Utopia.* Cambridge, Mass.: Harvard University Press, 1956.

STEINER, GEORGE. "It Happened Tomorrow," *The New Yorker,* November 16, 1968, pp. 237–246.

STEPHENS, WILLIAM N. *The Family in Cross-Cultural Perspective.* New York: Holt, Rinehart and Winston, 1963.

STINNET, NICK, AND JAMES E. MONTGOMERY. "Youths' Perceptions of Marriages of Older Persons," *Journal of Marriage and the Family,* 30 (August 1968), 392–396.

STOLLER, FREDERICK H. "The Intimate Network of Families as a New Structure," in Herbert A. Otto (ed.), *The Family in Search of a Future: Alternative Models for Moderns.* New York: Appleton-Century-Crofts, 1970.

STOODLEY, BARTLETT H. "Normative Family Orientations of Chinese College Students in Hong Kong," *Journal of Marriage and the Family,* 29 (November 1967), 773–782.

STOUFFER, SAMUEL A. "Intervening Opportunities: A Theory Relating Mobility and Distance," *American Sociological Review,* 5 (December 1940), 845–867.

STRAUS, JACQUELINE H. AND MURRAY A. "Family Roles and Sex Differences in

Creativity of Children in Bombay and Minneapolis," *Journal of Marriage and the Family*, 30 (February 1968), 46–53.

STREIB, GORDON F. "Intergenerational Relations: Perspectives of the Two Generations on the Older Parent," *Journal of Marriage and the Family*, 27 (November 1965), 469–476.

———. "Disengagement: Scientific Theory or Sociological Interpretation?" Paper read at meetings of the *Southern Sociological Association*, New Orleans, April 12, 1969.

STYCOS, J. MAYONE. *Family and Fertility in Puerto Rico*. New York: Columbia University Press, 1955.

STYRON, WILLIAM. "The Vice That Has No Name," *Harper's*, February 1968, pp. 97–100.

SUCHMAN, EDWARD A. "Man—Health, Attitudes and Behavior," paper read at colloquium on *Man's Health and His Environment*, University of Illinois, December 6, 1968.

SULLIVAN, HARRY STACK. *The Interpersonal Theory of Psychiatry*. New York: Norton, 1953.

SUSSMAN, MARVIN B. "Parental Participation in Mate Selection and Its Effect Upon Family Continuity," *Social Forces*, 32 (October 1953), 76–81.

———, AND LEE G. BURCHINAL. "Kin Family Network: Unheralded Structure in Current Conceptualizations of Family Functioning," *Marriage and Family Living*, 24 (August 1962), 231–240.

SWEETSER, DORRIAN APPLE. "The Effect of Industrialization on Intergenerational Solidarity," *Rural Sociology*, 31 (June 1966), 156–170.

TALMON, YONINA. "Aging in Israel, A Planned Society," *American Journal of Sociology*, 67 (November 1961), 284–295.

———. "Mate Selection in Collective Settlements," *American Sociological Review*, 29 (August 1964), 491–508.

———. "The Family in a Revolutionary Movement—The Case of the Kibbutz in Israel," in M. F. Nimkoff (ed.), *Comparative Family Systems*. Boston: Houghton Mifflin, 1965, pp. 259–286.

TAWNEY, R. H. *Religion and the Rise of Capitalism*. Harmondsworth, England: Pelican Books, 1938.

TAYLOR, GORDAN RATTRAY. *The Biological Time-Bomb*. London: Thames and Hudson, 1968.

TERMAN, LEWIS M., *et al. Psychological Factors in Marital Happiness*. New York: McGraw-Hill, 1938.

THIBAUT, JOHN W., AND HAROLD H. KELLEY. *The Social Psychology of Groups*. New York: Wiley, 1959.

THOMAS, DYLAN. "Do Not Go Gentle into That Good Night," in Oscar Williams (ed.), *The Pocket Book of Modern Verse*. Rev. ed. New York: Washington Square Press, 1958, p. 574.

THOMPSON, HUNTER. *Hell's Angels*. New York: Random House, 1966.

THOMPSON, PRESCOTT W., AND RONALD CHEN. "Experiences with Older Psychiatric Patients and Spouses Together in a Residential Treatment Setting," *Bulletin of the Menninger Clinic*, 30 (January 1966), 23–31.

THOMPSON, WAYNE E., AND GORDON F. STREIB. "Meaningful Activity in a Family

Context," in Robert W. Kleemeier (ed.), *Aging and Leisure: A Research Perspective into the Meaningful Use of Time.* New York: Oxford University Press, 1961, pp. 177–211.

TIGER, LIONEL. "Patterns of Male Association," *Current Anthropology,* 8 (June 1967), 268–269.

————. *Men in Groups.* New York: Random House, 1969.

Time Magazine, "Communes Go to Court," February 1, 1971, pp. 53–54.

TOFFLER, ALVIN. *Future Shock.* New York: Random House, 1970.

TOMEH, AIDA K. "The Impact of Reference Groups on the Educational and Occupational Aspirations of Women College Students," *Journal of Marriage and the Family,* 30 (February 1968), 102–110.

————. "Birth Order and Kinship Affiliation," *Journal of Marriage and the Family,* 31 (February 1969), 19–26.

TOWNSEND, PETER. *The Family Life of Old People.* London: Routledge and Kegan Paul, 1957.

————. "The Emergence of the Four-Generation Family in Industrial Society," in Bernice L. Neugarten (ed.), *Middle Age and Aging.* Chicago: University of Chicago Press, 1968, pp. 255–257.

TROST, JAN. "Some Data on Mate-Selection: Complementarity," *Journal of Marriage and the Family,* 29 (November 1967), 730–738.

TURNER, RALPH H. "Some Aspects of Women's Ambition," *American Journal of Sociology,* 70 (November 1964), 271–285.

UDRY, J. RICHARD. "Marital Instability by Race, Sex, Education, and Occupation Using 1960 Census Data," *American Journal of Sociology.* 72 (September 1966), 203–209.

————. "Marital Instability by Race and Income Based on 1960 Census Data," *American Journal of Sociology,* 72 (May 1967a), 673–674.

————. "Personality Match and Interpersonal Perception as Predictors of Marriage," *Journal of Marriage and the Family,* 29 (November 1967b), 722–725.

————. "Marital Instability by Race, Sex, Education, Occupation, and Income Using 1960 Census Data," in Robert F. Winch and Louis Wolf Goodman (eds.), *Selected Studies in Marriage and the Family.* New York: Holt, Rinehart and Winston, 1968.

ULLERSTAM, LARS. *The Erotic Minorities.* New York: Grove Press, 1966.

United States Bureau of the Census, U.S. Census of Population, PC (1), ID, 1960.

UPDIKE, JOHN. "Van Loves Ada, Ada Loves Van," *The New Yorker,* (August 2, 1969), pp. 67–75.

VAN DEN BAN, A. W. "Family Structure and Modernization," *Journal of Marriage and the Family,* 29 (November 1967), 771–773.

VAN DEN HAAG, ERNEST. "Love or Marriage?" *Harper's,* 224, May 1962, pp. 43–47.

VIDEBECK, R., AND ALAN B. KNOX. "Alternative Participatory Responses to Aging," in Arnold M. Rose and Warren A. Peterson (eds.), *Older People and Their Social World.* Philadelphia: F. A. Davis Co., 1965.

VINCENT, CLARK E. "Ego Involvement in Sexual Relations: Implications for

Research on Illegitimacy," *American Journal of Sociology*, 65 (November 1959), 287–295.

———. "Unmarried Fathers and the Mores: 'Sexual Exploiter' as an Ex Post Facto Label," *American Sociological Review*, 25 (February 1960), 40–46.

———. *Unmarried Mothers*. New York: Free Press, 1961.

———. "Mental Health and the Family," *Journal of Marriage and the Family*, 29 (February 1967), 18–39.

WAINWRIGHT, WILLIAM H. "Fatherhood as a Precipitant of Mental Illness," *Scientific Proceedings in Summary Form*, American Psychiatric Association (1964), pp. 96–97.

WALLACE, KARL MILES. "An Experiment in Scientific Matchmaking," *Marriage and Family Living*, 21 (November 1959), 342–348.

WALLER, WILLARD. "The Rating-Dating Complex," *American Journal of Sociology*, 2 (October 1937), 727–734.

———. *The Family: A Dynamic Interpretation*. Revised by Reuben Hill. New York: Dryden, 1951.

WALLIN, PAUL. "Marital Happiness of Parents and Their Children's Attitude to Marriage," *American Sociological Review*, 19 (February 1954), 20–23.

———. "Religiosity, Sexual Gratification, and Marital Satisfaction," *American Sociological Review*, 22 (June 1957), 300–305.

WARD, DAVID A., AND GENE G. KASSEBAUM. *Women's Prison: Sex and Social Structure*. Chicago: Aldine, 1965.

WASHBURN, SHERWOOD L., AND IRVEN DEVORE. "Social Behavior of Baboons and Early Man," in Sherwood L. Washburn (ed.), *Social Life of Early Man*. New York: Wenner-Gren Foundation, 1961.

WASSINK, M. W. GRAEFF. "Opinion Survey on Mixed Marriages in Morocco," *Journal of Marriage and the Family*, 29 (August 1967), 578–589.

WEBER, MAX. *The Protestant Ethic*. Talcott Parsons (tr.). London: Allen and Unwin, 1930.

WESTERMARCK, EDWARD. *The History of Human Marriage*. New York: Macmillan, 1891.

WESTOFF, CHARLES F., ROBERT G. POTTER, JR., AND PHILIP C. SAGI. *The Third Child: A Study in the Prediction of Fertility*. Princeton, N.J.: Princeton University Press, 1963.

———, AND ELLIOT G. MISHLER. *Family Growth in Metropolitan America*. Princeton, N.J.: Princeton University Press, 1966.

WHITE, LESLIE A. *The Evolution of Culture*. New York: McGraw-Hill, 1959.

WHITEHURST, ROBERT N. "Premarital Reference-Group Orientation and Marriage Adjustment," *Journal of Marriage and the Family*, 30 (August 1968), 397–401.

WHYTE, WILLIAM H., JR. *The Organization Man*. New York: Simon and Schuster, 1956.

WILLIAMS, MELVIN J. "Personal and Familial Problems of High School Youths and Their Bearing upon Family Education Needs," *Social Forces*, 27 (March 1949), 279–285.

WILLIAMS, ROBIN M., JR. *American Society: A Sociological Interpretation*. New York: Knopf, 1965.

WINCH, ROBERT F. "The Theory of Complementary Needs in Mate-Selection: Final Results on the Test of the General Hypothesis," *American Sociological Review*, 20 (October 1955), 552–555.

————. *Mate Selection*. New York: Harper and Row, 1958.

————. "Another Look at the Theory of Complementary Needs in Mate-Selection," *Journal of Marriage and the Family*, 29 (November 1967), 756–762.

————. "Some Observations on Extended Familism in the United States," in Robert F. Winch and Louis Wolf Goodman (eds.), *Selected Studies in Marriage and the Family*. New York: Holt, Rinehart and Winston, 1968.

————, AND RAE LESSER BLUMBERG. "Societal Complexity and Familial Organization," in Robert F. Winch and Louis Wolf Goodman (eds.), *Selected Studies in Marriage and the Family*. New York: Holt, Rinehart and Winston, 1968, pp. 70–92.

————, AND THOMAS AND VIRGINIA KTSANES. "The Theory of Complementary Needs in Mate-Selection: An Analytic and Descriptive Study," *American Sociological Review*, 19 (June 1954), 241–249.

WOLFENDEN REPORT, *Report of the Committee on Homosexual Offences and Prostitution*. London: Her Majesty's Stationery Office, 1957.

WOMBLE, DALE L. "Trends in Falsification of Age at Marriage in Ohio," *Journal of Marriage and the Family*, 28 (February 1966), 54–56.

YOUMANS, E. GRANT. "Some Perspectives on Disengagement Theory." Paper read at the meetings of the Southern Sociological Association, New Orleans, April 12, 1969.

YOUNG, MICHAEL D. *The Rise of the Meritocracy*. New York: Random House, 1959.

YOUNG, MICHAEL, AND PETER WILLMOTT. *Kinship and Family in East London*. New York: Free Press, 1957.

ZELDITCH, MORRIS, JR. "Family, Marriage, and Kinship," in Robert E. L. Faris (ed.), *Handbook of Modern Sociology*. Chicago: Rand McNally, 1964.

ZETTERBERG, HANS L. *On Sexual Life in Sweden*. Previewed in J. Robert Moskin, "The New Contraceptive Society," *Look*, February 4, 1969, pp. 50–53.

ZIMMERMAN, CARLE C. *Family and Civilization*. New York: Harper, 1947.

ZUKERMAN, JACOB T. "A Socio-Legal Approach to Family Desertion," *Marriage and Family Living*, 12 (August 1950), 83–84.